Changing anarchism

Published in our
centenary year
≈ 2004 ≈
MANCHESTER
UNIVERSITY
PRESS

Changing anarchism

Anarchist theory and practice in a global age

edited by Jonathan Purkis
and James Bowen

Manchester University Press
Manchester and New York

distributed exclusively in the USA by Palgrave

Published by Manchester University Press
Oxford Road, Manchester M13 9NR, UK
and Room 400, 175 Fifth Avenue, New York, NY 10010, USA
www.manchesteruniversitypress.co.uk

Distributed exclusively in the USA by
Palgrave, 175 Fifth Avenue, New York,
NY 10010, USA

Distributed exclusively in Canada by
UBC Press, University of British Columbia, 2029 West Mall,
Vancouver, BC, Canada V6T 1Z2

British Library Cataloguing-in-Publication Data
A catalogue record for this book is available from the British Library

Library of Congress Cataloging-in-Publication Data applied for

ISBN 0 7190 6694 8 *hardback*

First published 2004

13 12 11 10 09 08 07 06 05 04   10 9 8 7 6 5 4 3 2 1

Typeset in Sabon with Gill Sans display
by Servis Filmsetting Ltd, Manchester
Printed in Great Britain
by CPI, Bath

Dedicated to the memory of John Moore, who died suddenly while this book was in production. His lively, innovative and pioneering contributions to anarchist theory and practice will be greatly missed.

Contents

Contributors

James Bowen lives in West Yorkshire and works to promote literacy among children of all ages. His other interests include travel, speaking and learning foreign languages, writing songs and short stories, reading, and playing guitar and singing in radical folk-roots band Bar the Shouting. He is also a member of the Lib ED radical education publishing collective.

Colin Craig is a former senior international consultant in the subject of illicit drug use and the prevention of HIV transmission amongst injecting drug users. He has worked in the former Soviet Union, the United States and Western Europe on many different contracts relating to HIV prevention, research into drug trends, drug-using prisoners, drug user advocacy projects and developing health promotion amongst injecting drugs users. He is currently working on a history of the development of the War on Drugs.

Karen Goaman has written a PhD thesis in anthropology at University College London, on situationism and contemporary anarchism, and is a part-time lecturer in communications and cultural history at London Metropolitan University. She is interested in the strand of thought that opposes industrial civilisation and is active on the fringes of London's anti-capitalist milieu, including Rising Tide.

Joanna Gore teaches fine art at Middlesex University and is currently writing up her PhD thesis 'In the eye of the beholder: the role of the artist in the institutional dialectics of control, resistance and liberation'. She also works as a freelance artist/researcher in educational, health and community settings and tries to have fun.

David Gribble worked at a variety of schools during his teaching career, principally Dartington Hall School and Sands School (of which he was one of the founders). Since his retirement in 1992 he has visited free or democratic schools all round the world, written or edited several books and articles and spoken in many different countries. He played an important role in the establishment of the International Democratic Education Conferences, which take place each year in a different country.

Jamie Heckert is working towards a PhD in sociology at University of Edinburgh, exploring the concept of sexual orientation and how we can get over it. He teaches sex education, writes for *The Tartan Skirt*, *ScotsGay* and *Green Pepper* and enjoys yoga, swimming and reading science-fiction novels.

Steve Millett lives in York and works for a charity providing support and information to lone parents. He recently received his PhD in contemporary anarchist-communist political theory from the University of Central Lancashire.

John Moore (1957–2002) wrote extensively on contemporary anarchist theory in publications such as *Green Anarchist*, *Social Anarchism*, *Anarchist Studies* and was the author of several books, including *Anarchy and ecstasy* and *Book of levelling*. Until his death, he was regarded as one of the most eclectic and innovative anarchist thinkers around, and he did much to introduce a new generation to writings by Fredy Perlman, Max Stirner, the Situationist International and many other marginalised libertarian thinkers. He was also an entertaining and highly regarded poet.

Dave Morland teaches sociology and philosophy at the University of Teesside. He has written widely on anarchism and has campaigned on issues such as the poll tax, the miners' strike, nuclear arms and anti-capitalism. He lives with his partner and two children in north-east England, enjoys mountaineering and is a long-suffering Sunderland AFC fan.

Jonathan Purkis teaches media and cultural studies at Liverpool John Moores University. He has been active in various radical environmental, anticonsumerist and anarchist groups and written a PhD thesis and various articles on these movements. He is heavily involved with the journal *Anarchist Studies* and plays music with Huddersfield band Bar the Shouting.

Bronislaw Szerszynski is Lecturer in Environment and Culture at the Institute for Environment, Philosophy and Public Policy at Lancaster University, United Kingdom. He has researched and published work on: risk, environment and new technologies, citizenship and social movements, and religion and culture. He is also a singer, guitarist and songwriter.

Emma Tomalin is a lecturer in the School of Theology and Religious Studies at the University of Leeds and has pursued a research interest in the relationship between religion and environmentalism, particularly in South Asia and Britain. More recently she has begun to investigate issues concerning religion and international development, and links with gender and human rights concerns. She also works as a freelance researcher for radio productions and as a consultant for non-governmental organisations.

Acknowledgements

We would like to thank all of the contributors to this collection for providing an engaging and diverse collection of reflections on contemporary anarchism, as well as proving that co-operation and negotiation can work in practice. We would also like to thank Tony Mason and the staff at Manchester University Press for being supportive (and patient!) throughout the production of the book.

The help of Chayley Collis and Paul Fitzgerald has been particularly appreciated where technical, editorial and artistic matters have been concerned. Ongoing professional and personal support and interest has also been forthcoming (sometimes unwittingly) from Jacqueline Gaile, Ian Welsh, Sharif Gemie and the Lib Ed Network.

James Bowen and Jonathan Purkis

Introduction: why anarchism still matters

Global matters

In February 2002, Commander Brian Paddick, then Police Chief for the (London) Metropolitan Borough of Brixton, posted the following message on the direct action discussion forum www.urban75.com:

> The concept of anarchism has always appealed to me. The idea of the innate good-ness of the individual that is corrupted by society or the system. It is a theoretical argument but I am not sure everyone would behave well if there were no laws and no system. I believe there are many people forced into causing harm to others by the way society operates at the moment.

These comments, made by a senior British police officer already controversial for being openly gay and for extremely liberal drug enforcement policies, created something of a sensation in the mainstream media (where he also repeated them). The incident also prompted some sections of the slightly bemused alter-native media to react with outrage that a policeman was wasting valuable anar-chist discussion time on 'their' medium!

The controversy surrounding Paddick's comments provides a touchstone to explore matters that are becoming increasingly central to anarchist theory and practice. We live in an era where the politics of information are formulated and contested in a myriad of real and virtual locations and media, and where ascer-taining influence, apportioning blame, conceptualising and co-ordinating strat-egy has become an almost impossible business. Who knows what the impacts and influence of Paddick's remarks have been on the wider milieu?

The resurgence of interest in anarchism, which has been steadily percolating through often quite different social movements in the West over the last few decades, has now begun to form significant waves on a much wider scale, linking First and Third World struggles. This has resulted in the formation of a diversity of political alliances coalescing around the politics of globalisation. The so-called anti-globalisation movement (sometimes called the 'alternative globalisa-tion movement') that emerged in the mid-1990s includes indigenous peoples'

organisations, dispossessed or non-unionised workers, opponents of biotechnol-
ogies and militarism, environmentalists, squatters and campaigners against
debt. What unites them is a fundamental questioning of the viability of existing
mechanisms of decision-making, control, accountability and justice throughout
the world. The neoliberal economic and political hegemony that has held sway
for almost a generation is beginning to lose its legitimacy. Whilst it is clear that
the diverse concerns of these countermovements are not reducible to single political programmes or monolithic analytical tools, the theoretical concepts most
apparently to the fore appear to be those associated with anarchism. This is
something that has been acknowledged by people within those movements,
popular media commentators and even Marxist journals such as *New Left
Review* (Graeber, 2002).

It is when a liminal moment such as Paddick's occurs, when the barriers
between different forms of hierarchy and oppression relent to allow communication, about human nature, the desirability of particular political forms, the
practical problems of consistency between means and ends, that anarchism still
matters. It is when the Zapatistas in the Chiapas region of Mexico inspire
Western activists to flock, like so many did to join the International Brigades in
Spain in 1936, to participate in a complex struggle between indigenous cultures,
national interests and international corporate power that anarchism still
matters. When children on the streets of Delhi empower themselves through
alternative education, squatters create their 'occasional cafés' in English cities
such as Manchester and Leeds, needle exchange schemes flout repressive drug
laws in the USA and Australia, then theories of self-organisation and mutual aid
come into their own. When, after a pre-meditated State onslaught on protest
against international finance and development ends in murder, like at the 'G8'
Summit in Genoa, Italy during July 2001, activists regroup and rethink their
tactics, it is then that anarchism very definitely matters.

From there to here

These examples are separated by considerable temporal and spatial divisions yet
still retain a number of common themes. The fact that new generations seek out
and quote 'classical anarchist' literature such as that of Peter Kropotkin, Pierre-
Joseph Proudhon, William Godwin, Michael Bakunin, Errico Malatesta, Emma
Goldman or Alexander Berkman means that there are still issues and principles
that, despite different contexts, are still worthy of debate. Amidst the uncertain-
ties of globalisation and its culture of consumerism, people chance upon discourses of resistance: the accessible practicality of Colin Ward; the gentle reason
of Noam Chomsky; the challenge of the anticivilisational critique of John
Zerzan; and the enduring appeal of the Situationist International. Ecological
activists interested in permaculture make connections with social ecology and the
heroic and sometimes flawed attempt by Murray Bookchin to link Enlightenment

rationality with ecological thought. Experienced activists from campaigns in the 1970s and 1980s like Starhawk (2002b) help a new generation negotiate the pitfalls of protesting when the going gets tough. Postmodern and poststructural theory inspires artistic practitioners to problematise dominant representations of power and to construct more popular aesthetics based around grass roots activism. Scientific-minded activists are drawn to theories of chaos, complexity and emergence to help understand cause and effect in the social and natural worlds and the self-organising and yet unpredictable patterns that influence all life on earth.

The title of this book, *Changing anarchism*, attempts to convey the different sociological contexts for how contemporary anarchist theory and practice is to be understood. On the one hand, the contents epitomise many of the conceptual and practical concerns of this particular era, marking the changes in theories of power and offering strategies of resistance. Whilst we do not want to be accused of trying to map particular struggles on to certain sets of social, political or economic relations, it needs to be acknowledged that the contemporary political stage is both broader in scale and deeper in terms of critique than in the past. The much eulogised events of 'May 68' in France simply did not unite the diversity of political movements and oppressed groups across the world that currently challenge the rationale of globalisation.

We are increasingly living in what sociologists call 'world time', where particular events shape the future of whole populations instantaneously and not just those bound by nation states; this is a phenomenon perhaps first evidenced by the world's primary media war in Vietnam during the late 1960s. The construction of international events through increasingly subtle, far-reaching and effective media forces has amplified many of the ongoing concerns about the impact of mass culture and the forging of political consensus (Herman and Chomsky, 1988). The contestation of events that occur in 'world time' therefore takes on an added element of importance, whether this is enacted through existing notions of the global public sphere or the emerging alternatives to it. From the Oil Crisis of 1973, the 'Live Aid' spectacle of July 1985, the explosion of the Chernobyl nuclear power station in April 1986, or the protests at the World Trade Organisation conference in Seattle, United States, November 1999, there is a sense that 'the whole world is watching'.

In this respect, notions of 'risk' and 'contingency' as theorised by German sociologist Ulrich Beck (1992), help us to understand how social action, from the most private and individual through to the most collective and public, is constructed by the uncertainty of economic, political or technological relations. Managing the unpredictability of these forces is a challenge, Beck suggests, for governments, businesses and individuals, because of the global context within which most of them have to operate. As Colin Craig argues in this volume (chapter 7), it is this type of uncertainty that can be seized on by authority to legitimate new forms of repression and surveillance. This leads to the creation of 'wars of metaphor' which exist as much in the mind of the public as they do in the policies of Western governments, most obviously in America, Europe and Asia after 11 September 2001. The consequences of these events have on the one hand managed to intensify the pressure on already-existing relations of inequality, poverty and ecological devastation, but crucially demanded that anarchists reposition themselves according to the 'new world disorder'.

One such stance has been the gradual move away from the still persuasive insurrectionary models of political change born of the industrial era, frequently based around 'capturing' power. Although there is considerable imaginative appeal in this scenario, tackling the complexity of the established webs of power makes for far less romantic endgames. Anarchism in an era of globalisation requires vastly different conceptual and practical tools which are able to identify different sources of power and contest them using context specific methods. How anarchist praxis might be configured in relation to these changes is the subject of the conclusion in the collection: 'How anarchism still matters'. Yet in order to begin to construct a sense of strategy, there is an intellectual terrain that needs to be mapped and formulated into feasible and appropriate courses of action that can relate to large numbers of people in terms of their daily experience. To accomplish this, some brief assessment of the relationship that contemporary anarchism has with the past is necessary.

Classical matters

In 1971, the publishers of the collection *Anarchism today* (edited by David Apter and James Joll) put the face of Michael Bakunin on the cover of their book. A number of its contributors also alluded to the important influence that Bakunin had had on the events of 'May 68' and within the resurgence of interest in anarchism generally, in the New Left and the American counter culture. The choice of Bakunin as a political talisman was in some ways apt, given the power of his insurrectionary legacy and the momentary possibility of a revolution in the West (see also Joll, 1979: 264). In other ways it was massively inappropriate, for as Stafford (1971) notes, considerable development of anarchist thinking took place during the twentieth century, particularly around the idea of 'permanent protest' and the transformation of people's states of mind before, during and after a revolution. The words of Gustav Landauer (cited in Stafford, 1971: 84), that 'the State is not something that can be destroyed by revolution . . . but is a condition, a certain relationship between human beings', seemed much more apposite than the iconoclasm of Bakunin. The continuing relevance of nineteenth- and early twentieth-century anarchism is of course an evergreen debate and, over three decades on from May 1968, Bakunin would not necessarily be the choice of most ideal representative of the classical canon to inspire the latest wave of anarchist theory and practice.[1]

In any kind of new interpretation of the history of anarchism, sometimes awkward and arbitrary decisions have to be taken about the framing of 'contemporary' events in terms of those in the past. Although many of the concerns of the contributors in this collection stem from debates that have arisen from the mid-1990s, we are using the post-'May 68' era as being indicative of what might be understood as the period of 'global anarchism'. This is not to suggest that anarchists did not express solidarity with struggles on the other side of the globe in previous eras (they clearly did), nor is it a wholesale rejection of all anarchist theory in the past. We are not claiming any overnight transformation of politics, culture and theory; rather, that the events in France and beyond seemed to act as a lens for a number of emerging movements which, in addition to existing official anarchist movements, have given anarchism a new lease of life.[2] These include the environmental movement, the women's movement, the anti-nuclear (power and weapons) movement, the lesbian and gay rights movement and aspects of the civil rights struggle, whose impact has already been well documented and all of which have expressed aspects of anarchist praxis to some degree. Each of these movements have spawned their own theoretical insights that can only be briefly acknowledged (see below). However, they should be seen as concurrent with the emerging intellectual impact of the Situationist International, the reaction to structuralist interpretations of society, as well as shifts away from more production-oriented versions of Marxism (assisted by the 'Prague Spring' in 1968). As with any vibrant period in the history of ideas, attributing particular cause and effect is difficult, but the more general point is that the logic of many of these discourses only realised their potential in *the late 1990s*. So, just as Apter and Joll had legitimate grounds for defining a new era of anarchism – even though it still seemed rather couched within the framework of nineteenth-century political praxis – we believe that there is now enough conceptual and material evidence to claim a 'paradigm shift' within anarchism.

When we talk about a global anarchism, we mean that it is impossible for anarchist theory and practice to be formulated in ways that do not acknowledge its relationship with global flows of people, ideas, technology, economics and, crucially, resistance. Indeed, it is significant that anarchism can no longer be said to be the preserve of white Westerners. Globalisation might have been predicted by Karl Marx in the mid-nineteenth century, but the sociological and philosophical concepts of that era which are able to help us understand the early twenty-first century are somewhat limited. If anything, an era of global anarchism calls for a repositioning of the individual within these global flows and the need to respond to complex ethical and strategic problems which involves new formulations of classic divisions within anarchism, such as that of individual liberty versus collective responsibility.

Themes and schemes of *Changing anarchism*

The shifts within political cultures during the period which we are identifying as the era of global anarchism pose a number of questions regarding the weight that contemporary theorists and activists place on the classical anarchist canon. We regard it as self-evident that anarchist activities are constantly occurring throughout the world and do so without any knowledge of 'official' anarchist history, Western or otherwise. In this respect it is significant that several of the contributions to this book only briefly acknowledge the relationship that their themes have with the classical Western anarchist tradition. There are good methodological as well as rhetorical reasons for continually identifying new forms of 'anarchy in action', not least because it presents an opportunity to cast a different eye over the history of social organisation, politics and change.

In attempting to widen out definitions and manifestations of anarchism, we do not wish to dismiss the importance of the many writers and figureheads of official anarchist histories, or the unknown millions who have struggled to realise their ideals in a myriad of difficult and dangerous struggles. But this book is not about those people and our bibliography and glossary must serve as a signpost for those who wish to understand the nineteenth- and early twentieth-century anarchist tradition more clearly. Our intention has been to draw upon a number of valuable pointers that exist in the work of the classical anarchists, as well as a number of its enduring principles, and to frame them in new ways.

The value of couching present concerns to some extent within earlier debates is demonstrated in a number of the contributions here. Dave Morland's chapter (chapter 1) concentrates on the issue of broadening the parameters of how anarchist theory and practice is conceptualised, and compares the major philosophical differences and strategies between the classical period (what he calls 'social anarchism') and the contemporary anti-capitalist movements which he regards as being poststructuralist in nature. John Moore (chapter 3) acknowledges these epistemological differences in his argument that the often-overlooked figure of Max Stirner can be useful for understanding the impact of power on the formation of the Self, as well as prefiguring poststructuralist and situationist perspectives on revolutionary language. It is through an assessment of Stirner that Moore raises one of the critical questions about the relationship between anarchism and the Enlightenment: the extent to which a particular rational subject has dominated its theoretical *oeuvre*. Moore suggests that, by concentrating on writers who are embracing non-rational and individualistic perspectives, one can identify an 'anarcho-psychological' genealogy, constituting an alternative and antiauthoritarian *episteme*. This can be traced through Max Stirner and Friedrich Nietzsche to more recent writers such as Hakim Bey and is pivotal for understanding contemporary manifestations of anarchism, as well as posing important methodological questions about 'official' histories of anarchist and libertarian thought.

In a very different vein, David Gribble (chapter 10) assesses the viability of libertarian education a century on from the life and work of Spanish writer and activist Francisco Ferrer and finds considerable evidence for the endurance of these ideals. Instead of this form of education being the preserve of the privileged children of the Western middle classes, many of the experiments that he documents around the world were born out of adversity, from the poor Puerto Rican communities of Chicago to children on the streets of Delhi. The manner in which these projects emerge, with similar emphases in different parts of the globe, reprises arguments that were made by Kropotkin over a century ago about the 'natural' basis of anarchist ethics.

Even though Kropotkin's views of human nature as being naturally benign and co-operative might struggle to stand the test of time (see Morland, 1997, and this volume), there are still some grounds for claiming that Kropotkin is the 'classical anarchist' most worthy of continual attention. It is the current ecological crisis that makes Kropotkin's work continue to be relevant as well as his interdisciplinary methods. Whilst we do not want to prioritise eco-anarchism as such, some of the most intense debates within anarchist *milieux* have concentrated on the relationship between human and non-human eco-systems in terms of their respective evolution, intelligence and development of potential for 'freedom'. These ideas were pivotal to Kropotkin's work and form much of the basis for one of the most important developments out of them, Murray Bookchin's *The ecology of freedom* (1982). Bookchin and Colin Ward have been among the principal advocates of Kropotkin's ecological legacy and each has amassed considerable practical and theoretical material on the continuing relevance of these ideas. This legacy is also evidenced in his inspiration of several twentieth-century urban planners (Macauley, 1998), contemporary sociological theories of 'space' (Huston, 1997), and in anticipating the contemporary sciences of complexity and emergence (Purchase, 1994).

If some figures and concepts from over a century ago retain a degree of relevance and application in the present, the same can also be said for the principles upon which anarchists have premised their actions.

Power and principles

In chapter 1, Dave Morland outlines the continuing importance of key anarchist principles of the era of 'classical anarchism'. These can be summarised as: an opposition to all forms of representative politics; an opposition to one class or group assuming a privileged role in the political struggle (classically the proletariat); and the opposition to all forms of power, not just political or economic. In addition, one might also add: an advocacy of self-organisation, direct action and spontaneity; equating the means of an action with its ends; and plans for the future being determined by activists *in situ* rather than via revolutionary blueprints.

Whilst these are ideals recognised by many anarchists the world over, in the period that we have identified as that of 'global anarchism', these principles become firstly transformed by the re-emergence of critiques of power based on gender, ethnicity or sexuality and then by ecological discourses. In this context, the acceptance of difference – always part of the anarchist *raison d'être* – becomes essential, particularly in the kind of alliance politics between global North and South described by Karen Goaman in her chapter (chapter 9). This applies on a theoretical as well as a practical level, so that new forms of analysis do not become deterministic, and particular interpretations come to dominate alliance politics. As Jamie Heckert's discussion of the actions of Gay Pride in Scotland indicates (chapter 5), sexual identity politics can easily become essentialist and simply end up reproducing dominant notions of difference and oppression by another route.

The balance between collective strategies and individual freedom has always been a classic tension of all politics, yet because of the commitment of anarchists to notions of individual liberty and responsibility, it has often been more visible in the anarchist *milieu* than other parts of the political landscape. These difficulties are observed in a number of places in this collection, ranging from the practical implications of John Moore's interpretation of Stirner, David Gribble's discussion of pupil-designed education strategies to James Bowen's (chapter 6) advocacy of tolerance in the face of dogmatic praxis. Bronislaw Szerszynski and Emma Tomalin (chapter 11) note how, on protest camps and at alternative festivals, the freedom to develop one's identity through available spiritual 'resources' can occasionally clash with what is assumed to be collectively acceptable. The question of individual liberty and collective needs raises an equally important anarchist principle: equating the means of an action with its ends.

Personalised politics

For 'lifestyle anarchism'

If acknowledging difference has been one challenge in the era of global anarchism, an important added dimension has been the implication of anarchist critiques for living one's life in accordance to particular principles. Here we feel the need to consider how the 'politics of consumption' has become a central part of contemporary anarchist praxis, especially in terms of the impact that the actions of individuals and institutions have on human and non-human eco-systems. There are a number of critical positions that differentiate ecological forms of anarchism from their more mainstream counterparts. These have included social ecology, deep ecology and anarcho-primitivism as well as a number of permutations of these perspectives such as the 'inclusive democracy' project of Fotopoulos (1997).[3] Despite huge differences between these positions as well as within them, there are serious attempts within each to utilise 'holistic' perspectives on the impact of capitalism and industrialisation on non-human eco-systems and human interrelationships. These critiques affect anarchist strategy and many of their advocates consider matters of principle to extend to the minimisation of harm inflicted on social or non-human eco-systems through the adoption of lifestyles based on reduced carbon consumption.[4]

To many, the extension of the feminist adage that the 'personal is political' seems both necessary and obvious; it is simply part of anarchist process that operates on a micro- and macro-sociological level simultaneously. However, the issue of 'lifestyle anarchism' has been even more hotly debated since the publication of Murray Bookchin's book *Social anarchism or lifestyle anarchism: an unbridgeable chasm* (1995). The book is largely a defence of rationalism as part of the (collective) liberatory project and an onslaught on irrational and individualistic forms of anarchism, one of which is 'lifestyle anarchism' (in itself something of an umbrella term). Space prevents a comprehensive study of the history of this particular debate, but its existence is a useful indicator as to where the boundaries of 'legitimate' anarchist action are perceived to be.

Current research into radical movements, however, indicates the extent to which activists individually realise ethical codes and 'personalised politics' as part of their collective political struggles. This is most clearly argued in Paul Lichterman's excellent *The search for political community* (1996) and is illustrative of the extent to which political action takes place on many different levels, increasingly based around the politics of consumption as much as the politics of production. So, just as rationality and irrationality are not clear-cut states of mind, neither are social anarchism and 'lifestyle anarchism' mutually exclusive categories. This is most clearly demonstrated in Szerszynski and Tomalin's discussion of how activists knowingly construct their identities through a complex *bricolage* of 'irrational' ideas and unusual lifestyle politics.

Technology and violence

Personalised politics also extends to two related theoretical issues, regarding the extent to which the use of both technology and violence is so implicated in the reproduction of power relations that advocacy of the use of either is to be rejected out of hand. In the first instance, it is important to acknowledge the critique of technology that emerged from the Detroit-based *Fifth Estate* collective and writers such as Fredy and Lorraine Perlman, John Zerzan and George Bradford, initially in the 1970s but particularly during the 1980s. They drew upon earlier writers such as Lewis Mumford and Jacques Ellul who examined technological systems as being much more than just instruments of capitalism but sets of relationships in themselves able to shape consciousness itself. The argument asserts that technology cannot be neutral and must be rejected and that human societies must be organised on completely different lines.

This constitutes a significant departure from large swathes of ecological thought which have frequently adopted the position that technology can be liberatory if part of anarchist social relations. As Steve Millett (2003, and chapter 4, this volume) notes, this is a hugely controversial issue and although sometimes the critique lacks a practical application, it is extremely powerful in terms of raising questions about psychological dependency and alienation, in addition to its primary claims. Regardless of whether the premises of these arguments are accepted, a theoretical Pandora's Box has been opened. It is also hugely ironic that this critique has enjoyed considerable exposure, particularly through Zerzan, but also the Unabomber Manifesto (2001)[5] at a time when considerable weight has been placed on the importance of Internet and mobile 'phone technology in co-ordinating actions at the global summit protests described in Goaman's chapter (chapter 9).

If these particular technologies can be seen to be committing violence on the planet in terms of their exploitation of natural and human resources, those opposing the destruction are themselves locked into a number of debates as to the respective violence of their own protest tactics. In such circumstances we have seen the reappearance of long-established anarchist debates that have been reinvigorated through exposure to tactics used by the peace movement, the civil rights movement and the women's movement in particular. These have built on arguments used by Leo Tolstoy and Mahatma Gandhi (see Randle, 1994) that nonviolence can have extremely positive effects in the carrying out of civil disobedience and direct action strategies. In addition to the frequently made points that violence begets further violence and creates even more alienated activists, there are more complex matters when addressing issues of violence on property and violence as being appropriate or inappropriate for all circumstances (Hart, 1997). Considerable debate has occurred within the alternative globalisation movement about the tactics of the 'Black Block' anarchists, particularly in Seattle in November 1999 and at Genoa in July 2001. In the first instance the debates focused on the extent to which the trashing of multinationals such as Nike, McDonald's or Starbucks was useful to the overall message of the protests. In the second instance, the brutal policing tactics turned 'peaceful' protesters into victims, regardless of their intentions on the day. One journalist caught up in the violence compared the situation to Pinochet's Chile (Porter, 2001: 79). In the circumstances, hundreds of people were faced with the choice of defending themselves or facing serious injury, whilst the media focused on the Black Block for allegedly provoking violence. Research into anarchist attitudes towards violence in the past has been mixed, with the response often based around the relative short- or long-term vision of the person(s) in question (Chan, 1995). On balance, however, the internationalisation of much anarchist action has produced a greater inclination towards nonviolence, bearing witness (in Mexico and Palestine for instance) and the sharing of experiences. Although some writers have equated nonviolence and pacifism with 'pathology' (Churchill, 1999), the case for recognising violence as being multifaceted and operating on many levels appears to be made, something that Heckert notes in this collection with respect to 'forcing' political messages on to the general public.

It is our contention that the critical mass of these ethical matters and points of principle rising out of different analyses of power constitute a significant shift within anarchist theory and practice.

Theoretical matters

Definitional issues

If the sociological contexts within which the aforementioned key anarchist principles operate have changed so much, then to what extent are existing definitions
of anarchism useful? We have already intimated at the beginning of this
Introduction that the issue of whether anarchism as a single ideology can be said
to exist is one of considerable contemporary relevance. The choice of book title
further challenges this notion of shared critique and practice, but this would be
to misunderstand the diversity of perspectives that have always been present
within anarchist politics. Even a cursory glance at anarchist history reveals the
existence (and frequent coexistence) of mutualists, communists, collectivists,
syndicalists and individualists during the heyday of 'classical anarchism'
between 1860 and 1939. Moreover, these versions of anarchism offered different
interpretations of the classical principles outlined above. In this respect we note
the endurance of a number of debates: the relative importance of individual
versus collective liberation; the option to prioritise manifestations of political or
economic power; and the eternal dilemma of whether the right road of change
must be carried out through violent or nonviolent means. Whilst these theoretical and practical dilemmas prevail today, the world in which they are interpreted
and the criteria employed to do so are massively more sophisticated and diverse.
To this extent, we believe that it is only in the era of global anarchism that the
concept of *anarchisms* can really hold any weight. The analytical difference can
be demonstrated through considering the emphases placed within definitions of
anarchism itself.

In the introduction to his anthology *For anarchism*, the historian David
Goodway captures the parameters of classical anarchist epistemology very effectively. Anarchism manages to:

> Combin[e] a socialist critique of capitalism with a liberal critique of socialism, a
> (*laissez-faire*) liberal rejection of the State, both as status quo and as a vehicle for
> social change, with a socialist insistence upon human solidarity and communitar-
> ianism. (1989: 1)

Such frames of reference are by no means uncommon (see Apter, 1971; Walter,
1979) and, whilst important, do demonstrate the extent to which theorists of revolution have tended to prioritise particular characteristics of the critique of
modernity. Economic and political analyses continue to be important and in
some situations are perhaps the most visible constituencies of power, yet this
should not obviate responsibility from recognising other discourses. That anarchists have focused on a wide range of issues and have often declared their critique of capitalist society to be exhaustive and comprehensive is not a new
phenomenon. Debates about the relationship between patriarchy and capitalism
were important in the theory and practice of anarchism over a century ago
(Marsh, 1981) and one of its principal figures, Emma Goldman, also wrote

about racism in (American) society (1977). Indeed, the ecological influence of Kropotkin (and to some extent Proudhon) manifested itself practically in a number of sustainable living experiments in both rural and urban locations (see Hardy, 1979). Animal rights and vegetarianism were also emerging as part of a libertarian critique during this time period, particularly through figures such as Louise Michel in France and Edward Carpenter in England.

What becomes clear during the era of global anarchism is the consolidation of many of these latter critiques within distinctive anarchist movements and networks. Indeed, this period also saw the emergence of new claims for a more comprehensive analysis of power than those offered by the classical era.

Challenging anarchism

During the 1960s, the concept of 'totality'[6] began to gain intellectual weight, largely as a result of the critique of consumer capitalism offered by the Situationist International. However, whilst their contribution to anarchist theory is well established and acknowledged,[7] a number of their contemporaries have only recently began to accrue the same degree of critical appraisal. The aforementioned *Fifth Estate* collective (outlined in chapter 4 by Millett), comprised part of a *milieu* of radical communist intellectuals, including Jacques Camatte, Jean Baudrillard,[8] Cornelius Castoriadis and the 'Socialism or barbarism' group[9] who were all exploring ways to extend the critique of capitalism into new areas. One of the significant positions to emerge from some of these writers was to challenge the Marxist position that the aim of revolution was to capture 'capital' for the proletariat. Instead, the point was to abolish it and all of its attendant relations.

So, whereas some of the aforementioned new social movements brought new critiques of power to understanding oppression in terms of gender, race or ecology, these radical communists sought to encapsulate all relations of authority within the same conceptual space. For instance, based on a reading of the 'lost sixth chapter' of Karl Marx's *Capital* (see Millett, 2003), Camatte sought to explain how the economic relationships inherent in capitalism also percolated into all other areas of life as well. This was a starting point for writers such as Perlman (1983) and John Zerzan (1999) to question power on much more ontological levels.

Perlman's metaphor of 'Leviathan' as a giant machine, of which the State, capitalism and technology are all part, is an attempt to understand power relations as systems that arose with the early civilisations. It essentially merges Thomas Hobbes' (seventeenth-century) idea of a sovereign authority (1968 edition) with Lewis Mumford's notion of the 'megamachine' (1988). Mumford talked about the existence of an authoritarian (as opposed to democratic) 'technics' that organised all human relationships in the period of the early civilisations. It has been through such systems that societies have internalised and reproduced alienated power relationships.

Whilst clearly enjoying considerable appeal during an age of globalisation and American supremacy, these ideas can be seen to form the backbone of the contemporary anti-civilisational and anti-technological anarchist critique. In particular, they raise questions about human dependency upon technology, relations of authority, fetishisation of work and alienation from nature. Moreover, as Goaman points out (chapter 9), the kinds of new political alliances that are taking place between groups from the often impoverished global South and the 'developed' North suggest a rethinking of many of these notions, particularly where there are assumptions about technology as being beneficial. This is not a new argument and it is interesting to note a re-emergence of 1960s radical anthropology, such as the 'original affluent society' thesis offered by Marshall Sahlins in *Stone age economics* (1972).

The writer most aligned with this particular position in the contemporary anarchist milieu is John Zerzan, who has suggested that contemporary activists are looking for a 'theory that is pitched at a deeper level' (Campbell, 2001: 2). In his books *Future primitive* (1995) and *Elements of refusal* (1999), he has tried to provide such a theory. In the former work, Zerzan embraces Sahlin's thesis, arguing that pre-agricultural hunter-gatherer societies had an intelligence, health and social stability, a fact ignored by generations of anthropologists and archaeologists on account of its implications for the alleged 'progress' of civilisation. In the latter book, he extends this position through systematic attacks on the supposedly liberatory benefits of the invention of language, art, technology, numerical systems and concepts of 'time'. Each of these he sees as having a role in legitimising the exploitative relations that emerged in the 'cradle of civilisation' with agriculture and domestication, and which have, according to Zerzan, continued to feed the alienation of people from each other and from the natural world ever since.

These 'total' critiques of civilisation and technology offered by anarcho-primitivists certainly suggest new ways of conceptualising power that have hitherto been largely absent from the anarchist critique. What cannot be underestimated though is how controversial and problematic some of these positions are (note the different interpretations taken by Goaman, Millett and Bowen in this book for instance). The value of these 'deeper' critiques is that they offer a significant challenge to entrenched anarchist positions, particularly around questions of alienation, attitudes to nature and psychological reliance on technological systems. Whether they offer tangible strategies for remaking society is a moot point and one that we shall return to in the conclusion of the book. For now it is worth noting that in the period of global anarchism, there has been something of an acceleration in analytical frameworks which claim new interpretations of power, but the anti-civilisation critique is not one that necessarily holds sway.

Poststructuralism, anarchy and chaos

Two other philosophical perspectives that have begun to have an impact in the era of global anarchism are poststructuralism and theories of complexity and chaos from the natural sciences. These are also extremely problematic, but as Jonathan Purkis argues (2001, and this volume, chapter 2) they offer important new methods for thinking about the constitution of power in contemporary societies and how one can affect change in all kinds of ways simultaneously.

In *The Political philosophy of poststructural anarchism* (1994), the American author Todd May has argued that the poststructural move away from analytical frameworks which rely on a single explanatory 'hinge' is extremely compatible with anarchism. Both May and Andrew Koch (1997) have suggested that the theoretical tradition which includes Michel Foucault, Gilles Deleuze, Felix Guattari, Jean-François Lyotard and Jacques Derrida offers ways of problematising the rationalistic, humanistic and scientific assumptions behind classical anarchism and conceptualising power in unique ways. Certainly, all of these have critiques of the Enlightenment and particular 'meta-narratives' that may be of use to some anarchists. Foucault's work on the reproduction and perpetuation of social power through discourses specific to particular historical situations offers insights into the diverse manifestations of power and levels of complicity involved, willing and unwilling. Similarly the micro-sociological observations inherent in Deleuze and Guattari's (1988) concept of the 'rhizome' and the decentred, lattice-like and non-deterministic nature of power is attractive when we are trying to understand the ever-increasing complexities of global forces.

Ironically, the aforementioned associations are embraced more enthusiastically by non-anarchists than anarchists, and this may well be on the grounds that poststructuralism is not a philosophy of praxis.[10] In a review of May's book. Moore (1997a) notes the propensity for poststructuralists to talk about power as something that can be divided into negative and positive forms, a situation that most anarchists would feel uncomfortable with, but, in terms of praxis, anarchists also must engage with. As Moore points out in his own chapter in this collection (chapter 3), Foucault's seductive analysis of power/knowledge (1980) presumes that countercultural and antipolitical forces actually want to negotiate with those in power as opposed to desiring the abolition of power and organising in spite of them. It is this kind of reasoning which leads anarchists to see the areas of poststructuralism and also postmodernism as more of a conceptual toolbox than a particular advancement in anarchist theory and praxis as such (Goaman and Dodson, 2000; Zerzan, 1991).

In a very different vein, many contemporary anarchist theorists have tried to draw on the natural and physical scientific notions of chaos and complexity. The significant 'hook' here is the existence of 'self-organising' systems as an integral part of the ordering of life itself, that there are 'mutualistic' processes at work which allow other patterns to 'emerge' according to their own internal dynamics (rather than being imposed on from outside). As already indicated, there is considerable debt to Kropotkin here, although this is rarely acknowledged within the scientific community who 'discovered' these processes, perhaps because research into complex systems takes place in extremely hierarchical and profit-driven knowledge communities. As Chesters (2003) has recently noted, the concerns in some radical quarters[11] that complexity will be become comprehensively adopted by business cultures (as opposed to being a passing fad) is of less concern than it might otherwise have been. Competitive, hierarchical money-making enterprises cannot exist with 'flat structures' or 'complex adaptive systems' that allow new cultures to emerge simply because they do not have the rationale or organisational flexibility to do so. However, Chesters suggests, it is precisely in the organisational cultures of the 'alternative globalisation movement' (AGM) that these processes will begin to be visible:

> [The movement']s reliance upon flat structures, network forms, its antipathy to institutionalisation and leaders *per se*, its generation and proliferation of events, gatherings, e-mail lists and web sites has created a structure that is dynamic, resilient and actualises through 'weak ties' the potential of those belonging to it. The apparent disorganisation . . . masks a deeper truth – an emergent order on the edge of chaos. (Chesters, 2003: 56)

These concepts are still in their infancy, but are in a long line of 'holistic' perspectives frequently linked to ecological thought that have interested anarchists to varying degrees. Curiously, some areas of eco-anarchist philosophy – and especially Bookchin's version of social ecology – have expressed distrust to an uncritical embracing of concepts from the natural sciences, although there often appears to be more of an overlap than is sometimes acknowledged.[12]

Deconstructing old themes with new tools

Despite their different assumptions and trajectories, each of the aforementioned theoretical perspectives offers useful ways of rethinking the enduring areas of anarchist concern. In a sense, it is the generic idea of 'complexity' that differentiates the classical era of anarchism from the global one. This is perhaps best realised through the idea of the 'emergence' of pre-existing 'total critiques' into temporal and spatial contexts within which they make far more sense and impact. In particular, the deconstruction of dualistic and deterministic philosophy has to become a starting point for theories of global anarchism and this is evident in many of the contributions that follow.

Firstly, the importance of transcending dualistic philosophy is central to the arguments of Heckert (chapter 5), who, following very much in the footsteps of sexual revolutionaries such as Emma Goldman and Alex Comfort, offers some potentially unpopular but extremely important words for established Leftist practitioners of identity politics. For Heckert, any analysis of sexual politics should transcend critiques of political economy as well as essentialist positions that are culturally exclusive; indeed, in both theoretical and practical senses (on the streets), these discourses effectively reinforce the oppressive oppositions of Self and Other. Such questions of normality and the politics of intimacy are pivotal to Joanna Gore's (chapter 8) exposition on the boundaries of oppression as defined by both the educational and psychiatric professions. Gore embraces the often overlooked tradition of 1960s pioneers R. D. Laing, David Cooper and Thomas Szasz, whose anti-dualistic theories helped to deconstruct dominant definitions of normality and socialisation. Her argument, however, also makes important comparisons with the way that young people learn about the most appropriate forms of emotional expression within society, especially through artistic media. Here Gore draws on the radical tradition of 'community arts' that in the 1970s was a political force to be reckoned with before the evolution of a 'commissioning culture' in the 1980s. The former was a time when boundaries between artist and audience were being experimented with in many areas of politics and popular culture continuing the work of the Situationist International, the Living Theatre and drama theorist Augusto Boal. Interestingly, from different trajectories, both Gore and Heckert are effectively elaborating on a theme raised by Colin Ward in his essay 'Play as an anarchist parable' (1982). Undermining the serious and rational sentiments of political discourse is of course a fine situationist tactic, and in this context it is an effective one: sexuality without a sense of fun is as dull as everyday life without laughter. These arguments are central to Gribble's consideration of the philosophy of libertarian education and the importance of student-*defined* as opposed to student-centred forms of learning: education should be a pleasure, not a duty.

Contesting oppression in such micro-sociological contexts forms an essential part of Moore's evocation of the need for 'lived poetry' (chapter 3), a fantastically optimistic glimpse of how the Self could develop without the clutter of everyday power relations. The permeation of oppression through all areas of contemporary living is something that many of the essays here identify, regardless of which philosophical premises they draw upon, and is symptomatic of the limitations of and move away from dualistic thinking. If there is one particular area that defines much contemporary anarchist thought, it is the need to challenge existing divisions between humanity and non-human nature, long a concern of ecological critiques.

This relationship is addressed here in a number of different ways: by Millett in terms of the anti-technological position of the influential *Fifth Estate* collective; by Goaman in terms of bridging the distance between Western perspectives and movements in the global South; by Heckert through the deconstruction of debates about natural and unnatural sexuality; by Purkis in terms of the theoretical perspectives utilised by social scientists; and by Szerszynski and Tomalin through the notion of 'enchantment'. The latter authors raise the thorny question of spirituality within radical political discourse, asking what insight contemporary activists can glean from the adoption of apparently 'irrational' perspectives.

Such positions are not unusual in radical thought, and Szerszynski and Tomalin note some of the overlapping relationships between millenarianism, environmentalism and anarchism. The history of anarchism has been periodically peppered with advocates of non-aligned or anti-institutional forms of religious belief. Of the classical anarchists, Leo Tolstoy was perhaps the most sympathetic to religious beliefs, although some of his ideas are problematic (Hopton, 2000). More recently Taoism has become linked to anarchist ideas by a number of thinkers (Clark, 1984; Rapp, 1998) and in the science fiction novels of Ursula LeGuin.

Oppositional gambits

A key issue in these ecologically conscious, antidualistic currents is the extent to which the body becomes a focus and a vehicle for identifying and contesting power and oppression. Since the mid-1980s this has become a fashionable part of academic discourse, particularly in the humanities and social sciences. For our purposes, it is possible to identify a definite 'anarchist politics of the body' in a number of the contributions to this book. In his assessment of the role that the regulation of drugs has in wider forms of social control, Craig notes the manner in which the taking of narcotics can constitute a form of radical opposition. This can be couched in terms of individual self-determined acts of recreational resistance, or more soberingly a rejection of the very organisation of capitalist reality. In terms of the physical intervention of individuals in a protest situation, the body has always been an inspiring symbol of resistance, be this in the classic Gandhian-inspired form of civil disobedience (identified by Szerszynski and Tomalin) or the inventive symbolic interventions of protestors against globalisation, here discussed by Goaman. For many, the body is a central focus for the kinds of activist politics of consumption that intensified in the 1990s. As individuals have adopted non-exploitative lifestyles to co-exist with the protest tactics and philosophies of animal liberation, ecological direct action, anti-militarism and so forth, so the body becomes defined in new ways.

The theoretical matters that define the global age of anarchism are complex, controversial and constantly adapting to new forms of conflict and struggle in ways that seem impossible to articulate coherently. This has often been the problem of anarchist epistemology in a general sense, and being dismayed by the difficulties of categorisation and comprehensive analysis is perhaps to miss a crucial point about the need for indeterminacy in the world. For too long, anarchists have been burdened by embarrassingly simplistic, redundant visions of political analysis and engagement. Some of these may still be applicable in certain contexts, but, for the most part, the application of modernist and Enlightenment anarchism to the plethora of struggles around the globe requires at best a healthy degree of scepticism. The possibilities for influence and change are, to paraphrase an old situationist quote, endless and bizarre and are, in all probability, indicative of a paradigm shift that we are suitably unable to recognise at this point in history. Nevertheless, the issue of contesting and abolishing power wherever it is located is of course another matter and it is to these strategic considerations that we return in the conclusion. The diversity of perspectives on anarchism that follow serves to illustrate that the pursuit of libertarian forms of human organisation is a complex, challenging, but enriching and worthwhile matter.

Notes

1 Bakunin does feature, by default, in the argument made by Goaman, that there has often been an affinity between anarchism and the politicisation of the peasantry, something that connects seventeenth-century English radicals like the Diggers and contemporary indigenous movements like the Zapatistas.
2 Some theorists, whilst not discounting these events as indicating a sea-change in political cultures, have downplayed the idea that the new movements sprang up quite so dramatically. Jan Willem Duyvendak, for instance, suggests that 'May 68' was largely a battle over 'old movement politics' and the repositioning of the Left wing of French politics (1995: 113ff.).
3 In the 1980s, these debates were about the relative merits of social and deep ecology, with the political positions of the US Earth First! movement coming under scrutiny (see Bookchin and Foreman, 1991). The 1990s were characterised more by the growing impact that anarcho-primitivism had on the radical environmental movement and some within the growing alternative globalisation movement. One of the common denominators in many of these debates was the figure of Murray Bookchin, whose attacks on other theorists have received more attention than the ideas which he has tried to defend (see 1995 in particular). Good summaries of (some) of these debates can be found in Watson (1996) and Light (1998).
4 These positions are obviously culturally relative. In particular, critiques of anthropocentrism have been vociferous in Britain where animal liberation and rights movements have been very effective, but this has not been true even within the West, let alone the wider world.
5 'The Unabomber' (Theodore Kaczynski) is currently serving three life sentences in American prisons for a seventeen-year long war on technological society (which included fatalities). He has become a cult figure for some anarcho-primitivists.
6 The concept of 'totality' can be traced back to the Marxism of Georg Lukács.
7 The Situationist International and the work of Guy Debord (1987 [1957]) and Raoul Vaneigem (1967, 1994) in particular has been the focus of a number of high-profile treatments such as Plant (1992).
8 Baudrillard's legacy on social theory in general has been immense, although anecdotal evidence often suggests that his 'early work' such as *For a critique of the political economy of the sign* (1972) has a lasting relevance that some of his 1990s works lack. *Simulations* (1983) and its discussion of simulacra and hyper-reality are a constant reminder of the fluid and shallow nature of post-modern living, with more than a nod to the Situationist International along the way.
9 *Socialism or barbarism* was a radical communist journal edited by Castoriadis that ran from 1948 to 1967. Figures closely associated with it in the late 1960s included J. F. Lyotard and Daniel Cohn-Bendit.
10 The somewhat inward-looking dimension to poststructuralism, perhaps in reaction to the failures of 'May '68', has been pointed out many times (see Berman, 1992; Eagleton, 1996).

11 See for instance Fotopoulos (2000).
12 Many of the concepts that Bookchin discusses, such as non-human and human eco-systems having their own potential to 'actualise' through self-organisation and unfolding processes, feel a lot closer to these reference points than he himself acknowledges.

Part I

Thinking

One of the principal reasons for the endurance of anarchism is the fact that regardless of context it asks challenging questions about the nature of power. This collection premises itself on the idea that anarchist concepts of power are changing to reflect the extensive and varied shifts that are taking place in political culture, and on increasingly larger stages. The anarchist critique, as will be argued in this first section of the book, has deepened in terms of its willingness to consider power as having multiple and interconnected determinants, rather than single sources exercised by the State or the economy. In the opening chapter of this section, Dave Morland outlines the philosophical shifts that have occurred within anarchism and shows how different political voices have emerged to mobilise around an increasing plurality of injustices. Whilst anarchism has always, in theory, contested power wherever it appears, Morland argues that what we are witnessing in the era of poststructural anarchism are new concepts of 'totality' where power is constructed and resisted in all manner of social and cultural contexts (in this instance, the anti-capitalist movement). In such circumstances, the notion of a single anarchist subjectivity or human nature becomes problematic, with significant implications for the forms of political action that one might take.

This is one of the principal themes of John Moore's piece in terms of his analysis of how power imprints itself on the anarchist 'subject' in some of the first moments of life (and even before). Moore poses questions about power that explore the interface between form and content, time and space, history and memory in ways that stretch the imagination. His formulation of the 'anarcho-psychological critique', as an alternative to the principal narrative of modernity, which is driven by authority, scientific progress and mediated experience, is an important approach to thinking about anarchism and ontology.

Alternative perspectives on modernity are also provided in the chapters by Steve Millett and Jonathan Purkis, albeit from considerably different standpoints. Millett's comprehensive study of the *Fifth Estate* publishing project documents the emergence of the now highly influential anti-technological and anti-civilisational strand in anarchist thought. This offers something of a challenge to anarchism as a political philosophy of the Enlightenment, as well as to other contemporary versions of ecological anarchism and, to some extent, anarcho-communism. Millett, like Moore, identifies a psychological and psychoanalytic dimension to understanding authority, alienation and history, which is a powerful and still underacknowledged aspect of contemporary anarchism. Purkis addresses similar issues in his chapter, but from the perspective of the sociologist trying to understand the authoritarian and ecologically damaging premises behind sociological theory. He argues the case for an anarchist sociology which pays much more attention to how social experience is researched, theorised and represented. Like Morland, he finds poststructuralist literature a potentially useful tool for understanding power, particularly when theorising contemporary social movements.

The difficulties of doing anarchist theory is not lost on any of these authors, particularly when their starting points are sometimes challenging. The diversity of the contributions which follow are, however, indicative of some of the ways that anarchist theory is responding to a more globally conscious and 'complex' period of history.

I Dave Morland

Anti-capitalism and poststructuralist anarchism[1]

Introduction

Social anarchism has a long reputation as a disparate and incoherent ideology. Commentators, sympathetic and objective alike, have frequently accused social anarchism of being too diverse to constitute a singular, recognisable ideology at all (Chomsky, 1970; Miller, 1984; Ball and Dagger, 1991). To a degree this is true: social anarchism is a loose and diverse ideology that may be too elusive for some commentators to categorise neatly and clearly. However, other commentators, myself included, have taken the view that there *is* sufficient rigour and coherence within social anarchism to label this as an identifiable ideology (Morland, 1997; Woodcock, 1975). Notwithstanding that social anarchism is fraught with difficulties as an agreed academic construct, the task of defining anarchy itself remains problematic. Having progressed from nineteenth-century social anarchism, the last century witnessed the proliferation of a number of divergent strands within anarchist thought. Principal among these is social ecology, expounded largely by Murray Bookchin, but there are many other strands, including primitivism (e.g., John Zerzan) and poststructuralist anarchism (e.g., Todd May).

Differences concerning the definition of anarchy and social anarchism permeate anarchist thought and writings. Consensus is usually achieved, however, over what anarchists oppose. A common starting point is the issue of power. Drawing on rational choice theory, Michael Taylor (1982: 11–13) defines power as the ability to change the range of available actions that face people. In this respect, threats or rewards are instances of power. However, as Taylor acknowledges, power is also to do with the position of groups within society and their capacity to secure their own preferred outcomes. This corresponds to Marshall's understanding of the types of power within society: traditional power based on custom; newly acquired power grounded in the law, the State or the military, for example; and revolutionary power, frequently associated with vanguard political parties (Marshall, 1992: 45–6). Certainly, power is central to anarchist theory, and anarchists, whether old or new, are united in their belief that it should, wherever possible, be uprooted and eliminated. In particular, social anarchists have attacked power where it is most concentrated, in the hands of the State. Indeed, power is integral to social anarchists' critique of Marxism and its insistence on the dictatorship of the proletariat as pivotal to the success of revolutionary strategy. Similarly, anarchists are occasionally defined by dint of their opposition to the State. This accounts for social anarchism's reputation as an anti-State ideology. For most, if not all, anarchists, social anarchism is equivalent to constructing a future society without the State. (See, for example, the classic statement by Malatesta from the 1890s (Malatesta, 1974).) In etymological terms, anarchy refers to the absence of rule or government. Therefore, when we talk of anarchy we generally talk of 'a stateless society' (Carter, 1993: 141).

This chapter is not an attempt to resolve or settle the difficulties associated with defining anarchy or social anarchism. It will suggest that, when situated alongside the practices of new social movements associated with the recent anti-capitalist protests, the poststructuralist perspective affords insight into how new modes of anarchist practice are emerging. Bookchin attempted to delineate this debate in *Social anarchism or lifestyle anarchism: an unbridgeable chasm* (1995) thus denouncing postmodernism or lifestyle anarchism. Unsurprisingly, Bookchin's analysis is not accepted universally within anarchist circles, and a trenchant critique of that work may be found in Bob Black's *Anarchy after Leftism* (1997). In focusing on the relationship between social anarchism and poststructuralist anarchism, it is not my intention to make proprietorial claims about the nature of anarchism *per se*. This purpose of this chapter is to illustrate the importance of broadening the understanding of social anarchism. The intention is not to dismiss or discount other modes of anarchism, but simply to highlight how anarchist theory and practice (focusing on its postmodern and/or poststructuralist manifestations) is evolving into something distinct and is, at the same time, nurturing contemporary modes of resistance against traditional social, political and economic forms of oppression.

Social anarchism

Resisting power

For the purposes of this chapter, social anarchism is defined essentially in line with the writings and practices associated with nineteenth-century figures such as Proudhon, Bakunin and Kropotkin. One thing that the recent anti-capitalist groups and social anarchism often have in common is a shared alignment along an axis of negative unity. By that I mean that social anarchists and the temporary alliances that have been characteristic of recent anti-capitalist demonstrations are united by virtue of what they stand against. For the anti-capitalists, capitalism, globalisation and trans-national corporations are the adversaries most regularly cited. Social anarchists target similar enemies. More importantly, both social anarchists and anti-capitalists stress that a cartography of power relations does not yield a map in which there is one dominant epicentre of power.

Anarchists, old and new alike, insist that power relations saturate multiple networks and must be resisted accordingly.

Arguments against hierarchy, inequality and against capitalism itself are abundant in anarchist literature. It is here that we find evidence both of social anarchism's indebtedness to and its repudiation of Marxist theory. Bakunin is a splendid example of the way in which social anarchism on the one hand embraces Marx's moral critique of capitalism and on the other rejects its preferred revolutionary strategy. Although there are serious differences between the anarchist and Marxist conceptions of human nature, Bakunin readily draws on Marx's account of alienation in his attack on the dehumanising consequences of capitalist production. The importance here (in terms of the differences between social and poststructuralist anarchism) is that the adoption of this Marxist concept reflects social anarchism's foundationalist perspective. Here social anarchism and Marxism converge in assuming that the scale of the dehumanising effects of capitalism can be measured against some notion of human nature. Even though the conception of human nature differs between social anarchism and Marxism, the critical common reference point is the centrality of human nature to both ideologies. Human nature is the foundation upon which Marx builds his moral critique of the alienating and exploitative features of capitalism, which is a foundationalist perspective that social anarchists like Bakunin share.

However, the commonality is soon displaced by contestation when it comes to identifying an appropriate revolutionary strategy. The core of the debate between Marx and Bakunin in the First International and the subsequent wider disagreement about means and ends in revolutionary methodology hinges on rival conceptions of human nature. Accordingly, Miller (1984: 93) judges that anarchists possess a more realistic perspective of human nature, precisely because of their fears that a Marxist 'dictatorship of the proletariat' would lead to the development of a new ruling élite. The corrupting effects of power on human nature are well documented in the anarchist writings of Bakunin and others and are integral to the split between Marxists and anarchists after the First International.

In essence, what social anarchism is arguing against here is Marxism's mode of representational politics. Establishing themselves as the representatives and voice of the oppressed masses, Marxist revolutionary leaders assume a vanguard role in securing the victory of the proletariat. The creation of a centralised, hierarchical political party to lead the workers to victory is anathema to most anarchists for three principal reasons. The first of these is the issue of representation. As writers such as Bakunin (1990: 135–6) and Malatesta (1974: 44–7) stress, anarchists are not in the business of drawing up blueprints or establishing themselves as prophetic revolutionary leaders. This would be tantamount to anarchists becoming a priestly class governing the rest of humanity.[2] Malatesta writes: 'we would be declaring ourselves the government and would be prescribing, as do religious legislators, a universal code for present and future generations' (1974: 44).

Revolutionary agencies

The second reason why anarchists eschew Marxist visions of revolution is that anarchists have been somewhat reluctant to ascribe the role of revolutionary saviour to the proletariat. Anarchists were much more inclined to look beyond the industrialised working class as the embodiment of revolutionary destiny. Rather, figures such as Bakunin identified with what contemporary sociologists would now term the socially excluded as the source of revolutionary potential, much in the way that Marcuse (1968) did in the following century.

Locating power

The third reason follows naturally from the second for social anarchists. In visualising a potential revolutionary role for classes other than the proletariat, social anarchists express their belief that resistance is not solely and perhaps not even primarily political in nature. Power, for instance, resonates within social institutions and economic and cultural relations as much as the political realm. With that in mind, social anarchists stress that all forms of power, hierarchy and oppression, whether they be political, social, cultural or economic, are to be resisted and subverted. Consequently, modes of resistance transcend the political. Nonetheless, social anarchists have invariably identified the State as the locus of power to be resisted.

Direct action

A defining feature of social anarchism has been its commitment to spontaneous direct action. Driven by grassroots activists without bureaucratised revolutionary leadership, direct action has been cherished as an effective tool in the social anarchists' strategic armoury. Participatory by nature, direct action encourages anarchists' faith in the capacity of individuals to do things for themselves. As Ward (1988) has argued, even acts such as self-build housing projects or tenant co-operatives afford anarchists comfort simply because they provide convincing evidence of people's capacity to live without oppressive agencies such as the State. Self-organisation, then, has been fundamental both to social anarchism's promotion of direct action as an effective tool of resistance and subversion and to its assumptions about the feasibility of life without a State after the downfall of capitalism.

Poststructuralist anarchism

How then does poststructuralist anarchism differ from its predecessor in terms of its theory and praxis? Poststructuralist anarchism is equally committed to the elimination of power, inequality and capitalism as social anarchism is. To argue the converse would be to imagine a rupture of seismic proportions within the movement and within its theoretical narratives. Such a rupture has not taken place. Social anarchism has shifted its ground as it has embraced some elements of poststructuralist philosophy.

Rejecting foundationalist discourses

This shift in territory from social to poststructuralist anarchism is most notice-able and particularly important at three levels of theory. The first, and the one that underscores the others, is the poststructuralist denunciation of foundation-alist discourses or narratives. Poststructuralism, closely associated with the writ-ings of Foucault and Derrida, is a rejection of explanations (such as those found in Marx's writings) that the human condition can be explained by reference to underlying structures, such as economics, that are subject to objective analysis outside the discourse that constructs these structures. In *The political philoso-phy of poststructuralist anarchism*, Todd May (1994) exemplifies how poststruc-turalism has jettisoned all forms of humanism. For poststructuralists, 'subjects and structures are sedimentations of practices whose source cannot be discov-ered in a privileged ontological domain but that must be sought, rather, among the specific practices in which they arise' (May, 1994: 78).

There are two ineluctable strategic (in May's terms) difficulties in social anar-chist thought. The first is the subscription to a benign human essence or human nature, although, as I have argued elsewhere (Morland, 1997), to identify anar-chism as the proprietor of a benign assumption concerning human nature is sim-plistic and erroneous. The second difficulty concerns social anarchism's ascription to a suppressive notion of power, which will be addressed below. The former inescapably associates social anarchism with foundationalist discourses, and it is the abandonment of such discourses that facilitates the separation of social anarchism from poststructuralist anarchism.

Locating power

The second shift in theoretical territory is less pronounced but nonetheless real. It flows out of the transition to a poststructuralist philosophy that defines power as operating at multiple levels and in multiple modes. To be sure, social anar-chists have long conceived of power as a relation that permeates political, social and economic institutions. However, as May argues, social anarchism advocates the decentralisation of power precisely because it sees this as an alternative to the centralisation of power in the hands of the State. In this regard, social anar-chism is what May terms a strategic political philosophy, whereas for a tactical philosophy, such as poststructuralist anarchism,

> there is no centre within which power is to be located. Otherwise put, power, and consequently politics, are irreducible. There are many different sites from which it arises, and there is an interplay among these various sites in the creation of the

social world. This is not to deny that there are points of concentration of power or, to keep with the spatial image, points where various (and perhaps bolder) lines intersect. Power does not, however, originate at those points, rather, it conglomerates around them. (May, 1994: 11)

Within poststructuralist philosophy, power is conceptualised as existing in the rhizome of political, social, economic and cultural networks. Its distribution along the flows of these networks may result in occasional concentrations of power at interconnections between different networks. How different is this assessment from that of the social anarchists? Were the social anarchists too immersed in Marxian economics to perceive the power dynamics at play in social and cultural networks? Is it that poststructuralist philosophy identifies flows of power in the socio-cultural nexus because that nexus is more visibly central to our lives than it was in the nineteenth century? It is beyond the remit of this chapter to address such questions in detail, but it is imperative that consideration be given to the relationship between social and poststructuralist anarchism, if only to determine the degree to which poststructuralist anarchism is more than the arguments of social anarchism writ large.

That power inhabits the flows of networks is indicative of poststructuralist philosophy's perspective on totalities. Here there is a subtle shift of emphasis in how social and poststructuralist anarchism visualise the nature of systems oppression. For some social anarchists, such as Bakunin, the principal enemy is capital. Despite his difference with Marx over revolutionary strategy, Bakunin is indebted to Marx for his appraisal of where power lies and how to overturn the oppression that it brings. In nineteenth-century social anarchism, capitalism and the bourgeoisie are clearly identified as the source of the economic, social and moral wrongdoings that are committed against humanity. Whilst capital is not absolved of its responsibility in poststructuralist anarchism, there is a shift of emphasis that renders the narrow focus on capitalism and its governing classes as obsolete. Goaman (1999: 73), for example, has argued that we 'are oppressed and alienated by the totality of existing conditions . . . [and for that reason we] . . . need to examine the socio-economic-cultural framework underpinning the contemporary system of power relations and late capitalism'.

Passages such as this reveal how anarchists now look beyond capitalism to a broader and perhaps more insidious system that perpetuates oppression. Here metaphors of interconnectivity abound as anarchists uncover oppression and power across a wider totality. Thus Moore (1997a: 159) suggests that 'the focus of anarchism is not the abolition of the State, but the abolition of the totality, of life structured by governance and coercion, of power itself in all its multiple forms'.[3]

At times Moore's 'totality' is explained by reference to an underlying scientific-technological rationale that provides a framework within which capitalism thrives. However, the crucial point here is that anarchists are now persuaded that capital shares this totality with others. Indeed, it is often the logic and the myth that drives the system forward that must be resisted. It is for this reason that resistance should occur at multiple levels and at multiple points across these total-ities.

Redefining the State

Poststructuralist arguments on power are integral to its consideration of the State and the practices within which power and the State are situated. It is at this juncture that the shift in territory on the State and hierarchies becomes evident in poststructuralist anarchism. Thus, May contends that thinkers like Lyotard, Deleuze and Foucault have developed:

> a new type of anarchism. This new anarchism retains the ideas of intersecting and irreducible local struggles, of a wariness about representation, of the political as investing the entire field of social relationships, and of the social as a network rather than a closed holism, a concentric field, or a hierarchy. (1994: 85)

Certainly, the work of Deleuze and Guattari injects 'a radical notion of multi-plicity into phenomena which we traditionally approach as being discretely bounded, structured and stable' (Haggerty and Ericson, 2000: 608). One phe-nomenon that Deleuze and Guattari approach in this manner is the State. Their distinctive approach to the State emerges in their philosophical distinction between deterritorialisation and reterritorialisation. In *What is philosophy?*, Deleuze and Guattari (1994: 67–8) argue that we 'need to see how everyone, at every age, in the smallest things as in the greatest challenges, seeks a territory, tolerates or carries out deterritorialisations, and is reterritorialised on almost anything – memory, fetish or dream'. This process of deterritorialisation and reterritorialisation permeates the State and the city.

> State and City, on the contrary, carry out a deterritorialisation because the former juxtaposes and compares agricultural territories by relating them to a higher arith-metical Unity, and the latter adapts the territory to a geometrical extensiveness that can be continued in commercial circuits. The *imperial spatium* of the State and the *political extensio* of the city are not so much forms of a territorial principle as a deterritorialisation that takes place on the spot when the State appropriates the ter-ritory of local groups or when the city turns its back on its hinterland. In one case, there is reterritorialisation on the palace and its supplies, and in the other, on the agora and commercial networks. (1984: 86)

States are not uniform or identical in terms of appearance or organisation. States 'are made up not only of people but also of wood, fields, gardens, animals and com-modities' (Deleuze and Guattari, 1988: 385). But 'every State carries within itself the essential moments of its existence' (p. 385). The reason for that is that the State, for Deleuze and Guattari, did not evolve over the course of some defined historical period but 'appears fully armed, a master stroke executed all at once' (1984: 217). The primordial despotic State that accompanies Marx's Asiatic mode of production is the original abstraction that is realised in concrete existence in different settings. Now, the State is 'subordinated to a field of forces whose flows it co-ordinates and whose autonomous relations of domination and subordination it expresses' (1984: 221). Today, then, the State is formed out of the decoded flows it invents for money and property; it is formed out of the dominating classes; it cowers behind the things it signifies, and 'is itself produced inside the field of decoded flows' (p. 221). Accordingly, the State is now determined by the system within which it becomes concrete in the exercise of its functions, but in which it also remains subordinate to those very forces it decodes. Essentially, there are 'two aspects of becoming of the State: its internalisation in a field of increasingly decoded social forces forming a physical system; its spiritualisation in a supraterrestrial field that increasingly overcodes, forming a metaphysical system' (p. 222). Herein lies the totality that social anarchists must now address. Resistance against the State alone in a crude political stratagem makes little sense in face of new understanding of the State.

Poststructuralist resistance

Within poststructuralist anarchism, then, resistance is designed to reflect the nature of power and to confront it wherever it materialises. In this respect, post-structuralist resistance draws on the situationist heritage which confronted and simultaneously subverted the spectacle of capitalism, and in so doing signalled a shift away from economistic attacks on capital as the structural epicentre of power. Consequently, alternative modes of opposition are utilised to subvert the dynamics of the totalities. Resistance no longer confines itself to the political, to expressing itself against the bourgeoisie as the representatives of capital. Resistance now assumes social and cultural forms. These modes of resistance and subversion are central to the new social movements that constitute recent radical opposition, expressed through, among other things, the anti-capitalist movement.

Recent media coverage of anti-capitalist protests would have us believe that anarchists linger on the fringes of such movements as throwbacks to some nineteenth-century clandestine terrorist organisation, much as they have been painted in early twentieth-century literature such as Joseph Conrad's *The secret agent* (1978 [1907]). Indeed, as Apter has noted, anarchism 'is associated with unreason and bombs, violence and irresponsibility' (Apter and Joll, 1971: 1). It is futile to deny that violence often accompanies direct action as a mode of protest, but whether violence is any more acceptable remains a moot point. Here social anarchism appears as a broad church, with some proponents counselling against the use of violence, such as Kropotkin, and others ready to engage in a physical battle with the police and other opponents (see, for example, Miller, 1984, chapter 8).

New social movements

Formations and rationales

Although undoubtedly a construct of academics' analyses of popular protest, new social movements are real and tangible. Defining precisely the ontology of new social movements is beyond the scope of this chapter, but it seems fairly evident that the recent wave of anti-capitalist protests across the globe has illustrated the vitality of such movements, even if they are more complex than the label or construct suggests. As Whittier (2002: 289) comments, social movements 'are made up of shifting clusters of organizations, networks, communities, and activist individuals, connected by participation in challenges and collective identities through which participants define the boundaries and significance of their group'. Social movements are neither static nor monolithic. Rather, they are dynamic entities that frequently possess an organic and acephalous organisation. Moreover, movements of various and often quite radically different political hues have come together in recent protests against capitalism and globalisation. The anti-capitalist movement would be more accurately described as a movement of movements. Nonetheless, it is plain to anyone who has participated in recent anti-capitalist protests that anarchism is pivotal to the movement. As Graeber (2002: 62) opines, 'anarchism is the heart of the movement, its soul; the source of most of what's new and hopeful about it'. The mapping of social anarchism across social movements is not new. Murray Bookchin, for example, identified a number of anarchist principles and practices that may be located within the new social movements of the 1980s. For Bookchin, these are principally:

(a) that the literature of these groups resonates with Kropotkin's recommendations of decentralised society and the rejection of capitalism;
(b) that municipalist movements in particular adopt Bakunin's principle that anarchists can participate in local politics;
(c) that they are anti-hierarchical; and
(d) that the 'principle that unites these seemingly independent movements is the notion of participation and mutual aid'. (Bookchin, 1989: 271)

To be sure, Bookchin's analysis remains valid even when examining those movements associated with the recent anti-capitalist protests. Bookchin's analysis does, however, begin to lose significance with the recognition that the anti-capitalist movement is more poststructuralist in nature. As Ruggiero (2000) has noted, increasingly two schools of thought are emerging on social movements. The first suggests that social movements are concerned with resource mobilisation or distribution. This argument is advanced by writers such as McCarthy and Zald (1977) and Bluechler (1993). The second is led principally by Melucci (1996), who contends that new social movements are occupied less by political actions than by symbolic and cultural challenges.[4] A preferred categorisation depends much on the definition of 'new' in new social movements. According to Melucci (1996: 5), the 'new' is meant to signify multiple 'comparative differences between the historical forms of class conflict and today's emergent forms of collective action'.

Cautious of investing in these movements a unitary objectivity where none exists, Melucci observes that new social movements are:

systems of action, complex networks among the different levels and meanings of social action. Collective identity allowing them to become actors is not a datum or an essence; it is the outcome of exchanges, negotiations, decisions, and conflicts among actors. (1996: 4)

Melucci is right to emphasise the absence of political actions here, if only because new social movements, and especially the anti-capitalist movement, are explicitly anti-political. As Ruggiero (2000: 181) discovered in his study of the 'centri sociali' in Milan, the newness of these movements is encapsulated 'in their refusal to engage in building up a superior representative entity, such as a party or an all-embracing organization'. Establishing an organisational structure akin to groups like Friends of the Earth or Greenpeace, for example, is not the objective of new social movements (although this is probably less true of some of the Trotskyist organisations involved with the anti-capitalist movement, such as Globalize Resistance). Rather, their organisational modes are 'multifarious, fragile, transient and inconsistent' (Ruggiero, 2000: 181). They do not aspire to represent a majority; moreover, they have thrown off the shackles of representational politics completely.

Recognition of what constitutes the 'new', however, is occasionally lost, even among sympathetic commentators. Brady (2002: 58), for instance, applauds the anti-capitalist movement for engaging 'in refreshing forms of creative, extemporaneous protest' that encourages participatory politics whilst circumnavigating political spin. Appreciation of new modes of protest needs to be accompanied by a similar awareness of a sense of new purpose. In countenancing a move into the democratic arena to extend the democratic appeal of the movement, it is clear that Brady (2002: 65) has fundamentally misunderstood the nature and purpose of the anti-capitalist movement. Brady either has misjudged the centrality of anarchism within this movement or has misconceptualised the nature of anarchism as a political entity. Insofar as the anti-capitalist movement is anarchist, it has no intention of entering the democratic arena of electoral politics, or of aspiring to a broader cosmopolitanism grounded in democratic politics. Additionally, the movement does not pretend to speak for or represent anyone, never mind the world's people. The whole idea of representational politics is anathema to anarchist movements.

Certainly, the anti-capitalist movement in Britain has very visible origins. It has

emerged from a convergence between radical environmentalists and anarchists, aided by a growing sense of unease amongst some liberal organizations and commentators. It has been joined by left groups, some earlier (Workers Power) than others (the SWP[5]). (Jazz, 2001: 96)

Tactics, praxis and 'Black Block'

That the movement comprises groups of varying political standpoints is without question. This results, of course, in diverging tactics and praxis when confronting capitalism. There has been much discussion concerning the role of 'Black Block' in

Genoa and other anti-capitalist protests. Marked by a commitment to confront the police with violence if necessary, 'Black Block' were not welcomed by all quarters of the movement. Although not uniquely anarchist, 'Black Block' exemplifies the recrudescence of a social anarchist strategy that is at the heart of the anti-capitalist movement. Spontaneity, autonomy and direct action are the attributes of 'Black Block' and others in the movement. Indeed for some, 'Black Block' is no more than a tactic (K, 2001). For others (Porter, 2001), 'Black Block' has too readily adopted the stereotype identity of anarchists as instigators of chaos and destruction. To be sure, there is disagreement over tactics and targets in the anti-capitalist movement. Less contentious by far, however, is the recognition that 'Black Block':

> is no sort of organization, no sort of group. It does not exist outside the demonstration and is united only on that demonstration by some minimal unity of tactics – people who are up for property destruction and for fighting the police. (Anonymous, 2001: 45)

Such characterisations engender disquiet within the movement, but this unease is reflective of social anarchism's heritage that underscores anti-capitalist protest. As Kamura has noted, the consistence of means and ends within the movement is important. The prospect of violence becoming the defining statement of anti-capitalist protest threatens to jeopardise the whole direction of the movement: 'We want a fair world so we don't play dirty' (Kamura, 2001: 60). Violence has a long and ambiguous history within social anarchism, and it will undoubtedly continue to play an integral role in anarchist protest.

'Black Block' is also representative of another feature of the anti-capitalist movement: the absence of an obvious or hierarchical structure. Fleeting and temporary unity signifies the coming together of this movement of movements, both at the level of the broader movement itself during protests, and frequently within the individual groups or movements themselves. As Ian Welsh has illustrated, we are beginning to witness

> the arrival of the self-organising movement which exists without anything which can be identified as a traditional organisational structure. The existence of movements as networks capable of producing fleeting mobilisations to perform quite specific direct actions at short notice represents a very different model of cultural contestation compared to the essentially 1970s models which have shaped much social movement research. (Welsh, 1999: 79)

Moreover, today's activists are seemingly less likely to compromise their own commitment by ushering the movement into forms of engagement delimited by traditional structures and practices. As Welsh (1999: 79) observes, contemporary protests 'are increasingly staged on movements' own terms.' To date, groups such as Reclaim the Streets, Earth First! and the Anarchist Travelling Circus do not appear to be following in the footsteps of organisations like Friends of the Earth and Greenpeace, in either establishing dominant bureaucratic governing structures or by transferring to insider status and negotiating directly with government and its agencies.

This is not to say that all the groups or movements that have participated in recent anti-capitalist protests conform to this model. Frequently, and perhaps significantly at a local level, movements with fundamentally different outlooks combine forces during these protests. As research by Plows and Wall (2001: 4) illustrates, one of the distinctive features 'of protests against neo-liberalism is the hybrid character of the networks involved. Over 700 groups from many countries were co-ordinated by the Genoa Social Forum.' Nonetheless, a new dynamic is emerging within the protest movement. This is the drive to map out the interrelated mechanisms and practices of globalisation. Consequently, articulating the bigger picture is an integral element of the campaigns mounted by protest groups from the late 1990s (Plows and Wall, 2001: 8).

As these latter writers suggest, we are not witnessing the emergence here of entirely new groups who share nothing in common with their predecessors. The tactics and strategies they employ have often cascaded down from previous movements and groups active in the 1990s and 1980s, if not before. Insofar as those strategies invoke an engagement in political protest, it is possible to suggest, as Goaman and Dodson (1997) have done, that these new social movements are practising a tried and tested mode of orthodox socialist politics. However, the degree to which they eschew such traditional modes of action and reject the representation and vanguardism at the heart of Marxist politics, and conversely embrace new modes of socio-cultural contestation, the more sensible it becomes to regard such movements as exhibiting new poststructuralist modes of anarchism.

New social movements and poststructuralist anarchism

It is not just the fluidity and ephemerality of these alliances that makes them different; rather, it is in their strategies of resistance that they become visibly poststructuralist. At the heart of these strategies is what Welsh (1999: 80) refers to as the 'long-term process of autonomous capacity building'. The principle of acting for yourself has long been treasured by social anarchists and was the message enunciated by Kropotkin in his article 'Act for yourselves' in *Freedom* in 1887 (Kropotkin, 1988). To the extent that local communities and movements mobilise against capital and globalisation, for instance, such actions are a clear reinforcement of this anarchist principle. In this form, resistance resides at the core of new social movements' strategies. It occurs at multiple levels, assumes many different guises, and 'represents a point of convergence between anarchist and postmodern thought' (Amster, 1998: 109).

Building anarchist capacity

In essence, then, there are two features of new social movements that may be classified as anarchist in nature. The first, what Welsh refers to as 'autonomous capacity building', is that which links the old with the new: the rejection of representation. Anarchists have always been suspicious of vanguardism. Whether it appears in the form of a revolutionary élite or the veiled vampirism of an organisation that thinks it knows better, representation has been and remains an unwelcome reference in the anarchist lexicon of resistance. The reluctance of new social movements to be drawn into hackneyed strategies of political protest signals an invigorating commitment towards anarchism in action. It is precisely this ethos that underlines what Graeber (2002: 66) refers to as the movement's quest 'to map out a completely new territory'. Groups like the Direct Action Network and Tute Bianche are striving to construct 'a 'new language' of civil disobedience, combining elements of street theatre, festival and what can only be called non-violent warfare' (Graeber, 2002: 66). Such activities contrast sharply with traditional forms of protest associated with the social democratic Left and trades union politics over the last forty years. If nothing else, these protests have a very different feel about them. When compared to the prearranged march and rally, more recent protests certainly induce a sense of organic autonomy within their participants. Nonetheless, these tactics converge with the anarchist culture of 'delegitimizing and dismantling mechanisms of rule while winning ever-larger spaces of autonomy from' the State (Graeber, 2002: 68).

New forms of protest

The second feature is that which delineates contemporary social movements as converging with poststructuralist anarchism. As Goaman and Dodson (1997) rightly point out, if new social movements remain locked into tired modes of political protest, they will fail to transcend the parameters of orthodox socialist politics. By its very nature, anarchism has sought out alternative modes of opposition. Establishing communes, building free schools, publishing radical tracts, writing anti-hierarchical lyrics, planting flowers, living in trees, growing organic food, squatting in unused properties, and recycling cooking oil into green diesel are evidence of how resistance within anarchist circles assumes symbolic and cultural forms. It is also demonstrative of how both social anarchism and poststructuralism converge and are mediated by resistance. As May (1994) has argued, it is precisely through the promotion and cherishing of alternative practices that poststructuralism and social anarchism come together. In doing so they form a backdrop in front of which the new social movements surrounding the anti-capitalist debate play out modes of socio-cultural resistance.[6]

This socio-cultural movement amounts to more than a just penchant for carnival-style resistance. In the wake of communism's downfall across the former Soviet bloc and the general retreat of the Left when faced with a virulent neoliberalism, opposition to capitalism has transformed itself from endeavours to construct a brave new world (for much of the time premised on a centrally planned economy) to local and internal resistance. As Sader (2002: 97) comments, resistance in this changed environment has become separated from historical metanarratives and crude economism and has transformed itself into the 'local and sectoral'. Even if we cannot agree a name for it, society is certainly in transition and social movements reflect this change. This is not to say that traditional social movements have suddenly vanished. To be sure there is overlap between the old and the new in contemporary anti-capitalist protest, but there is also a real sense in which new social movements are distinct from their predecessors. As Melucci has observed, there are a number of common factors one may identify here:

> the diversity and low negotiability of the movement's goals; eschewing political power; questioning the partition between public and private; the convergence of protest and deviance; reaching for solidarity through action; and the repudiation of representation in favour of direct action. (Melucci, 1996: 102–3)

Echoing social anarchist sentiments through their own contemporary praxis, new social movements are also deeply reflective of new modes of anarchism. In targeting nodes of power across social, cultural and political networks, by way of organising into non-hierarchical and decentralised networks themselves, the anti-capitalist movement not only reinforces the customary anarchist approach to resistance but also confirms 'what is to be resisted' (May, 1994: 52). Here, we witness the emergence of poststructuralist anarchism. Subjects and structures obtain meaning through the specific practices from which they arise. In spurning representation, in shunning the quest for political power, and in focusing on the present and the specific (Melucci, 1996: 116), the anti-capitalist movement encompasses a series of attempts to carve out social spaces of autonomy that, by their very nature, oppose the dominant paradigm of neoliberal economic and social commodification. This search for auonomous zones unfolds itself at the level of the local and the specific intersections of social, cultural, economic and political networks. Essentially, the anti-capitalist movement has embarked on a poststructuralist voyage to 'construct power relationships that can be lived with' (May, 1994: 114). Recognition that power pervades multiple networks is recognition that power can never be eliminated. Social anarchists have long realised that. In building alternative practices, poststructuralist anarchists are engaged in what Deleuze and Guattari (1988: 291) term 'becoming minoritarian'. By developing alternative practices through social forums and other networks and organisations, contemporary anarchists are challenging dominant practices and simultaneously escaping oppression. As Deleuze and Guattari contend in *A thousand plateaux*, the concept of majority 'assumes a state of power and domination, not the other way around. It assumes the standard means, not the other way around.' With that in mind, it is important to distinguish between 'the majoritarian as a constant and homogenous system; minorities as subsystems; and the minoritarian as a potential, creative and created, becoming' (1988: 105–6). In becoming minor, 'a nondenumerable and proliferating minority . . . threatens to destroy the very concept of majority' (1988: 469).

Referring to Deleuze and Guattari's concept of nomadology, Paul Virilio has recently commented on the relevance of an understanding of the world as in flux.

'Today's world no longer has any kind of stability; it is shifting, straddling, gliding away all the time' (Armitage, 1999: 48). Poststructuralist analyses premised on concepts such as networks, rhizomes, cross-currents and deterritorialisation overlap significantly with social anarchism. Tracing its strategic origins to its reluctance to solely support the industrialised proletariat (precisely because power permeates other arenas in life), social anarchism has long been conscious of the need to assemble resistance across networks. As Ward (1988: 22) observes, anarchists 'have to build networks instead of pyramids . . . Anarchism does not demand the changing of the labels on the layers, it doesn't want different people on top, it wants us to clamber out from underneath.' This intellectual heritage is deeply rooted within social anarchism and pushes it away from strategic thinking towards what May terms a 'tactical political philosophy'. Strategic political philosophy, such as Marxism, situates various oppressions and inequalities in one basic problematic; by contrast, tactical thinking 'pictures the social and political world not as a circle but instead as an intersecting network of lines' (May, 1994: 10–11). Rather than focusing resistance on one apparent nucleus of power, tactical thinking opposes emancipation led by a vanguard élite. Observing that power inhabits networks instead of originating from one centre or source, 'the poststructuralist critique of representation' is plainly anarchist in nature (May, 1994: 12). Both social anarchists and poststructuralists envisage social spaces as comprised of 'intersections of power rather than emanations from a source' (p. 52).

Conclusion

In engaging in multiple modes of resistance to confront the numerous accumulations of power at different nodes that intersect across social, cultural, political and economic networks, social anarchism and poststructuralism share a common outlook and a common assessment of how to construct spaces of autonomy. In establishing sites of resistance, activists, including those allied to the anti-capitalist movement, are simultaneously undermining dominant or major discourses of power. In attacking lines of police officers with pink feather dusters, for example, anti-capitalist protesters are not only creating social spaces marked by theatre and autonomy, they are also delegitimising violent forms of State oppression. To be sure, not all anarchists engage in such practices, but increasingly they are adopting carnival-style protest and resistance. Equally, not all anarchists would agree with the assessment that social anarchism is converging with poststructuralism in the twenty-first century. This chapter does not pretend to proffer a narrative that applies to all branches of anarchist practice and theory. It is, however (if I can borrow a phrase from one scholar who would have certainly disagreed with this piece), testimony to the fact that anarchism should be regarded as a 'living, thriving project' (Moore, 1997a: 159). Unquestionably, anarchist praxis is evidenced through recent anti-capitalist protests. Consequently, as social anarchism adapts to life in a new century, it is a project that now possesses a distinctively poststructuralist dynamic.

Notes

1 I would like to thank John Armitage and John Carter for their comments on an earlier draft of this chapter.
2 The irony of Bakunin's occasional recommendation of Secret Brotherhoods (see for example Dolgoff, 1973: 148–55) that assume an essentially Leninist leadership role will not be lost on readers and signals one of the ambiguities in his writings. Another uncertainty surfaces in relation to the role of violence and propaganda by the deed, which does not always sit comfortably with anarchism's insistence on the commensurability of means and ends in revolutionary methodology.
3 It should be noted that Moore was not a subscriber to poststructuralist anarchism. Rather, he identified himself with what he termed 'the second wave of anarchism' incorporating figures like Guy Debord, Raoul Vaneigem, John Zerzan and Fredy Perlman. This is not a consistent grouping and ranges from situationists to primitivists.
4 *Editorial note*. The death of Alberto Melucci in October 2001 to cancer has deprived social movement theory of one of its most versatile and imaginative figures. Another assessment of the importance of his work for understanding contemporary anarchism is Atton (1999).
5 The Socialist Workers' Party, probably the largest and most highly organised of the far Left groups in Britain today.
6 It is also worth noting that Laclau's (1988) and Mouffe's (1988) writings on radical democracy emphasise the importance of multiple sites of resistance and struggle from a poststructuralist perspective.

2 Jonathan Purkis

Towards an anarchist sociology[1]

A serious scholar is one who takes the Pope at his word and discounts the words of rebels. A ranter is one who takes rebels at their word and discounts every word of the Pope. (Fredy Perlman, 1983: 183)

Objectivism and relativism not only are untenable as philosophies, they are bad guides for fruitful cultural collaboration. (Paul Feyerabend, 1995: 152)

Introduction

The 'politics' of knowledge has long been a concern of the humanities and social sciences. The decisions taken about which areas of society are regarded as being worthy of study, how they should be researched and the relative usefulness of the findings raise many questions about power and how it is manifested within particular societies. The ideological implications of these issues extend to questioning the role of the academic just as much as the legitimacy of State agencies who might turn research recommendations into potentially harmful social policies. In recent decades such questions have become part of the Marxist project to look at the intellectual means of reproduction in modern capitalist societies, as much as they have informed a generation of feminist sociologists keen to critique the politics of knowledge for their patriarchal assumptions. At the same time, however, the neoliberal economic agenda, in the ascendancy since the late 1970s, has asked its own questions about the politics of knowledge, to the extent that it has posed serious challenges to both established academic practice *and* socialist and feminist resistances to it.

As both Zygmunt Bauman (1987) and George Monbiot (2000) have noted, in recent times the priorities within the academy have changed, and the intervention of corporate interests into the production of knowledge has raised questions about its very constituency, particularly claims for 'value freedom'. Moreover, the role of the academy, at least in many Western countries, has changed to incorporate these new priorities. Not only are there particular priorities to maximise student intake at all costs, but any research that is allowed to be conducted requires framing within the intellectual rationale and financial remits of corporate competitiveness. To many on the Left, these market-driven and frequently anti-intellectual agendas have destroyed genuine research cultures and the search for knowledge as an exercise in itself.

The argument that follows takes a somewhat different and perhaps less nostalgic view of these matters. From an anarchist view, none of these things are particularly surprising, mainly because the parameters of what is being debated are limited by their assumptions about the organisation of society itself. So, regardless of whether the academy is being organised around market-driven, or State-orchestrated philanthropy, the assumptions that underpin it are based upon many of the same premises. This is to say that the social structures and sets of relations integral to sociological theory are as hierarchically based as those bodies that fund such methods of intellectual inquiry. There is, then, a mutually reinforcing intellectual agenda that sometimes, perhaps unknowingly, reproduces itself.

How one attempts to pursue a sociological method of inquiry without succumbing to either the interests of power structures, or their intellectual worldview, is a pertinent, and extremely complex, set of concerns. To accomplish this in a manner that is consistent with anarchist principles is therefore a significant challenge. Nevertheless, the potential benefits that could emerge from such a venture extend further than a hypothetical enclave of academic anarchists; there are areas of mainstream and even progressive sociology that can be assisted to resolve apparent contradictions within their own research. This is especially the case within the fields of the study of social movements and theories of 'reflexivity', but more broadly into the study of organisations and the nature of power itself. Some of these will be discussed in greater detail below, but it is first worth reflecting on where there are existing areas of sociology that might offer assistance in the development of an anarchist sociology.

Early indicators

On first viewing, the evidence is not good. To date, the role of anarchism in researching and analysing societies past and present has been rather marginal, and apparently ineffectual, outside of the anarchist milieu itself. There are a number of reasons for this. Firstly, an explanatory framework deriving from such obviously politicised assumptions forming the basis of any understanding of the world can be seen to transgress the sociological notion of value freedom. This is in spite of the institutionalisation of an equally politicised, but apparently more developed set of analyses of the world, Marxism. This forms something of a second reason: that Marxism has had a very long and dominating influence in the social sciences and humanities, especially since the 1960s. Anarchism has never achieved more than a toehold in the academic sphere and its intellectual depth has constantly been called into question, mainly because, as Alan Carter

(1989) points out, its concepts of history and society are seen to be too fluid and less sophisticated.

Moreover, any move away from exclusively materialist accounts of change to consider matters of psychology, human nature and people's 'need' for authority is seen to be too unscientific. Ironically, such materialist accounts are utterly unable to reconcile the disparity between their *own* justification for hierarchies and the social-constructed 'naturalness of competition' which is used by those who seek intellectual legitimacy for capitalism. In this respect, a sociology that examines the social construction of authority and its meaning in an authoritarian environment is inevitably going to be marginalised.

A third reason has been the integration or misuse of anarchist or anarchist-related literature, the most famous of which is Guy Debord's *The society of the spectacle*, (1987 [1957]), the full implications of which have been subsumed into postmodernist treatises on the processes of signification within consumer culture. Indeed, it is through the controversial discourses of postmodernism and poststructuralism that anarchism has been referenced in the social and philo-sophical sciences, sometimes as an argument for relativism. However, this has often taken the form of a *commentary on* the work of French poststructuralist philosophers of the 1970s and 1980s rather than an *engagement with* the anarchist canon itself.

However, some poststructuralist writers are now beginning to explore the relationship between their own premises and those of anarchism. As is discussed below in more detail, the work of Andrew Koch (1993, 1997) and Todd May (1994) can be usefully employed in analysing the micro-politics of power, which in turn can feed into larger questions about societal structures and ideology.

Questions of methodological power have been central to the concerns of feminist sociologists, who in the 1980s began to reformulate old conundrums about objectivity, the politics of research and the academic litmus test of value freedom. This overlapped to some degree with work in radical (social) anthropology circles. In different ways, these viewpoints challenged the right of 'experts' to speak on behalf of the people that they were researching and raised questions about the value of the research to those people.

A final area for consideration is science, which has had its fair share of political debates about method, truth and research communities. The increasing breakdown of disciplinary boundaries since the 1960s has meant that some of these issues have impacted on the social sciences, especially work by Karl Popper, Thomas Kuhn and particularly Paul Feyerabend. For our purposes, it is the latter's development of an 'anarchist epistemology' in *Against method* (1988) as well as his calls for public accountability of science (1979), which can provide something of a touchstone to developing sociological inquiry in this area.

More recently, the popularity of chaos and complexity theories in the natural sciences has prompted an equal (and sometimes opposite!) reaction in their social scientific counterparts. The radically different view of the role of cause and effect in the organisation of natural and social phenomena, coupled with the apparent vindication of the anarchist tenet of self-organisation in the natural world, has made these philosophies something of a theoretical hot potato.

The usefulness of poststructuralism and complexity will be assessed in due course, but firstly it is necessary to establish why these critiques have emerged in the first place. To accomplish this, we must return to the foundations of sociology as an academic discipline, look at its relationship with anarchist methods of inquiry, and then consider why an anarchist sociology must be guided by very different criteria.

From Enlightenment to deception: what's right and wrong with sociology?

Common histories

Anarchism and sociology share something of a common intellectual background as ideas shaped by Enlightenment developments in philosophy, science and technology during the late eighteenth century. Both succeeded in harnessing the new rational perspectives, in conjunction with the liberatory political philosophies of the spirit of the French Revolution, and evolved a particular set of ideas about how the world could be investigated and changed. From their origins, both anarchism as a political philosophy and sociology as a discipline have been preoccupied with the interrelationship between the individual as an active creator of social meaning and the organisation and construction of collective meaning within either a specific group or society in general.

Their differences lie in their respective founding intentions. Anarchism emerged as a revolutionary ideology that linked an age-old current in political radicalism with resistance to new forms of State surveillance and bureaucracy, the growing power of industrial capital and the limitations of the parliamentary system as a vehicle for progressive social change. Anarchism formed a rationalistic philosophy based around the benefits of a Stateless, self-determined form of social organisation, which respected the freedom of the (responsible) individual and legitimised the 'natural' tendency towards co-operation. Crucially, it embraced the 'darker' side of the Enlightenment, theorising that real change could only be truly realised if revolutionaries acknowledged the problems that the ego might pose for political organisation.

Conversely, sociology began as both a 'response to the demand of the modern State aiming at the "total administration" of society' (Bauman, 1988: 228) and as a form of inquiry linked to the need for social reform. On the one hand it was geared towards providing 'a huge apparatus of "social management" . . . [and] expert social management knowledge' through 'mass, statistical research' (Bauman, 1988: 228). On the other, it was concerned about the social impact of the new urban ways of living, of the consequences of the loss of traditional rural communities and cultures, of the alienation of the work practices of the industrial era, and the problems of sanitation, disease, poverty and crime. The commitment to social reform as well as legitimisation of the status quo is an important aspect of the history of sociology – from Durkheim's classic study of suicide (1970 [1897]), to the Chicago School's work with the urban marginals and drifters in the 1930s (Bulmer, 1984; Atkinson, 1990). Even within the most conservative and reactionary of all of its perspectives – Functionalism – there is an attempt to reintegrate the dysfunctional parts of the social structure – i.e., criminals – into the social body. Early sociology, however, unlike early anarchism, was less likely to see dysfunction as an institutional rather than an individual matter.

Similarities did exist in terms of support for the role of science. Sociology made it quite clear from early in its history that it was a 'science of society' with many of its early practitioners following a 'positivist' method of inquiry. This commitment to objectivity, through pursuit of the same laws of observable cause and effect that governed the natural sciences, was also seen as a value-free one. Equally committed to such ideas were a number of the 'classical' anarchists. For instance, both Pierre-Joseph Proudhon (1923: 150ff.) and Mikhail Bakunin suggested that it was through science that humans could realise their true social natures, the latter arguing that 'natural laws were in harmony with human liberty' (1985: 34). He did, however, question the right of these *savants* to use it to rule, as science should be 'the property of everybody' (1985: 62). These ideas about science and power were not lost on Peter Kropotkin who worked within the fields of natural biology, geography and sociology, and whose most famous work *Mutual aid* (1993) was designed to test Darwin's ideas on the competitive nature of the non-human (and by default) human world.

The application of the respective ideas of sociology and anarchism into either social policy or the realm of everyday life is clearly something where the former has enjoyed more success. However, the ideals of anarchism have also trickled into the public realm, particularly in town planning at the end of the nineteenth and beginning of the twentieth centuries (Hall, 1988; Ward, 1992). Indeed the utopian dreams of several generations of planners, architects and builders seem to have been touched by the anarchist or libertarian socialist ideas of writers from Kropotkin to Patrick Geddes, Lewis Mumford, Paul Goodman and Colin Ward.

The completely different aspirations of sociology and anarchism, as well as their respective positions within society, do mean that there are a number of barriers – intellectual and practical – that lie in the way of developing a radical, anarchist sociology. The following discussion considers some of these differences by looking at the assumptions behind the established sociological literature on social movements and offering some suggestions as to how anarchist theory would be of advantage to developing a more tangible understanding of this area of study.

Problematic assumptions (I) – the natural (social) order of things

In *American power and the New Mandarins* (1969), Noam Chomsky makes the point that when bourgeois historians interpret turbulent moments in history they typically ignore movements that utilise co-operative strategies because they

are alien to the liberal-bourgeois concept of historical change. A similar observation is made by Michael Maffesoli (1996: 56) with respect to theorists of social
movements who are unable to acknowledge the existence of social or political
groups who organise without hierarchies. Such assumptions can be illustrated
using the now well-established debate about the so-called 'new social movements' and the various analytical approaches to them (a good overview of many
of these debates is provided in Welsh, 2000).

The principal claim of the initiators of this debate was that the environmental, women's, peace and civil rights movements since the 1960s constituted a new
distinctiveness in protest history. These new movements were the harbingers of
major social, cultural and technological shifts within Western societies, through
which new contestations around information and particular quality of life issues
were beginning to take place. According to such writers as Jürgen Habermas
(1981), Alain Touraine (1981), Claus Offe (1985) and Alberto Melucci (1989),
these movements not only contrasted with 'old' social movements that were
more connected to the struggles and concerns of the labour movement, but their
organisational rationale was somewhat different. In particular, the new social
movements were anti-hierarchical, self-organising and pursued non-instrumen-
tal goals that were linked to politicised lifestyles and so-called 'post-material'
values. Political activism was seen to be more 'direct' than those using conventional political channels and carried out in a media-friendly manner.

Problems within this first wave of new social movement theorists are well documented, particularly in terms of the ahistorical nature of such claims, given that
the movements in question all have long histories themselves, most of which
demonstrate the same characteristics (D'Anieri et. al., 1990; Bagguley, 1992;
Lichterman, 1996). Such a macro-sociological and historical approach gives little
impression of what movements think and feel, and it overlooks how movements
reproduce themselves over time and fulfil multiple functions at the same time.
Nevertheless, many of the assumptions of its leading thinkers remain, such as
Melucci's claim that the purpose of these movements is to pose a symbolic challenge to authority and then go on to produce new élite groups (or simply wither
away).

Whilst the predominantly European Marxist writers behind 'new social
movement' theory were focusing on the large-scale changes, an emerging North
American school of political scientists was concentrating on *how* such contemporary movements mobilised (McCarthy and Zald, 1977). What has become
known as the 'resource mobilisation theory' (RMT) considered social movements as rational enterprises whose driving force is the 'pursuit of limited interests based on utilitarian cost-benefit calculations' (Joppke, 1993: 5) with the
intention of inclusion in or influence upon the mainstream political process.
Thus, collective action can be accounted for only by changes in resources, organisations and opportunities within a given set of parameters. Such a critique leaves
out other mobilisation issues: motivation, solidarity within movements, egalitarian sensibilities and the kinds of meanings that individuals attach to political

action. Given RMT's concentration upon organisational efficiency and lobbying and funding strategies it is not surprising that movements possessing different structures, agenda and broad visions of social change are under-investigated or sidelined. Moreover, such assumptions about intention and access to the public sphere are really only a mirror of the ideological hegemony of US liberal pluralism (Meyer, 1995: 169).

A variation on these themes is the Political Opportunity Structure (POS) model, originally coined by Eisinger (1973) and evolved in particular by Tarrow (1994) and Kriesi *et al.* (1995). The theory assesses a movement's opportunities for political action on the basis of electoral potential, ability to lobby/alter decision-making at an élite level, and the actual power of the State to repress or tolerate political movements. The wider the range of options for the campaigning group, the more likely it is that they will have some access to the political structures. Conversely, the fewer political options available for a movement, the more likely it is that they will operate outside the political system. In POS, the particular group is conceptualised in terms of how it plans and organises depending on the relative strength or openness of the State and political system. This is, of course, to presume many things about how the people in political movements choose to participate and what they think about the things that they actually do.

The POS model can also be seen as too instrumental: it assumes that there are certain steps taken by particular types of groups which necessarily aim to engage with the political mainstream. It also ignores the cultural dimension to the movement. Clearly, some movements will 'fail' to influence the apparatus of the State yet possibly enjoy widespread cultural influence, motivate large numbers of people and create new lifestyle practices and ideas. For instance, the anti-roads movement of the 1990s in the UK 'failed' to stop many of the roads it contested, yet its influence on society was massive, influencing other movements, launching political bands and publications, and even leading to soap opera representations within the media.

To date, many of the assumptions behind new social movement theory, RMT and POS remain intact, although there have been attempts to develop models acknowledging culturally-specific formations and rationales (Koopmans, 1995; Duyvendak, 1995) and to synthesise these main approaches (McAdam *et al.*, 1999).

The instrumentalism behind much of the aforementioned theoretical material raises a more general problem within sociology: the prevalence of 'rational choice' or 'game theory' as viable explanations for human action. One such example of this, which has generated considerable debate, is the so-called 'Prisoner's dilemma', whereby the most logical and least risky course of action for an individual is always the one that does not involve co-operation with other people. Whilst this is an extremely complex area of theory, it is worth noting Graham's (1989) observation that this kind of thinking can easily become a justification for the intervention of the State because it legitimises the egotistical

side of individuals (and implicitly justifies sovereign authority). The individualistic tendencies of this position have been noted by a number of commentators,
including Singer (1997).

Thus again we see sets of assumptions influencing how particular sociological phenomena might be investigated, despite the fact that some of the aforementioned literatures are broadly sympathetic to the aims and objectives of the
movements in question, yet they leave huge questions unanswered. It is to the
broader ramifications of this lack of sophistication that the discussion now
turns.

Problematic assumptions (II) – instrumental thought

An additional area of concern is the use of instrumental and rational choice
approaches within much of sociological theory. In his studies of rationality and
modernity, Max Weber (1930) argued that much of the development of Western
industrial societies involved an instrumental approach which prioritised the
'ends' of actions over their 'means' (see also Szerszynski and Tomalin, chapter
11 in this volume). Later theorists such as Theodor Adorno and Max
Horkheimer (1979) argued that this type of rationalisation lay behind the domination of nature by humans, an idea that has been influential on a number of
contemporary ecological thinkers (Dobson, 1990). Indeed, for Jürgen Habermas
(1981) the emergence of new social movements can be attributed to the instrumental processes of the increasingly interventionist State during the 1960s.

Yet sociology *itself* can also be seen to reflect this instrumental approach. The
eco-sociologist Alwyn Jones (1987) has suggested that instrumental and anthropocentric positions are prevalent in sociology and support what he calls the
'industrial growth model' of society. Jones draws on some of the psychoanalytical aspects of Herbert Marcuse's work, those of libertarian socialist and radical
Catholic Ivan Illich, as well as ecologists such as E. F. Schumacher (1976) and
Fritjof Capra (1982). He claims that sociology still prioritises technological as
opposed to human-based strategies for social organisation and everyday life, to
the detriment of the environment, human values, community and politics.
Indeed, Jones points to the problem of dualistic concepts that lie at the heart of
sociological assumptions – as well as much of Western thought in general – as
being something of a barrier to developing a more holistic method of inquiry.
The obvious dualism is one of human and nature. Bart Van Steenbergen (1990)
is sympathetic to this position, and talks about the need to develop a completely
different paradigm in the social sciences based on acceptance of new notions of
'holism'.

Clearly, sociology has always worked with notions of 'holism', the principle
that in order to understand any complex system you had to first understand its
parts, from which more general rules could be advanced. Van Steenbergen sees
traditional efforts within sociology to be holistic as being too deterministic and
reductionist, unable to grasp the fact that society is an interdependent network

of processes that constantly influence each other. In other words, he seeks to understand the parts through the workings of the whole (although not to the exclusion of the parts). Despite the fact that sociology attempts to problematise dualistic approaches, much of it is still based on an anthropocentric worldview that places the rational or scientific in opposition to the religious or spiritual, nature against culture, and, in terms of methodology, divides the subjective and objective positions.

Whilst sociology has been slow to address the instrumental elements within itself, a number of sociologists have begun to address the wider implications of instrumental approaches within society. In particular, the work of Ulrich Beck (1992) and Beck *et al.* (1994) – who might loosely be described as the 'reflexive modernisation school' – suggests that recent decades have witnessed a radicalisation of the very processes that formed modernity. So, as societies become aware of their own contradictions (such as pollution, health scares, addictions and stress at work), their policies become less instrumental and are increasingly organised around managing these difficulties. This is the era of what Beck calls the 'risk society', in which the new social movements are prime movers in ushering in post-instrumental values and policies.

There are, however, a number of limitations to the 'reflexive modernisation' thesis. It suggests that new social movements are helping to radicalise the thinking of those who administer the scientific, technological policies of State and capital. This might be said to be a 'limited' notion of reflexivity, in that the very people who are causing the social and ecological problems of the world are being asked to solve them (McKechnie and Welsh, 1994). From an anarchist perspective, it is important to acknowledge the part that hierarchical structures and the profit motive have in perpetuating these problems. That the reflexive modernists do not really get to grips with the antiauthoritarian and non-hierarchical nature of some of the contemporary 'new social movements' is perhaps indicative of this.

In the language of environmental political theory, the assumptions of Beck *et al.* might be construed as part of a 'shallow' rather than 'deep' ecological critique, which ignores the fact that instrumental attitudes to the natural world and the social worlds are fundamentally linked.[2] So, even in some of its more progressive areas, we see instrumentalism underpinning basic assumptions.

Problematic assumptions (III) – what is good research and who is it for?

If anarchist sociology is concerned with analysing the construction of authority in a variety of different contexts, from a methodological point of view, the relationship between the researcher and the researched must be central. The issues discussed in the previous section on instrumental rationality are therefore extremely pertinent to the means and ends of research: what gets studied, who funds it, who benefits from it? And, above all, how is it carried out, and by whom?

A useful starting point is the aforementioned work of philosopher of science

Paul Feyerabend in the 1960s and 1970s. In *Against method: outline of an anarchistic theory of knowledge* (1988 [1975]), Feyerabend argues that scientific claims of objectivity need to be demystified and that science should be placed alongside rather than above other forms of knowledge or beliefs about the world. He suggests that, far from being objective and rationalistic, many scientists are actually anti-rationalist, and authoritarian with it too. Feyerabend's commitment to the democratisation of information, anti-élitist perspectives and flexibility of method have been seen to be in the spirit of anarchism even though he rejected anarchism as a political philosophy. Although he was often associated with his famously misunderstood slogan from *Against method* – 'anything goes' – Feyerabend was a staunch advocate of the value of demystifying the boundaries of the researcher and the researched. Influential across the disciplines, his work also needs to be seen in the context of the breaking down of the disciplinary boundaries between the natural and social sciences during the 1960s.

One example of this has been the critiques of science from feminist and ecological perspectives that emerged in the 1980s, leading to a new academic branch of sociology (Bijker *et al.*, 1987; Woolgar, 1988). Developments in 'post-colonial' anthropology (Clifford and Marcus, 1986) can also be seen as illustrative of the shifts in conceptual as well as disciplinary boundaries, with the 'authority' of the white European male voice increasingly coming under fire from both marginalised academic communities and 'research subjects'. This issue of accountability has been particularly developed by feminist sociologists, including Stanley and Wise (1993) and Roseneil (1995).

This feminist strand of sociology acknowledges the importance, in qualitative and especially ethnographic research, of the relationship between the evolution of ideas in the research process and the emotional journey undertaken by the researcher. For Roseneil (1995), this must preface the whole research process, in the form of an 'intellectual autobiography', which documents the personal reasons for the research. As well as collapsing the old dualism of 'individual' and 'society' (Ribbens, 1993: 88), it also provides the opportunity for new forms of sociological discourse to emerge from personal writing, assuming that it is more comment than catharsis. It also tackles the issue of the hegemony of particular schools or methods within sociological circles which often 'forbid' non-scientific ways of representing data (Chaplin, 1994).

It is perhaps the respective relationships that exist between the researcher and the researched that have caused most controversy, and in particular, questions of obligation, responsibility and emotional involvement. Much has been written on this particular topic: when does one stop researching and will this affect anybody, if, for instance, the researcher is involved in a sensitive subject area, such as staffing a 'help-line'? Here we can see the debate about rationality and reason re-emerging so that one does not take such an instrumental approach to one's research 'subjects'. Or, to locate this within an anarchist framework, one attempts to equate the means of an action (or method) with its ends.

A useful pointer in these matters is Michael Burawoy's observation on contemporary ethnography: that the research process is more a type of collaboration than objectification (1991: 291). Whilst this is something to be aspired to, the parameters of a researcher's involvement is a controversial point. Most famous in this regard is French sociologist Alain Touraine who sees the research process as an opportunity, suggesting that the researcher is vitally placed to give the 'subjects' a 'greater capacity for historical action' (1981: 145). This method, which Touraine calls 'sociological interventionism', is one that acknowledges the fact that the researcher is *already* immersed within and influencing the culture in question. Touraine is not interested in the partiality question and believes that new spaces for knowledge open up in such situations. However, sometimes too much reflexivity creates problems, with the presence of the researcher fuelling existing conflicts (Ferguson, 1991; Armstrong, 1993: 30), or creating resentment if too much collaboration leads to an accusation of misrepresentation (Kurzman, 1991: 265ff.).

In addition, there are structural factors that can impact on any idealised anarchist research practice, and these may ultimately invalidate claims for an anarchist sociology within a formal academic context. Research organisations and universities might 'own' the research that gets done in their name with the final veto as to its future usefulness. Moreover, there are grey areas in terms of researching sensitive topics legally. Academics investigating football hooligans (Armstrong, 1993), drug dealer activity (Fountain, 1993) and sexual harassment in sports clubs (Yorganci, 1995), all found themselves in difficulties in respect of either wanting to report findings to the police or trying to avoid police interference with their research. In America, one researcher (Scarce, 1994) went to jail in order to protect his sources (animal liberation activists).

Recent developments: poststructuralism, chaos theory and anarchism

Disregarding the reasons why anarchist perspectives in the social sciences may have been either deliberately excluded or just failed to make an impact, two areas of theory in the last two decades or so have effectively began to change this. This is not because poststructuralist or chaos theorists have any gravitation towards an anarchist perspective, more that the theories lend themselves to such interpretations. The principal reason for this is because at the heart of these paradigms are critiques of hierarchical, predictable and generalised theories of both the natural and social worlds. These theories fundamentally question the temporal, spatial and ontological assumptions of the Enlightenment, of Modernism, and of Cartesian and Newtonian world-views. They have impacted on everything from microbes and weather systems to theories of revolution. The main purpose, therefore, of engaging with these areas of theory is because they offer a variety of analytical tools that can be of assistance in conceptualising the place of power in contemporary (as well as past) society. Moreover, the application of these concepts can add to and enhance the kind of perspectives that have been discussed so far.

Poststructuralism and anarchism

Poststructuralism stems principally from a group of predominantly French theorists who have exerted considerable influence on cultural and political theory in the last thirty or so years, much of it emerging out of critical reflection about the 'failures' of May '68. The main writers are Jean-François Lyotard, Jean Baudrillard, Jacques Derrida, Michel Foucault, Gilles Deleuze, Felix Guattari, Julia Kristeva and (the later work of) Roland Barthes. In different ways they came to be labelled as poststructuralist on account of the fact that they broke with the rigorousness of existing structuralist, Marxist, linguistic and psychoanalytical models of historical explanation, models that posited particular 'fixed ideas' about subjectivity, meaning and social change. Poststructuralists have regarded such rigidity as oppressive on account of the fact that it can lead to objectification and the exertion of power (Koch, 1997: 102). As with postmodernist theorists, there is a perceived need to deconstruct the absolutism that underpinned or emerged from the humanistic Enlightenment, as well as any notion of general historical laws or patterns. This has resulted in a commitment to critiquing dominant conceptual dualisms such as nature/culture and Self/Other, in order to reveal the extent to which such oppositions are social constructions. Moreover, poststructuralism favours a view of the 'decentred' subject that is far more dynamic in its construction than under structuralism, and this is seen to reflect the increasing heterogeneity of subject positions in a multi-cultural, postcolonial world.

The aforementioned writers are often associated with anarchism because of their antiauthoritarian and micro-sociological analysis, which considers how people are shaped by, but also implicated in, power relations which do not derive solely from State and capital. For instance, in their book *A thousand plateaux* (1988) Gilles Deleuze and Felix Guattari use a biological metaphor to illustrate that power is not determined by a single set of influences – the rhizome. This, according to the *Oxford English Dictionary*, is a 'an underground rootlike stem bearing both roots and shoots' (1996 edition: p. 1225). Rather than being interested in the role of structures, Deleuze and Guattari talk about the 'lines' that make up the constitution of contemporary relations. So, a 'rhizome connects any point to any other point, . . . its traits are not necessarily linked to traits of the same nature; it brings into play very different regimes of signs, and even nonsign states' (1988: 21).

Michel Foucault set out to identify the way that societies articulated and reproduced power relations through different 'discourses' such as sexuality, madness, punishment and medicine. He looked at how these were constructed in different historical 'epistemes' (or knowledge moments). Foucault's metaphor was that of a body, where power seeps through millions of capillaries, except there are no real identifiable determining forces driving the flow of power and that they are highly localised to particular epistemes (1980: 142). For Foucault, power was so omnipresent in these epistemes that it also determined any form of resistance to it on its own terms. The term he used was *agonism*: two forces that circle each other, defining each other and unable to exist without the other (1982: 221). This is an interesting notion and one which has much in common with the anarchist critique of how authoritarian relations (particularly the Marxist and Leninist models of political change) inevitably reproduce themselves through mirroring the (capitalist bureaucratic) structures which they are supposedly opposing.

The value of these perspectives to an anarchist sociology is, however, a mixed one. The poststructuralist approach to the understanding of power is useful insomuch that it forges a better understanding of how power becomes reproduced in all kinds of complex ways and the extent to which people are implicated within these processes (Goaman and Dodson, 1997: 87). However, since poststructuralism tends not to prioritise wider historical contexts, there are problems relating a micro-historical and sociological perspective to the kind of understanding of historical change of relations of authority which would be of interest to anarchist sociologists. For instance, to return to the social movement literature, the question of how movements learn from each other or why some radical movements become institutionalised and others do not is difficult to answer from such a standpoint. Indeed, one of the more controversial poststructural interpretations of power – May's idea that not all of it is necessarily bad and it is a question of identifying the more legitimate forms (1994: 123) – is somewhat problematic from an anarchist perspective.

Chaos, complexity and anarchism

By contrast, recent developments in the natural sciences point to the need to fundamentally rewrite the assumed 'laws' of the physical universe and by implication the social one. Since the 1960s, similar discoveries, firstly in mathematics, and then physics, biology, chemistry, astronomy and meteorology, have come to be regarded by many as equal to or of greater importance than Einstein's work on relativity or Werner Heisenburg and Niels Bohr's on quantum mechanics early in the twentieth century. Although a full discussion of the science behind complexity and chaos theory is beyond the scope of this article, a number of pertinent observations can be made.

The principal idea behind these theories is that everything upwards from the smallest particle in the natural world to the migration of birds and the behaviour of weather systems is ordered in an extremely dynamic and complex manner. Simple systems can give rise to complex behaviour but complex systems can also give rise to simple behaviour. The point is that the universe pursues non-linear and non-determining patterns that make reductionist scientific explanations impossible. The examples most used to illustrate this vary from the famous butterfly flapping its wings on one side of the world and causing tidal waves on the other, to calculating mathematical equations to six rather than seven decimal places and dramatically changing the application of the subsequent formula.

The implication of this, suggests Arran Gare (2000), is that all disciplines will have to take notice because these theories imply a removal of the boundaries of all disciplines, if not the creation of a new form of scientific investigation itself. Here we can return to Van Steenbergen's (1990) discussion of contemporary holism and the characteristics that he attributes to the social world. The implications are that the social world can also be understood in terms of self-organising and spontaneous processes, where unity rather than conflict is a better analytical device and the determinism of many theories of historical change must be resisted. From an anarchist perspective this can be seen to vindicate the work of both Charles Fourier and Peter Kropotkin, some of it carried out well over a century ago. As Purchase points out (1994: 163), all of the current trendy scientific concepts such as complexity, diversity, emergence and self-assembly were researched by these writers and placed in the context of balanced natural and social eco-systems. These have long been part of eco-political and anarchist thought. Moreover, Purchase suggests that the fact that computer-generated particles *self-organise* when only supplied with a few programmed instructions as to how to function in a group further legitimates the anarchist claims for such 'holistic' kind of thinking.

The fact that such a holistic approach has been overlooked or under-acknowledged is a moot point, but there are clearly huge implications for *any* kind of sociological theorising. How, for instance, does one evaluate the effects of particular events or sets of circumstances on people and how their ideas are subsequently diffused into the rest of society? How does one begin to research this, setting aside the aforementioned problems of 'intervention' and value freedom aside? Many sociological perspectives are hierarchical in their assumptions about both the structure of society and the analytic tools best suited to understand it. However, more flexible perspectives based on the complexity sciences are beginning to make an impact on the social sciences, particularly in terms of thinking about historical contingency and the potential that people have at conceptualising their own likely impact on events (Smith, 1998). It is also, as Urry (2003) notes, an increasingly valuable theoretical tool in understanding the process of globalisation and people's diverse experience of it.

Although it is possible that this supposedly new scientific paradigm might well revolutionise social theory, it is also possible that it will not. There is already evidence to suggest that, as with Darwinism and socio-biology, chaos and complexity have been used to justify free market philosophies and competitive theories of human organisation and behaviour by management theorists and stock market analysts. However, as Chesters (2003) notes, there is only a certain amount of conceptual applicability, as it becomes hard to talk about autonomy, self-organisation and networks meaningfully in hopelessly hierarchical contexts. Happily, as he indicates, there is considerably more 'fit' between these theories and the mobilisations of the alternative globalisation movement. Certainly theorising in terms of the self-organisational activities of large groups of people who may be otherwise 'hidden from history' but have unacknowledged impact on events would clearly serve sociology better.

Why develop an anarchist sociology?

This chapter has considered the possibility of developing an anarchist sociology and acknowledged some of the theoretical terrain on which it might be formulated or, alternatively, organised in opposition to. I have suggested that some of the founding rationales behind sociology in the nineteenth century, such as instrumental attitudes towards pursuing research in the name of industrial progress and social cohesion, might have negative impact on those being studied and their environment. The fact that sociology can be seen to have often mirrored the hierarchical structures of society in terms of its assumptions about organisation and change, mitigates against interpretations of history that might prioritise alternatives to dominant currents. By examining social movements, for instance, it is often possible to locate the political assumptions of the powerful in the analytical assessment of the phenomena in question. Theories of new social movements, resource mobilisation and political opportunities can all be seen to have overlooked the possibilities that political movement cultures are highly complex and dynamic processes that do not necessarily behave in ways consistent with static or generalised models of protest.

An additional area of concern for anarchist sociologists has been how research is carried out and the extent to which methodological processes can become forms of power. Although academic research is frequently linked to dominant corporate or State-related interests, the last twenty or so years has witnessed the evolution of much more reflexive forms of sociology. This has largely emerged through feminist research agendas, which have tended to treat fieldwork as though it is a collaborative and mutually beneficial experience, for those being studied as well as the researchers.

Whilst these developments offer great potential in terms of the breaking down of pre-existing structural barriers in society, there have also been a number of theoretical perspectives such as poststructuralism and complexity, whose philosophical premises have been seized on by anarchists as being potentially beneficial. The reason for this is down to the perception that discourses which emphasise analytical flexibility, multi-interpretations of power and influence rather than determinism and statis, are far more accurate interpretations of the world. From a sociological perspective this makes a lot of sense, particularly if these theories can assist in the unmasking of power and can contribute to a better understanding of the world.

To develop an anarchist sociology is to offer a different explanation of why particular social problems emerge, based on a different vision of how society is and ought to be. The development of an anarchist sociology is, however, still in its infancy, and the institutional possibilities for its emergence are probably somewhat limited. However, what is important is that there is enough evidence already to be able to advocate a substantial anarchist research agenda. There are endless research questions to be formulated: how is power formed and perpetuated? why do people desire their own oppression? how should we research these things sensitively? and what should we do with the results when we get them? If anarchists stick to the kind of principles that most have long held in their hearts, then there may well be answers to these questions. The opportunity for an anarchist sociology to emerge in a contemporary context should therefore not be underestimated.

Notes

1 Many thanks to Chayley Collis and James Bowen who have long suffered my preoccupation with this subject area and made significant contributions along the way. A number of these ideas were presented to the Anarchist Research Group in London in January 2001. Thanks to all those who attended the meeting and provided useful feedback. Much of the work in this chapter can be found in my PhD thesis: 'A sociology of environmental protest: Earth First! and the theory and practice of anarchism', Manchester Metropolitan University, 2001. Electronic copies are available from the author at jonathanpurkis@yahoo.co.uk.
2 I am using the phrases 'shallow' and 'deep' ecology in a very generalised manner. My use of 'deep ecology', for instance, is much more similar to the social ecology perspective of Bookchin (1982, 1996a) than to the deep ecology thinkers such as Naess (1973, 1989) or Devall and Sessions (1985).

Lived poetry: Stirner, anarchy, subjectivity and the art of living[1]

Introduction

At the heart of the new anarchism(s) there lies a concern with developing a whole new way of being in and acting upon the world.[2] Contemporary revolutionary anarchism is not merely interested in effecting changes in socioeconomic relations or dismantling the State, but in developing an entire art of living, which is simultaneously anti-authoritarian, anti-ideological and antipolitical. The development of a distinctively anarchist *savoir-vivre* is a profoundly existential and ontological concern and one rich in implication for the definition of contemporary anarchist practice, activity and projects. Central to this process is the issue of anarchist subjectivity and intersubjectivity, as well as related concerns about language and creativity.

Hakim Bey, language and ontological anarchy

Hakim Bey's essay 'Ontological anarchy in a nutshell' (1994) provides a concise but landmark formulation of this issue. The opening passage of the essay focuses on the existential status of the anarchist and anarchist practice:

> Since absolutely nothing can be predicated with any certainty as to the 'true nature of things,' all projects (as Nietzsche says) can only be 'founded on nothing.' And yet *there must be a project* – if only because we ourselves resist being categorized as 'nothing.' Out of nothing we will make something: the Uprising, the revolt against everything which proclaims: 'The Nature of Things is such-&-such'. (Bey, 1994: 1)

Drawing upon Nietzschean perspectivism, Bey mounts an anti-foundationalist argument: given the collapse of the philosophical concept of truth, there is no foundation, no basis upon which anarchist subjectivity or activity can be grounded – no foundation, that is, except nothingness itself. Developing his perspective from this epistemological premise, Bey identifies a distinctively anarchist mode of being: ontological anarchy. The anarchist hangs suspended in space above the abyss, certain of nothing except the nothing over which s/he hovers and from which s/he springs. But this existential condition, rather than a cause for despair, remains the source of limitless freedom. For, as Bey indicates, 'Out of nothing we will imagine our *values*, and by this act of invention we shall live' (Bey, 1994: 1). Being and nothingness are not binary oppositions in this formulation, but elements of an overarching complementarity:

> Individual vs. Group – Self vs. Other – a false dichotomy propagated through the Media of Control, and above all through language . . . Self and Other complement and complete one another. There is no Absolute Category, no Ego, no Society – but only a chaotically complex web of relation – and the 'Strange Attractor', *attraction itself*, which evokes resonances and patterns in the flow of becoming. (Bey, 1994: 3)

Nothing can be said about the nothingness underlying existence. Language cannot penetrate and organise this space, except tentatively perhaps through poetry and metaphor: 'As we meditate on the *nothing* we notice that although it cannot be de-fined, nevertheless paradoxically we *can* say something about it (even if only metaphorically): it appears to be a "chaos"'. Through wordplay, through ludic and poetic language, Bey attempts, not to *define* nothingness, but to *evoke* it. Nothingness emerges in his account, not as an empty void, but as a chaos of plenitude and abundance: 'chaos-as-becoming, chaos-as-excess, the generous outpouring of nothing into something'. Or, to put it more succinctly: 'chaos is life'. Binarist language, unable to constellate a chaos which everywhere overflows its boundaries, seeks to control, contain and domesticate it through the deployment of dualistic categories. Against this language of order and stasis, Bey proposes the language of poetry – a fluid language based on metaphor and thus appropriate to the expression of the flows and patterns of passion, desire and attraction which characterise chaos – and a *'utopian poetics'* (Bey, 1994: 1–4).

Rooted in nothingness, the dynamic chaos that underpins existence, anarchist subjectivity is a life-affirmative expression of becoming. For Bey (1994: 1) 'all *movement* . . . is chaos' whereas stasis remains the characteristic of order. But the anarchist subject is not merely a subject-in-process, but a subject-in-rebellion, and as a result remains nothing without a project. The anarchist affirmation of nothingness simultaneously enacts a refusal of being categorised as a (mere) nothing – or as a *mere* being. But, further, the anarchist affirmation of nothingness is a 'revolt against everything' – in short an insurrection against the totality, against the entire assemblage of social relations structured by governance and control. In other words, the anarchist project affirms nothing(ness) against everything that *exists*, precisely because anarchy (or its synonym, chaos) is always in a condition of becoming.

The anarchist subject – and by extension the anarchist project – is necessarily in a constant state of flux and mutability. Characterised by spontaneous creativity, anarchist subjectivity is marked for Bey by imagination and invention, and hence finds its most appropriate mode of expression in poetic language.

Anarchist subjectivity emerges in his work as a synonym for poetic subjectivity, and anarchist revolt as a synonym for the immediate realisation of the creative or poetic imagination in everyday life. Anarchy, in short, remains a condition of embodied or lived poetry. The notion of lived poetry originates with the situationists, who contrast lived poetry with the language-form of the poem. Lived poetry is a form of activity, not merely a mode of writing, and springs up in moments of revolt and rebellion. It is life lived as an act of spontaneous creativity and the complete embodiment of radical theory in action (see Moore, 1997b; 2002).

The anarchist-as-poet aims to create and recreate the world endlessly through motility and revolt. In part, this project becomes realisable because the anarchist affirms (rather than denies) the nothingness that underlies all things, and openly founds the anarchist project on this nothing. This affirmation re-situates the individual within the matrix of chaos and makes available – to itself and others – the plenitude of its creative energy. Freedom consists of the capacity to shape this creative energy in everyday life according to will and desire: 'Any form of "order" which we have not imagined and produced directly and spontaneously in sheer "existential freedom" for our own celebratory purposes – is an illusion.' (Bey, 1994: 2). But in order to achieve a generalisation of chaos, the anarchist needs to form affinities and create insurrectional projects based on these affinities: 'From Stirner's "Union of Self-Owning Ones" we proceed to Nietzsche's circle of "Free Spirits" and thence to Fourier's "Passional Series", doubling and redoubling ourselves even as the Other multiplies itself in the *eros* of the group.' (Bey, 1994: 4). Anarchist subjectivity, then, is defined by a complex web of inter-relations between the autonomous individual, passional affinities, and the matrix of chaos which 'lies at the heart of our project'. (Bey, 1994: 1). Anarchist subjectivity, in other words, remains inseparable from anarchist intersubjectivity. The anarchist project is formed through interactions that occur between those who desire to dispel the illusory stases of order – those illusions which obscure the unlimited creative potentials of chaos, which manifest themselves as lived poetry in daily life. As Bey says of affinities formed through free association: 'the activity of such a group will come to replace Art as we poor PoMo bastards know it. Gratuitous creativity, or "play", and the exchange of gifts, will cause the withering-away of Art as the reproduction of commodities' (Bey, 1994: 4). Anarchy, a condition of free creativity generated through motility and revolt, can only be conceived and realised by the poetic imagination and, as far as words are concerned, can only find expression in poetic language.

In Bey's formulations, the anarchist subject is simultaneously unary, multiple and heterogeneous. Under conditions of power, the multiplicity of the subject is denied and erased. Through the production of psychosocial stases, power manufactures an apparently unified identity for each individual, containing and channelling otherwise free energies on to the territories of governance and control. These stases of order are illusory, however, in that the organised appearance of unitary identity is based upon the introduction of division into the subject. Power disrupts the free flows of energy within the holistic field of subjectivity: it carves up this field and delimits the split subject, divided from and turned against itself in ways which enhance profit maximisation and social control. A language structured around binary oppositions – and principally the polarity between self and other – maintains a regime based on separation and alienation. Anarchist revolt seeks to abolish all forms of power and control structures. In terms of subjectivity, this project entails destruction of the illusions of a separate self and recovery of a free-flowing and holistic sense of subjectivity. Insurrection aims to dismantle staticity, overcome blockages and put the subject back into process. As part of realising this project, the anarchist uses poetic language in order to combat the language of control and its sociolinguistic construction of the divided self. For the anarchist, poetic language – in all its apparent illogicality – provides the logical mode of expression for the creation of a life of lived poetry, a means for breaking through the dominant logic, and a repository for the *savoir-vivre* necessary to live in conditions of chaos.

Ontological anarchy, modernity and postmodernity

As a synthetic thinker, Bey constructs a *bricolage* of materials derived from a variety of sources including anarchism, situationism, existentialism and surrealism. However, his formulations concerning ontological anarchy remain exemplary and indicative of the philosophical underpinnings of the new anarchism(s). Although the range of sources upon which he draws suggests that the ideational matrix from which the new anarchism(s) emerge is not in itself particularly new, it is nevertheless associated with newness.

In an important essay entitled 'Anarchy as modernist aesthetic', Carol Vanderveer Hamilton (1995) has identified a discourse of anarchy which runs through modernism and shapes and informs its aesthetics. Subsequently obscured by liberal and Marxist interpretations of modernism, Hamilton maintains that the discourse of anarchy structured modernist representation through a cultural identification of the signifier of the anarchist bomb with modernity. In modernism, then, anarchy became a synonym for newness.

Hamilton's groundbreaking text opens up crucial issues, but given its preliminary nature the discussion inevitably remains generalised. Although the analysis is remarkably wide ranging, the focus on propaganda by deed and the bomb as metonym for anarchism is ultimately restrictive. Hamilton has crucially identified the existence of a discourse of anarchy and established its significance within modernity, yet in her account anarchism emerges as a seemingly uniform doctrine. The reasons for this are not hard to detect. A survey of the anarchist figures who are namechecked – notably Kropotkin, Goldman, Berkman, De Cleyre and Reclus – suggests that the focus of Hamilton's essay is effectively anarcho-communism. The Stirnerian individualist strand within classical anarchism does not appear within Hamilton's discussion of the discourse of anarchy, despite the widespread acknowledgement of the influence of this strand on modernist thought and aesthetics.[3] In the current context, this remains unfortunate, as it is clear that Stirner remains not merely a crucial influence on modernist anarchism and more generally on modernity, but (more importantly for current purposes) also the key figure underpinning the new anarchism(s) in the period of postmodernity. Even Murray Bookchin, the major ideological opponent of the new anarchism(s), admits the latter point in his splenetic survey of current developments within contemporary anarchy, *Social anarchism or lifestyle anarchism: an unbridgeable chasm* (Bookchin, 1995).[4] In order to understand the significance of Stirner to both modernist anarchism and (more pertinently) the new anarchism(s), the nature and significance of his thought needs to be radically revised.

Stirner and the anarcho-psychological episteme

In *The order of things* and *The archaeology of knowledge*, Michel Foucault develops a discursive archaeological methodology which 'attempts to study the structure of the discourses of the various disciplines that have claimed to put forth theories of society, individuals, and language' (Dreyfus and Rabinow, 1982: 17).

To achieve this aim, he introduces the notion of the *episteme*, which he defines as follows:

> By *episteme*, we mean . . . the total set of relations that unite, at a given period, the discursive practices that give rise to epistemological figures, sciences, and possibly formalized systems . . . The episteme is not a form of knowledge (*connaissance*) or type of rationality which, crossing the boundaries of the most varied sciences, manifests the sovereign unity of a subject, a spirit, or a period; it is the totality of relations that can be discovered, for a given period, between the sciences when one analyses them at the level of discursive regularities. (Foucault, 1972: 191)

On this basis, Foucault then attempts to 'isolate and describe the epistemic systems that underlie three major epochs in Western thought': the Renaissance, the Classical Age, and Modernity (Dreyfus and Rabinow, 1982: 18). In analysing these epistemic systems, however, he remains largely concerned with the operations and regimes of power rather than projects aimed at the abolition of power; and, where he is interested in struggles against power, the struggles considered are usually of a partial or reformist nature.[5] In examining any one epistemic system, he *is* interested in conflicts and resistances, but the historical course of these conflicts remain of limited concern, and he neglects entirely to examine those discursive – and extra-discursive – practices which seek to overthrow any ruling episteme and the social formation which it articulates. In his account of modernity, for example, those anarchist projects – and particularly the Stirnerian strain – which attempt to initiate a total transformation of life are completely absent from Foucault's discussion.

John Carroll's seminal study *Break out from the crystal palace: the anarcho-psychological critique: Stirner, Nietzsche, Dostoevsky* provides an invaluable corrective to Foucault's failures, and indicates the centrality of the Stirnerian – or what Carroll more broadly calls the anarcho-psychological – critique to both the anarchist project and modernity/postmodernity. Although he does not frame his analysis in Foucauldian terms, Carroll's study investigates the discursive conflicts that took place within the emerging episteme of modernity during the nineteenth century. Carroll focuses on the struggle that occurred between what he variously terms three different intellectual, theoretical or ideological traditions, competing social theories, perspectives, world-views, or bodies of social theory (Carroll, 1974: 1, 2, 3, 6, 13, 14 *passim*). Two of these conflicting perspectives – British, liberal, utilitarian rationalist social philosophy and Marxist socialism – are well known and widely acknowledged elements of the episteme of modernity. The third, however, the anarcho-psychological critique, has been scandalously neglected and written out of accounts of the formation of modernity.[6]

Carroll's text restores the anarcho-psychological critique to its rightful place as a key element in the discursive – and by extension, extra-discursive – contestations over the modern/postmodern condition. *Break Out* convincingly demonstrates that although the anarcho-psychological critique has been obscured by the political conflicts of the two dominant paradigms of capitalist liberal-rationalism and Marxist socialism, its antipolitics has acted as a persistent underground presence, exerting a barely acknowledged and sometimes unsuspected but often widespread influence. Taking Carroll's analysis further, it can be argued that with the collapse of the Marxist paradigm, the anarcho-psychological critique is finally emerging from its subterranean hideout and, in contemporary anarchy, catalysing the breakout from the crystal palace of the control complex.

Carroll argues that the anarcho-psychological critique commences with the publication of Stirner's *Der Einzige und sein Eigentum* in 1845 (translated as *The ego and its own*). This text 'inaugurates the reconstitution of philosophical debate' and constitutes 'a crossroads in nineteenth-century intellectual history' (Carroll, 1974: 26, 88).[7] The distinctive and innovative feature of Stirner's formulations in particular and the anarcho-psychological critique in general remains its emphasis on a unique ontology or, rather, an ontology of uniqueness:

> At the basis of the philosophical innovations of Stirner and Nietzsche is ontology: their radically new perspective on religion, on morals, on political and social life, stems from their attitude to *being*. Their entire work branches out from the stem conviction that there is a primary order of reality about which all that can be said is that the individual exists, that 'I am!' The individual first exists, and then begins to define himself [*sic*]. Essences, the communicable, socially mediated dimension of individual character belong to the second order of reality. Behind them lies an unconscious, irreducible, never realizable or comprehensible force, an inviolable coherency: the *individuum*. This is the ground of *der Einzige*, the unique one, the realm of what Stirner calls his 'creative nothing'. (Carroll, 1974: 39)

Carroll's analysis proceeds from an examination of ontology to a discussion of the epistemological anarchy developed within the anarcho-psychological critique.

If this cluster of ideas seems familiar, this is because the anarcho-psychological critique clearly underlies Hakim Bey's contemporary formulation of ontological anarchy in particular and the new anarchism(s) more generally. Carroll makes it clear that the antipolitics characteristic of the anarcho-psychological critique[8] remains rooted in its ontological commitments, but this is evidently as true for Bey as it is for Stirner:

> The political anarchism of Stirner and Nietzsche is a logical development of their ontological anarchism: their denigration of social authorities represents one dimension of their endeavour to displace the authority of essences and stress the primacy of the *I*. Both see the springs of the human condition as anarchic, willful, problematical, a complex of forces with their deeply individual source beneath the superstructure of social mediation; both recognize what Plato referred to as the 'unutterable' in each individual, a noumenal core which makes of human thinking, of necessity, an isolated, introspective activity. The social or essentialist superstructure is by itself lifeless; its function is to provide the *I* with a means of expression. (Carroll, 1974: 39)

Stirner anticipates the Heideggerian/Sartrean emphasis on existence preceding essence. In fact, 'Stirner illustrates how the individual ego, whose ontological ground is simply the self-reflection that it exists, is fettered as soon as it subordinates itself to qualities or essences' (Carroll, 1974: 21). Historically, the Stirnerian ego comes to consciousness in a world of socio-existential alienation. *Historically* this is the case because, as Stirner's broad overview of history indicates (1993: 15–151), individuals have always been subject to governance, order and control. The anti-authoritarian insurrection proposed in *The ego and its own*, however, aims to bring about a historically unprecedented world in which socio-existential alienation will be abolished. Born out of a creative nothingness (or non-existence), the ego comes into existence by asserting itself, affirming its existence – in other words, asserting the only thing which, for the individual, has any ontological foundation: its self.

The subject, then, is self-created: it creates itself as an individual by and through its assertion of its self. Language acquisition and use remains crucial to this act of self-affirmation. In emerging from a condition of non-existence to one of existence, a being issues forth spontaneously, but then finds itself in a world requiring introspection and self-reflection. Or, to put it another way: being emerges from a condition of ineffability into a world of language. In some respects this account of the construction of the self concurs with the theories developed by Jacques Lacan (see Payne, 1993). However, on the issue of language, the two thinkers diverge radically. Both agree that language is the major force through which the individual is constituted and structured. However, while Lacan maintains that the entry into language entails a simultaneous submission to social authority, and the beginning of alienation as the self passes from full self-presence to the condition of absence characteristic of language systems predicated on the signifier/signified division, Stirner's perspective on this issue remains rather more radical.

Emerging from non-existence into self-consciousness, the Stirnerian being creates itself as an individual by *appropriating* language: or, more accurately, by appropriating in the first instance only those words which it needs to bring itself into existence as an individual and express its self-affirmation: I am! The Stirnerian being possesses the (self-)confidence to undertake this act of (self-) assertion because, at the deepest levels of being, it never becomes separated from the creative nothingness which is the ontological (non-)ground of its existence. The creative nothingness of the unutterable void beneath all existence underlies and precedes all notions of self, signifying systems, social mediations and authority structures. But its inexhaustible creativity remains a wellspring at the source of the individual being and fills the latter with confidence in its capacities and energy with which to fulfil its potentials:

> I am *owner* of my might, and I am so when I know myself as *unique*. In the *unique one* the owner himself returns into his creative nothing, of which he is born. Every higher essence above me, be it God, be it man, weakens the feeling of my unique-ness, and pales before the sun of this consciousness. If I concern myself for myself, the unique one, then my concern rests on its transitory, mortal creator, who con-sumes himself, and I may say: 'All things are nothing to me.' (Stirner, 1993: 366)

This sonorous passage, the closing words of Stirner's symphonic *The ego and its own*, articulates some key themes concerning the self-creation and self-real-isation of the individual. The individual is defined by the capacity to own, and primarily by the ability to own him or herself – that is to say, to dispose of the self and act in any way congruent with one's will, desire or interest. Ownership of self is primary; other forms of ownership are secondary and derive from this fundamental form. As a subject-in-process (indeed, a subject-in-rebellion, for reasons that will become apparent subsequently), the Stirnerian self is con-stantly re-creating itself and revising its modes of activity in accordance with its changing desires and interests, but throughout these continual changes one con-stant persists: the need to own oneself or be in a condition of ownness. Being in a condition of ownness means first and foremost that an individual is able to draw upon the fund of creative energies which are loaned to it by the nothing-ness at the basis of its being. These energies are then available at the free dispo-sal of the individual. The capacity to make free and unhindered use of these energies defines the individual as unique. The individual becomes a unique one at the moment of self-reflexivity, in the instant in which she or he realises his or her ownness.[9] The self-created individual wilfully creates and destroys itself. Although the energies of the void are inexhaustible, those energies loaned to the individual are finite. The individual uses up those energies in its progress toward self-realisation: it creates but also consumes and ultimately burns itself out. The individual comes from nothing and returns to nothing. The turning point in this voyage of self-creation and self-destruction occurs at the apogee of its attainment. At the very moment when the individual realises itself as unique, at the exact moment when the maximum degree of individuation and differentiation has taken place, then 'the owner himself returns into his creative nothing, of which he is born'. But at the peak of its powers the individual is less like a comet than a sun – 'the sun of this consciousness' – a burning orb which illuminates, by contrast, the dark void which contains it.

This process is set in motion with each individual's primal assertion of selfhood. By appropriating the words 'I am!', the Stirnerian self takes ownership of language, or at least that little corner that she or he can make their own at this stage of maturation. Confidently rooted in the unutterability of the roots of its being, the Stirnerian individual creates a self through owning language. The origins of selfhood are thus indistinguishable from ownership. The self achieves its initial sense of ownness through making language its own, and exalts in this first victory of its will. The Stirnerian subject is neither intimidated nor victimised by language as the individual is in the Lacanian schema. The reasons for this are clear: the Stirnerian subject is not a split subject, divided by language, because its identity is not wholly defined by language, but remains rooted in the creative nothingness from which it springs.[10] Hence the attitude of such a subject to language – as to the world in general – is not one of victim or dependent, but that of conqueror. Identity is not to be sought in and through language, because it has not been lost; the Stirnerian subject does not need to search for a self, but starts from it: 'the question runs, not how one can acquire life, but how one can squander, enjoy it; or, not how one is to produce the self in himself, but how one is to dissolve himself, to live himself out' (Stirner, 1993: 320).

However, in seeking self-realisation, the Stirnerian ego is immediately confronted with other wills and forces which seek to delimit, contain and control the self-willed individual, and hence 'the *combat* of self-assertion is inevitable' (p. 9). The Stirnerian ego maintains that 'Nothing is more to me than myself!' (p. 5), but finds itself in a world where power, in all its varied shapes and forms, wants the ego to accept that 'It is more to me than myself' (p. 305). In such a world, conflict remains inevitable unless the individual consents to submit to a life of alienation, subordination and self-renunciation. 'A human life,' the opening chapter of *The ego and its own*, traces the stages of this lifelong struggle which commences at birth: 'From the moment when he catches sight of the light of the world a man seeks to find out *himself* and get hold of *himself* out of its confusion, in which he, with everything else, is tossed about in motley mixture' (p. 9) (all italics are from the original work). The ego is born into a world of illusions which ensnare and blind the individual, and from which the ego must disentangle itself if it is to realise itself. These delusions are caused by the dominance of abstractions – what Stirner calls spooks ('*Spuke*') – over concrete individuals. Abstractions – concepts, ideas, beliefs and so on – that were once attributes and thus possessions of individuals, now control their one-time owners, and crystallise as fixed ideas which prevent the free flows of subjective will and desire. They are, in short, power relations. Stirner's entire insurrectional project – which, as Carroll indicates, is envisaged as a revolution against the totality of power relations, not merely the State[11] – thus directly derives from the ontological status of the individual. The ramifications of this insurrectional project are manifold and beyond the scope of this chapter. In what follows, attention will be limited to the key issue of language.

Stirner, language and subjectivity

Stirnerian ontology postulates a radical monism. The Stirnerian ego, as indicated above, embodies a paradoxical reconciliation of opposites, as it is simultaneously being and nothingness: a self-created autonomous but ephemeral individual *and* an inexhaustible creative nothingness. The crucial moment in the emergence of the former from the latter, however, remains the simultaneous act of self-assertion and the subject's insertion (or perhaps more accurately, incursion) into language. At this moment, the primary instance of self-expression, but also the moment when self-expression and self-assertion become identical, the ego moves from the realm of the unutterable into the world of utterance (while not, of course, entirely abandoning the former world). From that moment onward, however, the ego increasingly discovers that the world of utterance is characterised by conflict and delusion, and that she or he must adopt a combative stance and a contestatory mode of procedure if self-realisation is to occur. In the first instance, this contestation takes place within language or in activities whose structures and parameters are defined through language. Language, then, becomes a key area requiring mastery by the Stirnerian ego because it remains essential to the devising of insurrectional projects.

The importance of language in Stirner's work cannot be overestimated. The world of utterance (or, at least in historical terms, the world of power) is a world haunted by spooks – disembodied ideas, principles and concepts, abstractions which take the form of words. The spook is a revenant who assumes the insubstantial shape of the dominant discourse, the language of governance, before it manifests itself in more material forms. It is the language of order, management, utility and rationality. Hence, the ego seeks to find and express itself in a language of insurrection, a language of radical otherness which negates dominant discourses and their expressive modes, as well as embodying the ego's self-affirmation in a style commensurate with its uniqueness.

Carroll refers to Stirner's 'constant concern with revitalizing language, repossessing it as a creative force' (Carroll, 1974: 36). Power drains language of its vitality and creativity: it captures words, domesticates them, debilitates them, debases them, instrumentalises them, makes them prosaic, so that they may act as a means for maintaining social control. The Stirnerian ego seeks to liberate language, or rather repossess it so that it once again becomes available for the free self-expression and enjoyment of the individual. However, it is not sufficient for the egoist merely to reappropriate an enervated or aridly rationalistic language: in making language its own, the egoist must regenerate and reinfuse it with the creativity which lies at the depths of his/her being. The Stirnerian ego, in other words, *transforms* language: she or he does not speak in the prosaic language of authority, but in the only language suitable for an insurrection against authority: the language of poetry.

Stirner dreams of a 'literature that deals blows at the State itself' (1993: 226) and *The ego and its own* is an attempt to generate such a text. Even in translation,[12] Stirner's distinctive, poetic style of writing remains evident. Although it is a work of philosophy, it is not composed in the 'stiff, concept-strictured' writing style characteristic of the discourse, but has instead a 'highly flexible aphoristic style' full of 'gaiety and buoyancy' (Carroll, 1974: 27–35). As in many other respects, Stirner anticipates Nietzsche in becoming the first *Dichterphilosoph* (poet-philosopher), penning passages of pure poetry, such as the following indictment of the ego's historical self-alienation and dispossession:

> I, who am really I, must pull off the lion-skin of the I from the stalking thistle-eater [Power]. What manifold robbery have I not put up with in the history of the world! There I let sun, moon, and stars, cats and crocodiles, receive the honour of ranking as I; there Jehovah, Allah, and Our Father came and were invested with the I; there families, tribes, peoples, and at last actually mankind, came and were honoured as I's; there the Church, the State, came with the pretension to be I – and I gazed calmly on all. What wonder if then there was always a real I too that joined the company and affirmed in my face that it was not my *you* but my real *I*. Why *the* Son of Man *par excellence* had done the like; why should not *a* son of man do it too? So I saw my I always above me and outside me, and could never really come to myself. (Stirner, 1993: 224–5)

Due to the central value placed upon creativity by Stirner, Carroll maintains that 'the artist is the most appropriate paradigm for . . . the egoist' (1974: 4). But this formulation could equally be reversed so that the egoist becomes the paradigmatic artist. However, the art with which the egoist remains primarily concerned is the *ars vitae* (the art of living) because as a subject in process (of constant self-creation) – 'I am every moment just positing or creating myself' – his/her life is a work of art (Stirner, 1993: 150). But an authentic *ars vitae* remains impossible without a certain *savoir-vivre* – and such knowledge can only be born of reflection; hence, given the decisive role of language acquisition to individuation for Stirner, the importance of the text as a means for self-expression. The *ars vitae* and the *ars poetica* are not antithetical in Stirner, but intimately interconnected.

Although presumably possessing some kind of genealogical link with the eighteenth-century German Romantic prose poems of Novalis, *The ego and its own* is appropriately *sui generis*. It is not a work of poetry in the conventionally accepted sense of the term at the time of its publication.[13] Nevertheless, it remains a work couched in poetic language. In order to appreciate the significance of Stirner's innovation and the magnitude of his achievement in this text, it is necessary to relate *The ego and its own* to the analysis of literary discourse undertaken by Julia Kristeva in *Revolution in poetic language*.

Stirner and poetic language

For Kristeva, poetic language and poetry are not coterminous: 'neither confined to poetry as a genre nor inclusive of all poetry, poetic language inscribes the signifying process and manifests the negativity, rejection, and heterogeneity of the subject' (in Payne, 1993: 40). Poetic language 'stands for the infinite possibilities of language' whereas 'all other language acts are merely partial realizations of the possibilities inherent in "poetic language"' (in Roudiez, 1984: 2). Kristevan textual analysis consists of investigating the relations between two interdependent modalities within the signifying process that constitutes language: the semiotic and the symbolic. These modes manifest two aspects of the subject. The semiotic refers to the rhythms, flows and pulsations which play across and within the body of the subject prior to language acquisition. Semiotic rhythms are never entirely lost, even when they are overlaid and hidden by the symbolic – the order and syntax characteristic of language. Indeed, Kristevan textual analysis focuses on the interplay between semiotic and symbolic dispositions within any text. When the symbolic disposition predominates, a text becomes a phenotext, in other words bound by 'societal, cultural, syntactical, and other grammatical constraints' (in Roudiez, 1984: 5); when the semiotic disposition predominates, a text becomes a genotext, a space for the actualisation of poetic language, an anarchic language which irrupts in rebellion against the constraints of social and semantic order. 'By erupting from its repressed or marginalised place and by thus displacing established signifying practices, poetic discourse corresponds, in its effects, in terms of the subject, to revolution in the socioeconomic order' (in Payne, 1993: 165).

Historically, commencing with the texts of Lautréamont and Mallarmé in the last third of the nineteenth century, Kristeva discerns in the work of certain avant-garde writers a shift in emphasis towards the deliberate creation of genotexts which, by actuating the revolutionary potential inherent in poetic discourse, brings about a revolution in poetic language. This kind of avant-garde text 'may be interpreted as an affirmation of freedom, as an anarchic revolt (even though it openly advocates neither freedom nor revolution) against a society that extols material goods and profit' (in Roudiez, 1984: 3). This remains precisely the problem which Kristeva, her focus inclined entirely on literary texts, remains unable to resolve. Although it

> dissents from the dominant economic and ideological system, the [avant-garde] text also plays into its hands: through the text, the system provides itself with what it lacks – rejection – but keeps it in a domain apart, confining it to the ego, to the 'inner experience' of an élite, and to esotericism. The text becomes the agent of a new religion that is no longer universal but élitist and esoteric. (Kristeva, 1984: 186)

The avant-garde text, lacking any commitment to revolutionary social transformation at the level of content, confines its revolution to language and form, and thus remains subject to recuperation. Equally, the conventional political tract, failing to draw upon the revolutionary capacities of poetic language, confines its incendiary appeals to the level of content, and moreover stultifies itself by embodying them in the language of order and rule. Opaque to one another, these two forms of discourse remain trapped within their limitations and thus incapable of enacting radical psychosocial transformation.

Kristeva borrows from Plato the term *chora* to designate the space which Stirner calls 'creative nothingness'. The *chora* is 'the place where the subject is both generated and negated, the place where his [*sic*] unity succumbs before the process of charges and stases that produce him' (Kristeva, 1984: 28). Like the creative nothing, it remains unrepresentable because it is impermeable to language: 'although the *chora* can be designated and regulated, it can never be definitively posited' (Kristeva, 1984: 26). 'Indifferent to language, enigmatic and feminine, this space underlying the written is rhythmic, unfettered, irreducible to its intelligible verbal translation; it is musical, anterior to judgment, but restrained by a single guarantee: syntax' (Kristeva, 1984: 29). While language (and the realm of the symbolic in general) tends to generate a fixed identity around the personal pronoun *I*, the semiotic rhythms derived from the *chora* undermine these tendencies and ensure a heterogeneous subjectivity which 'cannot be grasped, contained, or synthesized by linguistic or ideological structures' (in Payne, 1993: 239). As a result, the heterogeneous subject remains continually in process, free of the stases typical of a unary subjectivity; but, further, in terms of representation, the signifying practices produced by such a subject set off an 'explosion of the semiotic in the symbolic' (Kristeva, 1984: 69).

Kristeva's discussion helps to clarify the revolutionary nature of the charged poetic language which runs through *The ego and its own* as well as the significance of Stirner's concern with subjectivity and the emergence, formation and ongoing development of the subject. Stirner's consideration of these issues, however, extends beyond issues of subjectivity to encompass an interest in intersubjectivity and its role in shaping the self and projects for self-realisation. Contrary to the opinion of Stirner's detractors, the Stirnerian egoist is not an isolated, selfish ego*tist*. The egoist seeks self-realisation through owning him/herself and thus becoming unique. But from the beginning this project is thwarted, and thus the egoist declares war on society, the State and all the other forms of power which attempt to obstruct or limit his/her will to self-enjoyment. At a certain stage, however, the egoist realises that she or he does not have the capacity to combat Power on her/his own, but must link up with other egoists who are similarly seeking self-realisation through free activity. Stirner recommends that the egoist seek affinities within a union of egos. The individual egoist cannot achieve self-realisation in isolation, nor within current social arrangements, and so, through union, egoists mutually pursue the insurrectionary project of 'the liberation of the world' (Stirner, 1993: 305) – but each for entirely egoistic reasons.

Stirner does not regard the union, however, as merely an unavoidable and perhaps unpleasant expedient, but as a mode of affinity rooted in the subject's ontological condition:

> Not isolation or being alone, but society, is man's original state. Our existence begins with the most intimate conjunction, as we are already living with our mother before we breathe; when we see the light of the world, we at once lie on a human being's breast again, her love cradles us in the lap, spoon-feeds us, and chains us to her person with a thousand ties. Society is our *state of nature*. And this is why, the more we learn to feel ourselves, the connection that was formerly most intimate becomes ever looser and the dissolution of the original society more unmistakable. To have once again for herself the child that once lay under her heart, the mother must fetch it from the street and from the midst of its playmates. The child prefers the *intercourse* that it enters into with *its fellows* to the *society* that it has not entered into, but been born into.
>
> But the dissolution of *society* is *intercourse* or *union*. A society does assuredly arise by union too, but only as a fixed idea arises by a thought . . . If a union has crystallized into a society, it has ceased to become a coalition; for coalition is an incessant self-uniting; it has become a unitedness, come to a standstill, degenerated into a fixity; it is – *dead* as a union, it is the corpse of the union or the coalition, it is – society, community. (Stirner, (1993: 305–6)[14]

In Kristevan terms, the Stirnerian subject can be seen to inhabit the realm of the semiotic before and immediately succeeding birth. Intimately connected with the *chora*, the mother's body, the pre-linguistic subject lives in a condition of immediacy. However, in the course of time, this condition comes to be regarded as a restriction, a limitation, a shackle. The subject, made aware of its individuality through the self-assertion and self-reflexivity provided by language acquisition, asserts its independence in order to quit a narrow for a wider form of interdependence. The (speaking) subject prefers (social/sexual) intercourse or union with companions in a sphere that has been chosen or willed, rather than one that has been purely given. Language, openly but playfully conflated with sexuality, provides the means whereby erotic energies are directed away from the mother's body and into the space of the union.[15] However, as these energies derive *from* the *chora*, they are not lost or denied, but incorporated *into* the union. As a result, the union is not a fixed but a fluid mode of practice. The subject is formed by the synergy of the diverse erotic fluxes which flow in and through the intercourse of the union, just as much as, if not more than, in the initial condition of sociality with the mother. The union acts as a means for multiplying and magnifying as well as diversifying these motile flows and directing them toward a maximisation of uniqueness for each participant. Language – more specifically, poetic language – plays a central role in achieving this aim. As a fluid mode of practice, the union requires a signifying practice commensurate with its form. The union is not based on unanimity ('unitedness') but resemblance – a resemblance of interests. If metaphor, the basic figure of poetry, comprises a pattern of resemblances, then the union is a living metaphor, an embodiment of lived poetry, and the words spoken in the union are in the (m)other tongue of poetic language.

Conclusion

In terms of representation, Kristeva claims that investments of erotic energy in revolutionary or reactionary projects are 'textually enacted processes that are manifested in prosody and syntax' (in Payne, 1993: 193). Although a close analysis of the physical, material aspects of the language of *The ego and its own* would be necessary for purposes of substantiating the presence of the genotext in Stirner's work, it is my contention that this text constitutes a veritable embodiment of the revolution in poetic language. Further, I maintain that Stirner's text not only prefigures but initiates the revolution in poetic language which Kristeva detects in late-nineteenth-century avant-garde writing. Stirner's key role in the formation of the episteme of modernity has already been established: his inauguration of the revolution in poetic language can now be recognised as an important aspect of that epistemic shift. Further still, I contend that Stirner has, in advance, anticipated *and* resolved the issues which for Kristeva stultify the revolutionary impetus in textual and by extension extra-textual terms. These are large claims, but following Carroll's recovery of Stirner's unacknowledged but seminal participation in and influence on the discursive formation of modernity/postmodernity, I would go so far as to claim that the insurrectionary impulse articulated and embodied in *The ego and its own* constitutes – to adapt Conrad's term – the secret agent of (modern) history. Although driven underground by the clash of rival political ideologies for much of the twentieth century, the anti-ideological antipolitics of this revolutionary perspective is once again surfacing in the new anarchism(s). And the revolution in poetic language at the core of its textuality remains central to its insurrectionary purpose.

Notes

1 Editors' note: this was the second draft of John's chapter, completed about two months before his death. Whilst we believe that this stands as a finished piece in itself, because a substantial proportion of the text is dependent on a translation of Max Stirner's *The ego and its own* from the German, there are a number of areas which we hoped to clarify prior to publication. This should not be seen as a weakness, but more in the spirit of ongoing debates about the relationship between theory, method and practice, which were always central to John's concerns. We have edited the chapter sparingly and in keeping with the writing style to which many around the world have become accustomed.

2 The usefulness of the term 'new anarchism(s)' – or indeed 'anarchism' *per se* in the current context remains somewhat dubious. Like many contemporary radical antiauthoritarians, Stirner refused any reductive ideological labelling, and neither referred

to himself as an anarchist nor labelled his perspectives as anarchist. This label has only retrospectively – and rather unfortunately – been appended to his writings. Some contemporary radical theorists (notably Fredy Perlman) have not only refused labelling but have distanced themselves from the (classical) anarchist tradition. Others have attempted to define various post-(classical) anarchist positions and terminologies. Bob Black, for example, has posited a 'Type-3 anarchism', neither collectivist nor individualist – a label which Hakim Bey has characterised as a useful 'pro-tem slogan' (Bey, 1991: 62). Black also authored an essay with the self-explanatory title 'Anarchism and other impediments to anarchy' and in a subsequent critique of 'anarcho-leftism' termed contemporary proponents of anarchy as 'post-leftist anarchists' (Black, 1997: 150). Bey has similarly written an essay entitled 'Post-anarchism anarchy' (in Bey, 1991) which distances contemporary anarchy from a moribund, dogmatic and outdated classical anarchism, and has attempted to launch the term 'chaote' (a proponent of chaos) as an alternative to the term 'anarchist'. In my 1998 essay 'Maximalist anarchism/anarchist maximalism', I adapted the terms 'maximalist anarchism' and 'minimalist anarchism' to draw a comparable distinction between the first wave of (classical) anarchism which effectively climaxed at the moment of the Spanish Revolution, and the second wave of post-Situationist anarchy which emerged in the wake of May 1968 (Moore, 1998a). I have since abandoned the use of the terms 'anarchism' and 'anarchist' in my theoretical and creative work, although like Perlman, Black and Bey (among others), I have retained the use of the word 'anarchy.'

In the present chapter, however, I use the term 'anarchist' and the label 'new anarchism(s)' as a kind of shorthand and for the sake of convenience. They are not necessarily the most accurate or suitable terms, not least because they do not do justice either to Stirner's thought or the range of contemporary radical antiauthoritarian formulations, but they are perhaps the best currently available. Readers should bear this caveat in mind.

3 Malcolm Green, for example, notes that Stirner 'was forgotten until the turn of the [twentieth] century when his work influenced among others: Scheerbart, Hausmann, Wedekind, B. Traven, Shaw, Gide, Breton, Picabia, Kubin, indeed the whole November 1918 generation, and later Sartre, Camus and Heidegger. Also, of course, the Vienna Group' (Green, 1989: 241). This roll call of modernist figures influenced by Stirner remains very selective, however, and excludes several major names (e.g., Nietzsche), as well as a diverse range of individuals and currents within the radical anti-authoritarian milieu (e.g., John Henry Mackay, Otto Gross, Albert Libertad, and the Bonnot Gang). Stirner's influence on modernism should not – perhaps cannot – be underestimated.

In scholarly terms, Redding (1998) continues the tradition of marginalising Stirner in terms of both anarchism and modernism, but Weir (1997) and Antliff (1997, 2001) redress the balance somewhat by re-establishing Stirner's significance in both discursive spheres and at their points of intersection.

4 'Today's reactionary social context greatly explains the emergence of a phenomenon in Euro-American anarchism that cannot be ignored: the spread of individualist anarchism . . . In the traditionally individualist-liberal United States and Britain, the 1990s are awash in self-styled anarchists who . . . are cultivating a latter-day anarcho-individualism that I will call *lifestyle anarchism*' (Bookchin, 1995: 8–9). Bookchin's jaundiced and distorted account has rightly received numerous trenchant critiques within the anarchist press, notably Watson (1996) and Black (1997). The accuracy of his

observation concerning the resurgence of Stirnerian anarchist individualism, even though he sees this as a negative phenomenon, cannot be contested.

5 See for example pp. 211–13 of Foucault's 'Afterword on "The subject and power"' in Dreyfus and Rabinow (1982) which focuses entirely on 'forms of resistance' (p. 211) – i.e., struggles which are essentially negotiations with power instead of seeking its abolition.

6 And accounts of anarchism too. Bookchin, for example, devotes several ill-tempered pages vainly trying to dismiss individualist anarchism or cast it as reactionary (Bookchin, 1995: 7–11).

7 Others – notably, for Carroll, figures as diverse as Nietzsche and Dostoevsky (but also Freud and the existentialists) – are to develop the anarcho-psychological paradigm in various directions, which are beyond the scope of this chapter, but Stirner's formulations are originary.

8 On the contrast between politics and antipolitics, I refer the reader to my text *Anarchy and ecstasy*: 'by antipolitical I do not mean an approach that pretends it has no ideological dimensions. I do, however, mean an approach that is not political. The *Concise Oxford Dictionary* defines politics as the "science and art of government" and political as "of the State or its government". Political praxis, in this definition, thus remains the ideology of governance, and as such it remains appropriate to the shared discursive territory of the forces of control and counter-control. In attempting to transcend that territory, therefore, it is necessary to construct an antipolitics, an anarchic praxis that is more germane for those whose aim is the dissolution, not the seizure, of control' (Moore (1988: 5–6)).

9 The issue of gender – i.e., the question of whether the Stirnerian notion of the individual is gendered or whether it escapes gendering, as well as the question of the relationship between language acquisition and gender identity in Stirner's work – requires consideration in its own right, and unfortunately lies beyond the scope of this chapter.

10 The Stirnerian entity appears to be a divided or unary subject, but might more appropriately be characterised as a heterogeneous subject. Despite the emphasis in *The ego and its own* on the ego and uniqueness, the Stirnerian subject is not unitary because it has no essence, no basis in being. 'Nothing at all is justified by *being*. What is thought of *is* as well as what is not thought of; the stone in the street *is*, and my notion of it *is* too. Both are only in different *spaces*, the former in airy space, the latter in my head, in *me*; for I am space like the street' (Stirner, 1993: 341). The Stirnerian subject remains a space, a void, within which heterogeneous desires, wills and impulses arise and are then consciously *owned*. Hence Stirner's paradoxical self-characterisation as 'I the unspeakable' or the assertion that 'neither you and [*sic*] I are speakable, we are unutterable' (Stirner, 1993: 355; 311). In this way, Stirner eludes the Derridean charge of logocentrism, despite the importance of the logos in his work.

11 'Stirner at times uses "State" as no more than a convenient shorthand for supraindividual authority' (Carroll, 1974: 136n).

12 Green, who has himself translated the opening passage of *The ego and its own*, regards the standard Byington translation as 'hopelessly turgid' (Green, 1989: 241). Editors' note: having referred to the original German ourselves, we feel that Byington's translation *is* a reasonably faithful representation of Stirner's (complex and technical) original; therefore, we would have sought to question and clarify John Moore's (secondhand) claim here. Again, we believe that John would have relished the debate.

13 The specifically French tradition of the prose poem, made famous later in the nineteenth century by Baudelaire, Lautréamont and Rimbaud, seems to have been initiated by Aloysius Bertrand in 1842 – only three years prior to the publication of *The
ego and its own* – and is therefore unlikely to have influenced Stirner.
14 For sound rhetorical reasons, Stirner employs the same term – 'society' ('*Gesellschaft*'
in the original) – to designate both the mother–child relationship and the organised
social aggregation of individuals and groups.
15 The dissolution of the initial mother–child 'society' forms a paradigm for the disin-
tegration of (the totality of power relations which comprise) society. For Stirner,
however, society is a form of mass psychological regression. Social formations arise
when unions lose their motility and become subject to stasis. The erotic energies
invested in the union are no longer fluid but 'crystallised' and fixed – or, rather fixated
– on a reunion with the mother's body. In contrast to the life-affirming erotic drives
characteristic of the union, society constitutes a mass reactivation of death drives, a
psychological atavism whose sociopolitical expression is obedience to authority and
support for totalitarian projects (here, John is paraphrasing p. 306 of Stirner (1993)).

Technology is capital: *Fifth Estate*'s critique of the megamachine

Introduction

'How do we begin to discuss something as immense as technology?', writes T. Fulano at the beginning of his essay 'Against the megamachine' (1981a: 4). Indeed, the degree to which the technological apparatus penetrates all elements of contemporary society does make such an undertaking a daunting one. Nevertheless, it is an undertaking that the US journal and collective *Fifth Estate* has attempted. In so doing, it has developed arguably the most sophisticated and challenging anarchist approach to technology currently available.[1]

Starting from the late 1970s, the *Fifth Estate* (hereafter *FE*) began to put forward the argument that the technologies of capitalism cannot be separated from the socioeconomic system itself. Inspired and influenced by a number of writers, including Karl Marx, Jacques Ellul and Jacques Camatte, it began to conceptualise modern technology as constituting a system of domination itself, one which interlinks and interacts with the economic processes of capitalism to create a new social form, a 'megamachine' which integrates not only capitalism and technology, but also State, bureaucracy and military. For the *FE*, technology and capital, although not identical, are more similar than different, and cannot be separated into an 'evil' capitalism and an essentially neutral technology. Any critique of capitalism and the State must recognise the importance of contemporary technology and the crucial role it plays in the development of new forms of domination, oppression and exploitation. Concepts of 'capital' and 'megamachine' are also explored later in this chapter.

The *Fifth Estate*

The *FE* began in Detroit in 1965, started by seventeen-year-old high-school student Harvey Ovshinsky. Set-up with the help of a $300 loan from Ovshinsky's father, over the course of the next five years it grew to became a focus for Detroit's burgeoning radical and countercultural milieu.

> As the anti-war, civil rights, hippie, New Left and alternative culture movements
> grew in Detroit, so did the paper. Our pages became the forum for the new and
> rebellious ideas that characterized the era . . . The early paper's content was a mix
> of articles about psychedelic drugs, the anti-war movement, rock and roll, the alter-
> native culture, and anything that was anti-authority. (Werbe, 1996: 1)

At one point, having a weekly circulation of over 15,000, the *FE* was an integral part of the increasingly confrontational political scene of the late 1960s and
early 1970s. Despite, or perhaps because of its high circulation, the paper struggled to maintain production. The sheer workload and the pressure on staff,
many of whom did not take a holiday from political work for years, was beginning to take its toll. Worse, the indications were that the political climate in the
US was changing. The landslide re-election of Nixon in 1973 signalled the
increasing conservatism of the electorate, and the ending of the draft removed
one of the main motivating forces behind the popular radicalism of the 1960s.

Many people left the *FE*, and it was soon on the verge of collapsing. It sur-
vived by taking on a militant socialist/labour perspective, and later by becoming
a bi-weekly alternative arts and political publication. By 1975, the paper was in
debt to printers and suppliers, it had lost some of its staff through personality
clashes and it was now dependent on revenue from commercial advertising.
Faced with impending collapse, the remaining staff members put an advert in the
paper stating that without new members the paper would close. Peter Werbe,
who had worked at the *FE* previously, was one of those who decided to join the
paper.

> A number of us, including several other former staffers and friends . . . answered
> the call. Eleven of us had constituted ourselves as the Eat the Rich Gang and under-
> took a number of projects in 1974–75, including . . . producing a number of *Fifth
> Estate* inserts, setting up study groups, as well as some sabotage activity and radical
> pranks. (Werbe, 1996: 5)

These eleven new members effectively carried out a coup which involved a
dramatic series of changes in the running of the paper, and led to the resignation
of the three existing staffers. These changes included the paper becoming
monthly, no longer accepting advertising, and abolishing all paid positions (the
new members arguing, 'We will no longer relate to people in this way' (Hippler,
1993: 35)).[2]

The new staff had diverse political outlooks and influences, but it was decided
that 'the politics of the paper would reflect a "libertarian communist" viewpoint'
(*Fifth Estate*, 1979a: 15). Through the late 1970s and early 1980s, the *FE* staff
began to expand and develop their political perspective, based on their own lived
experience, on an analysis of relevant events elsewhere and through the study of
any texts that seemed to throw light on developments of State and capital in the
late twentieth century.

One element that defined the new radical *FE* from early on was its rejection
of ideologies, arguing that 'all isms are wasms'. Ideologies were abstract systems

that ended up telling people what they could or could not do or think, and tended to become ossified and not receptive to changing historical conditions. Consequently the *FE* rejected anarch*ism*, but not anarchy as a goal. As it stated in 'Renew the earthly paradise' in 1986: 'We are not anarchists *per se* but rather pro-*anarchy*, which is for us a living, integral experience, incommensurate with Power and refusing all ideology'(*Fifth Estate*, 1986: 10). As their perspective developed, *FE* staff came to criticise not only the State and capital but also technology and the entire edifice of industrial civilisation. Their influences were diverse, and in developing the position on technology outlined below they drew on a variety of sources, from the fields of social science, philosophy, politics and anthropology. In order to contextualise their position, as well as suggesting its origins and outlining its trajectory, I will first offer an overview of three writers whose works (even when much was rejected) were central to the emerging *FE* position: Karl Marx, and two French writers, the theologian and social critic Jacques Ellul, and the ultra-Leftist theoretician Jacques Camatte.[3]

Marx – capital and technology

Many *FE* members were aware of Marx's ideas and retained some central elements of his outlook while rejecting much that was seen to be irrelevant or incorrect. One aspect that was retained was the significance of social relations in identifying forms of power and oppression, as Marx did with capital.

In conventional terminology, capital is simply 'an asset owned by an individual as wealth' and could be money, machinery or property (Bottomore, 1991: 68). As such it is ahistorical, and could exist in any society at any time; it is capital by virtue of its intrinsic properties. Marx argued instead that 'capital is not a thing at all, but a social relation which appears in the form of a thing' (*Capital III* cited in Bottomore, 1991: 68). By social relation – or more specifically, social relation of production – Marx meant 'the way people organise in order to produce'. While this organisation could be relatively informal, in the capitalist system the most important relation is the bourgeoisie's ownership of the means of production (leaving the proletariat with only its labour to sell). It is this relation that allows capital to produce wealth, and that is something that is historically specific. For Marx, what defined a particular historical epoch was a combination of the forces or means of production – that is, machinery, plus the available labour power – and these social relations. Together these constitute the 'mode of production'.

Marx focused on production as the key element of human existence, and insisted that it was central to determining the consciousness of individuals:

> The mode of production of material life determines the general character of the social, political and spiritual process of life. It is not the consciousness of men that determines their being, but, on the other hand, their social being determines their consciousness. (Preface to 'A contribution to the critique of political economy', in Bottomore and Rubel, 1963: 67)

He argued that the mode of production 'should not be regarded simply as the reproduction of the physical existence of individuals. It is already a definite form of activity of these individuals, a definite way of expressing their life, a definite *mode of life*' (*German ideology*, in Bottomore and Rubel, 1963: 69). For Marx, you are what, and how, you produce.

Since Marx focused on the relations of production, he did not consider that the machinery had to be examined in and of itself, outside of the relations of production. In *Wage labour and capital* he wrote:

> The cotton-spinning machine is a machine for spinning cotton. Only under certain conditions does it become *capital*. Torn away from these conditions, it is as little capital as *gold* by itself is *money*, or as sugar is the *price* of sugar ('Wage labour and capital' in Bottomore and Rubel, 1963: 155)

Because the central determining factor was the social relations, the technology itself could be looked on as effectively neutral. As such it could be a significant element in the revolutionary process and in turn vital to any future communist society. Marx saw communist society emerging as a historical necessity out of the contradictions of capitalism. Technology would play a key role, since it had within it the potential to free humans from the problems of scarcity and usher in a realm of freedom:

> Marx anticipates that technology will play a central and essential role in the communist society. In a highly efficient manner it will provide the level of productivity required so that people can develop as free and creative individuals. (Fischer, 1982: 121)

However, this would not happen under capitalism since the social order was organised for the benefit of the few, not for the good of the many. In fact, the forces of production would be held back by the illogicality of capitalism, and could only be freed for the benefit of all humanity by a proletarian revolution.

So although technology was crucial for Marx's vision, he saw it ultimately as subservient to economic social relations, and a change in these relations would enable the existing technology to be used and developed for the good of humanity.

Jacques Ellul – the autonomy of technique[4]

Ellul has been one of the most important writers on technology since the mid-twentieth century. His most well-known work, *The technological society*, has been described as 'one of the most ambitious and widely read attempts to analyze the relation between technology and modern society, and to try to understand modern technology in terms of that relationship' (Mitcham and Mackey, 1971: 102–3). His work in general has been considered as 'among the most important in . . . a vast literature on the nature of technological society and the effects of technology on the life of man' (Lovekin, 1977: 251).

Ellul was a Marxist at 19, but converted to Christianity at 22. He found it impossible to reconcile Marxism and Christianity, with the result that he abandoned the former as an over-arching philosophical system. However, he was aware that biblical texts were unable to offer a tool for analysing contemporary society. In attempting to 'deduce . . . political or social consequences valid for our epoch', he still relied on a Marxian approach: 'I did not see why I should have to give up the things that Marx said about society and explained about economy and injustice in the world. I saw no reason to reject them just because I was now a Christian' (Vanderburg, 1997: 14).

However, Ellul was unconvinced by Marx's emphasis on economics and production, believing instead that: 'on the sociological plane, technique was by far the most important phenomenon, and that it was necessary to start from there to understand everything else' (Ellul, 1970: 5).

What does Ellul mean by *technique*? It is an opaque term, and his definitions often conceal as much as they reveal. The most commonly used definition provided by Ellul appears in a 'Note to the Reader' of his book *The technological society*:

> The term *technique*, as I use it, does not mean machines, technology, or this or that procedure for attaining an end. In our technological society, *technique* is the *totality of methods rationally arrived at and having absolute efficiency* (for a given stage of development) in *every* field of human activity. Its characteristics are new; the technique of the present has no common measure with that of the past. (Ellul, 1965: 3)[5]

There are three important points to make here. The first is that *technique* is not synonymous with individual pieces of technology. 'Technique is radically different from the machine,' he writes, 'it is a radical error to think of technique and machine as interchangeable.' *Technique* is not something external to but is rather a part of human activity – it is 'the consciousness of the mechanized world'. 'Technique', writes Ellul, 'integrates the machine into society' (Ellul, 1965: 5–7).

The second point, demonstrated by Ellul's definition of *technique* being limited to 'our technological society', is that Ellul analyses *technique* historically. *Technique* has always existed, but in previous societies it was contained by a variety of factors which prevented it from achieving autonomy: primarily, that it had a definite and relatively insignificant role in society; that technological means were limited; that it was local; that technological evolution was slow; and that individuals' lives were not constrained and defined by technique, i.e., they could escape (Ellul, 1965: 65–77). *Technique* started to develop its modern, unique form in England and France towards the end of the eighteenth century, and in the United States at the beginning of the nineteenth. However, the above conditions no longer apply to modern *technique*. This historical perspective means is that what Ellul is interested in is not technical action, but the interaction between *technique*, individual and society. It is the nature and degree of this interaction that, Ellul argues, defines contemporary society as 'technological'.

The third point, leading on from the first two, is that Ellul's emphasis is on humans and human society, a perspective on the world, or even a way of being, and this is located within humans, rather than as something outside of them.[6] When Ellul refers to *technique* as being autonomous, therefore, he is not referring to an external entity that acts on humans but as something which is part of human society. As Durkheim saw society as 'a specific reality with its own characteristics', so Ellul also believes in a 'collective sociological reality, which is independent of the individual' (Winner, 1977: 62; Ellul, 1965: xxvi). *Technique*, for Ellul, represents one such 'collective reality'; it can be considered, therefore, from a sociological perspective as an autonomous agent, not dependent on the social relations of other spheres. However, *technique* no longer competes with the other spheres, or is limited by them: in technological society *technique* 'encloses' all other human activity. 'In a word, what determines our politics, our economics, our science, our social activities is technique' (Holloway, 1970: 23).

In some respects, *technique* is similar to Marx's idea of the mode of production in that it represents a totality that includes consciousness as well as artefacts; but, as mentioned above, Ellul does not believe that economic or productive factors are preeminent. 'It is self-deception to put economics at the base of the Marxist system. It is technique upon which all the rest depends . . . It is useless to rail against capitalism. Capitalism did not create our world; the machine did' (Ellul, 1965: 150).

In attempting to clarify the relationship between *technique*, society and the individual in the 'technological society', Ellul develops a set of 'characteristics'. The first two of these he refers to as 'well known', and does not go into them further; they are rationality and artificiality. By rationality, Ellul means here the application of logic and design to overcome spontaneity: 'Every intervention of technique is, in effect, a reduction of facts, phenomena, means, and instruments to the schema of logic'. By artificiality he means that 'technique is opposed to nature', and it 'destroys, eliminates, or subordinates the natural world' (Ellul, 1965: 79). There are a further five characteristics, however, that Ellul refers to as 'new' and which are the defining characteristics of modern, autonomous *technique* (Ellul, 1965, chapter 2). I will outline these because they are central to Ellul's approach and because they were referred to in the first major exposition of the *Fifth Estate* 'anti-tech' position (see Fulano, 1981a).

It is *automatic*. The one law of *technique* is the search for efficiency, or what Ellul calls the 'one best means'. This is the only principle for action, and therefore human judgement and spontaneity are irrelevant and unnecessary.

It is *self-augmenting*. Since every invention leads to other inventions, there is a knock-on effect such that technical progress occurs by a geometric rather than an arithmetic progression. This process is unpredictable and outside of human control. It is also irreversible. *Technique* creates new, technologically-dependent ways of doing things, replacing traditional methods; once certain skills are lost, they are rarely recovered.

It is *unitary* or *holistic*. All the different *techniques* combine to form a whole.

Ellul refers to 'the necessary linking together of techniques' (1965: 111). There can be no distinction made between different *techniques*, or between *techniques* and the use to which they are put.

It is *universal*. *Technique* is a civilisation or culture. As such, it must take over and destroy indigenous cultures with which it comes into contact. Everywhere, technique produces the same results, and cannot therefore be assimilated.

It is *autonomous*. Since efficiency is the only criterion for success, *technique* is autonomous of morality, and of politics and economics, which will change to suit its needs and requirements. Humans, as a potential source of error and inefficiency, must be eliminated from technical systems wherever possible; where humans are still necessary for the functioning of the system they must capitulate to the necessity of *technique*. Consequently, human freedom is constrained by *technique*. For Ellul, 'there can be no human autonomy in the face of technical autonomy' (Ellul, 1965: 138).

These five characteristics in effect offer an expanded definition of technique *in the current technological society*, and have been utilised by the *FE*, as will be seen. However, before moving on to examine their position, it is first necessary to consider the work of the third main influence, the French ultra-Leftist Jacques Camatte.

Jacques Camatte – the real domination of capital

The third influence on the FE was Jacques Camatte. Camatte's ideas were not specifically about technology, so I will only touch on them briefly, but they are important in the development of the FE view of the nature of capital as a culture and civilisation, rather than simply as an economic system.

Camatte was originally a follower of the Italian Marxist and active member of the Italian Socialist Party (PSI), Amadeo Bordiga.[7] Bordiga developed his own views on a number of key political and economic issues, but largely he stuck closely to the communist programme as laid down by Marx and Engels in 1848 (Buick, 1987: 13). He stressed that socialism was a non-market, propertyless and moneyless social form, and it was this that inspired many pro-communist groups, particularly in France, in the 1960s and 1970s, groups that can be classed under the rubric 'neo-Bordigists'.[8] What is significant theoretically is that 'all the French currents put at centre stage . . . the so-called "Unpublished Sixth Chapter" of Volume I of *Capital*' (Goldner, 1999). This was the originally planned Part Seven of Volume I of *Capital* (Marx intended the present Part One to be an introduction, hence it was originally Chapter Six). It is entitled 'Results of the immediate process of production', and was first published in Russian and German in Moscow in 1933. It did not attract attention in Western Europe until republished in German and other Western languages in late 1960s. Its first English publication was in 1976 as an appendix to the Penguin edition of *Capital I* (Marx, 1976).

A central element of the Sixth Chapter is Marx's identification of two period-isations of capitalism, namely the formal domination of capital and the real domination of capital (also known as the 'formal and real subsumption of labour under capital'). The formal domination of capital involves pre-capitalist forms of production being maintained under capitalism: the relationships of production have changed (i.e., become worker-capitalist) but the nature of the production process remains the same. However, under 'real domination' an entirely new mode of production comes into existence, with new technologies and forms of social organisation promoted by and beneficial to capitalism. What Camatte extrapolates from this is that, as the process of revolutionising production continues under the conditions of 'real domination', it gradually permeates all aspects of society.

> In Camatte's version, capital moved on from real domination over the economy and politics (bourgeois society) to real domination over humans in their biological being (material community of capital). (Trotter, 1995: 13)

Rather than being riven with, and eventually destroyed by, contradictions, capital is able to absorb them and utilise them to its advantage. The proletariat is not, under the conditions of real domination, an opposition to capital, but part of it. Capital becomes representation, that is represented in the minds and bodies of human beings. It becomes anthropomorphised and therefore escapes the previous limitations that held it in check, including natural barriers which cannot be regarded as insurmountable. For Camatte, 'capital has run away . . . it has escaped' (Camatte, 1975: 13).

The separation of the forces of production from humans (since these are controlled by capital) and the absorption of the proletariat mean that the growth of productive forces is no longer a means to the formation of community (*Gemeinwesen*):

> Communism is not a new mode of production; it is the affirmation of a new community . . . Until now men and women have been alienated by this production. They will not gain mastery over production, but will create new relations among themselves which will determine an entirely different activity. (Camatte, 1975: 36)

Camatte uses the term 'domestication' to describe the condition of humans who have internalised the rationality of capital. For Camatte, historical materialism represents only 'a glorification of the wandering in which humanity has been engaged for more than a century: growth of productive forces as the condition *sine-qua-non* for liberation' (Camatte, 1975: 23). The development of productive forces is carried out by capitalism, and there is no clear way in which to differentiate capitalism from communism. As such, there are no negating forces within capitalism and these can only arise outside of it. The only way to overcome domestication is 'to reject the entire product of the development of class societies' (Camatte, 1975: 61–4).

So autonomous capital is no longer capital controlled by the ruling class: it is a material community which is all-encompassing and does not hold its contradictory nemesis (the proletariat) within it. The revolution will therefore be a human revolution to abandon capital, not a proletarian one to claim it for its own.

These three thinkers gave the *FE* a framework in which to develop their critique of technology – from Marx, that the key to the systems of oppression in any epoch are to be found in social relations; from Ellul that *technique*, as a form of consciousness and social entity could have a key role to play in the development and maintenance of such systems, independent of the socioeconomic form; and from Camatte, that Marxian ideas of the limitations of capital, the revolutionary role of the proletariat, the necessity of developing the means of production were invalid for the late twentieth century.

The *FE* now attempted to integrate these strands into a perspective that sought to illuminate the links between culture, economics and technology, between capital and *technique*.

Technology, *technique*, and capital

As Ellul uses the term *technique* to describe the technological system and outlook, the *FE* has tended instead to use *technology* in the same way, i.e., as a system rather than as individual tools or machines. David Watson has referred to it as 'an interlocking system of apparatus, rational techniques and organization' (1995: 11). Elsewhere, writing as George Bradford, Watson has attempted a more formal definition, utilising the words *technique*, technics and technology. Here, it is technology that comes closest to Ellul's idea of *technique*:

> Probably, the most workable approach for our purposes would be to suggest a provisional definition of these terms, considering *technique* to be that procedural instrumentality . . . which is shared by all human societies but which is not necessarily identical in its motives or its role in those societies; *technics* to be technical operations using tools or machines . . .; and *technology* to be the *rationalization* or science of techniques . . . , the geometric linking together, systematization and universalization of technical instrumentality and applied science within society, which brings to light its emergence as an autonomous power and social body. (Bradford, 1984a: 11)

Here we have the essence of Ellul's approach: a differentiation between a simple instrumentality and operation and a 'social body' which involves the 'systematization and universalization' of this instrumentality into a form greater than the sum of its parts, i.e., a focus on the social relations of technology/technique under specific historical conditions. Unfortunately, this does appear to complicate the discussion. The problem is that the terms used can be taken in three ways: they have everyday meanings, more specialist meanings, and then the radical analytical meanings used here. As George Bradford replied to a Marxist critic who argued that the *FE*'s concept of technology made no sense since it did not conform to the dictionary definition of the term:

If [he] were to look up capitalism in his dictionary, he would find nothing about
exploitation, alienation, or domination, only a reference to the private ownership
of the means of production. Would he therefore conclude that discussion of capitalism as more than private ownership, as a system of domination, is merely a
'theoretical device?' (Bradford, 1984a: 11)

A problem also arises regarding Ellul's work with the use of the French
word *technique* and its translation as 'technology'. It has been pointed out
that:

for Ellul technique equals a systematic unity of all rationalized means, an idea
which is not necessarily implied by the English 'technology', nor precontained in
the French *technique*. In each case there is an extension of the common sense
meaning of the term which must be argued for. (Mitcham and MacKey, 1971: 105)

'Technology' is used in the FE presumably because that is the term most familiar to English-speaking readers, and because the debate in the FE referred to
'technology' before the introduction of Ellul's ideas in the paper in 1981.

Like Marx, the FE recognises the primacy of social relations in defining a historical epoch, and, like Ellul, it recognises the importance of technology independent of other social factors. From Camatte comes the recognition of the
over-arching dominance of the techno-capitalist system and its ability to escape
its limitations. However, unlike Marx it does not see technology as being
neutral; and unlike Ellul it does not give complete primacy to technology,
instead seeing it as integral to a system that is driven by both technology *and*
capital:

'The capitalist system has been swallowed up by the technological system,' writes
Ellul. But he misses the point: technology and capital are both surpassing their lim-
itations in runaway fashion, but neither has been swallowed by the other.
(Bradford, 1992: 19)

The term the FE uses to describe this system is 'megamachine', a term bor-
rowed from Lewis Mumford. Mumford argued that the first machines were not
the mechanical products of the Industrial Revolution, but rather belonged to the
civilisations of the ancient world. Megamachines were forms of social organisation, organised by élites, with the aim of achieving particular ends that would be
beyond the means of small-scale community activity. After the collapse of these
early civilisations, the megamachine disappeared from history, only to re-emerge
in our own time. Mumford argues that both new and old megamachines '[are]
mass organizations able to perform tasks that lie outside the range of small work
collectives and loose tribal or territorial groups . . . [which] aim to ultimately
exert control over the entire community at every point of human existence . . .
[with an underlying ideology that] ignores the needs and purposes of life in order
to fortify the power complex and extend its domination' (Miller, 1995: 345–6).
The FE uses this term to describe the contemporary interlocking system of the
State, corporations, bureaucracies, the military and technology.

Technology as historical agent

The *FE*'s critique of technology is applicable, like Ellul's, only to the current soci-oeconomic form of organisation, that is, it is a historical manifestation. Technology is not, therefore, strictly deterministic: technology has not *necessarily* determined the course of history, since it is only autonomous under certain specific historical conditions.[9] In earlier, non-technological societies, technology was absorbed within the social matrix and did not occupy a separate sphere (something that was also true of other abstract forms such as 'production').

> Technical operations existed (and exist) in societies which are non-technological. The technical phenomenon does not come to define all activity in the society, does not shape the social content. Rather, it is a secondary, sporadic mediation, embedded in culture. (Bradford, 1984a: 11)

The clearest example of this is found in 'primitive' societies. The FE does not offer a definition of the primitive. It is a characterological category (located in the characteristics of primitive society), rather than a chronological one (located in time), although there is a chronological element to the extent that primitive society was the first form of human society and has subsequently been replaced by civilisation. These characteristics are: the absence of a formal economy; the preeminence of the symbolic and the absence of a separate sphere of production; the absence of coercive political power; a participatory and egalitarian epistemology; a harmonious ecology; and the active limitation of needs and the refusal of power and civilization. The term primitive, or sometimes primal, is also used to mean original, i.e., the original form of human social existence (see Millett, 2003).

> The two-fold character of primitive technics – its adequacy (or appropriateness) to its environment, and its relative insignificance in terms of the constitution of primitive society – point to its fundamental quality: primitive technics is simply a modality of human being. (Brubaker, 1981: 19)

Technology was only allowed to emerge as a potentially autonomous entity with the breakdown of the community structures which had held it in place, possibly through the emergence of a system of labour and production (an argument also offered in Fredy Perlman's (1983) *Against His-story, against Leviathan!*)

Consequently it would be a mistake to accuse the *FE* of criticising technology *as such*, since no such ahistorical form exists (in the same way that there can be no capital *as such*). As the *FE* responded to some of its critics:

> You accuse us of advocating destroying all machines, something we have never done . . . We don't define the nomad's shoulder strap or spear as technology. If it is, and everything from rubbing flints to computerized nuclear reactors is defined in the same category, then th[e] word is incoherent. We are talking about advanced, industrial technology, the stuff of civilization. (St Jaques *et al.*, 1980: 14)

The emergence of technology as a separate sphere created the potential for a technological society, although it required a complete breakdown of the old communal forms to permit its complete emergence. This breakdown was brought about by a combination of technology and capitalism, neither being dominant overall, but with one or the other having a crucial effect at a particular time and place.

> Although there has been controversy over whether new technologies and time-keeping spurred early-capitalist mercantilism, or whether the reverse was the case, there is no reason to choose one interpretation over the other. Synergism was here in effect: technical development and capitalism went hand-in-hand, creating in their wake the technological civilization of today. (Fulano, 1981a: 5–6)

Capitalism and industrial technologies emerged together, one reinforcing the other, synergistically (i.e., the total effect being greater than the sum of its parts). The ultimate origins of the technological society, then, lie in the breakdown of primitive society and the rise of civilisation; but technology did not begin to appear as a separate social entity until the rise of capitalism. From that point, both evolved together as interlinked, mutually supporting systems of domination.

The critique of technology – realities and considerations

The *FE* view of technology was developed over many years, and although it has been treated in some depth it has never been set out systematically. The seven elements outlined below, which the *FE* identifies as crucial to any consideration of the modern technological system, have been consolidated from a number of different articles. The *FE* itself has not catalogued its critique in this way. This is a representation of an overview of its position as it has developed.

I Social production

The *FE* maintain that all goods and manufacture have to be looked at in the context of social production – that is, from their genesis on the drawing board to their delivery to the shop or wherever. There may also be additional elements required for their use, such as fuel for powered goods. The production process requires human parts, a division of labour between scientists, engineers and designers at one end and shop-floor workers, miners, labourers and so on at the other. It also requires an apparatus of communication and distribution that in itself entails other technologies and productive processes. In addition, raw materials have to be extracted and petroleum products refined and transported. Fulano notes that 'technology encompasses the entire social process, the means and the instruments of production of these products, not just the products alone'(1981b: 6).

It is, therefore, never possible to assess a product simply by looking at the product alone, outside of the complexities of the system in which is was produced.

2 Social use

The principle of the social use of technology is summed up by Langdon Winner in his book *Autonomous technology*. He writes:

> The human encounter with artificial means cannot be summarized solely (or even primarily) as a matter of 'use'. One must notice that certain kinds of regularized service must be rendered to an instrument before it has any utility at all. One must be aware of the patterns of behaviour demanded of the individual or of society in order to accommodate the instrument within the life process. (Winner, 1977: 194–5)

For small technologies, integrated in society, this need not be a problem. For example, a cup is designed with a handle which will encourage it being used in a particular way, although picking it up without the handle is quite possible and will not have any great consequences (except possibly burnt fingers). Larger, more complex technologies suggest ever more limited ways in which they may be used efficiently (or indeed, at all) as well as requiring a greater social adaptation to their use (i.e., the human and natural environment is altered to suit the technology). When these technologies assume the scale of telecommunications systems, for example, they demand high levels of conformity of both those who use them and those who operate and maintain them – spontaneity is effectively 'designed out'.

As we become increasingly dependent on technology, and as it generates new needs which can only be satisfied technologically, we are left with no choice but to use the technologies and conform to their requirements. In fact, in the end we end up adapting ourselves to the technologies, not the other way around.

> Technology is not a simple tool which can be used in any way we like. It is a form of social organization, a set of social relations. It has its own laws. If we are to engage in its use, we must accept its authority. (Fulano, 1981b: 6)

How these two characteristics combine is illustrated in the quotation below in which George Bradford examines the difference between 'tools' and 'technology', between the spear and the missile. A spear has inherent limitations, and the damage that can be done with it is limited without a complete reorganisation of the society in which it is used (demonstrated by the armies of ancient civilisations). But in the case of the missile:

> the organization of human beings as a machine, as a network of production and destruction, is fundamental to what is produced, and the only limit implied is that which is attained with the ultimate annihilation of the human race by its technology. (Bradford, 1984a: 11)

3 Social and political organisation

For the *FE*, an authoritarian and hierarchical social and political form is implicit in technology, and cannot be separated from it. This is the wider implication of the two previous characteristics given above, that the technological system demands a division of labour and a hierarchical and authoritarian political structure.

> The enormous size, complex interconnection and stratification of tasks which make up modern technological systems make authoritarian command necessary and independent, individual decision-making impossible . . . The massified technical structure can only exist through extreme specialization of labor, stratification of tasks, and bureaucratic management techniques. (Bradford, 1984a: 11)

The political organisation of any society which utilises this technology is therefore given, and cannot be reorganised along decentralised and community lines as long as such a system is maintained.

Furthermore, the *FE* questions why anyone in a free society would decide, voluntarily, to work in a factory or a mine. Following Solzhenitsyn in *The Gulag Archipelago*, they refer to forced labourers as 'zeks'.

> Every middle-class Marxist I've ever met has expressed the same desires for a multifaceted life after the revolution. It doesn't sound bad, but I've never heard one of them say that they wanted to be a coal miner in the morning, a forge operator in the afternoon and a micro chip board assembler after dinner. Tasks like these, done by zeks, are the foundation of industrial capitalism and if we drag the same old shit into our new society, they will also be done by zeks. (Maple, 1983: 2)[10]

The maintenance of a technical-industrial system will require a division of labour that will inevitably result in a worker-class, and it is unlikely that this could exist without an authoritarian political structure.

4 Dependency and expertise

The nature of the technological systems requires a dependency of humans both on the system itself and on the experts who run it. The complexities of this system mean that it is impossible for an individual to understand how anything but a small part of it works (although this in itself presumes a willingness to immerse oneself in technological know-how). In all other areas it will be necessary to defer to the knowledge of experts in the field. This is particularly difficult because one of the problems with expertise is not simply the profit motive but a determination to succeed at the technical task at hand, a determination which may well outweigh any commitment to the wider social good.

> Even technicians who are not out simply to preserve the privileges and the power which come from their project . . . believe in their system and will change figures, make errors of omission, and argue for solutions which are actually untenable. Those of us who are not there with the expertise and the information . . . will have to take their word for it. (Fulano, 1981b: 6)

A society based on high technology will therefore inevitably operate with a high degree of opacity regarding technical, and therefore social, issues which will undermine any attempts at transparent direct-democratic participation.

5 Ecology and technology

Modern technological systems are inherently complex. This suggests four possible roots of potential environmental problems.

Firstly, *indeterminacy of ends*: when the technologies are very large-scale and/or deal with extremely complex systems (such as the human body or natural ecosystems), the possible outcomes of their use are impossible to determine with any degree of accuracy. In fact, such unforeseen outcomes may be extremely damaging, as in the cases of DDT and the Thalidomide drug. This epistemological problem is not surmountable, since there is no way to study technology outside of the totality of the 'megamachine'.

> Technology cannot be isolated from itself and studied with its own techniques. The laboratory experiment in a given geographical or social area performed by the huge, powerful, bureaucratic hierarchy of technicians and managers *is* technology and carries its own social implications within it. The results of innovation will necessarily have multiple and unpredictable significance to the different sectors of the megamachine. (Fulano, 1981a: 8)

The second problem is that *solutions are not inevitable*: the focus on the supposed efficacy of technology and applied science generates a belief that, eventually, solutions can be found to any and all problems. Ironically, more technology is often seen as the only solution for problems that have been technologically induced.

> What is to be done with chemical and nuclear wastes? Here the technicians smile and say, 'You need us.' But their 'solutions' not only legitimize and tend to prolong the original causes of the disaster, but tend to aggravate it even further. Now we are faced with the innovation of chemical waste dumps to solve the problem of toxic wastes, which is already proving to lead to other difficulties. But we need technology, they argue, we've got to put this stuff somewhere! And to not join in the chorus is to seek 'easy answers'. (Fulano, 1981b: 8)

The third problem is that *whereas solutions may not be inevitable, mistakes are*: whatever attempts are made to prevent mistakes, mechanical or human error is inevitable at some stage. When highly toxic or explosive materials are involved, or with high-capacity forms of travel, such mistakes can have catastrophic consequences. The blame for these mistakes is often laid at the door of corporate greed, the profit motive, or the irrationality of the market, implying that if the system was not run along capitalist lines ecological disasters would not occur. Dave Watson writes: 'Global industrial production might possibly be accomplished without capitalist economic relations, but it cannot avoid honest mistakes . . . [I]ndustrialism . . . makes disasters inevitable' (Watson, 1996: 137).

The fourth problem is that *contamination* is an *inevitable* by-product of large, industrial technologies. After the release of a deadly gas cloud from the Union Carbide factory in Bhopal, India, which killed 3,000 people and disabled 20,000 more, George Bradford made a number of points which indicted industrialism: he noted that this was not a 'one off' in the Third World where predominantly Western companies have operational standards below what would be tolerated in the US and Europe; that similar, if smaller, 'accidents' also occur in the US and other 'developed' countries; and that the constant usage of chemicals contaminates the environment to a dangerous level even without the occurrence of such disasters.

When a residentof the US living with a risk of hydrogen-cyanide poisoning from factory wastes referred to the use of this gas in Nazi extermination camps, Bradford commented:

> A powerful image: industrial civilization as one vast, stinking extermination camp. We all live in Bhopal, some closer to the gas chambers and to the mass graves, but all of us close enough to be victims. And Union Carbide is obviously not a fluke – the poisons are vented in the air and water, dumped in rivers, ponds and streams, fed to animals going to market, sprayed on lawns and roadways, sprayed on food crops, every day, everywhere. The result may not be as dramatic as Bhopal . . . but it is as deadly. (Bradford, 1988: 50)

Although this currently applies to a system organised under market-capitalist social relations, the *FE* is clear that these problems are inherent in the technological and industrial system.

> You cannot have petrochemicals without colonies and sacrifice zones . . . waste pits, oil spills, refinery row, ruined areas and lives . . . Show me the non-polluting, convivial, democratic, peaceful model in which industrialism and technology could exist after a revolution. I don't think it can be done. (Watson, 1995: 10)

6 Human subjectivity

Another aspect of the *FE* critique is its argument that how humans view their world is determined by the prevalent social relations – following Marx, people are how they live: 'As individuals express their life, so they are' (in Bottomore and Rubel, 1963: 69). When humans are enclosed in a mass technological apparatus, their subjectivity becomes adapted to this – i.e. humans change to suit the technological world. In the technological society, all reference points are technological. Human needs and expectations are conditioned by what is technologically possible.

> The human being is transformed along with the content of social life . . . [the means of production are] the daily activities of the people who participate in these systems, and . . . require the inevitable characterological internalization of these means in human beings. (Bradford, 1984a: 11)

Dogbane Campion refers to Joseph Weizenbaum's book *Computer power and human reason:*

> Tools and machines are not mere instruments, he argues, 'they are pregnant symbols in themselves . . . A tool is a model for its own reproduction and a script for the re-enactment of the skills its symbolizes . . . [it] thus transcends its role as a practical means towards certain ends: it is a constituent of man's symbolic re-creation of his world'. (Campion, 1988: 17. The quote is from Weizenbaum, 1984: 18)

Elsewhere David Watson argues: 'Neither tools nor technology are neutral. They are inevitably powerful constituents of our symbolic world. Technology imposes not only form but content wherever it comes into use' (Watson, 1995: 11).

The human imagination will necessarily see possibilities for interacting with and changing the world on the basis of the tools available. The tools therefore offer a template for their own replication, which is the externalisation of the internal technological consciousness. Furthermore, if it is accepted that this imaginative content also defines how the human individuals sees themselves, the technological world also inevitably means the internalisation of a technological human being.

This is particularly noticeable in the case of the media, what Watson terms 'capital's global village'.

> A sky reminds us of a film; witnessing the death of a human being finds meaning in a media episode, replete with musical score. An irreal experience becomes our measure of the real . . . The formation of subjectivity, once the result of complex interaction between human beings participating in a symbolic order, has been replaced by media . . . we are becoming machine-like, more and more determined by technological necessities beyond our control. (Watson, 1999: 131)

7 Computer and information systems

One area of modern technology which is often cited as being both of importance to radicals and activists today, and also potentially indispensable to an anarchist society, is information technology (IT). The *FE* questions this assertion, firstly on the basis of the points raised above regarding social production, use and organisation – 'How do you expect this sophisticated equipment to be produced? What will be the role of the experts who supervise the production of the machinery was well as the dissemination of . . . information?' – but also regarding the very nature of the technology itself (St Jaques *et al.*, 1980: 3). For the *FE*, computers and information systems are not simply a way of communicating neutral information. Information, in the way that it is understood today, is itself a development and manifestation of capital. Computers effectively act as filters which only allow certain forms of communication, and these forms themselves are central parts of the social relations of the techno-capitalist society.

> *Information* is no more neutral than technology. It is a form which capital has taken since the technological revolutions beginning in the middle of this century . . . The kind of information which is transmitted through satellites and computer systems is a form of domination and power, inherently centralized, authoritarian and technocratic. (St Jaques *et al.*, 1980: 3)

Modern communication techniques promote cultural homogeneity through demanding a universalised form of communication based on the requirements of *technique*. Rather than diversifying human experience it standardises it, imposing 'a universal impoverishment and homogenization of human experience' (Fulano, 1981a: 7).

Arguing that 'technology does not increase choices', but 'imposes its own limited technological range of choices', the *FE* does not see cyberspace as an area of contestation:

> The notion that this 'information field' is a contested terrain is naïve, to say the least. The very existence of such a 'field' – in reality a web of abstract, instrumentalized social relations in which 'information' reproduces itself through alienated human activity, just as the system of value reproduces itself through the false reciprocity of commodity exchange – is itself the essence of domination. (Bradford, 1984b: 8)

Technology is capital

To sum up the *FE* position as outlined so far, there are seven areas regarding modern technology that need to be considered in any analysis.

1 *Social Production:* Individual products and technologies cannot be considered in isolation from the productive processes which produced them.
2 *Social use:* Technology cannot be separated from its use. Technology demands that humans conform to laws implicit in the technology itself.
3 *Social and political organisation:* Modern technologies require hierarchical and authoritarian forms of social organisation in order to function.
4 *Dependency and expertise:* Technological systems require a dependence of humans on these systems, and on the experts that develop and run them.
5 *Ecology and technology:* Industrial technologies are inherently damaging to the environment: outcomes are not foreseeable; there are not solutions to all problems; mistakes are inevitable; contamination is an inevitable part of the industrial system.
6 *Human subjectivity:* The ways in which humans view the world, their imaginations and perceptions, become adapted to the technological world. Humans begin to think and act in terms of the machine.
7 *Computerisation and information technology:* Computers and IT do not represent a potentially liberatory technology. As well as being the product of a vast technological structure, they channel a limited form of information which is amenable to, and representative of, capital.

Obviously, the above characteristics describe a technology which is radically different from that commonly held to be a neutral and potentially beneficial set of tools. This is a view held by many libertarian socialists and anarchists who still see the primary focus of their political critique as being the State and capitalism. This is, of course, rejected by the *FE*, for whom, 'opposing the state while at the same time defending technology or remaining indifferent to it is comparable to opposing the police force while saying nothing about the military. They are part of a unitary whole' (Bradford, 1981: 10).

It was noted earlier that the Marxian view of capital is that it is a social relation not a thing. However, Marx also saw technological things as not being capital – that is, the means of production were separate from the relations of production i.e how production, and society, was organised. But, as George Bradford points out, if modern technology is theorised with the characteristics noted above, then the idea of the means and relations of production (in the Marxian sense) being different makes little sense:

> When the 'means of production' are in actuality interlocking elements of a danger-ously complex, interdependent global system, made up not only of technological apparatus and human operatives as working parts in that apparatus, but of forms of culture and communication and even the landscape itself, it makes no sense to speak of 'relations of production' as a separate sphere. (Bradford, 1990: 10)

Clearly, from this perspective, changing the formal ownership of the 'means of production' will be of little consequence if the technological apparatus remains in place:

> It is not a question of 'evil men' but the totality of a system . . . Naturally, capital is more than just technology, but *it is also the technology and the human relations it creates*. No such apparatus could appear out of nothing; it presupposes relations of hierarchy and domination irrespective of the formal and juridical property forms. (Bradford, 1981: 10, emphasis in the original)

Here the *FE* makes its point explicit: the properties of modern technology to act on social life make it a form of social relations, and as such a clear distinc-tion between capital and its technology is impossible. Technology is able to swallow up all attempts to control it. It is not that the *FE* disagrees with Marx when he argues that the problem is not with 'things' but with social relations – but it sees technology as social relations, not as things. '*Technology is capital*, the triumph of the inorganic, humanity separated from its tools and universally dependent on the apparatus' (Fulano, 1981a: 5).[11]

Possibilities

The *FE*'s critique of the technological society is comprehensive. After the cri-tique, however, the question arises as to what alternatives are possible, and how these could come about.

Alternatives

As with much of the revolutionary Left, the *FE* has avoided blueprints of its alter-native society. In part, this is consistent with its determination to avoid a politi-cal programme, a programme which would be, in effect, an extension of the society which it criticises.

> We are proposing nothing less than the radical deconstruction of society, but this cannot come about through a political and technological program with its blue-prints and agendas, for that would be more of the same . . . *all* programs, by their

nature of emanating from a central source outward to the 'masses', are inherently authoritarian and conservative. (Fulano, 1981a: 8)

There is clearly the implication, though, that a workable anarchist society would be based on small communities, and that tools and pieces of technology would be small and/or simple enough to be integrated fully into such a society. David Watson refers to 'a world in which human beings create their own subsistence and culture in their own back yards with convivial tools in which technical matters play only a minuscule and sporadic role in their lives and where nature looms large' (*Fifth Estate*, 1983: 4).[12]

Their aim is not only a society free of the State (or any authoritarian political structures) and capital, but also free of technology. This is not a society without tools, but one not ordered around the technological system either. Instead, the social should have priority: 'Reduced to its most basic elements, discussions about the future sensibly should be predicated on what we desire *socially* and from that determine what technology is possible' (*Fifth Estate*, 1979b: 6). Because of this emphasis, alternative or appropriate technologies are treated with scepticism. The *FE* agrees that there are 'forms of technics that humans can understand and control' and that the development of these represents 'some of the practical activities which will help to make our escape from technological civilization a reality' (Brubaker, 1983: 2). But the problem is social and cultural – it cannot be solved by pieces of technology, and the belief that it can is simply another manifestation of the technological consciousness.

A further criticism of 'alternative' technologies is that they are not inherently in opposition to capitalism or mass society – solar, wind and wave power could be developed on a massive scale, and functionally integrated with modern industry. Large and/or high-tech 'alternative' technologies would still have the characteristics of technology outlined above; they could even be utilised by State and capital to achieve the transformation of capitalism into a new, more 'sustainable' form. The *FE* argues that, although certain types of technology will be useful, even necessary, in a free, post-civilisation society, there should be no technological prerequisites for the desired social form: 'Whether or not such communities decide, say, to turn into windmills the automobiles left behind by this civilization, is ultimately a secondary, local and technical problem' (*Fifth Estate*, 1983: 4).

Another perspective commonly associated with the Left, and often argued for by those in favour of post-revolutionary high tech, is the need for planning, that is for a planned society to replace the 'anarchy', as it is often unfortunately termed, of the market. However, for the *FE* this is a false promise, based on the premises of mass technology. Firstly, it assumes that such planning is actually possible, assumes that large-scale systems are manageable and all problems can be reduced to logical (i.e., technical soluble) components. Secondly, it assumes that these planned systems can operate within a libertarian social structure. The *FE* disagrees:

> Let me say it in clear terms: planning is *impossible* anywhere but at the most local-ized level and can only take place in a democratic fashion when shared by people who enjoy face-to-face relationships. A computerized, planned world will be a dreadful nightmare . . . We must opt for a non-administered world . . . the schemes of the planners will never work. (Maple, 1982: 7)

Here to there

There is little in the *FE* to suggest how this state of non-technological society should be reached. Since the *FE* has broken away from the idea of progress, par-ticularly in its Marxian, dialectical materialist form, it does not see anything spe-cific in the present social environment that is necessary for the transition to communism. The revolutionary change therefore does not emerge from within contemporary capitalist civilisation but rather, as Camatte argues, from outside of it. The revolutionary change will be a break with the old order, not a devel-opment of it.[13]

Who, or what, though, is 'outside' of capital or civilisation? How does one know if one's group or activity is part or, or in opposition to, capital? This is a problematical area that the *FE* has itself acknowledged in a debate over an article written by Camatte and Gianni Collu. 'On organisation' identified all forms of formal political organisation as 'gangs' or 'rackets' fighting over the spoils of capital. In reviewing this pamphlet, E. B. Maple agreed with Camatte and Collu that that formal organisations at best mirror, at worst increase, the hierarchies present in the rest of society. When it was pointed out that this implied that the *FE* might itself be a 'gang' activity, and therefore a part of capital, Maple replied:

> One answer that often strikes me at very cynical points in my life is, very possibly yes. As to the charge that if we accept the [Camatte and Collu] contention, *all* polit-ical activity becomes gang activity; again, very possibly yes . . . So, the big question is, if some activity becomes human and does not fall into a unity with capital, who gets tarred and who doesn't? It would seem that any statement from me on that would be arbitrary . . . and self-serving. (Maple and Clarke, 1976: 14)

Nevertheless, the *FE* does make some suggestions about challenging or breaking with, technological civilisation. One obvious option is simply to *stop*.

> We'd like a moratorium on industrialization starting right now – a mass strike for the abolition of industrial civilization. Stop the plastics, the steel, the cars, the chem-icals, the paint, the logging, the construction of dams and roads, the mining, the exploration of new territories, the computerization. Let's all get in the streets and start discussing what needs to be done, in an anarchic, liberatory way. Let's reforest and refarm the cities themselves . . . Stop the exponential growth of information, pull the plug on the communications system. Obviously, we'll need to decide in these assemblies what is absolutely essential for the time being. *But we have a vision of a nontechnological world – let us make that foremost.* (Solis, 1985: 25–6)

There are two aspects to this emphasis: firstly, it is a conscious break with the current order of 'progress' and production, not a continuation of it; secondly, it requires, and is within the ability of human beings, to *choose* a different path:

> I believe in the possibility of a conscious break with this civilization and its tech-
> nology . . . I am not sure how even to begin except to state the existence of such a
> possibility . . . a new cultural vision must be forged in the rejection of the techno-
> logical world view and in the struggle against the power of technology over our
> lives. (Fulano, 1981b: 21)

Resistance to capital may take many forms, including workers' struggles, although its possibilities are limited without the creation of a wider culture of resistance to challenge global techno-capitalism. Class struggle as such does not offer the possibility of radical change, since the proletariat has now been absorbed by capital, and is frequently in the front line of the battle to preserve industrial capitalism. As Camatte argues, following the trajectory of capital leads eventually to either slavery or annihilation. In the end, resistance is the necessity of all humanity, not simply the province of a particular group or class:

> We are all slaves of capital. Liberation begins with the refusal to perceive oneself
> in terms of the categories of capital, namely as proletarian, as member of the new
> middle class, as capitalist, etc. Thus we also stop perceiving the other . . . in terms
> of those same categories. At this point the movement of recognition of human
> beings can begin. (Camatte, 1975: 40)

The first step of any change is to begin to formulate a radical critique of the entire global system of oppression, including modern technology, and challenge its basic assumptions:

> asking the kinds of questions and raising the kinds of issues that make no sense
> either to business-as-usual or to palliative reform . . . We have to talk tentatively
> about how an unprecedented, megatechnic empire and its corresponding constel-
> lation of cultures might become an organic weave of diverse, egalitarian, commu-
> nal societies; and how an atomized, mass human being might become a whole
> person embedded in a community. (Watson, 1995: 12)

Conclusion

The *FE* has attempted to disentangle capital and technology, and to create the basis for an analysis of technology as an autonomous social agent. Basing its theoretical position on Marx, Ellul and Camatte, it has created a theoretical amalgam which explores the crucial role played by technology in the breakdown of community and the ascendancy of capitalism, and the way it links with capital in an over-arching system of domination. It stresses the inherently authoritarian elements of such technology, and in so doing warns of the dangers of importing it into any future anarchist society.

However, there are obvious problems with the *FE* critique. It is underdeveloped, and has not been systematically explored. In fact, much of the work has been in reply to critical responses to the paper. It also offers no obvious path to change. Additionally, the relationship between capital and technology may be more complex than the *FE* suggests. There is only a small amount of evidence presented to support its claims, in line with the polemical and propagandist nature of the work. It does, however, refer to several other writers, such as Ellul, Weizenbaum and Winner, who can be approached to support its arguments. Further, this work was developed in the 1970s and 1980s, and is based on ideas that were formulated in the 1960s and 1970s. It does not, therefore, consider more recent debates regarding technology, but is primarily involved with opposing Marxist and syndicalist arguments that argue for the neutrality of technology and its continuing relevance to the revolutionary project. There seems no reason to believe, though, that this necessarily undermines any validity its argument might have, since the trajectory of techno-capitalism does not appear to be greatly different in the twenty-first century than in the late-twentieth; certainly, the increasing ubiquity and expansion of electronic information and communication systems is encouraging the penetration of the realm of technology into people's lives at a rate greater than before. Secondly, the breadth of the *FE* critique, indicting a system of social relations rather than individual technologies, makes it applicable to conditions and circumstances beyond those originally explored by the *FE*.

Ellul conceives of *technique* as a civilisation that must, by nature and necessity, extinguish other cultures and civilisations with which it comes into contact. Consequently, 'globalisation' implies not only the spread of capitalism, but also of technology. Watson (citing Ellul) states that exporting technology is not really about exporting machines: it is about exporting 'the ensemble of the technological world' (Watson, 1999: 111). Referring to a photograph of a traditionally dressed New Guinea tribesman with a modern camera, Watson comments: 'What is he becoming, if not another cloned copy of what we are all becoming?' (111, 131).[14]

There are terminological problems and ambiguities relating to capital, *technique*/technology, and the relationship between the two. Although the overall link between technology and capital as advocated in the *FE* is clear enough, the exact relationship between the two is less obvious. One of the problems is that it is not entirely clear what the *FE* mean by capital. Despite the centrality of the concept to his work, even Marx does not provide a straightforward definition: 'Capital is . . . a complex category, not amenable to a simple definition, and the major part of Marx's writings was devoted to exploring its ramifications' (Bottomore, 1991: 68). Clearly, the *FE* does not mean exactly what Marx means by the term, that capital relates entirely to the economic order. Rather, it appears to follow Camatte's extension of capital to imply a culture or civilisation, a material human community. In this vein, and emphasising the cultural aspect, Watson has suggested that, 'capitalism isn't simply an "economic system" –

though that is how it names itself. It is a disorder of the Spirit', while elsewhere, writing as George Bradford, he has refered to 'capital' and 'technology' as being 'metaphors, partial descriptions which represent the modern organization of life'. A fuller examination of capital, its characteristics and development in the modern world, and its manifestation as a cultural rather than an economic form – as 'a culture and a way of being' – would be useful here (see Watson, 1992: 1; Bradford, 1984a: 11 and Watson, 1995: 111).

One criticism that could be levelled at the *FE* is that it concentrates almost entirely on critique, and does not attempt to outline either how any change might come about, or what tools or technologies might be useful or necessary in a non-technological society. In answer to this, the *FE* uses two arguments. The first, already noted, is intrinsic to its critique: programmes and plans are a part of the system it is attacking, and the essence of overthrowing technological society, as a form of consciousness, is to relegate technological matters to second place behind social organisation. Focusing on technological prerequisites is therefore still think-ing in a technological way. The *FE* argues that what is important is the social form, and that what technologies will be used are dependent on that, not *vice versa*.

The second argument, which is related to the first, is that simply because the members of the *FE* editorial group have read Marx, Ellul, Camatte and others, and filtered them through their own life-experiences to come to the conclusions outlined above, they have not subsequently been given any greater insight into how to effect fundamental and wide-ranging change than anyone else. David Watson points out that: 'our critical perspectives on civilization and technology, like our philosophical and ethical orientation in general, give us no qualitatively special insight into how to transform or dismantle mass society' (Watson, 1996: 18). They do not have a 'special insight', and do not wish to be considered to have one: 'We're a group of friends putting out this paper, not a political group or organizing center, or "voice" of anyone other than ourselves and don't want to be' (Maple, 1983: 2). Certainly, they themselves have been unable to resist the technological juggernaut, producing the paper on a computer since 1993, when their old manual equipment had become unserviceable. Their feelings about this were made clear by the heading to the article explaining this conversion: 'The Fifth Estate enters the 20th century. We get a computer and hate it!' (Maple, 1993: 6–7).

Whether or not the *FE*'s refusal to attempt to provide concrete solutions is seen as some sort of 'cop-out', it certainly means that they keep within their own limitations, and avoid grandiosity or the temptation to lay down a proto-ideol-ogy. Those who wish to develop this critique further are left with their own prob-lems, ambiguities and opinions. Here Watson and the *FE* find themselves in agreement with the 'technicians', although for different reasons: it is clear there are no 'easy answers':

> So, what to do? I'm glad I'm no political organization with a need to invent a nuts-and-bolts plan for everything from what to do with toxic waste to the health care system to a green party program . . . [M]uch of the transformation is already going

on around us, within us. People in wide-ranging projects are already answering the question, 'what to do'. I wouldn't presume to tell them. Mistakes will surely be made, but the important point is to *keep* doing what we think enhances community, solidarity, the nurturance of life – to endure. (Watson, 1999: 20)

Notes

1 Although only the work of the *Fifth Estate* collective is considered here (much of which was written by David Watson), there were other crucial elements in the development of these views. Two collaborators and contributors of particular significance were Fredy Perlman and John Zerzan, both of whom had pieces published in the paper (see Perlman, 1983; 1992; Zerzan, 1988). The *Fifth Estate* is a newspaper produced by a group of friends organised into a publishing collective. As such there is no 'party line' or ideological view to be adhered to. Equally, there is no 'Fifth Estate' group outside of the collective that publishes the paper (although individuals, particularly David Watson, have published elsewhere). Because of this, the paper and collective will be treated as synonymous and the italicised *Fifth Estate* (FE) will be used to refer to both.

2 For another insight into the *FE* and Detroit radical milieu at this time see Perlman, 1989.

3 There were many writers and thinkers influential on the *FE*; the three noted here were most significant for the critique of technology. Other important works were Giedion, 1969; Winner, 1977; Mumford, 1969, 1971; Illich, 1990.

4 For a brief introduction to Ellul see Ferkiss, 1993: 167–73. On the significance of Ellul on the *FE*, John Zerzan writes 'there has been a willingness in the *Fifth Estate* to consider the sense in which present and future technology tend toward a life of their own. Here there has been an effort to critically assess the extent to which Jacques Ellul is correct that technology is becoming itself an independent system dominating society' (Zerzan, 1982: 2).

5 This definition was inspired by that of Harold Lasswell – technique is 'the ensemble of practices by which one uses available resources in order to achieve certain valued ends' (see Ellul, 1965: 18).

6 According to one commentator, 'Ellul contends that *technique*, which he regards as a unique mode of consciousness, makes the machine possible, and while the machine aids in the perpetuation of that consciousness, it is not the cause of it; rather, it represents the ultimate ideal towards which all technique strives' (Lovekin (1977: 254); see also Menninger (1981: 114)).

7 Amadeo Bordiga and the theoreticians close to him were known as the Italian communist Left. For his relevance and context, see the translator's note to Camatte and Collu's 'On organization', in Camatte (1995: 28–9).

8 Goldner describes these as: 'French currents influenced by Bordiga, but not slavishly; the best of them attempted to synthesize Bordiga, who was oblivious to the historical significance of soviets, workers' councils, and workers' democracy, and who placed everything in the Party, with the German and Dutch ultra-Left who glorified workers' councils and explained everything that had gone wrong after 1917 in terms of "Leninism"' (Goldner, 1999).

 9 Early *FE* statements veered more towards determinism, but this has been less evident
    in later works. See *Fifth Estate*, 1978; *Fifth Estate*, 1979b. Here technology is seen as
    an inherently alienating form of mediation with the natural world. This perspective
    has been developed by John Zerzan (see Zerzan, 1988 and 1994).
10 The term 'zeks' was first employed in this way by Perlman (1983).
11 Fulano also makes the point that it is technology that opposes tools, since the system
    of technology makes human-centred tools irrelevant. A rejection of technology need
    not entail a rejection of science. See for examples Ellul's discussion of the Ancient
    Greeks (Ellul, 1965: 28ff.). Refering to this, Fulano argues that 'the notion that a sci-
    entific world view demands a technological outlook is simply not necessarily so. It is
    pure technological propaganda . . . the fact that the Greeks could have a scientific
    outlook without a technological-utilitarian basis proves . . . that such a conception of
    life is possible, and therefore a scientific society without slavery and without technol-
    ogy is also possible' (Fulano, 1981b: 7).
12 The term 'convivial tools' comes from Ivan Illich. Illich argues that tools are a neces-
    sary and important part of human society, but may be either mastered by people or
    masters of them. 'Convivial tools are those which give each person who uses them the
    greatest opportunity to enrich the environment with the fruits o f his or her vision'
    (Illich, 1990: 21). However, Illich tends to focus on the tools and machines themselves,
    rather than on the social relationships of their construction, maintenance and use. So,
    for example, a telephone is a 'structurally convivial tool', because it allows commu-
    nication and the conversations carried are not amenable to bureaucratic or govern-
    ment control.
13 Jean Baudrillard has argued a similar point. The fundamental historical break was
    between symbolic societies and productivist societies; the next (revolutionary) break
    must entail a return to a society organised around symbolic exchange (see Kellner,
    1989: 43–5).
14 Technologies always have an effect on the societies into which they are introduced.
    The *FE* uses the example of the snowmobiles introduced into Finland in the early
    1960s, which resulted in enormous changes in the way reindeer were herded. The tra-
    ditional methods were soon superseded by quicker methods, and non-mechanised
    herders were forced to buy snowmobiles to maintain economic parity. But the disrup-
    tion caused by the new methods disrupted the natural rhythms of the herds to such
    an extent that fertility and population fell dramatically. Economically, the herders are
    largely no better off than before the introduction of the snowmobiles, but once intro-
    duced, the new speed of activity forces all the herders to buy snowmobiles and
    increase their own rate of activity, whether they want to or not (St Jacques, 1981). For
    critiques of the implementation of modern technologies in 'developing' countries, see
    Taghi Farver and Milton, 1972; Shiva, 1991.

Part II
Doing

The following four chapters provide a snapshot of a number of debates and critical positions which inform contemporary anarchist practice. The specific areas covered offer unique perspectives on aspects of socialisation – sexuality, education, addiction and mental health – and how this can be challenged at a number of different levels. Each of the contributors comes from a specialist professional or activist background (rather than an established academic one), and to varying degrees the chapters bear out points made in Part I, 'Thinking' regarding biographical positioning of the author in terms of carrying out research. This is particularly the case with Jamie Heckert's chapter on sexuality (chapter 5), which also demonstrates the sensitivity and ethical dilemmas that must accompany any libertarian sociological method. Whilst this is a background consideration of the other authors in this section, the principal threads which run through this part of the book concern taking action on an everyday basis, and the need to move away from outdated models of change.

In different ways, each of the chapters is indicative of the movement away from deterministic theorisation towards more holistic, ecological and complex visions of reality. As we have suggested in our Introduction to the volume, these re-emerging views complement much of contemporary anarchist theory and practice, which has itself always posed challenging questions about the social and natural construction of reality. Although acknowledging the role of particular classes and élites within society in the perpetuation of exploitation and oppression, all these authors explore the complexity of the boundaries of complicity in power relations. Devising useful political strategies therefore requires breaking with classical dualistic categories that posed revolutionary actions against reformist ones, a model of a political world long departed.

The result is not as clear-cut as one would always want it to be, theoretically, strategically or ethically. For example, despite a challenging look at the social construction of addiction, Colin Craig's chapter (chapter 7) still appears to be supporting 'liberal' local courses of action such as harm reduction through needle exchange schemes. He also suggests that sometimes the positions adopted by the Left tend not always to be the most libertarian ones and we should sometimes listen to other voices. In addition, when one looks at the unpleasant picture of the narcotics trade, political repression and millions of people dying of AIDS, doing something seems better than doing nothing. This sentiment is echoed in James Bowen's chapter (chapter 6) in terms of acting against militarism and racism. Often one actually opposes such forms of power by means of a variety of political alliances, some of which contain libertarian elements and some of which clearly do not. Sometimes one acts in an entirely personal capacity where the effects are perhaps hard to discern. In such instances, the squaring of means and ends does not work for every situation, and there actually might be tactical reasons for opting for less dogmatic 'anarchist' strategies simply to facilitate useful group co-operation.

Of course, none of these situations are at all unique to the era we have identified as that of global anarchism. It is more the case that actions cannot be framed in simple notions of cause and effect, in a world characterised by increasing complexity and uncertainty. Each of the chapters here notes how identities and the construction of reality are equally unstable, often mutually reinforcing concepts. Heckert's chapter (chapter 5) looks at how this occurs through campaigning on issues of sexuality, both in terms of the identity of the individuals concerned, but also how successful the strategies adopted are in conveying a coherent and libertarian message to the rest of society. In her discussion of mental health and creativity, Joanna Gore (chapter 8) taps into a radical psychiatric tradition which has frequently appealed to anarchists for its critique of dominant constructed notions of reality. This is one of the reasons for the attraction of Michel Foucault's work to many anarchists. Certainly the way that Gore looks at the discourses around creativity and art, as well as those of mental health and normality, is reminiscent of this analytic approach. Gore's and Bowen's chapters concentrate on education, age, communication and the importance of art and creativity in the libertarian struggle, something that places them in the tradition of writers like Herbert Read (1970).

The importance of locating young people within the wider debates about anarchist strategy and socialisation is still, as all the authors in this section allude to, highly controversial in the extreme. In the light of the often-paralysing dominant constructions of childhood as representing innocence, naïveté and ignorance, there is a pleasing symmetry in the way that these articles cover young people's protests against war and injustice from school walkouts in 1911 to opposition to imperialism post-9/11.

5 Jamie Heckert

Sexuality/identity/politics[1]

Introduction

At an anarchist discussion group, I confessed to working for the council. I explained that I felt justified because the sexual health programme in which I was involved was so incredibly progressive. The person to whom I had made this admission replied, rather haughtily, 'I hardly think sex education is revolutionary.' Putting aside the idea that something is only worthwhile if it will bring on 'the revolution', I was concerned with the apparent attitude that sex education cannot be 'anarchist'. Perhaps this is because anarchism has traditionally focused on formal hierarchy, especially in the forms of the State and capital.

Academically and politically, my primary interest is sexuality. By this I include sexual or erotic desires, behaviours and relationships. I often ask myself how I can justify putting my energy into sexuality. Climate change, nuclear weapons and other forms of environmental catastrophe could have disastrous effects for all forms of life on this planet. Capitalism, as a system of institutionalised competition, supports abuse of the individual, unsustainable consumption, and inhibits co-operative social efforts. Racial hatred, nationalism and xenophobia are central to violence and war. How can sexuality be seen to be nearly as important? I say this is because any attempt to build a society where people are comfortable with themselves and each other *must* include a radical reorganisation of sexuality.

Sexuality is not separate from these other issues which are more commonly considered political. Our collective discomfort and obsession with sex is capitalised upon by advertising agencies further fuelling consumerism (Connell, 1997), which plays a key role in climate change (Marshall, G., 2001). The gendered division of labour is partly justified through expectations of reproductive roles (Lorber, 1991). In Britain and elsewhere, belief in 'racial purity' and the fear of 'whites' becoming a minority plays a role in the stigmatisation of mixed-race relationships and the almost eugenic tendencies sometimes found in the distribution of contraceptives and birth control propaganda (Weeks, 1995b). Also during times of crisis or more rapid social change, people tend to become very anxious, often about sex. The McCarthy era of American history offers one obvious example of this, when fears of communism became tied up with anxieties about 'deviant' sexuality. In the event of drastic climate change or the collapse of unsustainable economic and political institutions, sexuality could well become increasingly the focus of social anxiety. Today, in our rapidly changing world, anxieties about sexuality are apparent in advertising, media intrigue and sex panics surrounding sex education, homosexuality and paedophilia. In our obsession, we talk about sex all the time. Unfortunately, constructive dialogue about the personal and political issues of sexuality is disproportionately limited in relation to our everyday discourse.

Anarchism needs to move beyond its traditional focus on the State and the market in order to address hierarchy throughout society, not just in the public sphere. Sexuality is constructed into hierarchies and is interconnected with other forms of social divisions including gender, sexual orientation, class and ethnicity. Any efforts to build a society that includes among its values non-hierarchical organisation, appreciation of difference, comfort with bodies and the elimination of categorical social divisions must acknowledge the importance of sexuality. Furthermore, sexuality must be recognised as its own specific realm of hierarchy and oppression, rather than merely a subset of more 'fundamental' divisions such as class or gender.

The key problems in both recognising sexuality as being political and developing an effective political strategy can be understood to derive from dualistic thought. Sexuality is not perceived as political either because it is natural (the opposite of social) or because it is personal (not political). Efforts to politicise sexuality largely rely on strategies of identity politics, suggesting that the issues affect *us*, not *them*. This chapter provides an overview of the limitations of dualistic thought followed by a specific exploration of the constructions of natural/social and personal/political in terms of sexuality. I then explore criticisms of identity politics, drawing on a case study of Pride Scotland as well as my own activist experience in that organisation and elsewhere. Finally, I conclude with a call for an anarchist, issue-based politics of sexuality.

Opposites and sex

In structuralism, following Levi-Strauss, 'binary oppositions were thought to structure psychic and social life in a patterned, universal way' (Seidman, 1998: 221). Thus, those who were among the first to challenge dualist thought (e.g., Derrida, 1976) provided the basis for poststructuralism. Criticism of dualist thought has since become central to much feminist theory (especially critiques of the division between public and private), postcolonial theory (in that the 'universal truths' of dualism were imposed upon local knowledges through Western imperialism), sociology and queer theory (e.g., Seidman 1996, 1997). It is essential that anarchism also take into account criticisms of dualism. This has been taken up in certain respects, for example, the anarchist critique of the work/play division (e.g., Bowen, 1997). Here I suggest we should understand anarchism as a theory and practice that promotes the development of non-hierarchical social organisation. Hierarchy does not exist only in the public sphere as anarchist emphasis on the State and market suggests.

> Different modes for the classification of populations, differential treatment on the basis of labelling or attributions of capacities and needs, and modes of exclusion that operate on this basis (the core features of what may be called social divisions) are characteristic of modern social formations. They permeate the social order and indeed lie at the very heart of discursive, symbolic, psychic, economic and political practices. (Anthias, 1998: 506)

Dualist thought underlies and sustains the dual processes of social divisions: 'the process of differentiation (and identification)' and 'the process of positionality' (Anthias, 1998: 511). The first refers to the way in which people are placed (and place themselves) in social categories. The second refers to the way in which the relationships between categories, within particular social divisions, are hierarchically constituted. Furthermore, oppositional dualist thought inhibits the possibility of recognising complex political positions that involve more than one form of hierarchy.

In dualist opposites, one is valued while the other is perceived as being dangerous or uncomfortable and requiring control: mind/body, human/animal, love/lust, rational/emotional, educated/ignorant, civilisation/nature, political/personal, normal/deviant, law/anarchy, man/woman, straight/queer, white/black, etc. People in positions of authority in countries like Britain and the United States are predominantly educated, rich, straight, white and male; these categories are associated with rational thought and civilisation. Sex is strongly tied up in this binary system. Note the scandal when a politician is found to have been involved in a sexual activity too far outside of the carefully controlled institution of monogamous heterosexual marriage. (Of course, how far is *too far* varies according to social context.) This is because any other form of sexuality is at odds with the dominant series of concepts. Exhibiting (sexual) deviance, queerness or lust is seen as a fall from grace, a slip into the dark side of human nature.

Discomfort, fear and obsession with bodies, lust, emotions and queerness are central to the maintenance of this system of dualist thought and thus to the basis of our selves, our values and our institutions. Anxieties about bodies (and, by association, sexuality) being 'out of control' are used to support a variety of hierarchical institutions and practices. If anarchism is the promotion of non-hierarchical social organisation, it must problematise dualism as well as addressing the key role of sexuality in maintaining hierarchies. The construction of 'civilisation' and 'nature' as opposites is a good place to start.

Unnatural sex

Sexuality is generally perceived to be essential – a natural, pre-social and irrational force. From this perspective, it is our human society that controls our powerful sexual desires. Two opposing camps have adopted this understanding of sexuality. On one side, conservatives argue that society must regulate sexuality or else we will collapse into immoral, hedonistic 'anarchy'. On the other side, liberationists argue that society has no right to control sexuality but that we should be free to express ourselves naturally. Although for supporters of anarchism, the second argument may be rather appealing, I argue that both are based on a misunderstanding of the 'nature' of sexuality. Like any other aspect of society, sexuality is organised. Of course, it could be organised very differently.

Sexuality is unnatural. Like any other social practice, it does not express a biological truth; nor does it deny biology (Connell, 1995). Biology sets the limits of sexual possibilities (Weeks, 1995b) as it does for all social possibilities; we are all biological creatures. However, very few would argue that we can understand other social phenomena (such as the State, labour or families) primarily in terms of biology, even though they all depend upon it. Much like hunger, the desire for sexual pleasure may well be inherent in the human condition. However, what you eat, how you eat, with whom you eat and where you eat are socially defined, not naturally determined. Likewise, expectations about appropriate sexual partners, location of sexual activities, and even what constitutes a sexual act are all socially defined. Societies across time and space have very different understandings of what we would call sexuality (Weeks, 1995b). For example, among the Sambia people of Papua New Guinea, a rite of passage for boys to become adults involves them performing what we would call oral sex on adult men and swallowing their semen. In our culture, this would be constructed as paedophilia. For the Sambia people, semen is considered the essence of masculinity that must be passed on to a younger generation in order for them to become men (Herdt, 1982, 1987). Even in our own culture, certain acts may be considered sexual in some contexts but not in others. A finger inside a man's rectum in order to touch his prostate gland may be a sexual act or a medical examination. Sexuality is not defined by nature, but by society. Associating sexuality with nature rather than civilisation is indicative of our collective belief that certain aspects of our selves and our society are natural and therefore cannot be challenged or changed. From Thomas Hobbes and Darwin through to the authoritarian populism of Thatcherism, ideas about 'human nature' and the 'natural order of things' have been used to justify various institutions including the state, imperialism, the market, the gender order (Connell, 1995) and competition (Kohn, 1992).

Public sex

Sexuality is not simply a personal or private concern; it is also a public (political) issue. Just as anarchism argues that being unhappy with one's job should be understood in terms of the organisation of paid labour, the obsession and discomfort that so many people feel about sexuality should be recognised in social terms. The liberal ideology of individualism underpins not only constructions of sexuality, but also the market and the 'democratic' State. However, the personal and the political are not entirely separate. Relegating certain issues (e.g., gender and sexuality) to the private sphere serves to maintain hierarchical social divisions. The apparently tempting liberal argument – that as long as sex is done in private between consenting adults, it is outside the realm of politics – is flawed in its failure to recognise the fact that definitions of 'privacy', 'consent' and 'adult' are political (see, e.g., Califia, 2000). For anarchism to be successful, it must acknowledge the political nature of sexuality.

Identity politics

Identity provides a problematic starting point for any form of political movement. It is true that 'there can be no politics without some sense of identity because it is through a wider identification (with a party, a movement, a specific goal) that political practice is made possible' (Weeks, 1995a: 101). However, as Weeks notes, identities develop from social movements rather than the other way around. Thus it is possible to roughly differentiate between social movements that imagine a pre-existing identity (identity politics) and those that do not. Although I am focusing specifically on the politics of sexual orientation, these arguments also apply to politics based on other identities such as 'working class', 'women', 'people of colour' and possibly even 'anarchists'.

Lesbian, gay, bisexual and transgender (LGBT) politics depend on a politicised subject defined in opposition to institutionalised heterosexuality. Identity (for both individuals and groups) is defined in terms of sameness and difference: Self as opposed to Other; us as opposed to them (Jenkins, 1996). Oppositional politics is based upon the same terms as that which it opposes. Thus, it serves to maintain the definition of the situation imposed by its opposition. In identity politics, the categories upon which social divisions depend are reified. The concept of heterosexuality cannot exist without homosexuality, just as man cannot exist without woman, rich without poor, or whiteness without colour. Identity politics serves to maintain the series of conceptual binaries upon which much of Western thought rests. The second central problem with identity politics is its interpretation of 'the personal is political'. Although the two are not entirely separate, they are not identical either.

Identity politics is not the source of these problems. The concepts of heterosexuality, homosexuality, bisexuality and transgenderism are inventions of the psychiatric profession and a range of other social forces. Before that, particular sexual acts were sanctioned or criminalised, but were not considered the basis for a sexual identity (Foucault, 1990). The medical model of sexuality has redefined sexual acts as symptoms of a sexual (dis)order. (Approved) sexual acts with only members of the other sex are defined as the healthy and normal state of heterosexuality. Sex with members of the same sex leads to the diagnosis of bisexuality or homosexuality. Encouraged by the individualism inherent in representative democracy (Rahman, 2000), LGBT politics maintains these categories: it intends to invert their meaning, redefining sexual deviance as sexual identity of which one should be proud and sexual normality as boring/oppressive. While the strategy has undoubtedly had some benefit, it is nonetheless limited at best and exceedingly problematic at worst.

Pride Scotland

In order to develop an understanding of how participants in LGBT identity politics position themselves in relation to these aforementioned critiques, it is useful to draw upon my own qualitative research data. This was conducted in 1999 using participant observation and semi-structured in-depth interviews with seven organisers and seven participants of the annual Pride Scotland March and Festival. These ranged in age from early twenties to early forties and included gay, lesbian, bisexual and heterosexual identified individuals (all represented here with pseudonyms). During this research project and the year prior to its beginning, I was an organiser for Pride Scotland (Heckert, 2000).

The first Pride Scotland was held in Edinburgh in 1995. Since then, events have alternated between Edinburgh and Glasgow. I became a Pride Scotland volunteer in the spring of 1998, helping to organise the Health Area in general and the Safer Sex Cinema specifically. Although my relationship with sexual orientation identity politics had always been complex, it was during these months that I really began to question the politics of Pride. Reading gender activist Riki Anne Wilchins' critique of identity politics (1997) and seeing performance artist The Divine David, whose commentary included the fact that he could not afford to be gay, offered me a new lens through which to see this Pride event that I had helped organise. Shortly after, I offered my letter of resignation. However, my partner convinced me that it would be more constructive to try to promote an alternative point of view within Pride Scotland rather than simply quitting. I returned to organise the Diversity Area for 1999 and carry out the interviews with Pride Scotland organisers and participants. The Diversity Area was an attempt to move beyond the limits of identity politics by providing an interactive space including performance, discussion and stalls for a variety of community and political organisations addressing issues that are not considered LGBT-specific (e.g., nuclear weapons).

Problems of transgression

In order to explore the argument that identity politics reinforces the processes that define 'normal' sexuality, it is important to examine the relationship between the ends and means of Pride Scotland, especially the strategy of the Pride March and its participants' goals of social change. The Pride March can be said to serve as a demonstration of difference by those who march for those who watch. Thus, it serves as an example of a long-standing tendency in 'sexual minority' politics, from gay liberation of the 1970 to queer theory in the 1990s, to view transgression and opposition as strategic methods to subvert identity categories and the heterosexual/homosexual division (Weeks, 1995a).

Visibility was a key theme in the interviewees' explanations of the value of the Pride March. Most of them suggested that simply being seen was perhaps the most important part of the event. Betty put it quite succinctly: 'If society doesn't know you are there, it can't respond to you.' The best way to be seen by (heterosexual) 'society' is to occupy public space. Thus, the Pride March winds its way through the most occupied and most public areas of the city. This demonstration of difference is not only a spectacle, but also a political and oppositional act. Richard emphasises this in his militaristic comment: 'The March is the reclaiming [of] public space . . . The thing that gets the adrenaline going for the March is that you are walking through the same street you might have walked down yesterday alone, but your with x-thousand other people and it's *your* space. *You've taken it over*' (my emphasis). These participants seem to agree with Lynda Johnston (1997) in her argument that, with this transgression (i.e., the breaking of rules or the defiance of authority), Pride Marches disrupt the public/private duality that maintains queer invisibility in public spaces.

However, not all the participants were convinced that the March has a purely positive effect. Gloria was concerned that visibility does not necessarily lead to acceptance: 'I think it can be ridiculed sometimes . . . Like the Christian guy who hangs out in university. He's kind of . . . like a weird person that you're kind of interested in but kind of ridicule as well. I think that [the March] can encourage . . . people [who] are already going to react negatively.' Fiona, who was generally supportive of Pride, also had reservations: 'We mustn't confuse our . . . more obvious . . . profile in society as . . . necessarily being one of more acceptance . . . . People [may] feel threatened . . . feeling we're on a take-over of their . . . traditional values or way of life.' John Holmwood similarly noted, 'with the politicisation of marginality and the assertion of "deviant" lifestyles, social problems are, indeed, made matters of "public debate", but there is no guarantee that the public will share the radical affirmation of the "identities" being presented' (Holmwood, 1999: 281).

I'm not suggesting, as some have (Onion, 2001) that Pride Marches simply need to be made more 'straight' by getting rid of explicit sexual references or sexualised bodies, drag queens, or dykes on bikes. To do so would be to suggest that there are two opposing options: break the rules or follow the rules (see Weeks, 1995a: 108–23 for a discussion of these two tendencies in LGBT/queer politics). Furthermore, even if all the men wore suits and all the women wore dresses, the very act of publicly presenting themselves as LGBT reinforces the idea that these people are different from 'normal' people. While Pride Marches are transgressive, I would suggest that they do not disrupt the public/private and dominant/minority dualisms, but rather reinforce them.

Strategies focused on transgression ultimately maintain the rule that they attempt to break down. As Wilson argues, 'just as the only true blasphemer is the individual who really believes in God, so transgression depends on, and may even reinforce, conventional understandings of what it is that is to be transgressed' (1993: 109). Pride Marches do nothing to question the organisation of normal and queer, of public and private; rather they provide the opposition necessary to the norm. Normal cannot exist without queer (or otherwise deviant). A successful radical politics, I suggest, must not rely upon transgression and opposition if its goal is to reconstruct society around a different set of norms (e.g., co-operative, non-hierarchical, comfortable with sexuality, consensual, etc.). The importance of consistency between ends and means is an important theme in anarchist theory. Bookchin notes: 'it is plain that the goal of revolution today must be the liberation of daily life . . . there *can be no separation of the revolutionary process from the revolutionary goal*' (1974: 44–5 original emphasis). More recently, Cindy Milstein has argued that the contemporary anarchist 'movement is quietly yet crucially supplying the outlines of a freer society . . . where the means themselves are understood to also be the ends' (2000). Rather than expending energy by defying the forms of authority that maintain the current form of social organisation characterised by social divisions, it is more consistent to develop and support ideas and institutions that promote alternative values and forms of organisation. Of course, in situations of violent repression by the State or others, transgression and opposition may well be necessary effects of political action. However, they should never become emphasised over more constructive strategies.

Pride Marches suffer from this break between ends and means. The participants and organisers with whom I spoke all desired a world where people weren't divided up depending upon whom they fancied. However, the means of the Pride March are not consistent with the desired ends of a world where sexual orientation and gender expression were not forms of social division. This inconsistency can be seen most explicitly in Darryn's argument that 'you've still got to have the gay message *rammed down* people's throat during the March until . . . it becomes more accepted' (my emphasis). The contradiction between a symbolically violent means (ramming, taking over) and a desired peaceful end (acceptance) could not be much more blatant. Neither, I think, could the problems with this contradiction. How often do people accept things that are rammed down their throats? It seems to me that people are much more likely to reject anything that is (perceived to be) forced upon them. Any kind of attack (including symbolic transgression) leads to defensiveness that inhibits, rather than promotes, change. I believe this is especially the case where these attacks are perceived as based around identity. People tend to take criticisms of their identities personally.

Taking the political too personally

While the first critique of identity politics is the way in which it reinforces social divisions through opposition and transgression, the second problem is that it takes the feminist slogan 'the personal is political' too literally. Certainly, the personal and the political are intertwined. Since the late 1960s, a key aspect of feminist theory has been challenging the assumption that the personal and private (e.g., family, sexuality and gender issues) formed a completely separate sphere of reality from the political and public. However, the relationship between the personal and political is complex. Fuss (1989: 101) argues that

> we should not . . . lose sight of the historical importance of the slogan which galvanised and energised an entire political movement . . . But the problem with attributing political significance to every personal action is that the political is soon voided of any meaning or specificity at all, and the personal is paradoxically de-personalised.

Coming out is a key example of equating the personal and the political in LGBT politics. Labelling oneself to others as lesbian, gay, bisexual or transgender is fundamental to LGBT identity and politics (Plummer, 1997). Coming out is often defined as politically beneficial and is thus encouraged (as in the US 'National Coming Out Day') or enforced (as in 'outing'). But should individual desires be made political? And why are only certain desires seen as political? I address these questions and others here by exploring the attitudes towards the personal and political in coming out amongst the participants of Pride Scotland.

The primary focus on the value of coming out was, for most of the participants, personal rather than political. Many of them spoke about the positive impact this had upon their lives. Henry, although he did not agree with the metaphor of the closet, spoke powerfully about his experiences: 'The butterfly and chrysalis scenario – that's what it felt like. Coming from a caterpillar into a butterfly – that's what it felt like. To be able to just float off. That first summer when I came out, that was what it felt like. It was amazing. Absolutely amazing.' Relief and freedom were themes that came up in many people's stories, as was the idea of being able to be one's true self. Betty said: 'I don't think you can ever be yourself until you come out on some level.' Although most of the participants focused on the personal aspects, many of them addressed the political as well.

Attitudes toward 'outing' (i.e., declaring someone else's 'queerness' without their consent as a political act) were mixed. Most of the participants asked about outing were opposed to it, placing importance on personal choice. Two others would be willing to make an exception in the case of an authority figure that they perceived to be 'hypocritical'. Most of the participants agreed that freely choosing to come out was politically beneficial. Betty, for example, spoke about using her identity to challenge heterosexist comments. 'I have no problem with outing myself to challenge someone . . . [But] I think that's very difficult for some people because some people . . . will then think that they are gay. I think it's probably a bit harder for straight people [laughs] to do that.' Outing oneself refers to informing another or others of one's own 'queerness' for political reasons. In general usage, only people who are 'really' queer are able to do this – hence Betty's comment on the difficulty for 'straight' people to challenge homophobia with their identities. Richard argued that coming out was inherently political rather than just a potential political tool. For him, coming out as LGBT was the basis for both the Pride movement and individual pride:

> R: Well if you are talking in terms of sexuality being just another personal attrib-
> ute, then being gay is nothing . . . But the . . . ways of dealing with [issues] that you
> are usually proud of [include] being honest with people and so on. That would be
> the distinction I'm trying to make. The out gay person as opposed to the closet gay
> person is a similar sort of thing. Although there are different levels of being out.
> J: Does that mean the more out person should be more proud?
> R: Well it's interesting to quantify it, but probably, yes [laughs]. Ah well, that's quite
> difficult. There are different reasons for people to be differently closeted and so on.
> But I would say in general that's a reasonably good rule of thumb.

Others spoke about the general benefits of coming out. They felt that more people knowing others who were identified as LGBT would lead to changes in attitudes. Fiona suggested that coming out 'breaks down prejudices because people know . . . or know of, individuals. They are the sons and daughters of their friends . . . I think knowing individuals takes away people's fears of the unknown and therefore breaks down intolerance.' According to this logic, changing attitudes of individuals leads to social change, which leads to the creation of a better world for future generations of LGBT people. Gloria makes a similar statement:

> the fact is that still probably the majority of the population is fairly anti-gay, so I
> think if you are [LGBT] then [to be proud of that] can be a responsibility if you
> choose it to be . . . because I think it will ultimately make it easier for people . . .
> later on . . . to be out and gay and for it to be accepted.

But not everyone was convinced that coming out was an entirely positive political strategy. Four of the participants described their concerns about political pressure placed on individuals. Although Fiona spoke in favour of coming out, she was worried about people being pressured to act for the good of the cause:

> I don't see why people individually should all be political markers for an explana-
> tion. They can only do as much as they feel comfortable with. And I don't think
> people's lives should be made a misery for . . . a greater good . . . I think people
> should be encouraged to, and supported to, to be strong for themselves and for
> others. But they shouldn't be kind of bullied into having to be sacrifices . . . they
> deal with enough without having to be charged with not being . . . *gay* enough.
> [original emphasis]

Mark was also worried about the emphasis on coming out as political. He felt that it could be quite harmful to the individual. He explicitly mocks the political slogan 'come out, come out, whoever you are.'

> Sometimes martyrdom can be very important and can be a very powerful motiva-
> tor for political change but it tends to be a bit of a fucker for the martyr . . . Come

out, come out, whoever you hurt, you know. Not least of all yourself. To say nothing of people that are close to you.

Finally, Patrick demonstrated that coming out can have an impact, though not necessarily the one intended:

> I was through in Glasgow a couple of weeks ago. My parents live in a Glasgow housing area [laughs]. So not exactly the most liberal of environments on Earth. As ever, some mates of my brother started talking about gay . . . talking about the Soho bombing[2] and stuff. And they were still making a point that for a lot of them, I am still the only gay they have ever met. Although they still managed to bring it down to, 'We hate poofs, but we know Patrick so he's fine'. I have this protective bubble from the fact that they've known me for the last 20-odd years . . . I've got a get out of jail free card with them.

When the personal is made political, it will not necessarily be interpreted as such. Here was an example where general attitudes towards homosexuality were apparently not affected by knowing someone who happened to identify as gay. Although Patrick may have intended coming out to be a political statement, to his brother's mates it was interpreted as a personal one.

Most of my interviewees felt that coming out should be a personal choice and were concerned about political pressures. At the same time, the conflict between promoting coming out as beneficial to LGBT politics and suggesting that it should be a free choice is obvious. Not only are LGBT the people pressured to come out, only they are able to do so. This conception mimics and maintains the medical idea that homosexuality, bisexuality and transgenderism need to be explained while heterosexuality often does not. In fact, the idea of 'normal' people coming out is absurd. One participant made a joke of this. I said to Walter, 'some say that if everyone came out, the world would be a better place'. He replied, 'I think if *everyone* came out things could get confusing' (original emphasis). Although obviously privileged in relation to homosexuality and bisexuality, heterosexuality is not as straightforward as it may seem.

Heterosexuality

Hierarchies exist within heterosexuality as well. Mixed sex desire across generations or 'racial' categories may well be stigmatised. A heterosexual identified woman who rejects the sexual advances of a man may well be labelled dyke or frigid, not because she is believed to identify as lesbian or asexual, but because she does not seem to identify with ideological norms of passive heterosexual femininity. Likewise, a heterosexual identified man may be less likely to brag to his friends about the sexual pleasure he receives from anal stimulation from his female partner then he would be to brag about pleasure from vaginal intercourse (Morin, 1998). This deviates from the ideological norm of penetrative heterosexual masculinity with which straight men are expected to identify.

LGBT identity politics helps to maintain the illusion that heterosexuality is monolithic and unproblematic while LGBT identities are problematic and therefore political:

> Heterosexuality is *seen* to be devoid of politics, embroiled in no relations of dominance and subordination, and to affect no form of coercion. In contrast, because homosexuality is the marked, subordinate one, it is constructed as political. (Brickell, 2000: 171, my emphasis)

Heterosexuality is political and complex, though this is rarely acknowledged explicitly outside of gay/queer and feminist theory. Because of its dominance within the sexual orientation hierarchy and its status as 'normal', heterosexuality is constantly visible to the point of being invisible. Heterosexuality is presumed and therefore not perceived.

Maintaining the illusion of heterosexuality as apolitical has three very political effects. First, as long as normative heterosexuality is perceived to be apolitical, all other forms of gendered and sexual expression will remain politicised and problematised. Second, it discourages heterosexual identified people from being involved in the politics of gender and sexuality. As long as gender and sexuality are only issues for 'deviant' people, 'normal' people will see no reason to be involved. Third, it inhibits the questioning of normative heterosexual practice and traditional masculinity and femininity. Politicising coming out seems to me to have effects other than those intended by its proponents. Making the (queer) personal political may inhibit discussion of the underlying issues (e.g., gender and sexuality) as well as maintaining the division between LGBT (problematic/political) and straight (unproblematic/apolitical). Of course, politicising homosexuality is not the source of the problem; rather, to do so is to be uncritical of the roots of the problem. This is the social division called 'sexual orientation', within which normative heterosexuality is dominant.

Not only does 'sexual orientation' exist as a hierarchy of gendered desire, but, as a nexus of gender and sexuality it also serves to support (and at the same time it is supported by) both the gender order (Connell, 1995) and the hierarchical organisation of sexuality (Rubin, 1993). Much of our social organisation is based around expectations of and support for reproductive, monogamous traditionally gendered male–female couples (Connell, 1995). Thus, it appears that heterosexual identified people have a 'vested interest' in maintaining the social division of 'sexual orientation'. However, I would argue that heterosexual identified people also hold 'latent interests' (New, 2001) in challenging this division. Here are a few examples: pressure to conform to norms of heterosexuality (including ideals of what constitutes sex and gender expectations) leads to a continuation of unsafe sex practices, especially among young people (Holland, Ramazanoglu, Sharpe and Thomson, 1998). Institutionalised heterosexuality helps to support the gender order (Connell, 1995) which is oppressive to women and men (New, 2001) as well as everyone who doesn't fit neatly into one of those two options (Bornstein, 1996). Heterosexual identified people who are perceived to be 'queer' may also be the victims of queer bashing (National Coalition of Anti-Violence Programs, 1997). Close same-sex friendships may be interpreted as queer, while close mixed-sex friendships are seen as a potential romance; thus, all close friendships become charged with potentially damaging significance. Heterosexual identified people could find themselves attracted to someone of the same sex and lose their position of privilege. Young men in my sex education sessions have sometimes been comfortable enough with each other and with me to talk about fears of potential same-sex desires. Any system that limits or stigmatises our imaginings of the possible (be it anarchism or same-sex desires), much less act upon them, is oppressive to all of us. In short, identity does not determine interests, which are always complex (New, 2001).

Anarchist politics: incorporating sexuality

Ethics

One of anarchism's strengths is an emphasis on ethics. Why should some people have access to more resources than others? Why should some people get to make decisions over other people's lives? Why should some people be more valued than others? People who advocate anarchism should also recognise that the current social organisation of sexuality is also unethical. Why is sex considered a dangerous force? Why are some consensual sexual acts more socially acceptable than others? Those advocating a radical change to this organisation must offer an alternative ethics of sexuality.

American sex radical and feminist anthropologist Gayle Rubin argues that:

> a democratic morality should judge sexual acts by the way partners treat one another, the level of mutual consideration, the presence or absence of coercion, and the quantity and quality of the pleasures they provide. (Rubin, 1993: 283)

Other aspects of sexual behaviour, she argues, should not be of ethical concern. For queer theorist Michael Warner, sexual ethics are also of central importance. He criticises sexual identity politics for focusing on identity to the exclusion of sex. For him, sexual shame is the key issue to be addressed in a politics of sexuality. The political value of queer and public sex cultures is not in their transgressive nature, but in their development of alternative sexual values that attempt to move beyond sexual shame. 'In queer circles . . . sex is understood to be as various as the people who have it' (Warner, 2000: 35). As Rubin noted, many of the forms of sexual pleasure expressed in these queer circles (e.g., sex in parks or toilets, SM, role playing, making or using pornography, having sex with friends, etc.) are perceived to be immoral at best and amoral at worst. Respect, empathy, informed consent and shared pleasure are arguably values to be supported in all relationships, sexual or otherwise. Indeed, these values must be central in any efforts to produce and sustain non-hierarchical relationships, organisations and societies.

Issues not identities

A politics of issues could avoid the problems inherent to identity politics. Firstly, while politics of issues will necessarily involve conflict, they will not necessarily be oppositional, as identity politics must be. Politics of issues could allow for the exploration and development of alternative systems not dependent on social divisions. Secondly, the social organisation of sexuality could be recognised as fundamental to all of our lives rather than a minority concern. Thirdly, a politics of issues is not *inherently* exclusive. Small minority movements could be replaced by mass efforts of people who are involved because of the interests and their passions instead of their categories. These criticisms and their alternatives are not limited to the politics of sexuality, but also to political theories and actions based around any other form of identity. However, just as participants in non-hierarchical organisation must continually be aware of the possibility of hierarchies developing (a theme explored in anarchist literature (Le Guin, 1974) and political action (Roseneil, 2000)), those who participate in issue politics must be wary of slipping into the logic of identity politics.

Much as homosexuality is constructed as a deviant, minority sexual desire, anarchism is constructed as a deviant, minority political ideology. Thus, it is unsurprising that many people who advocate anarchism come to identify themselves as 'anarchists'. This results in a reification of a dualist division between the 'anarchists' and the 'non-anarchists'. The 'anarchist' becomes a type of person; such identities are inherently normative. What is an anarchist? Who qualifies and who does not? Furthermore, why else would I have felt the need to confess and justify working for a council, if not to defend my anarchist identity? How could the response be interpreted, if not a criticism for not being *anarchist enough*? Anarchist identity is often constructed in opposition to other identities (e.g., liberals, hippies, bosses, politicians, middle-class people). This construction of boundaries around an anarchist identity thus excludes people based on their status, rather than their (potential) political views. Once upon a time, I identified as a 'liberal'. If my first encounter with anarchism had been an attack on 'liberals', would I be writing this now? People and politics are continually evolving and changing processes. Anarchism depends on change; fixing people with static labels inhibits it. (For a similar critique of 'feminist' identity, see hooks (1984).) Anarchism will never become a mass movement if we waste limited energy arguing over who the real (or potential) 'anarchists' are, or worse, thinking of potential allies as enemies (Edwards, 1998). The aim should not be to recruit 'anarchists' into our exclusive club. Rather, we should work together to promote anarchist thought and create anarchist organisation now, focusing on social issues, offering ethical alternatives and unifying ends and means.

Conclusions

The social organisation of sexuality is a political phenomenon that must be addressed in anarchism. Not only is the organisation of sexuality in itself hierarchical, it also helps to maintain other social divisions. Furthermore, anxieties around sex and sexuality are used to promote consumerism, to justify State violence and to discourage solidarity. If, as I suggested earlier, we understand anarchism as a theory and practice that promotes the development of non-hierarchical social organisation, then anarchism must work to eliminate all social divisions. Identity politics, rooted in the very categories of social divisions, is fundamentally incompatible with this approach. Anarchism should move beyond the social division of 'sexual orientation' upon which LGBT politics depends. Anarchism should question the idea that queer is political while straight is not; meanwhile, the politicisation of LGBT identities maintains it. What identity politics is capable of is inverting the usual hierarchy, such that gay becomes good and straight becomes boring (at best) and oppressive (at worst). Identity politics is not the source of the problem but rather an inherently limited response to historically constructed social divisions. And while identity politics has its successes, any efforts to reduce or eliminate social divisions must find alternative means.

Furthermore, for anarchism to effectively offer an alternative to all forms of hierarchy and domination, it must incorporate sexuality. This includes addressing issues such as rape and sexual abuse, pornography, marriage, queer bashing, sex education, sex work and the tyranny of 'normal' sex/ualities. More profoundly, we must recognise that 'sexuality' is not an entirely separate aspect of life with its own list of issues, but integral to all aspects of our hierarchical society. Concepts such as respectability, normality, progress, evolution, change and organisation are infused with assumptions about sexuality (Weston, 1998). Efforts to understand and challenge hierarchy must incorporate sexuality.

Our thoughts, anxieties and experiences about sexuality, like so many other issues, so often remain unspoken. Whenever we are silent, we can continue to believe that social concerns are individual problems. The (predominantly) US-based direct action group ACT UP (AIDS Coalition To Unleash Power) had a powerful point with their slogan, 'Silence = Death, Action = Life'. Whether it is how much we suffer at work, how isolated we feel, or how much shame and anxiety we feel about our sexual desires, maintaining our silence helps to maintain the status quo. Chomsky makes a similar comment on the impact of media propaganda.

> You may think in your own head that there's got to be something more in life than this, but since you're watching the tube alone you assume, 'I must be crazy' because that's all that's going on over there. And since there is no organisation permitted – that's absolutely crucial – you never have a way of finding out whether you were crazy, and you just assume it, because it's the natural thing to assume. (1997: 22)

Again, if we want to build a society where people are able to co-operate and communicate, they must be comfortable with themselves and each other. If they are deeply uncomfortable with sexuality, such a society will be very difficult to organise and not as pleasurable as we might imagine anarchism to be. Encouraging people to be comfortable talking about sex and sexuality is a current focus of my political work. Besides talking with teenagers in schools, I am involved with a group called 'Intercourse: talking sex'. So far, we have organised public discussions on a variety of topics, had more informal outings to the cinema and pubs, and produced a leaflet promoting masturbation (Intercourse: talking sex, 2002). Sex education – in the broad sense of encouraging development of self-esteem, critical thought and knowledge through discussion rather than an expert imparting knowledge – is *revolutionary* if the aim is a society where relationships are valued for their respect, empathy, informed consent and shared pleasure. If I cannot talk about sex, I want no part in your revolution.

Notes

1 I would like to acknowledge the help of the following people in terms of comments on and contributions to earlier drafts of this chapter: James Bowen, George Daniels, Simon Eilbeck, Iain Lang, Diggsy Leitch, Hamish MacDonald, Anne K. G. Murphy, Samuel Porter, Jonathan Purkis, Paul Stevens and Mark B. Wise.
2 On 30 April 1999, the 'Admiral Duncan', a popular gay pub in Soho, London, was the target of a nail bomb attack in which three were killed and dozens left injured. David Copeland, a 24-year-old advocate of neo-Nazism, admitted guilt to this attack and two others targeted at ethnic minority groups.

Moving targets: rethinking anarchist strategies

Introduction

In the anarchist movement in Britain and across the world today, there are a number of reasonably prolific publishing projects and a few moderately successful groups and organisations. It is even true that the word *anarchism* has lost much of its popular perception as a source of terror and chaos, particularly in 'anti-globalisation' and environmental circles; but anarchism *per se* simply does not have an impact on the vast majority of the population. This is not to say that *change* is not happening all around us at all times, and that there aren't elements of that change relating to the central themes of anarchism, namely promoting liberty, equality, solidarity and community and opposing exploitation, oppression, dehumanisation and environmental degradation. However, the relatively marginal position that anarchism occupies in terms of both the popular and critical imagination suggests that the subject of anarchist strategy is one worthy of reassessment.

This chapter suggests that some of the impediments to the acceptability of anarchist ideas lie in often dogmatic, exclusive and fundamentalist approaches to effecting change. This is as true for the use of narrow conceptual categories that juxtapose 'revolutionary' strategies against 'reformist' ones as it is for unrealistic expectations about what people are capable of doing politically on a daily basis and whether some social groups are more likely to effect change than others. This is relevant both at the level of small-scale projects such as co-operative housing through to strategies for opposing globalisation or militarisation. For anarchist ideals to be either explicitly or implicitly practised, it is necessary to consider the potential for influence in areas other than those which anarchists are naturally prepared to consider. This necessitates a greater flexibility about notions of inclusion and community as well as a preparedness to take part in networks or broad-based coalitions.

What *is* 'the anarchist project'?

Any discussion of anarchist strategies must begin with the worldview of its principal protagonists. Given the historical diversity of anarchist theory and practice, whether in terms of its different analytical categories or its preoccupation
with either individualist or collective forms of action, definitions matter. As will
become clear, it is increasingly the case that definitions of anarchism which focus
on single loci of power are no longer viable in the twenty-first century. Whilst it
is important to acknowledge the respective impact that economic, political and
technological forms of power have on people and the planet, none of these are
monolithic and all-determining. As writers such as Newman (2001) show, power
encompasses all forms of authority in human relationships and this, I will
suggest, has major implications for thinking about strategy, both in terms of
everyday issues of community and identity, as well as on more international
stages.

Suggesting that power is present in *all* relationships and requires appropriate
theory and practice is slightly heretical, departing as it does from what for many
is still the heart of the anarchist project, the class struggle (see Guérin, 1970: 34–9
and *passim*). To move away from the class struggle is not to suggest that differentials of economics, culture, education, opportunity, perception and aspiration do
not still exist, since clearly they do, maintaining inequality in many global contexts. However, focusing on any one economic group as the agent of change is
misleading in the extreme, just as hanging on to notions of class more reminiscent of the era of George Orwell (1949, 1984) or Richard Hoggart (1957) is also
unhelpful. It is important to remember that in times of social change, the working
classes have been found to work both for the forces of liberation and reaction, as
have members of the other socio-economic classes. As George Walford notes: 'If
we keep on believing anarchism to be a class movement we shall be clinging to a
myth that never did work very well and is now losing whatever effectiveness it
once possessed' (Walford, 1990: 229).

A key ingredient in the myth of anarchism as a class movement has been the
belief in 'the revolution' as an 'event' carried out by a clearly identified class. This
idea of revolution as a 'short and specific social and political upheaval event that
will happen in an unspecified future situation' is both sociologically simple and
practically unhelpful. Only in a very limited number of historical circumstances
have such 'events' actually taken place. This is not to say that the nineteenth-
century insurrectionary model of change should be necessarily dispensed with,
since there may be circumstances – particularly in the Developing World – where
it might be entirely appropriate. Rather, it should not become the organising
basis of anarchist strategy.

One of the consequences of believing in 'the revolution as an event' is that it
has posited the anarchist project as a choice between revolutionary action and
'reformist' action, with all of the attendant accusations being levelled against
'liberal anarchists' whenever any apparently 'non-revolutionary' courses of

action have been advocated.[1] This also is a position based upon a limited view of how change happens and who carries it out, again belying the fact that power occurs in increasingly complex and diffuse ways, not according to predetermined historical laws. It is therefore more useful if we think about anarchism as not simply being about the redistribution of wealth (by certain historical forces at particular times) but also involving a change in our relationships with each other, institutions, technology and our environment. This is therefore where I believe the anarchist project begins, with the boring, small-scale, mundane business of making positive, non-alienated relationships with our friends and neighbours and remaining open to new people and ideas. This is the unglamorous but ultimately vital area of working against our own alienation and that of our communities, and one in keeping with the practical anarchist writings of people such as Paul Goodman (1971) and Colin Ward (1988). The emphasis on the everyday as an organisational basis for anarchism therefore draws upon the notions of 'mutual aid' developed by Kropotkin (1993), combined with the legacy of feminism whereby it is impossible to separate the personal from the political.

One of the implications of viewing the anarchist project as one that is rooted in the everyday is that the possibilities for political organisation and influence change, in particular concerning who takes part and what are the most appropriate and effective courses of action.

The politics of inclusion

Revolutionary politics has often drawn its support, at least initially, from the more marginalised strata of society, but this is not necessarily either the best way of thinking about change or one that is appropriate to the complexities of contemporary societies. If we perceive anarchism as a process rather than as a goal or an end product, any decisions about political alliances and the various strategic avenues that are open to us become more difficult. As soon as we start to exclude or reject people according to other criteria than simply their willingness to participate, we will have failed at the first hurdle. As Donald Rooum has noted (1990: 237), one does not need to be a victim of social injustice to advocate revolution against it, as many key revolutionary figures of both Marxism and anarchism have demonstrated. It may well also be the case that people with the least to lose and the most to gain from major social change are actually the least open to radical ideas.

Socialisation, we have to remember, is a powerful force and one which influences our decisions about taking political action at different points in the life-cycle, depending on whether we are young, have families to support, have ties to people or places or feel motivated to act out of anger. Fear is an often under-acknowledged concept in thinking about political change, something to which increasing privatisation of space, time and social life in the West is certainly contributing. Our potential for change is therefore perhaps better conceptualised in terms of a 'continuum' where we sometimes have vested interests in the status quo but equally might desire particular changes and be prepared to fight for them. We may well *all* stand to benefit from certain circumstances, but communities and identities are not easily homogenised and anarchist history is already so littered with sectarianism and exclusivity that more is not needed. The rethinking of anarchist strategies needs to be done with an acknowledgment that this cannot be achieved solely using rational criteria: human beings are most often open to change when they feel good and confident about themselves, but people's identity and self-image fluctuate regularly and sometimes enormously. Interestingly, whilst social scientists are more receptive to the idea that radical change occurs during periods of rising expectations rather than increased immiseration, there is still largely a failure to acknowledge the possibility of fluctuating states of mental health and psychological preparedness to instigate social change on a micro-sociological level.

All of these factors need to be considered in the light of the vast differences that exist within communities. Indeed, understanding the socio-psychological identity of a community is an important step in terms of formulating realistic anarchist strategies, since invariably there will be local conditions which will determine particular responses and affect how one acts politically. We all identify as a whole range of different things, some of which are more salient for more of the time at certain periods in our lives, but none of which are the most important feature about ourselves at all times. How we 'fit' into a community also determines our identity, and we may alter our accent or dialect, dress differently, and even choose to suppress certain information about ourselves for the purpose of 'fitting in'. Conversely, many people have no idea how steeped they are in their community's culture until they have moved away from it, and are confronted with a different way of living which perhaps puts them in a 'minority' position. I myself (full of youthful idealism and internationalism!) did not really become aware of the extent to which I was actually 'English' until I lived in France. I then came to the conclusion that I was perhaps idiosyncratically but quintessentially an Englishman abroad; a majority of English people may well have perceived me as a spotty punkrocker with torn jeans giving 'we English' a bad name on the continent, and therefore someone with whom they imagined themselves to share no community. Communities, as Benedict Anderson (1983) famously pointed out, are frequently 'imagined', a perceived unity of disparate characteristics, often used for political expediency. Shifting identities and definitions of community have always been a social theorist's nightmare, and the development of virtual identities and communities further complicates this, but this should not result in strategic paralysis. A balance must be struck between believing that we belong to some kind of community, with all of the potential solidarity that this entails, *and* to be looking to radically transform that very community into something else. We also must feel positive about the political activities that we undertake.

In order to maximise inclusiveness in any 'anarchist activities' it is important to be sensitive towards such differences within communities, which may mean that sometimes it is more fruitful, as argued elsewhere in this volume by Jamie Heckert (chapter 5), to pursue issue-based rather than identity-based political change. Likewise, in order to facilitate inclusiveness, it might well be the case that sometimes we have to adopt forms of action which are not ones we would ideally pursue, and to avoid alienating people with inappropriate ideas, rhetoric and tactics.

For instance, socialisation and fear in Britain and Western Europe in recent years has led to often extremely hostile attitudes towards 'asylum seekers' which calls for considerable sensitivity when campaigning on issues of racism. Welcoming asylum seekers (be they political, economic or cultural) into our communities as equals and sharers in our good-fortune may not appear particularly radical, but their effects can be felt throughout society. Similarly, saying 'hello' to our neighbours (whoever they are, wherever they come from), writing a letter to the local paper, challenging a bigoted remark at work or responding with outrage to racist attacks all go a long way to challenging the racism within our society as well as building more progressive politics.

The politics of process

If the lesson from the above discussion is that anarchist strategies must be inclusive, tolerant and community-based, a nagging question remains as to the extent to which actions remain anarchist in terms of the principle of equating the means of an action with its ends. Historically and theoretically anarchists have based their strategies upon the views of human nature and political hierarchy inherited from Kropotkin, Proudhon and Bakunin and this has rightly led to an obsession with avoiding 'leadership' of any sort and rejecting political 'blueprints' of the future. This has been fine in the goldfish bowl of 'official' anarchist groups and networks, but is not necessarily applicable to the kind of popular alliance politics or community activism within which much contemporary anarchist action takes place. This is particularly important when remembering that people bring different skills and expectations to all political situations and many are ill-equipped to deal with having another set of alienating procedures foisted upon them (a mistake parties of the revolutionary Left repeatedly make). In such instances, the purity of anarchist principles might have to be sometimes tempered with the practicalities of inclusion, avoiding alienation and 'doing anarchism' by example rather than rhetoric. The principles of consensus and negotiation are thus retained, even if sometimes anarchist ideals are more of a yardstick to measure participation rather than being written in stone. This is not to say one should cease from monitoring and contesting any of the unavoidable inequalities present in political relationships (due to skill, knowledge and experience differentials, availability of time, economic or other resources).

   The politics of process also requires devising strategies which are tangible and achievable on an everyday level for people other than professional activists. This is especially the case with respect to not prioritising particular forms of political action, as though there were a hierarchy of legitimacy. Many anarchist and Leftist organisations favour demonstrations, strikes, pickets, attending meetings, publishing papers, books, magazines and Internet articles, throwing missiles at the police, and setting up support groups. These may or may not be useful in terms of either instigating social change for the better or in promoting self-confidence and solidarity among those participating. Paul Goodman (n.d., originally 1966: 28) notes that 'it is hard to tell when a riot or other lawlessness is a political act toward a new setup and when it is social pathology'. More publicly visible activities are of course loved and promoted by the Left, and are alternately loved and ignored by the mass media. However, these need not necessarily be the most effective, and with the cause and effect of political action being increasingly hard to judge, establishing a hierarchy of actions serves to create more divisions.

   By comparison, activities which are easily discounted might well include: living in families and communities with explicit (or implicit) ideals of equality; or working in non-exploitative or oppressive ways in formal work, voluntary and other situations. Such areas of life may not have the glamour of perceived 'political' acts (compare the media interest generated by, say, collectively growing some organic carrots as opposed to trashing a McDonald's), but it is in our personal and individual relationships that our ability to change the world begins. It is vital that we also recognise this fact, remembering that, as equals, we bring different skills and experiences to bear, but that *all* human interaction is potentially liberating or oppressive and that we should celebrate *all* our actions that serve to further our own and each other's liberation.

Educational influences

In the light of the above discussion, one of the areas of anarchist activity which is often overlooked in the face of more glamorous events such as anti-capitalist and anti-globalisation protests on a global stage, is education. Many writers have focused on the liberation of education as a means of promoting the core ideas of equality and freedom (from Ferrer (1913) to Freire (1972), Stirner (1967) to Shotton (1993), Neill (1962) to Illich (1971) to Gribble (1998) and so on). This is a key area of social change, in that an institution such as a school or college can serve to demonstrate ways in which we may be able to live, interact and relate to each other outside of the current 'normal' run of things as well as opening doors to new ideas and ways of empowering ourselves. Such alternative institutions, at no stage 'the finished article', highlight the point about anarchism and social change being a process, in that there are constantly problems, conflicts to resolve, misunderstandings and less-than-idealistic interactions, in spite of the high ideals in which the establishment may have been set up.

The classic work in this area is A. S. Neill's (1962) *Summerhill*, but David Gribble (1998; also chapter 10 in this volume) provides numerous contemporary examples of educational establishments and organisations across the world which explore 'varieties of freedom'. The work of Gribble is important for noting how progressive ideas can exist in areas other than self-identified radical education projects, further undermining simple juxtapositions of libertarian education as being solely practised in 'free schools' and places like Summerhill against the repressive offerings of the State sector.

It would be rhetorically and theoretically convenient to assume that the State has a monolithic stranglehold over the education of our children and young people. On a certain level this is true – National Curricula abound, along with inspectors and government directives – and it is also the case that the school plays a part in reinforcing existing inequalities of gender, class, ethnicity, sexuality and disability, as well as other aspects of socialisation (see Craig (this volume) on schools and the War on Terror and the War on Drugs). Schools are also often the places where people first experience bullying (by students or teachers) and feelings of inadequacy, failure and humiliation. However, it is also true that the State is never as all-powerful and all-encompassing as it (and some anarchists) would have us believe. Human systems are invented by humans, implemented by humans, screwed up by humans and subverted by humans. In terms of influencing the process of social change, both mainstream and alternative education systems offer enormous potential for developing responsible, human-scale and equal relationships among both students and teachers. For instance, the literacy development work that I do in schools provides tremendous opportunities for me to challenge different sources of prejudice and power, around race, gender, class and, importantly, age. The acquisition of language and literacy skills can act as a spur for the achievement of great things in life (both now and later) and the changes that I have observed in my own work puts paid to theories that claim language is universally oppressive, fixed and uncontestable. For many young people, the confidence and validation that comes from engaging in positive inter-action with perceived 'authority figures' can have an enormous impact upon all aspects of their lives. Often this is only possible where the 'educators' meet and interact with the young people on their own level and continue to validate their language and interaction while also trying to create a forum where they can extend and grow in new directions. Freire (1972) clearly outlined the liberatory power of literacy for liberation in modern societies, but it is vital that we don't forget issues of power, accessibility, alienation, culture and subculture when we look at the channels of communication within our communities. Many of the young people I work with express themselves through language and music, their chosen media being almost exclusively non-standard. It would be a disaster to ignore the liberatory power of such words and language in this context in favour of those analyses which only perceive language as oppressive and constraining.

The examples of education and language further reinforce the need to rethink the models of power which underpin anarchist strategies as well as recognising the diversity of the possible options and methods of change. However, whilst change on a small scale is hard to theorise and calculate, extending some of the aforementioned arguments to a global scale calls for even greater flexibility.

Democratic interventions

In trying to enact positive projects and relationships, it is easy to become pessimistic about the possibilities of wider social and political change for the better. The sheer psychological burden of trying to position oneself in terms of all of the murderous horrors inflicted by governments, corporations, fundamentalist religions and damaged individuals is in itself enough to put one off political activism. It is then extremely heartening when, despite all expectations, cracks appear in the edifices of power and popular protest gains a new legitimacy.

I am going to use the opposition to the war waged on Iraq by the US-led 'coalition' in 2003 as an illustration of why it is important to consider anarchist strategies alongside the tactics and philosophies of other movements campaigning on this issue and to maintain a stance of flexibility and non-dogmatism. It has already been established that in the context of community politics a slight 'dipping in anarchist standards' may be necessary simply in order to intervene in an important contemporary political environment. The mobilisations held on '15/2' in particular (the largest demonstrations ever held on this planet) provide something of a focus for the antiwar movement, providing a useful context regarding what is normally perceived of 'as anarchism'.

In early 2003, something occurred amongst the populations of Western societies (and beyond) which was a combination of the continued disillusionment with American foreign policy (especially in Afghanistan, Israel and Palestine) and the new political confidence generated by highly visible opposition to globalisation and the destruction of the environment. This was most evident in the huge waves of school children becoming involved in the opposition to the build up to war in Iraq. Organised and spontaneous walk-outs and sit-ins occurred throughout schools and colleges across the world, sometimes resulting in dozens of city centres coming to a complete standstill. In my hometown in West Yorkshire and the surrounding cities, there were regular demonstrations of thousands of people marching in opposition to the war and, perhaps more importantly, celebrating life, with humour, music and dance. The central organising groups in most urban centres consisted of the usual assortment of Trotskyists, anarchists, Leftists, trades unionists and students, but also present were members of the Muslim communities, Quakers, former soldiers and so on. The means of protest were perhaps less creative than some of us would have liked, but there seemed to be an acknowledgement by many that simply marching down the street with banners (selling newspapers) was not the only or necessarily the best form of protest, and that different people came at the subject with a huge variety of ideas and skills. Additionally, the celebratory nature of the mass demonstrations provided a forum for people to meet friends old and new, such that it was often suggested that we should perhaps block the ring road more often![2]

The antiwar mobilisation begs a number of enormous political questions: why were those people all there? what were they against? and, crucially, what did they want? It is still too early to answer these questions with any degree of academic certainty, but, in simple terms, the antiwar movement sought a number of things. Firstly, it sought freedom from: warmongering and dehumanisation; US economic and political arrogance and imperialism; fear of broadening conflict; Islamaphobia and racism; the cheapening of human life, especially when it's impersonalised and a long way away from here; the fear of terrorist repercussions (real or imagined). Secondly, although somewhat less coherently, it also sought the freedom to do a number of things, most particularly for people to have more control over the actions of governments, corporations and unelected trade organisations which seek to impose free market solutions on disadvantaged parts of the world.

The popularity of recent books like Naomi Klein's *No logo* (2000) suggest that the public has become increasingly willing to question the ethics and motives of large corporations and the logic of globalisation. Yet the clue towards asking what people are *for* lies in the parallel questioning of the legitimacy of democracy. In popular terms, Michael Moore's best-selling book *Stupid White Men* (2002; also Palast, *The best democracy money can buy*, 2003) has pushed the limitations of democracy and its hand-in-glove relationship with big business into the media spotlight. This has been compounded by the intentions of the United States and the United Kingdom to 'impose' democracy on the people of Iraq after the overthrow of the regime of Saddam Hussain, when the failures of the Western model of representative democracy have become so apparent.[3] Indeed, the exporting of democracy, under the guise of humanitarianism, has become one of the most insidious aspects of the post-Cold War era, in the Balkans, the Middle East and Africa; it is not however, a new story. Recently, I was reading about independence movements in sub-Saharan Africa in the second half of the twentieth century and the problems of grafting Euro-American political ideology and economic systems on to other parts of the world (with an unhealthy dose of colonial intervention, greed, mineral and human exploitation and so on). In a small isolated village (in the Congo in one case), for example, the adoption of US-style democracy resulted in 51 percent of the electorate achieving a democratic decision that they approved of, leaving 49 percent unsatisfied. In this case, democracy proves a recipe for disaster, since nearly half of the electorate remains unsatisfied with the outcome. Traditional decision-making often takes other forms.

It is of course easy for anarchists to denounce (representative) democracy as (Proudhon's) 'tyranny of the majority over the minority' and to celebrate the disdain with which it is increasingly regarded. However, in the midst of debates about enticing the apathetic voting publics of the West with improved forms of electoral participation − through emailing and SMS texting − a healthy degree of anarchist intervention is needed. Whilst we do not yet know the political biographies of those young people for whom the anti-war movement of 2002 provided their first activist experience, we do know that for their generation the shape of politics is changing fast. As David Graeber has noted, it has perhaps escaped the Left's attention that the political form of many contemporary movements, against war, against global-isation and environmental destruction are 'horizontal networks . . . based on prin-ciples of decentralized, non-hierarchical consensus democracy' (2002: 70). These may be pluralistic and alliance-driven, but since they constitute part of the debate about the nature of 'democracy' – representative, participatory or inclusive – and there are degrees of overlap with anarchist practice, they should not be dismissed as irrelevant. In a sense, this is just a continuation of the old anarchist argument for why squatting empty properties, attending town meetings or being involved with tenants associations or parish councils can be vital areas of activism.

A tapestry of oppositional threads

In keeping with the need to conceptualise and challenge power in as many con-texts as possible, it should not be forgotten that intervening in 'democratic' arenas is just one possible area of anarchist activity. Small-scale community politics is vital of course, but we cannot absolve ourselves of the responsibility of interven-ing at the global level, especially in terms of economics. How this takes place is again somewhat controversial. I have suggested that some forms of activism are perceived to be more valuable than others and it is in tackling corporate power that these kinds of hierarchies of action themselves need subverting. In particular, one of the 'successes' of the protests against the World Trade Organisation in Seattle 1999 was the diversity of strategies employed, and a recognition by many that this was an extremely effective way of maximising influence. It was also a good indi-cation of the difficulty of apportioning blame given the complex flows of people, money, technology and power that exist in the world system (although those acti-vists who 'pie' corporate leaders seem to have their own ideas about this!). On such a huge scale, the levels of culpability vary and this means that appropriate strate-gies are devised to target particular points of production and consumption.

It may not appear very attractive when we are wearing our 'political radical' colours, but, in pragmatic terms, a government or legal directive that limits capi-talism's excesses can be as vital to our movement as any explicit anti-globalisation protest. Sometimes the lobby of a politician or a letter in support of or in opposi-tion to a small legal change may have as far-reaching consequences in terms of quality of life as more overtly 'radical' forms of direct action such as physically stopping the destruction of a forest. One form of activism doesn't need to take precedence over the other: often both of them are essential parts of a tapestry of oppositional threads. It is also true that mobilisation within a not very radical local community can best be done using more moderate strategies, and the real radical action is actually empowering people to take action themselves. Judging who ben-efits from an action and what kind of change is taking place is particularly difficult.

A big failure of the Left in general is to acknowledge diversity of opposition, in terms of popular alliances and umbrella organisations, as opposition at all, particularly regarding the active implementation of relationships, systems, even laws. In terms of ideological purity, we might prefer to avoid sullying our hands with the tools of the State (laws, politicians, government and so on) but in pragmatic terms, we have to take our victories and allies where we find them, be they in the United Nations, the European Court of Human Rights, the Geneva Convention, trades union legislation or activity or among our friends and neighbours. The economic and political system that we oppose works on many different levels, and we therefore have to oppose it on these different levels. Burying our heads in the sands of ideological purity changes little and helps few, although it is understandable why many favour simplistic answers, since the complexity and comprehensiveness of capitalism is breathtaking. Our opposition has to be complex and breathtaking too.

I am treading on shaky ground here, particularly in terms of one of the oldest debates in the anarchist canon, namely the issue of means and ends. I would suggest that the examples provided in this chapter demonstrate that, in an increasingly complex world, clear-cut and all-embracing principles are hard to achieve. Anarchists are of course rightly wary of engaging with structures and organisations which appear (or indisputably are) opposed to their political ends. Unfortunately, it is usually only with hindsight that we can successfully evaluate the impact of our actions, but I would argue that it is better to have engaged on whatever level we feel able to and to have lost the battle than to have done nothing at all and then criticised the outcome.

The flexibility of our opposition must also apply at the level of our visions of the future and the practical realities of achieving them on an everyday basis. For instance, like most people I abhor political violence and would largely argue that violence begets violence and is not a means towards creating a peaceful society. However, it is very easy sitting in a relatively safe Western sitting room passing anarchist decrees which would seem ludicrous in parts of the world where political activists are routinely murdered or are necessarily engaged in an armed struggle. Similarly, the current appeal of primitivist forms of anarchism to Western activists is all very well if one is able to live a low-tech existence in a 'natural' location (with access to hi-tech solutions like piped drinking water, electricity, telecommunications and healthcare if required). However, for most people it is practically infeasible, not to say theoretically ill-conceived. It is true that we need to think hard about our relationship with technology and its relationship with capitalism, but to reject 'technology' out of hand indicates a failure to engage with most people's everyday existence, needs, aspirations and reality.

Conclusion

Any form of political (and social) action is fraught with pitfalls, since it involves interaction with other human beings, who, of course, often act in sadly predict-

able and unimaginative ways, but who also constantly amaze by their creativity.
Anarchists are no different, except they set themselves extremely high political
and ethical standards which have constantly confounded political theorists, activists and the general public. Despite its (self-appointed) role as 'the conscience
of politics', anarchism is still in need of constant revision, and in this chapter I
have suggested a number of ways that might be useful in the present political
climate. In accordance with models of power, influence and change in the social
sciences that are beginning to have an impact on political theory, so anarchism
needs to examine its strategies in the light of new political and intellectual contexts. Primarily this must consist of a distancing from simplistic dualisms such
as 'reform versus revolution' and monolithic perspectives on the power of the
State, capital, technology and even language. The kind of contemporary arenas
where anarchists are and can be (more) active requires flexibility of critique,
strategy and sometimes principle, simply on the grounds that anarchists have to
work with people who are not anarchists. Similarly, if we are genuinely interested
in achieving social change with the cornerstones of anarchism (freedom, equality, solidarity, community) providing a foundation of our society, world and economic system, we must engage in multiple, original and continual cultural,
social, political and economic interventions, avoiding sectarianism, dogmatism
and prejudice, such as those provided by Gribble (1998) and Shotton (1993) in
the arena of radical education.

   The breadth and power of international capitalism is awesome; the strength
of our opposition has to lie in our flexibility, our humour, our intelligence, our
doggedness, our humanity and our creativity, all of which we have in abundance
if we only care to tap into them and to share them.

Notes

1 This particular position has often dovetailed with debates about violence and nonviolence within anarchism. In Britain during the 1980s large amounts of print was
   devoted to this 'liberal'/reformist versus 'revolutionary' argument in the (respective)
   publications *Freedom* and *Black Flag*, a debate which seemed to be severely hampered
   by acrimonious exchanges between two well-known, now dead, English anarchists.
2 As a footnote to this, a neo-Nazi British National Party councillor has been elected
   to the local council in recent weeks (August 2003 in Heckmondwike), causing much
   soul-searching among local anti-racists. Hopefully, having learned from the antiwar
   experience, we will oppose the neo-Nazis more by a celebration of our humanity and
   multi-culturalism than by the usual tactic of a march followed by a dull rally with predictable speakers. However, there has already been a tendency from many on the Left
   to advocate the usual, often totally alienating and inappropriate means of expressing
   our opposition, rather than learning from the recent antiwar experience of existing
   within a broad church.
3 Both Moore (2002) and Palast (2003) give a fine account of how George W. Bush lost
   the 2000 election to Al Gore but still became president.

7 Colin Craig

What did you do in the Drug War, Daddy?

Inhaling metaphor

The War on Drugs has been going on since US President Richard Nixon coined the term in the late 1960s. It appears at first sight to be a completely illogical concept: how, we might ask ourselves, can a war be fought against a conceptual term that defies definition? Of course, the War on Drugs refers to those drugs that have been proscribed by law and therefore deemed illegal, and it represents a conflict with the express intention of eradicating illicit substance use from the face of the planet. In actual fact, since the outset of the War on Drugs, there has been both a proliferation of drug use across the whole world and an enormous growth in the numbers of consumers. Former Eastern Bloc nations where drug use was previously virtually unknown now have huge burgeoning drug markets fuelled by the breakdown of borders, the growth in trade and ultimately by mass populations with a desire to seek out new forms of oblivion.

Wars of metaphor are an important element in modern political culture and the War on Drugs and the War on Terror are the latest in a long line, which most famously included the War on Poverty in the United States of the 1960s (Piven and Cloward, 1977). For the purposes of this argument it is important to see the War on Drugs and the War on Terror as crucially interlinked. The use of these particular metaphors has enabled the same secretive governing forces to extend conflicts across international boundaries without declaring war in a conventional sense. The consequences of these 'wars' have been the subjecting of populations to ever-increasing repression, monitoring and control in the name of a 'drug-free' and 'terror-free' world (even as governments actually profit from the international drug trade in the process). Moreover, these conflicts of metaphor represent a new asymmetrical form of warfare; one that can never be won, yet which must be constantly fought.

Anarchists and libertarian socialists have been historically uncomfortable with how to position themselves in relation to these issues. When it comes to drugs, should they be prohibitionists or libertines? Is legalisation good, bad or irrelevant? How does one deal with a drug pusher at the school gates or a liberal police chief peddling a softly-softly approach on the streets of a city? And what happens if the people at the opposite end of the political spectrum have all the best tunes? Should we sing along or steal the hymn sheet?

This chapter argues that the War on Drugs has to be understood as a smoke screen for a wider war, on society in general, and on minorities in particular. This smoke screen has enabled recent US administrations to push forward aggressive foreign policy under the guise of fighting a metaphorical war, especially but not exclusively in Latin America. It is sustained by the myth of drug addiction and searches for 'cures' and 'treatments' that belie the fact that it is our everyday conditions of living which is the problem. Different governments, many of which have actively ignored the plight of millions of those caught up in the Drug War, such as HIV sufferers, fight the War on Drugs on many fronts. These governments increasingly choose surveillance strategies to police the bodies and minds of their populations. In the post-11 September 2001 political climate, the opportunities have arisen for an intensification of the confluence between the War on Drugs and the War on Terror, but active resistance to it remains.

To hell in a handcart

I was returning from a meeting in Spanish Harlem in New York City, on the hottest day of the year shortly after the millennium turned. On the pavement sitting just outside a shop that sold alcohol sat a whole family disconsolately arranged around a couple of large plastic travelling bags that might well have contained the family's total possessions. It was an awful sight filled with pathos. It reminded me that despite being the most prosperous and dynamic capitalist nation in the world, the United States of America takes very little care of those who fail to live up to the American dream.

Previously I had spent some time in the company of a fellow European who was living and working in New York attempting to prevent the spread of HIV amongst the urban poor of the city. The European said to me, 'Well, you can see the twin towers from here, but let me tell you, we are as far away from them here as they are in the Third World. This is the Third World here and don't let anyone tell you otherwise.' The European then went on to tell me about how Third World conditions had devastated the local Harlem and South Bronx communities in the world's richest nation and how the injecting of drugs had provided the vital vector for the transmission of HIV in particular.

Later the European's wife explained to me how the local police force had used the excuse of drugs and drug dealing to launch a campaign against all the local men of a particular ethnic origin in that district. She described how, in the early days of the epidemic, she had been forced to operate a needle exchange from the back of her car in contravention of the law, constantly harassed by the police. It took the fear of a full-blown epidemic, spilling out of the ghettos, to eventually force the New York State Authority to declare a state of public health emergency in order that the federal law could be ignored and needle exchanges established on a semi-legal basis. The majority of States in the United States still have not taken this action and hence, to this date, needle exchange remains illegal across the most of the United States. The following day I mentioned the destitute family that I had seen to a civil rights lawyer in downtown New York. She explained that they could quite conceivably have lost their city housing and public benefits as a result of drug use being discovered in the family. Increasingly across the whole of the world, the act of consuming illicit substances is enough to deprive the individual of any basic human rights that are guaranteed to ordinary citizens.

In the West, despite years of economic prosperity, drug markets have continued to grow. Two major economic forces drive these Western drug markets: a desire for new hedonistic experiences and a desire to escape immediate personal troubles. The combination of these two aspects of desire has proved to be a winning formula (for the drug dealers), despite all apparent attempts by Governments to counter the booming drug markets of the Western world.

Was it always like this? Apparently not. Many Victorians did not consider the issue of intoxication to be one of their public concerns. To quote Dr Colin Brewer and his submission to the recent Home Affairs Select Committee report:

> Until 1916 you could intoxicate yourself with whatever you liked. You could go to hell in your own handcart, but at least the law did not interfere. Personally I feel rather strongly we should go back to that set of Victorian values. (Evidence to Home Affairs Select Committee, 27 November 2001)[1]

Many Victorians, however, did not agree with this *laissez-faire* approach, particularly those middle-class elements that were active in the temperance movements of the late nineteenth century. Thus there began a general public debate about intoxication amongst the new urban poor of Britain's industrial cities. These concerns about intoxication were not unfounded, as terrible social conditions combined with poor public health gave the new inhabitants of industrial cities every reason to want to escape their reality. Public concern was further driven by many cases of deaths amongst infants due to the use of laudanum and other opiates. Primarily the public concern reflected not the actual issue of intoxication but rather a fear of the new urban poor who were living in the squalid conditions. This disorderly rabble had the very real potential to cause trouble of every order, from riots all the way to full-blown revolution. It is a common historical theme that during times of great economic upheaval there is public concern about the morals of the dispossessed. In our lifetimes we have seen about forty years of some of the largest economic, technological and social changes in the history of humanity. The locus of the means of production has increasingly moved from Western factory floors to the sweatshops of the Far East and into cyberspace. Globalisation has freed up capital beyond national borders and has thus created a massive transnational workforce with little to protect it from the whims of the free market. From Buenos Aires to Vladivostock people have found their labour casualised, resulting in greater uncertainty. For many, the changes in global markets have meant a slide into economic desperation. In this climate of desperation, there are opportunities both for those who want to corner the new illicit markets in drugs that are developing in such communities and those eager to seek the oblivion that these illicit products offer.

In response to public concerns about the British drug laws, the British Government commissioned a body of MPs to engage in a thorough review of British drug laws. The Select Committee was impressed by the contributions made in favour of the repeal of British drug laws, concluding thoughtfully that:

> We have listened carefully to the arguments. We acknowledge that there is force behind some of those advanced in favour of legalising and regulating. The criminal market might well be diminished (though not eliminated); likewise drug-related crime. (Report of the Home Affairs Select Committee, 2002)[2]

Despite obvious sympathy towards arguments that were tendered by individuals from every political hue, the Home Affairs Select Committee was not able to accept these arguments. To understand this, we need to understand some of the philosophies and theories that have informed drug policies in general.

State positions on drugs

There is a well-developed utilitarian argument against the ongoing prosecution of the War on Drugs. This opinion, expressed by the British organisation Liberty, is neatly summarised in the 2002 report that has just been quoted from:

> as part of a free, democratic society individuals should be able to make and carry out informed decisions as to their conduct, free of state interference, or in particular the criminal law, unless there are pressing social reasons otherwise . . . John Stuart Mill argued that the state has no right to intervene to prevent individuals from harming themselves, if no harm was thereby done to the rest of society. 'Over himself, over his own body and mind, the individual is sovereign.' Such fundamental rights are recognised by government, both in allowing individuals to partake of certain dangerous activities, for example drinking, extreme sports, and also in international treaties.[3]

This well-argued and perfectly reasonable position is, however, considered radical nowadays. The Home Affairs Select Committee in 2002 did reject Liberty's view but, to their credit, they were willing to include in their report the possibility that at some future point the tide might turn towards legalisation and liberty. This is an important change in the British discourse around the Drug War and it does represent a significant shift away from some of the more authoritarian positions adopted by other nations.

From a European perspective, the Swedes and the French are perhaps the most authoritarian in their attitude to illicit drug use. Sweden has inherited a paternalistic set of values from the temperance movements of the Victorian era, which assume that the State must protect the individual from the consequences of their own folly. French drivers will soon be subject to draconian drug testing regulations that will target cannabis smokers in a national crackdown. The Swiss, Germans and the Dutch are much more tolerant, all providing heroin users with a legal supply of pharmaceutical heroin and making drug treatment services as user-friendly as possible. (The Dutch also make cannabis use *de facto* legal via the licensing and toleration of 'coffee-shops'.)

The United Kingdom tends to swing between these two models and has only recently begun to shift away from a long period of American-influenced infatuation with the criminal justice system as a means of tackling drugs in UK communities. This new breeze of tolerance resulted in the advent of the 'Lambeth experiment' that concluded in 2002 (see below) and the much-trailed plan to reclassify cannabis by New Labour. *Daily Mail* columnists complain that the Government has gone soft on drugs and that the legalisers have captured the Home Office. Brian Paddick, the police chief of Brixton became an unlikely hero for dope smokers throughout the UK by single-handedly effectively decriminalising cannabis use within the London Borough of Lambeth, and instead concentrating on the dealers of harder drugs. Without wishing to add to Mr Paddick's current woes, it might also be noted that he admitted to having some regard for the concept of an anarchist society, although he did express concerns about how that society would be regulated (see the Introduction to this volume).

The 'Lambeth experiment' saw a clear distinction emerging between acceptable forms of drug use such as cannabis-smoking and even the use of Ecstasy whilst simultaneously subjecting the 'hard' drug-use of the non-working poor to ever more stringent and draconian controls. Paddick's attempt to reform our drug laws appears to have gone too far. The Lambeth experiment has been closed and, whilst the law is changing on cannabis, there has been such fudge about its implementation that even middle-class cannabis-smokers will not sleep any more easily in their beds. In the meantime, UK cannabis campaigner Colin Davies has been sent to prison for three years for his attempts to make the drug freely available. Despite Paddick's more liberal innovations in British drug policy, it still remains clear that the UK Government is committed to the policy of prohibition and that there will be little chance for major reform of the drug laws in the United Kingdom in the near future.

The prohibitionist paradox

The near-universality of contemporary drug cultures and problems does, however, necessitate a practical libertarian position on the prohibition or legalisation of particular drugs. At the core of these complex theoretical, ethical and moral dilemmas we find the issue of the libertarian response to authority. This subject has implications for our current activities in the world today but also for the world that future generations will inherit. Should we, as Left-leaning libertarians, back pressure groups and campaigning organisations that aim to change the drug laws? Should we support and work for organisations that aim to 'treat' drug users?

Clearly, prohibition is a blunt instrument of public policy that creates illegal markets for organised criminals and secretive governmental agencies to exploit. If we accept Liberty's utilitarian position outlined above in relation to prohibition, then the best reason to prohibit a particular behaviour is because it causes unhappiness and suffering to others. Although the majority of drug use may well constitute a 'victimless crime', there are three persuasive arguments in favour of continued prohibition: firstly, any loosening of control will result in a growth in the market; secondly, prohibition prevents vulnerable young people from getting involved in drug abuse; and thirdly, the use of certain substances will inevitably lead to criminal acts against others.

Cannabis and 'softer' drugs

It is probably true that if we legalise cannabis, for instance, people might well be more willing to try it. Evidence cited in Robert J. MacCoun and Peter Reuter's (2001) *Drug war heresies* shows that the liberalisation of cannabis markets in the Netherlands has resulted in increased use mainly due to increasing commercialisation. I do not see any reason why that should be a worry, given that we know that cannabis does not cause great damage to the individual beyond a few particular and specific cases. We therefore might argue that cannabis is a preferable alternative to alcohol, a drug with a well-documented link to violence and aggression.

Few commentators suggest that we should sell heroin at the cornershop, but many argue that heroin users should have legal access to their drug of choice rather than having to buy adulterated and unreliable products from the thriving criminal gangs who have occupied the gap in the market created by prohibition. The current emphasis on the frailty and vulnerability of the young in relation to their drug use does not stand up to much analysis. Young people are ignoring the law, taking substances whether they are proscribed or not. A majority of young people in the UK will inevitably experiment with illicit substances (European Monitoring Centre, 2001; Green Party, 2002) and a significant minority of young people are using these substances regularly (Drugscope, 2002). Most people however do not experience significant problems that relate to their drug use and will eventually grow out of the use of illicit substances or will develop norms around the use of certain substances. Experimentation might well be seen as simple youthful hedonism, a rite of passage through which most present day young people will pass. The fact that authorities attempt to stop them can only serve to alienate youth further from any sane authority that does exist. In this environment, prohibition only serves to further stigmatise youth, marking normal youthful behaviour as pathological and pushing young people into contact with organised criminals via prohibition. Normal youthful risk taking becomes pathological and ultimately encourages young people to consider their elders to be simple-minded and foolish. The Dutch have strong arguments in their favour when they indicate that their toleration of semi-legitimate cannabis cafés has ensured that there is a clear divide between this youthful kind of drug use and other potentially more dangerous forms.

Evidence for beneficial medical uses of cannabis continues to accumulate. Cannabis therapeutic clubs have sprung up in the United States and are now at the centre of a major storm, with authorities attempting to close these down. Some cannabis therapeutic advocates have even sought refuge in Canada, claiming that they are subject to politically-motivated oppression.

'Harder' drugs

Now let us consider other potentially more dangerous drugs such as cocaine and heroin. Heroin in its pure pharmacological form is not necessarily dangerous. Opium and its recent derivative heroin have provided a heaven-sent relief to many people suffering from chronic pain over the centuries. Should the UK Government decide to follow its Swiss counterpart and establish clinics where heroin users can gain free and legal access to heroin, we would most likely see a similar decline in the problems that are associated with this drug. We might, however, be concerned about the hidden agenda behind such programmes, especially as heroin use is found disproportionately amongst the poorest and most deprived communities.

However, if we were to legalise cocaine hydrochloride we might also see a rise in the use of this substance and its more powerful derivative crack cocaine. Cocaine hydrochloride users with no demonstrable problems probably do exist, but this drug has considerable potential to cause trouble to any user, especially in the form of crack. Dependency on this variety of the drug is frequently linked to violence and psychiatric disorder, and relapse is a common and frequent feature amongst users. Most commentators on the nature of crack cocaine accept that the use of this drug over a given period of time will eventually usually result in problems for the user and also for the user's family, friends and wider community. Some individuals claim that crack can be used recreationally and with control, but there are only a few people who would support this view, and this author is not one of them.

Myths of addiction; myths of cure

What we know about drug dependency is often what those in power want us to know. For instance, studies that do not agree with the *status quo* are quietly shelved whilst sensational and often highly skewed studies into, say, neonatal defects associated with whichever substance are trumpeted to the world as conclusive evidence that drugs are harmful. There is, however, now a significant body of knowledge that has begun to challenge these dominant definitions and is worth considering. The idiosyncratic but seminal *The Myth of Addiction* by J. Booth Davis (1993) and Elliot Currie's (1993) masterful *Reckoning* summarise much of the existing knowledge in this area. There are three important issues that we should consider in relation to drug dependency:

Firstly, there is no such thing as addiction and no such thing as an addict. Whilst drug dependency is a very real social phenomenon, we can find no convincing evidence of an underlying illness that is associated with the behaviour. The real social fact of drug dependency has been colonised by psychiatrists who have reduced this complicated phenomenon and individual drug users down to a set of symptoms.

Secondly, drug dependency appears to be the result of a complex set of interactions between our genes and the environment. We should be aware that some people are more prone to dependency through a complex set of interrelationships between their genes and the situation in which they live. Importantly we should be aware that the environment is a vital part of the equation, ameliorating or exacerbating the potential for the 'dependency' genes to express themselves.

Thirdly, there is strong and compelling evidence that people gain control of their drug dependency when they perceive themselves to have good reasons to stop. The recent history of attempting to control drug misuse in our communities provides a wealth of evidence to show that no amount of external control will stop the determined dope fiend from pursuing his or her poison. On the other hand, researchers cited by Elliot Currie have discovered that, on an annual basis, 10 per cent of the population of people with a drug problem will spontaneously desist. Currie also cites Charles Winick's (1962) classic study that indicates that people with drug problems tend to 'mature out' of their dependency. Is the challenge therefore not to stop drug use but simply to ensure that the drug user stays alive long enough to learn from their own experiences?

There is, of course, also much contrary evidence of drug users who continue a lifelong battle against dependency, and the reasons for 'relapse' are many and complex. Indeed, the relationship between addiction, desire and the experience of modernity is something that continues to interest sociologists (Giddens, 1991). That people may switch from one addictive focus to another is also an under-acknowledged point in drug policy debates. Clearly there are few simple facts and no simple answers in this area, and therefore we must tread carefully in our pursuit of reasonable and considered attitudes to such an emotive and complex subject.

Much current drug policy is predicated on the assumption that sufficient punishment will deter drug taking. Despite the fact that our prisons are stuffed with drug users, that drug users will risk death to continue their dependency and that drug use appears to be normal human behaviour, we still continue to threaten and exhort people towards 'the good'. Current drug policy is also predicated in the United States and the United Kingdom on the assumption that, once drug users are caught, they will be amenable to 'treatment'. There is very little reliable evidence that external pressure (whether it is the family, the community or the police) has any impact on drug users' intentions to use drugs.

Drug policy is also predicated on the notion that drug dependency can be 'treated'. Just as addiction can be said to be a flawed concept, what passes for 'treatment' is frequently based on poor research and little evidence and is based on the psychiatric/medical model of drug dependency that has held sway since the late 1960s.

Essentially, for the last 30 years drug users have effectively been dealt with as a sub-set of the population of people with mental health problems. There is no convincing rationale behind this other than the pressing concern at the time to move prescribing away from general practitioners towards a more tightly controlled and monitored system. Unfortunately this expedient was unable to prevent the rise in the numbers of heroin users that grew gradually during the late 1960s and early 1970s, leading to a dramatic increase in heroin use during the late 1970s and the 1980s.

By the mid-1990s, heroin use was endemic in most urban communities, and with increasing use emerging among rural populations. The response on the part of the British Government was to develop services that dovetailed with criminal justice agencies including: the development of arrest referral schemes; community-based drug treatment and testing orders whereby magistrates compelled drug users to access treatment; and prison-based 'CARATS' (Counselling, Assessment, Referral, Advice and Throughcare) programmes. Thus the latter half of the twentieth century saw UK governments using both a psychiatric-led medical model and the increased use of the police, prison and courts as a means of identifying, monitoring and controlling heroin users.

During the last three years in Britain, the health model of understanding drug issues in our society has started to re-establish after several years in the doldrums. The British Government has developed the 'National Treatment Agency', a special health authority with powers to oversee all aspects of drug treatment. Should libertarians support such moves? Clearly it is preferable to view drug-dependent users as people who need help rather than as criminals. Yet, according to the Right-wing libertarian Thomas Szasz (1996), the treatment paradigm is just as iniquitous as the crime and justice model for dealing with drug dependency. Szasz argues that this mode of thinking does not resolve the problems caused by prohibition and allows the psychiatric profession to extend their influence over people who do not have demonstrable psychiatric problems.

Harm reduction and the politics of HIV

Within the 'treatment' discourse, one truly libertarian thread has emerged: harm reduction. This side-steps the issue of the legal position of drugs and takes at its base the notion that the most important issue is not prohibition but the prevention of the worst harms that are associated with drug use. As a result of this perspective it is possible, for example, to develop programmes for the prescription of 'substitute' drugs such as methadone in the place of heroin and to establish needle exchanges.

The concept of harm reduction with methadone, however, amounts to the replacement of heroin with an opioid analogue which has few of heroin's finer qualities such as a sense of euphoria. This is a triumph for the temperance-minded amongst us who blanch at the idea that 'treatment' might also be pleasurable. Thus it is that an impartial observer of methadone treatment programmes would observe that very few 'patients' manage to avoid the continued use of heroin on top of the State-sponsored dependency formed by methadone use.

Needle exchange schemes in many Western nations have helped reduce HIV infection and have generally succeeded in giving injectors access to clean equipment. This strategy quickly became established in the UK and several other liberal democratic nations in Europe and further afield in Australia. In spite of opposition to these programmes from some quarters, those nations that have made needles freely available to injecting drug users since the outset of the HIV epidemic have low levels of HIV amongst their injecting drug users. The United States, however, has consistently failed to adopt this policy for the reason that it would be perceived as tacitly condoning injecting drug use. In 1998 the Governor of New Jersey sent in State troopers to close down a needle exchange service, arguing that HIV infection is a consequence of such deviant behaviour and therefore the transmission of such infections should not be prevented as they are an important potential deterrent for future drug injectors! (Day, 1998: 13).

Although HIV infection rates are considerable amongst drug injectors in the United States, they are held in relative check by a variety of factors mediated by the US federal government's ability to provide treatment and care to the infected individuals, combined with the effect of considerable social stratification. Outside of the United States, however, in poorer nations, where access to treatment is not available and where the majority of the population live in poverty, the HIV epidemic amongst injecting drug users has skyrocketed.

Harm reduction in the former Soviet Union is something of a luxury by comparison. HIV is a biological time bomb that has already begun to tick there, with various sources suggesting that the Russian Federation will have a million HIV positive individuals within the next decade. Experts predict that the nation's population might halve by the year 2050 (Hill, 2003). Just over the border in Ukraine, the HIV epidemic is developing even faster with the possibility that Eastern Europe will soon see an epidemic that will rival Africa's in the scale of its misery. In Eastern Europe, prescribed medicines as well as illicit substances are routinely administered by injection in order to save resources, which means that there are few population-wide taboos against the injection of drugs. An ideal vehicle thus exists for the dissemination of a virus across the whole of a nation. Drug users travel, tend to be young and sexually active, and some of them work in the sex industry to pay for their drugs. Those that spend time in jail help an already effective mechanism for HIV transmission. At the time of writing, a second wave of infection had already begun in the city of Kaliningrad where the epidemic was first discovered. This wave of infection is affecting heterosexuals who have never injected drugs and who do not work in the sex industry. The implications of this phenomenon, once it spreads to the rest of Eastern Europe, China and other Asian nations, are enormous.

If HIV was not invented as a means of hitting the poorest and the most deprived in the world then it is certainly doing that job very effectively now.

Crocodile tears

The War on Drugs might alternatively be viewed as a smoke screen and one where governments across the world shed crocodile tears at the devastation that drugs and HIV have caused in some places. They then use the 'scourge' of drugs as an opportunity to push forward a range of repressive measures against their own populations. From China to the United States, abuses of all forms are permitted under the cover of the prevention of this awful 'scourge'. During the national anti-drugs day in China during June 2001, over 60 drug dealers were publicly executed (CBS news, 26 June 2001).[4] In the United States in the same month, the Supreme Court legitimised the use of random drug testing on school children, something that corporations already carry out on their staff on a regular basis. An important barrier has thus been breached, giving to the panoptical State powers to develop surveillance of our bodily fluids.

The War on Drugs is of course also a war against Blacks, Latinos, the underclass and deviants of every hue. The United States has over a quarter of a million drug-related offenders currently behind bars. In 2000, drug law violators comprised 21 per cent of all adults serving time in State prisons – 251,100 out of 1,206,400 State prison inmates (Harrison and Beck, 2002: 12–13), with Black and Latino drug users far more likely to receive custodial penalties than their White counterparts (www.drugwarfacts.org/racepris.htm). It is also a war against the young, with the US Government recently rushing through the RAVE Act, with the aim of prohibiting dances that are related to the use of Ecstasy.

There is an even darker side to the Drug War in terms of secrets, organised criminals and covert sources of funding. The alcohol prohibition period of the 1920s in the United States enabled organised crime to flourish. Prohibition of illicit drugs in the early twenty-first century towers over that period in terms of the potential threat to undermine any just authority that may continue to exist. Nowadays, we should not be concerned about Al Capone holding Chicago City Authority in his pocket, but rather we should fear the role that drug prohibition has played in undermining what little democracy exists in the world. Colombian judges declare that cocaine cartels have enough money to buy off or to destroy the whole Colombian legislative body. Secret service agents in the pay of the American Government sign sworn affidavits (www.wethepeople.la/ciadrugs. htm) claiming that American intelligence services established a top-secret air link from Colombia with the express intention of importing cocaine (Dyncorp-sucks, 2002). Senate investigations into the Contra affair in Nicaragua proved links between the Central Intelligence Agency and cocaine dealing (Webb and Waters, 1999). Opium production in Afghanistan has boomed following the fall of the Taliban (Drugscope, 2002a). Who knows just what kind of unholy alliances are being forged in the ongoing War against Terror?

Neither Left nor Right

One of the great ironies of the War on Drugs is that, in the opposition to drug laws and State surveillance, some of the old-fashioned distinctions between Left and Right have become more and more blurred. Libertarians on the Left might well find surprising friends and some unusual enemies in this brave new world of ours. Noam Chomsky is at least one Left-leaning libertarian who has the Right-wing libertarians at the Cato Institute to thank for publishing his views. Chomsky himself has expressed the view that current policy on drugs has failed and he advocates the development of 'harm reduction' policies and of course radical re-thinking of the drug laws. Left-wing advocates of liberty might find common ground in the work of a non-governmental body such as the Drug Policy Alliance that campaigns for drug-law reform in the United States.

At the American National conference on harm reduction that took place in Miami during October 2000, the Director of the Drug Policy Alliance, Mr Ethan Nadelman presented a vision of the mission of the organisation that is funded by the Hungarian billionaire George Soros, a devotee of the neo-liberal libertarians: economist FA Hayek and political theorist Karl Popper. Thus it cannot be said that the Drug Policy Alliance truly represents the views of Left-wing libertarians; rather, it appears to be more concerned with establishing truly legitimate market forces in an unregulated and chaotic situation. Within a discourse that does not address the profound impact that drug dependency has on the poorest communities, the Drug Policy Alliance takes the view that drug use is no more than consumer behaviour and that, as consumers, drug users are being deprived of their rights to consume what they will. This position is not far removed from Liberty's utilitarian philosophy that so impressed the UK Parliament's Home Affairs Select Committee. Nadelman compared opposition to the ongoing prohibition of illegal drugs to the civil rights movement of the 1960s and obviously to the previous prohibition of alcohol in the States. Mr Nadelman is clearly correct in the scale of his comparisons but readers must ask themselves whether an organisation with such close links to a neo-liberal agenda can truly represent their views.

Is there clear blue water between the Right and Left wing of libertarian thought around the drug policy debate? I believe that Left-wing libertarians would generally hold the view that drug use and economics are far more complex in their relationships and that those existing features of inequity that exist in markets are mirrored when we look to drug markets. I would hope that Left-leaning libertarians would not consider the deregulation of markets a sufficient answer to the problems of drugs in our societies.

For example, let us look at crack cocaine. Right-wing libertarians would presumably argue that we have a right to consume whichever drugs we wish to consume and if there are negative social consequences as a result of this situation then markets will inevitably respond to correct imbalances. Thus, epidemics of crack cocaine in poor urban communities will effectively be self-limiting: those who will die will die; those who will get better will get better; and ultimately local consumers of these products will learn from their experiences not to use the substance or will find safer ways to use. There is logic to this argument, but this logic ignores the economic reality of oppression in the poorest communities across the globe and the role that drug use plays in these communities. The crack epidemic of the late 1980s and 1990s appeared to be self-limiting, with fewer and fewer new recruits as younger consumers reached the wise conclusion that crack use was not for them. This does not mean, however, that drugs are no longer an issue in Harlem and the South Bronx. Left-wing libertarians might consider the prevalence of crack cocaine and heroin use amongst the poorest communities and the persistence of these forms of drugs in those communities when compared with richer neighbourhoods and communities. We might also acknowledge the role that drug use has to play in the degradation of poorer neighbourhoods and communities. We might also worry that the creation of a free market in drugs would enable corporations to become richer and that these corporations would not necessarily have the best interests of their consumers at heart.

Despite the hypocrisy and repression that is associated with the Drug War, would libertarians really support the establishment of a free market in cocaine and its derivatives? Are there alternatives to the problems associated with cocaine hydrochloride that do not require the legalisation of cocaine, and could involve 'safer' supplies of the stimulant? This second question concerns an idealised future world where issues of economic injustice have been settled. Given our understanding of the potential effect of this cocaine on susceptible individuals, would we still wish to allow access to this substance even though we know that it might cause harm to others? Is the individual right to self-expression always paramount over the public good in a libertarian society? How would we 'police' such a policy, given our natural reluctance to exert power over others?

The Infinite War

Even as far back as the early twentieth century, Errico Malatesta, responding to the concerns about cocaine in his era, concluded that we might be better off liberalising the trade in cocaine and using taxation to fund the treatment of those who develop dependency. Spanish anarchists in the 1930s had a far less *laissez-faire* attitude: in Barcelona following a defeat of Franco's rebels during the Spanish Civil War, local anarchists went down to the docks and murdered every pimp and drug dealer that they could find, throwing their bodies into the water (Beevor, 2001). On the other hand, Aldous Huxley, a supporter of the (anarcho-syndicalist) CNT during the Spanish Civil War, considered psychedelic drugs such as mescaline extremely valuable to the inner development and even asked for the substance on his deathbed.

French playwright Jean Genet held the view that criminals are not only engaged in crime but are also actively opposing the oppression by dominant value systems. Whilst this might seem to be a subject for philosophers, in the Drug War there is a great truth in this view. Drug users all across the world on a daily basis act against authoritarian laws and oppressive political structures simply by continuing to express their desire to get high. They express their agency over their own bodies even though it might be only in a negative sense. The thousands of young people who take Ecstasy every weekend all over the world are engaging effectively in weekly civil disobedience.

In an era of what Gore Vidal (2002) (quoting Charles Beard) calls the 'Perpetual War For Perpetual Peace', the complexities of addiction, of treatment, of State surveillance of our bodies and of international politics require more flexible and comprehensive analyses that look beyond our parochial boundaries and towards a more far-reaching meta-analysis. Left-wing libertarians need to take as much interest in the emerging debates around the Drug War as their Right-wing libertarian counterparts do because there is potential 'business' in this for both sides. Whilst Right-wing libertarians may generally not take much interest in drug debates once the issue of economic liberalisation has been con-sidered, we on the Left have the opportunity to demonstrate that there are far deeper concerns. It will come as no surprise to the reader to discover that the use of heroin is found disproportionately within deprived communities (Drugscope, 2002b). We may ask ourselves about why impoverished people are more likely to seek solace in opiates and super stimulants? We may also want to ask ourselves why we on the Left of the libertarian spectrum have tended to ignore the issue of drugs. Does this say something about our response to the issue of pleasure and desire that needs addressing?

Now we are moving into a new age that began with those awful events of September 2001, spawning the War on Terror. The two wars of metaphor have begun to coalesce and develop into a global conflagration without borders. The twin wars of metaphor have begun to merge together in Colombia, Afghanistan, Russia, on every Western street and in every school and in the very living room of every family. Soon conventional warfare will also add to the woes of the people of the world as nation states move towards conflict too. Stan Goff, a former Green Beret and Special Forces soldier for the US army, provides us with an illuminating insight into this spooky world where metaphor and real violence coincide. Goff, writing about US anti-drug operations during the 1980s and 1990s in South America compares them to Vietnam: 'Democracy wasn't a goal then. We were stopping communists. Drugs are a great rationale too. But with FARC we can have our drug war and our war against communists' (2001).

Observing the situation in Colombia, Goff concludes that the United States more often than not ends up in league with drug lords rather than fighting them. He explains that the war in Colombia is primarily a war against communist insurgents; drugs simply provide the excuse for the intervention and the opportunity to make lots of money that will never be scrutinised by any Senate committee. Wryly he observes the role of the CIA in the international drug trade and says of the former Drug Czar of the United States: 'It might make more sense for McCaffrey to find $1 billion dollars to declare war on the CIA' (2001). Now there's an idea!

Conclusion

All over the world disadvantaged people are subject to ever-more draconian measures in the name of 'the public good'. In Western nations, the most disadvantaged groups are subject to the most extreme forms of repression under the guise of the Drug War. The so-called underclass knows what it is to live under occupation just as their counterparts in Colombia and all over the so-called developing world do. They also know the degree of hypocrisy and corruption that is to be found consistently within the hall of mirrors that is the War on Drugs. This oppressed group forms a natural constituency for libertarian socialists and anarchists of every hue; principled action against the War on Drugs might well help to galvanise these groups and their constituencies.

The process of resistance has already begun in the United States where it is currently being led by the Drug Policy Alliance, an organisation that is supported by neoliberal backers. In that enormous nation, the sheer number of incarcerated Black and Hispanic people is now beginning to create the opportunity for political resistance towards the War on Drugs. During the Vietnam conflict, drug politics and antiwar protest merged, resulting in a creative and dynamic counter culture that provided an effective resistance to the dominant interests of the powerful élite. That movement was strongly influenced by Left-leaning libertarians who saw no distinction between their desire to consume proscribed drugs and their opposition to Uncle Sam's ongoing prosecution of an imperialistic war: it was all about freedom of self-expression and liberty, the most fundamental of American concepts. So far, Left-wing libertarians have not made much of an impact on the present-day Drug War debates and there has been little connection between the two wars of metaphor in the minds of Left-leaning libertarians. Stan Goff (2002) has coined the term 'Infinite War' to describe the present situation that is emerging since the fall of the twin towers that once dominated the Manhattan skyline. We can only hope that this Infinite War will in its turn spawn an equally active and effective resistance.

What are the dimensions of resistance that Left-wing libertarians should consider? Firstly, we should consider the new plague that afflicts our era and concentrate our efforts on the care and support of people who are infected with HIV. This is an international concern and libertarians must develop a transnational response to the virus. One important area of attention is the prevention of its spread amongst drug injectors; in this respect the urgent need is to establish needle exchanges and 'helping services' for drug injectors, particularly in nations where such agencies do not exist. Those young Americans and Russians who currently operate illegal needle exchanges are engaged in a political struggle that is vital.

Secondly, libertarians should engage with drug policy debates and should support reformist movements that aim to move away from repressive policies. Civil disobedience against such laws must be perceived as a just response to unjust laws.

Thirdly, libertarians should address the connections between drug laws and the disproportionate use of these laws against underprivileged communities. The racialist and oppressive nature of the Drug War is plain to see in the numbers of Black and Hispanic people who are currently incarcerated in the United States.

Fourthly, we should resist the international assault on human rights that the War on Drugs represents. The threat to the right to privacy and the principle of freedom of speech that the Drug War and its twin, the War on Terror, represent should be of great concern to all libertarians.

The Infinite War will be fought on many fronts and it should be resisted on every level.

Notes

1   This source and those on the following pages which relate to the UK Government Select Committee investigation into the effectiveness of drug policy can all be found www.parliament.the-stationery-office.co.uk/pa/cm200102/cmselect/cmhaff/318/1112708.htm.

2   UK Parliament (2002), found at www.publications.parliament.uk/pa/cm200102/cmselect/cmhaff/318/31806.htm#a18.

3   Memorandum 36 – submitted by Liberty and found at www.parliament.the-stationery-office.co.uk/pa/cm200102/cmselect/cmhaff/318/318m52.htm.

4   Links between the death penalty in China and the lucrative trade in organs have been well documented (Amnesty International, 1996). China's history of the oppression of drug users goes way back and as many as 50,000 drug users may have been killed during the Cultural Revolution. There are few willing to speak in defence of drug dealers who are commonly vilified as the scum of the earth.

In the eye of the beholder – child, mad or artist?

Introduction

In a climate of capitalist control, exercised through education, notions of normality, categorisation, economic structure, inequality and so on, resistance manifests itself in many guises. This discussion concerns the role of art and how artistic expression can challenge dominant constructions of reality; specifically those adhered to by two sometimes remarkably similar institutions, the mental hospital and the school. Within Western societies these institutions are characterised by a structure, function and ideology which is intended to 'educate' or 'cure' inmates, moving them from invalid categories of 'negative subject' into institutional ideas of 'normality' and the 'ideal subject'. Artistic expression is often encouraged in this socialisation process and this is professionally justified through models of 'art therapy', 'art education' and 'client-led' or collaborative art practices.

I propose that it is possible to create a further, anarchist,[1] model which is based on the 'validation' (rather than stigmatisation) of the (artistic) viewpoints of those individuals who are constructed as 'invalid' by the dominant definitions operating within these institutions. This 'validation' model owes something to the grassroots-based community arts movement in Britain during the 1960s and 1970s, which utilised different philosophies about the nature and purpose of 'art' in society. It also rests upon the now unfashionable radical psychiatric perspectives of R. D. Laing, Thomas Szasz and others, who perceived mental illness as being created by society rather than being the product of personal problems.

For the sake of brevity I refer to people who have been labelled as mentally ill as 'the mentally ill' and young people as 'children'. These are the 'categories' in which people may find themselves at certain times in their life course; they are not realms of being.

Shared ideology, structure and function

Radical feminists and anarchists have often argued that authoritarian structures begin at home with the nuclear family. The voice of authority to be obeyed originates within the family unit, and children learn to obey father, teacher, boss and god. My concern here, however, is with the similarities between the institutions of school and mental health. Schools serve as the gateways to the outside adult world, a place where children learn and become 'civilised', that is to say, culturally and socially adept. Schools deliver a complex network of control exercised through hierarchical, disciplinary and educational structures in an attempt to make children conform to adult ideas of 'ideal' or 'normal' person. The mental health system is a gateway through which one who has diverged from the 'normal' can enter 'ill' and re-emerge 'whole' or 'normal'. This is done with the aid of mind-altering drugs, electric shock treatment, isolation and other forms of physical coercion. Alternatively, a mental hospital may be the end of the line, the rubbish tip for those people who are seen as being permanently 'subnormal'.

Mental hospitals and schools share an ideology that there is a 'normal' 'grown-up' 'ideal' being that some people (because of immaturity, incorrect perceptions, 'illness' or lack of sufficient education) have not yet achieved. Children and mentally ill people question the authority of the system in that they question the authority of the State that defines 'normal' 'grown-up' behaviour. They assert an autonomy of action that threatens the State's authority over 'normality'. They are not seen as responsible (autonomous) beings that purposely oppose authority, but as ill, confused, uneducated or undeveloped. They are therefore put into programmes of rehabilitation or education.

> It is quite appropriate that moral philosophers should group together children and madmen as beings not fully responsible for their actions, for as madmen are thought to lack freedom of choice, so children do not yet possess the power of reason in a developed form. (Wolff, 1998: 12)

Institutional interventions aim to move subjects from undesirable 'negative subjects' to mature, normal 'positive ideal subjects'. Their function is to help people achieve the 'normality' goal, and therefore to fit in and function in 'normal/adult' society. This is achieved through 'education' in the form of classes and/or workshops and 'cure' in the form of drugs and therapies. The increasing overlap and interconnected relationship between the two institutions is significant in the shaping of beliefs and attitudes towards notions of normality and the ideal person.

Shared inmate status

The American sociologist Erving Goffman argued that 'there is a current psychiatric view that the ward system is a kind of social hothouse in which patients start as social infants and end up, within the year, on convalescent wards as resocialized adults' (1961: 150). Inmates of schools and mental hospitals also share a status. The work of Goode (1991) demonstrates how 'retarded' people, even though biologically adult, can still inhabit the category of child, in that they are considered to have never grown up. This also applies to people who have been labelled 'mentally ill': they are considered to be people who, because of their illness, have become like children. Both the mentally ill and children are seen as having inferior, undeveloped, childlike behaviour, often regarded as over-emotional and unable to control the release of emotional discharge.

Western normality encompasses stillness, quietness and politeness and it is 'normal' to be non-emotional (whether angry, excessively happy or excessively sad). The ideal adult person is also well-educated and well-mannered. Neither children nor the mentally ill generally have these attributes. Many people labelled as 'mentally ill' are originally sectioned for displaying disruptive, 'unacceptable' public behaviour; they often have the same chaotic liveliness as children. Children move a lot; they jump around and make a lot of noise; they skip down the street; children approach and befriend strangers, chatting to them on buses and trains; they rarely hide their feelings and openly express opinions about other people's appearance, moods, disabilities and the like. 'Mentally ill' people often show this same open friendliness or lack of inhibition. In a child it is seen as innocence in that 'they don't know any better', or 'they haven't learned yet'. In an adult, such behaviour is weird, mad, crazy, scary or ill. People exhibiting such behaviour inhabit a category of 'negative subject'. Negative subjects are people who have been invalidated, and this, according to David Cooper, is part of a wider and much more systematic process of exclusion that in some circumstances leads to marginalisation, segregation and even extermination (1967: 11).

Erving Goffman, R. D. Laing, Thomas Szasz and Cooper were all pioneers in the anti-psychiatry movement and the Philadelphia Association of the 1960s and 1970s, which aimed to deconstruct the notion of mental illness as personal problem and reposition it as a consequence of social exclusion. However, their theories and experiments somehow became a *cul de sac*, being never quite disproved but never developed either. Acceptance of their theories would have required a shifting in social and political thinking. By turning an analytical eye on the society that the individual inhabits rather than on individuals themselves, this would have threatened capitalism at its core. Accordingly, the models of mental health that have dominated have tended to be those that emphasise the biological as opposed to the social dimension. Although the work of Laing (1978) and Szasz (1974) continues to be popular amongst students, the mainstream medical psychiatry profession often regards them as heretics. Fortunately, writers in UK publications such as *Asylum* (founded in 1986),[2] and the literature of the radical psychology group, Psychology Politics Resistance (founded in 1994), as well as a few small coalitions of mental health professionals, continue to refer to these perspectives (see Coppock and Hopton, 2000: 88).

The marginalisation of children and the mentally ill entails economic, social and political restrictions and serves as a backdrop to the two institutional systems that house them. Since invalidated persons are economically and socially unproductive, this legitimises their status as property of the institutions; their rights to full legal citizenship is delegated to legitimate 'owners' (doctors, teachers, parents and guardians) who decide on their charges' behalf what is good for them. This reinforces and condones the mistreatment of them as it is done in the guise of upholding the harmony of the rest of the social system.

If the potential exists that you can become an economic producer, everything will be done to ensure that you do. If the reverse is true, 'you're not only going to find it difficult to survive, you will confront an attitude of questionability as to whether you should be allowed to' (Evans, 1994: 93).

Shared notions of cure/education and resistance/liberation

The same behavioural models and sanctions are also used to control both children's and mentally ill people's conduct. This can be seen through practices such as 'grounding', detention and isolation in separate rooms, wards or exclusive spaces for 'bad' behaviour, or the giving and taking away of 'privileges' such as free movement, belongings, cigarettes, sweets, etc. Both children and the mentally ill are required to explain themselves to a grown-up or a 'normal' person if they are thought to have acted inappropriately. They are monitored to see how well they conform to society's norms. Being subjected to periodical reviews and reports, their behaviour is plotted on charts, and they are continually assessed and tested, while their 'development' is reported to their families or those in charge of their affairs.

The restriction of the movement of children in schools is a form of what Merleau-Ponty (1962) terms 'embodied control'. In mental hospitals freedom of movement is also controlled. Doorways are significant; those who pass through them freely have a higher status. The doors to the staffroom are often shut; you are only allowed in if a staff member says so. Access to your own room is often controlled by staff, as is access to the kitchen and food. You need to gain permission to move around the institution as you do in school and are often not allowed to do so without an escort. Fences erected around mental hospitals are similar to those around schools and prisons.

Since the 1960s, mental health programmes have attempted to be more humane, whether through the use of psychiatric drugs or through an emphasis on helping clients and children to understand the consequences of their 'maladaptive behaviour'. Despite many institutions advocating client-specific treatment and respect for the individuality of clients, many of the same rationales persist. For instance, schools increasingly play a role in the 'new' psychiatric diagnosis of Attention Deficit Disorder and the use of psychiatric drugs such as Ritalin to 'cure' the 'problem' of lively, rebellious, resisting young people. In the mental health system education is on the increase, with inmates encouraged, coerced, threatened and sometimes blackmailed into taking part in rehabilitation activities where they are to 'learn' how to function in society as 'normal' people.

Due to similarities in structure and function of the institutions, shared forms of everyday resistance also emerge. Here a comparison with Scott's (1985) work on everyday forms of resistance by 'peasant' communities is useful. In order to be effective and avoid severe repercussions by landowners, resistance by peasant activists has often had to be low key and not adopt more 'visible' hierarchically organised opposition.[3] Inmates in schools and mental hospitals partake in everyday forms of resistance such as purposely spilling drinks, tipping up ashtrays, burning furniture, writing on walls, ignoring instructions from staff, sabotage and disruption of 'classes', intentional lateness, making noise and so on. As Fillingham argues, resistance is not perceived by the authorities as a political statement but as uncooperative behaviour: 'Only acceptance of the power system and its terms will get patients classified as normal, and thus earn their release' (1993: 147).

Such everyday resistance is common in schools and other institutions, but occasionally 'low-level' resistance increases in magnitude and organisation to achieve wider influence. We can gain a sense of excitement and justice from liberating stories such as *One flew over the cuckoo's nest* (Kesey, 2003) or the excerpt below:

> At a tiny Welsh school on September 5th [1911] a note calling for a strike was passed round from hand to hand. When the culprit was punished by the teacher all his classmates deserted the schoolroom and took to the streets in protest. The next day Liverpool's schools were hit by strikes, and then Manchester's. From there a fever spread as far south as Portsmouth, north to Glasgow and Leith; by mid-September at least 62 towns and cities were affected. Throughout the country children of all ages, some as young as three years, went on strike. In Dundee alone, 1500 children were involved. The demands included end to corporal punishment, extra holidays, shorter hours and payment for coming to school. Completely self-organised, with their own methods of communication, the children formed strike committees, picketed and demonstrated, attacked school buildings, and fought battles with strike-breakers and police. (Harper, 1987: 104)

Similarly, despite attempts in many parts of the British media to belittle their significance, thousands of well-informed, organised and determined young people walked out of their schools and colleges and took to the streets across the United Kingdom (and across the world) in March 2003 in protest at the US and UK governments' war in Iraq.

The role of the arts and the artist – legitimisation of the 'abnormal'

Many of the aforementioned distinctions between normal and invalid categories of behaviour can also be seen in established perceptions of 'art' and how it intersects with everyday life. Understanding how this happens is therefore important if we want to claim that art can provide an opportunity for liberation. This section looks at how art comes to be categorised in ways that sometimes *prevent* liberation.

Radical art movements, from Dada, the Surrealists to the Situationist International have constantly emphasised the need to integrate 'art' into everyday life, believing that this helps to realise a creative subjectivity. Part of this process, according to these movements, has been to challenge normative categories through different media. By invention and creativity, people have the ability to express things that do not fit into and/or challenge preconceived 'normative' categories. This may result in new reflections on their own circumstances with a view to presenting potential solutions to particular problems. Moreover, creativity can also provide more accessible *forms* of expression and communication than some 'normative' methods of artistic production. This can be important for people who are less 'educated' or less adept at the manipulation of language, media and 'high status' means, which is often the case with the mentally ill, children and working-class people. Creativity therefore often provides useful tools for resistance.

When I refer here to 'creativity', I refer to it in the sense of individual expression, in any form or style, and unjudged and unrestricted by the art establishment's yardstick used to legitimise 'proper' art.[4] This is also similar to the Symbolists of the nineteenth century who

> insisted that poets must be absolutely free to create and use their own forms. More importantly, the guiding principles must be the poet's own unique, subjective experience. Poetry is best created and understood by allowing the imagination total freedom of interpretation. (Harper, 1987: 70)

To return to the work of Szasz, we can see a legitimisation of the above argument in his analysis of language. He suggests that 'non-discursive languages do not lend themselves to translation into other idioms, least of all into discursive forms'. Creativity can stand for itself as an expression 'not necessarily one that yet has meaning' (Szasz, 1974: 130). He argues for a language that comes before verbal or 'conscious' language, calling this lower level of language 'protolanguage' (see also Moore, chapter 3, this volume). Protolanguage is the thing that exists before it is interpreted into verbal language, the thing that is not yet named: 'While it is evidently impossible to speak about something one does not know, it is possible to express, by means of protolanguage, something which is not clearly understood, explicitly known, or socially acknowledged' (Szasz, 1974: 113). Psychoanalysis may call this the unconscious.

Szasz argues that attempting to communicate with people with 'hysteria' or other 'mental illnesses' is similar to communicating with people speaking a different language. It is not a bodily disease that can be diagnosed and treated, but rather a linguistic misunderstanding. Therefore looking for a cause, treatment or cure is as nonsensical as looking for a cause, treatment or cure for someone speaking French. It may make sense in some circumstances for a French person to begin to speak English to make communication clearer, but this is about learning rather than 'cure'. Although Szasz regards this different language as 'valid', he does not suggest, however, that it may be as useful for the English-speaking person to learn French. It is automatically presumed that the patient, child or non-English speaker should learn the ways of the dominant party rather than the dominant party investigating the possibility of learning and understanding those of the subservient party. The use of art as a platform for communication requires each party to communicate using the same language and on a similar level, allowing for the fact that, like any form of communication, art also remains open to interpretation by both producer and consumer.

The mistake that is often made is that we try to 'interpret' art into a rational and linguistic form. Art may communicate something emotional and you may only be able to feel it in the same way that music can invoke feeling. Trying to understand it in terms of spoken, written or thinking terms cannot always work because the translation is either not possible or gets misinterpreted in the process. The young child who simply produces a drawing and presents it to the world is creating something anew. However, we often require the child to attach concrete meaning to it so that we can categorise it and, ultimately, restrict it, a point also noted by Clifford Harper in his discussion of the Dadaist movement:

> [it] sought to break the shackles . . . that prevent the creation or recognition of freedom in a mind too confused by the absurd contradictions of a modern world – a world where, for example, governments execute criminals for the 'crime' of murder but mutually engage in mass slaughter. Dada recognised that these shackles could be broken by allowing chance, irrationality and disorder to develop, and this would reveal the possibilities of a new world, which would itself be one of constant change, of no rules, of constant spontaneous, individual creativity – a world of Art. (1987: 126)

The person categorized as 'artist' is perceived differently from the 'non-artist'; their 'eccentricity' is celebrated rather than scorned. The 'artist' is allowed or expected to inhabit a space outside the realm of everyday 'normality' and thus the category 'artist' or 'art' enables 'abnormality' to exist in the 'normal' sphere, legitimised by the categories of weird, fantastical, confrontational. If one can identify or categorise oneself as 'artist' or partaking in artistic expression, this changes the diagnosis of madness or the label of 'uneducated' or 'child' and vice versa: it allows an eccentricity that would otherwise be categorised as 'mad', 'ignorant', 'immature' or 'abnormal'.

An extremely poignant example of this is one documented by mental health survivor (and now 'Mad Pride' activist) Mark Roberts (2000) about his experience working on London buses. He recounts how one day he decided that the number 69 bus should not stop at the poor working-class area of North Woolwich but instead should go into the middle class area of Chingford. After thirty people had boarded, he decided not to stop at any other bus stops but to simply take the passengers (who were mostly on their way to work) straight to Epping Forest just to the north of London. He had noticed how mundane, drab and monotonous the journey to work and process of the working week had become for these people and decided to do something radical to change it. In effect, this amounted to 'kidnapping' thirty passengers. However, if this had been done in the name of art he still may have been questioned or even charged for doing it, but it would have been a sensational piece of performance/public art work that would have projected his career straight into the limelight; a similar case might have existed had it been done for a sensationalist 'reality TV' programme as a sociological joke. Unfortunately, Mark Roberts had a history of mental illness, which meant he was immediately charged with kidnapping; he was sectioned and locked into an institution to be treated with a number of damaging psychiatric interventions. His heroic (although it could be argued misguided) act of liberation for people whom he regarded as trapped in an 'insane' world of capitalism was swept under the carpet as a shameful and embarrassing episode carried out by a sick and pitiful man.

Under 'artistic licence', this incident could be categorised as a valid statement; without this legitimacy, it becomes invalid behavior. Calling actions 'art' can liberate and validate their creator's actions. The same potential for validation exists for children. A child is often seen as daft, stupid, naïve, ignorant, silly, loopy and so on for behaviour that is outside the normal adult ideal. It is harder for children to masquerade as 'normal' in the same way that a 'mad' adult can because their size exposes them; their 'invalid' status is more visible. Young people's opinions, creations, inventions and ideas are often disregarded as 'they lack knowledge' or 'they have too vivid an imagination' in the same way that mentally ill people's are called delusions. A young person thinking they can fly is put down to lack of knowledge of gravity whereas an adult discussing astral projection or a science fiction writer's character defying gravity is categorised as 'scientific phenomena' or 'creativity'. The child's status or the mentally ill person's status warrants their ideas as 'invalid', often without prior consideration.

However, children can and have covertly taken part in adult/normal discourse through art. There have been art projects designed specifically to do this by providing young people with a platform and media that cannot be recognised as having been produced by a child.

The Kidspace/SEEK and TELL Project in 1997 at Tidemill school, Deptford, South London involved sixteen 10 to 11-year-olds using photography to represent the world of childhood. Taking cameras into their homes and street-lives they photographed whatever was interesting and important to them. Their work was exhibited in the SEEK and TELL exhibition, an international exhibition including adult artists' work on the theme of childhood at the APT Gallery in Deptford. Due to the medium of photography and combination of work, it was difficult, if not impossible, to know which work was by an adult and which was by a child. The work therefore was viewed and valued from an equal standpoint of validity and importance. This, however, did not hold true for the catalogue, as artists wrote a statement to go alongside their work, thus exposing their age because of the difference in the written language they used.

The three models of art in institutions – and a fourth one

The aforementioned relationships between official definitions about the perceptions of art and reality are also evident in models used by professionals in existing mental health and educational institutions. These also suffer from many of
the weaknesses that I have already identified. Firstly, the so-called 'Arts Therapy'
model, is a medicalised perspective which sees arts practices as a form of diagnosis and 'cure' for the assumed pathologies of mental illness. A second model
is that of 'Arts Education' whereby the (visiting) artist is seen as a teacher helping
participants to 'develop' to a higher stage of competence and achievement
(within certain parameters). A third, and potentially more useful one is that
referred to as the 'Collaboration' or 'Client-led' model where there is a degree of
acceptance of the legitimacy of the perspective of the person identified as a
'problem'. This is related to my own work which tries to go beyond these definitions and find ways to re-validate those people who have been defined as 'invalid'
by particular institutions. I have termed this fourth perspective the 'Validation
Model', which has, I believe, considerable potential to change our way of relating to art and to mental health issues. However, in order to understand where
this model might fit into the above schemata, it is important to understand the
theory and practice of the original UK community arts movement whose work
can be related to anarchism.

The community arts movement

During the early 1960s and 1970s, a new form of arts was developing which was
termed 'community arts'. In Britain, the Association of Community Artists
(ACA) was founded by Bruce Birchall, Martin Goodrich and Maggie Pinhorn in
1971 and it became the recognised body that 'spoke' for community artists. The
ACA's main aim was to oppose the system of arts funding that they saw as élitist
and exclusive to 'high art'. In response to this movement and because of an
increasing number of applications for funding from community artists, the Arts
Council set up a 'Community Arts Working Party' in 1973, chaired by Professor
Harold Baldry, the objective being to determine whether 'community arts' was
distinguishable as a category and whether the Arts Council would support it.
The results of this research (The Baldry Report) prompted the legitimisation of
'community arts'.

> Community artists are distinguishable not by the techniques they use . . . but by
> their attitude towards the place of their activities in the life of society. Their
> primary concern is their impact on a community and their relationship with it: by
> assisting those with whom they make contact to become more aware of their situ-
> ation and of their own creative powers, and by providing them with the facilities
> they need to make use of their abilities, they hope to widen and deepen the sen-
> sibilities of the community in which they work and so to enrich its existence. To a
> varying degree they see this as a means of change, whether psychological, social or

political, within the community . . . [They] differ from practitioners of the more established arts in that they are chiefly concerned with a process rather than a finished product; a many-sided process including craft, sport, etc., in which the 'artistic' element is variable and often not clearly distinguishable from the rest. (Arts Council of Great Britain, 1974: 7)

Although community artists may object to this definition of themselves as people who want to 'increase awareness', it had an impact of legitimacy within the art world, albeit a distorted one of 'lower class' art.

'Community arts' was a movement in its own right before this 'legitimisation' by 'the Establishment'. Unfortunately, a theoretical framework for community arts practice was never developed, causing it to be somewhat disjointed and open to misinterpretation. In 1984, Kelly attempted to provide such a framework:

Community arts were woven, then, from three separate strands. Firstly there was the passionate interest in creating new and liberatory form of expression, which the Arts Labs both served and fuelled. Secondly there was the movement by groups of fine artists out of the galleries and into the streets. Thirdly there was the emergence of a new kind of political activist who believed that creativity was an essential tool in any kind of radical struggle. (at p. 11)

The community arts emphasis might have been on deprivation – financial, cultural, environmental or educational – but much of this was lost in the subsequent scramble by the artists to make money from their individual enterprises. The steady impact of the previously aloof 'fine art' community also had an effect, as funding originally intended for community artists tended to be diluted by these more prestigious 'professional artists'. Thus community artists advocating social change become supplanted by 'artists working in the community'.

Between the 1970s and 1990s, outreach projects from museums, galleries and various other institutions developed upon the initiatives of community artists. In the 1990 report *Arts and communities: the report of the national inquiry into arts and the community* by the Community Development Foundation (CDF) it was stated that, due to the expansion of community arts, it was no longer appropriate to call it community arts and it would have to be renamed 'Arts in the Community'. The CDF make this distinction clear:

Arts in the Community means those arts which emanate from or are created to serve people in a particular locality or community of interest. Thus it includes both community arts and other streams of development, such as: independent arts initiatives by local residents; arts in adult education; outreach work by professional companies; the arts aspects of social and religious life; the arts of cultural minorities; initiatives by arts entrepreneurs; arts initiatives by public authorities, including health, education, social services, prisons. (CDF, 1992: 87)

With the development of 'Arts in the Community', community arts has become institutionalised, controlled via funding organisations, government, arts boards, local authorities, health authorities, business sponsors, trusts, foundations, social organisations. There is also a rapidly expanding network of community arts organisations who are affiliated to and restricted by these same funding bodies and attached legalities. It is becoming increasingly difficult for individual community artists to gain funding for projects due to sponsors requiring that funding be managed by an arts organisation. Control is therefore moving from the hands of the artists as individual collaborating practitioners into the hands of the managerial committees of arts organisations. These committees are often made up of directors, managers and administrative staff who do not actually practise in the community themselves and so are often divorced from the needs and wants of the actual individuals within a community. They are kept busy justifying outputs in terms of numbers and product to their funders so as to keep any sort of arts in the community alive and of course to protect their own jobs. Unfortunately it often leads to them working in direct conflict to the process and humanistic base of 'community arts'.

In these processes the issue of class is never far from the surface. It seems no coincidence therefore that 'fine artists' are usually middle-class, coming from the academic positions operating from 'top down', whereas community artists were/ are usually working-class activists working from the 'bottom up':

> The institutions of the art world are built upon and are riddled with class bigotry, a prejudice often reciprocated. This duality becomes a situation of dominance and subordination where those in power can materially validate certain art forms according to subsidy whilst devaluing others . . . It has been easy for art world supremacists to dismiss whole areas of practice as 'social art' – seen as decoration, community work, art therapy or play. That it is not considered equal to those other 'proper' art forms which cater to a minority of tastes and to which the majority of funding goes, deflects any challenges to the mainstream. (Dickson, 1995: 11)

This is the fundamental problem with art as education in the community or in education projects. Non-dominant categories of people (be they the socially excluded poor, the mentally ill or children) are to be educated in the aesthetics and art etiquette or the history and culture of the 'Fine Arts': the 'community' is to be educated and enlightened in the arts of the élite.

However, Nicholas Lowe, a community artist, talks about work he did in partnership with another community artist, Alan McLean:

> We had both been collaborating with individuals who had no formal arts training. We had both understood that the changes our collaborators were going through were enhanced with an increase in their self-esteem. Also their developing practical understanding of our working processes meant they had begun to show their potential as autonomous visual artists. It was clear from this point that our work was not simply a matter of education but that it had as much to do with approaching our collaborators as equal human beings with valuable skills and experience to offer. (cited in Dickson, 1995: 85)

The original aims of the community arts movement have become lost as other imperatives have taken over: dependence on state funding grew, community artists learned to fit their projects into the funding applications, highlighting the funders' aims and glossing over their own. As there was no real framework to look at, subsequent community artists used these proposals, reports and documents as examples of community art, with the result that the initial impetus of social change became lost. Community arts became defined by the funding agencies. The activism of community art changed into helping disadvantaged people to become enlightened about 'proper' art taught by people who were experts in it. This process of institutionalisation of community arts has continued to grow, with an increasing number of universities developing modules and courses in 'community arts'.

The failure of 'community arts' as a radical movement could be said to be due to never having a theoretical framework or analysis with which to measure itself. Even so, the impact of community arts that many artists still desire is one of social change and they are debating what role they play. I hope that this movement develops a theoretical framework that defines different practices within the community (such as education, therapy, collaboration, facilitation, and validation) so that community art can reemerge as a movement for social change. The Validation Model outlined in this chapter attempts to do this.

The Validation Model

The Validation Model of arts education encourages a 'stepping out' of preconceived positions, a process which, whilst occurring at institutional sites, is in conflict with their tendential roles in producing 'ideal selves' through 'cure' and 'educational development'. The role of the artist in the Validation Model is not to 'teach' art or to analyse somebody's 'illness' but to inspire and encourage people to express their own inherent creativity. This also serves to educate staff and outsiders about the opinions, ideas, lives, interests and criticisms of the client group, thus inverting the 'top-down' process of 'education' and the perceptions of 'illness', 'cure' and 'normality'. It makes the arts education process one of shared experience and shared learning. Part of experiencing the art of 'outsiders' (such as that of children and the mentally ill) requires a letting-go of the idea that there is a right or 'normal' way of being.

I propose that, through such processes, creativity itself can become a neutral space, an antidote, an inverted space filled with obscured or non-existent normality; its function can be to cancel and suck out preconceived ideas of what we are. Arts practices can thus function in a deconstructive and liberating way, breaking down narrow prescriptions and challenging received and categorical ideas about what people are or should be.

The Validation Model, by focusing on the inmates of institutions, does go towards validating them. However, the model is limited due to the restriction of the category that they continue to inhabit. Real Validation may only begin when we turn the focus from the 'ill' or the 'child' as invalidated beings in need of help to the 'confused' society that excludes them. This means encouraging people to step out of their preconceived positions, widen their perspectives, deconstruct restrictive categories, allow statements, or expressions or *validations* of what we all are in our own terms, rather than as staging posts in a journey mapped out for us by other (expert) people.

Conclusion

I have suggested that institutions play a significant part in the constitution of self and others through shared notions of normality and ideal person, with particular reference to institutions for the 'mentally ill' and schools. (Re)categorisation of 'art' and 'artists' can legitimise the breakdown of restrictive and negative categories and, in the process, go towards validating if not the person, certainly the work and expressions of the artist who has been invalidated as 'mentally ill' or 'child'.

The activities and ambitions of the community arts movement in Britain in the 1960s and 1970s up to the present day provided us with an important lesson for developing genuinely liberatory arts practices, as well as lessons in the dangers of institutionalisation, or removal, of projects committed to social change.

Such processes of control also exist in social scientific attempts to translate children's and mentally ill people's perceptions into their own analytic categories of 'other' or 'outsider' rather than trying to understand these different perspectives. Instead of trying to understand the opinions of 'invalidated' persons from the 'valid' person's perspectives and communicating through 'valid' media, 'validated' persons must learn to look at and experience the world through the eyes of the 'invalid', through media that reduce misinterpretation by their immediacy and accessibility to both parties.

Children partake in the production of art and creativity throughout their daily lives. As 'sane' 'normal' 'adults', we have often simply forgotten how to recognise it and so we forget the importance of such things as listening to music, dancing down the street, climbing trees, staring at clouds, whistling with grass, picking scabs and popping tar bubbles with our toes. I propose that art has the potential to enable children and the mentally ill to express and communicate their experiences, whilst validating their perceptions on their own terms; it can also remind us of what we have forgotten in the process of becoming 'normal' 'adults'.

Notes

1 It is only with some qualification that I place my own political position within this milieu, but do so because I feel that my attitude towards authority, self-responsibility and autonomy warrants the broad label 'anarchist'.
2 *Editorial note*: this publication now has a website: www.asylumonline.net/about.htm.

3   By 'peasant', Scott refers to people of 'lower class status', presumably of rural origin; again this is not a realm of being.
4   See Willis's chapter entitled 'Grounded aesthetics' in Willis (1990).

Part III

Being

One of the ongoing attractions of anarchism is that it constantly raises questions about the nature of being in ways often sidelined or suppressed by other political perspectives. Why do people rebel against authority? Why do they also feel compelled to offer alternative solutions to collective problems through co-operation? How interrelated or separate are humans from nature, as well as from very different human cultures? To what extent are technological systems creating new forms of identity which are not necessarily liberatory? How can one develop more 'spiritual' aspects of oneself without succumbing to forms of oppression such as organised religion or personality cults? Such questions have led anarchists into many different directions, embracing existentialism, Taoism, paganism to extreme forms of isolationism and even hedonism. Yet, for most, the process of being in the world is inextricably linked to that of *becoming* and linked to questions of strategy developed in the previous section of the book. Moreover, the question of being must be part of a holistic and integrated critique.

The contributions in this section each address notions of being and becoming within different areas of anarchist theory and practice. Indeed, it is the ontological dimension of contemporary anarchism – especially the placing of Self within a wider ecology of global relations, human and non-human – which distinguishes anarchism from radical perspectives that retain too much focus on materialism and political economy. The fact that anarchism has largely premised its critique on a psychological dimension to power relations, not just a material one, has been an advantage in this respect. Ecological anarchism, which has been the driving force behind much contemporary anarchist theory and practice, has been committed to thinking about the relationships between people and 'nature' in new ways and this is evident in the chapters by Karen Goaman (chapter 9) and Bronislaw Szerszynski and Emma Tomalin (chapter 11).

In recent years, the political perspective of anarcho-primitivism has gained considerable appeal and notoriety for taking anarchist theory into areas of anthropology and trying to ask challenging questions about the nature of 'civilisation' by examining the 'deep past' and the roots of humanity. In this respect,

Goaman's contribution here complements arguments made by Steve Millett earlier (chapter 4) in his treatment of the anti-technological critique offered by the *Fifth Estate* collective. Goaman's focus in chapter 9 is a practical application of many of those ideas, examining contemporary protests against globalisation and suggesting that we can learn more than just lessons in solidarity from the ongoing alliances with the rural and land movements of the global South. We can, she suggests, use this as an opportunity to rethink our relationship with nature.

At the heart of this argument, and indeed at the heart of much of ecological anarchist thinking, is the problem of alienation. As the global ecological crisis has deepened, so commentators have tried to address the psychological as well as the practical impact that intensifying forms of global consumption are having. Whilst Goaman offers some practical suggestions to address these forms of alienation, Szerszynski and Tomalin in chapter 11 discuss some of the psychological strategies taken by political activists to cope with the burdens which contemporary Western societies bestow upon the individual. Their discussion of how activists involved in direct action protest utilise discourses of nature and spirituality as 'resources' to try to forge a more 'holistic' sense of Self is important in a number of respects. Firstly, it shows the complex nature of social movement culture, particularly the kind of affective dimensions that theorists frequently ignore. Secondly and relatedly, it counters the charge sometimes made by more 'traditional' anarchists that anarchism has 'regressed' into solipsism and hedonism. Clearly one cannot 'read' these forms of spiritual anarchism as evidence of this; rather they act as forms of empowerment, or as these authors call it, 'enchantment'. As Szerszynski and Tomalin themselves point out, anarchism has always entertained something of this spiritual dimension, as evidenced by the history of millenarianism, with which it shares a lot of common ground.

Chapters 9 and 11 also include material on the importance of the symbolic in contemporary anarchist practice. Given the global audience in front of whom the actions described by Goaman and Szerszynski and Tomalin are taking place, the symbolic economy is becoming increasingly crucial. This applies in terms of contesting particular spaces, subverting dominant imagery and, crucially, it is a significant aspect in the process of personal transformation. Here the symbolic terrain also is concerned with the global Other, the collective manifestation of those groups crushed by the processes of globalisation and with whom many of the Western activists discussed in this book try to identify. Being able to embrace difference is an important part of contemporary anarchist identity, in that there are numerous grounds for unity of purpose, but the diversity of the struggles and their respective contexts require considerable sensitivity.

The old ecological anarchist maxim of unity through diversity is also pertinent to David Gribble's examination (in chapter 10) of the endurance of anarchist ideals in education throughout the world. He takes up many of the points developed in Joanna Gore's chapter earlier in the book (chapter 8), demonstrating how libertarian education requires a different ontology, one that moves away from instrumental views on learning and how it is formalised. All of the institutional boundaries between art and life, child and adult, expert and novice, work and play that conventional education is predicated upon are challenged, sometimes even dissolved, within the bounds of libertarian education. Gribble's work (see also 1998) is also an important refutation of the charge that the ideals of libertarian education are somehow the preserve of privileged Westerners. Clearly the fact that different permutations of the ideals of pioneers like Ferrer have occurred in such diverse contexts raises important questions about the anarchist psyche as well as ongoing debates about the ecological basis of ethics (Light, 1998).

The anarchist travelling circus: reflections on contemporary anarchism, anti-capitalism and the international scene

Introduction

The phrase 'anarchist travelling circus' was uttered in stern tones by Tony Blair, as, after the European Union summit in Gothenburg, Sweden, in June 2001, he condemned the protests that have converged on every significant such gathering over the last few years. The unintentional note of joyfulness, play and spontaneity captured by this phrase was quickly recuperated by the movement itself, appearing on a banner, and reproduced for May Day 2002 in London. Here the May Day Collective called for an Anarchist Travelling Circus strand, a 'mobile, spontaneous and collective performance, reclaiming the roots and culture of mayday!' For future economic summits, more extensive itineraries, linking many cities and countries, are planned.

The echoes of play and pleasure evoked by the notion of the 'anarchist travelling circus' connect to the following discussion on the power of the symbolic to expose the hollowness of everyday capitalist existence by appropriating the spaces of power. The highly visible expressions of the Anarchist Travelling Circus at economic summits and beyond are analysed in terms of their significance in allowing a central drama to unfold; as examples of 'modern pilgrimages' with the capacity to defamiliarise the familiar; and as examples of an unlicensed carnival by inversion. Anarchism is a central characteristic of the 'anti-capitalist/anti-globalisation' movement, though much of the mainstream Left has had trouble acknowledging this. Another central feature of the anti-capitalist movement is the significance of grassroots movements of the global South, which have provided much of the inspiration for the movement, and with which networking and support are exchanged. The rural and 'peasant' dimensions of anarchist history and practice are often overlooked.

There is now a strand of anarchism which, as well as criticising hierarchy, capitalism and the State also opposes industrialisation, modernisation and the impact of technology. This strand is strongest, ironically, in the United States, expressed most coherently by theorists such as John Zerzan (1994, 1999) and the writers of the periodical *Fifth Estate* such as David Watson (1996, 1999). This strand is growing in importance in the anarchist movement, and looks to the lives of people living in small-scale societies, including primitive and rural village/peasant societies, to learn how to reclaim autonomous ways of life with a low impact on the earth. A crucial aspect of this anti-technological and anti-civilisational critique is the need to reclaim a relationship with the land and local economies, not only in the global South as a means of alleviating poverty, but also in the global North, as a means of alleviating alienation, pollution and misery.

After 11 September 2001 (or '9/11', to use the almost universally adopted American phrase), the anti-capitalist movement was declared dead by the mainstream. In reality, repressive bills had already begun to criminalise the movement and stifle dissent by intimidation well before 11 September 2001. This chapter considers the impact of the changing political scene in the last few years, and notes the way in which anarchism has come into its own in confronting the intensified alliances between states, corporate power and the military.

The anarchist travelling circus: summit hopping

Many mainstream commentators expressed consternation at the unexpectedness of the demonstrations against the World Trade Organisation (WTO) in Seattle in November 1999, at which protesters succeeded in derailing the conference talks despite being met by riot police and tear gas.[1] Journalists scrabbled to find out who were the people who had converged in such numbers ('Who are these guys anyway?' asked The Times in London). A distinction was quickly made between 'peaceful protesters' and the apparently more 'violent' anarchists. As anyone who has watched even mainstream news footage of the summit demonstrations will know, those engaged in property damage (construed as violence) did so with a variety of insignia – Maoist, communist and anarchist, for example.

The reality is that those who call themselves anarchists organise and participate in all sections of these summit demonstrations. This is a continuation of anarchist presence in many of the most visible struggles of our times, from the Anti-Poll Tax campaign in the United Kingdom in 1990 to the radical environmental protest scene of the 1990s. The difference with the anti-capitalist/anti-globalisation movement (I use the terms interchangeably here) is that the overwhelming ethos of summit demonstrations is the commitment to non-hierarchical organisation, and also to direct action, which goes beyond such orthodox protest forms as letters, petitions and rallies. This is anarchism in action, and many of those peaceful protesters who do not explicitly think of themselves as anarchists are nonetheless enacting the spirit and principles of anarchism.

Stalwarts of the Left have not easily acknowledged this overwhelming imprint of anarchism on the anti-globalisation movement. This was underlined by an American anthropologist, David Graeber, writing in the Marxist journal New Left Review. Graeber, a professor at Yale University and a founder of the Anti-Capitalist Convergence, notes the gulf between participants of the emerging movement and the old theorists of the Left who have for years been writing about 'vast social movements that do not in fact exist' (Graeber, 2002: 61). Such theorists find themselves confused or dismissive now that real movements are everywhere emerging. Graeber sees such theorists as either more liberal than they want to admit, or not entirely happy about having to accept that most of the creative energy for radical politics is now coming from anarchism – a tradition that they have hitherto mostly dismissed – and that taking this movement seriously will necessarily also mean a respectful engagement with it (Graeber, 2002: 61–2).

Graeber sees anarchism as 'the heart of the movement, its soul' (p. 62). He counters those critics who criticise the anti-globalisation movement for its lack of any central theme or coherent ideology. For him, the 'ideology' that connects those involved *is* the notion of reinventing democracy and daily life, with new forms of decentralised, non-hierarchical organisation. Graeber defines the anti-globalisation movement as a movement for global justice and against neoliberalism and corporate globalisation and he cites the following declaration by Subcomandante Marcos on behalf of the Zapatista movement: '"Let it be a network of voices that resist the war Power wages on them. A network of voices that not only speak, but also struggle and resist for humanity and against neo-liberalism"' (Graeber, 2002: 63).

Selected highlights and raised stakes

I turn now at the highlights of the main summit events, and changes in the use of space in the last few years. This introduces the symbolic and direct action involved, and the way in which the stakes are raised at each event, as numbers grow and police repression intensifies.

Seattle, United States, November 1999

Tens of thousands of people converge to demonstrate against the WTO. There are 200 activists dressed as green-blue-black sea turtles, marching beneath a huge inflatable turtle. Others are dressed as business tycoons on stilts, alongside monarch butterflies, vegetables, fish and pigs. Drummers beat out the rhythms of resistance in what was to become a significant element in major summit protests. Messages on banners and placards highlight the diversity of those present, with radical environmental groups alongside indigenous rights groups and so on (Slyk, 2002: 56).

The Direct Action Network has co-ordinated nonviolent direct action by ten thousand people to stop delegates entering the convention centre. The delegates to the conference are significantly outnumbered and those caught on video (*RIP WTO*, 2000) look confused, as though for the first time having their power challenged and their legitimacy stripped away.

The protests succeed in winding up the conference early. The world, through the media, sees people voice their concerns about globalisation, and sees the 'Robocop'-style riot police attempt to crush them.

Prague, Czech Republic, September 2000

The conference centre where the World Bank and International Monetary Fund are meeting is heavily sealed off. The demonstration organises itself in different sections, identified by colours denoting the different tactics. For example, the Yellow section consists mainly of the Italian Tute Bianche and the Pink and Silver section consists of a samba band, then recently formed in London, with dancers and people mainly from Britain's Earth First! and Reclaim the Streets network. One participant describes the Pink and Silver section as 'like marching along the streets with the contents of your local nightclub crossed with *It's a Knockout* and an anarcho version of *Dad's Army*' (*Do or Die*, 2000: 12).[2]

Attempts to push through police lines to reach the conference are met with police repression and arrests (although some demonstrators are successfully 'de-arrested' by fellow activists). The Pink and Silver section finds an entrance to the conference centre guarded only by a few ordinary police who temporarily retreat as pink fairies flash wands and feather dusters at them. Moments later the police lash out with truncheons (*Channel 4 News*, 26 September 2000).

Gothenburg, Sweden, June 2001

The year 2001 sees escalations in summit protests, numbers of protesters and police repression. At the European Union summit in Gothenburg, police surround a school that, by agreement with authorities, is to be used as a convergence centre for protesters. Police refuse to let people out.

On the following day, thousands of protesters attempt to reach the EU conference centre down a narrow street. Police attack with dogs and horses. The tone then is set for the demonstration, with mounting anger in some of the protests. Police seem out of control, using live ammunition and shooting three protesters. The 19-year-old son of a member of Doctors against Nuclear Weapons is shot in the back while standing alone, many metres from police, from whom he was turning away. He fights for his life, recovering after losing a kidney and his spleen. Protesters charged with violence are given prison sentences of up to five years whereas, prior to the anti-globalisation protests, sentences averaged one month.

Demonstrators never get near the conference centre.

Genoa, Italy, July 2001

Three hundred thousand demonstrators converge for the 'G8' (Group of Eight most economically developed nations) summit. A thirty-foot high fence is erected around a large zone surrounding the conference centre. Attempts to get near the fence are met with police water cannon.

Protests around the city are met with the worst police brutality for many years. Hundreds of protesters are truncheoned by police, with the resulting head wounds caught on video by activists for the Indymedia group. There is footage of lone protesters, despite their pleas and cries, being mercilessly beaten by police. One protester, Carlo Giuliani, the 23-year old son of a trade union official, is shot dead.

In all this, amidst intense tear gas from canisters fired by police, the different sections attempt to carry on with their chosen themes, from the Pink and Silver carnivalesque to the hundreds of Tute Bianche with their white overalls, padding and makeshift armour.

Post-11 September and anti-capitalism

After 11 September 2001, and the severe repression of civil liberties, the media declares the movement dead. Nonetheless, a demonstration in January in Washington DC, at the World Economic Forum summit, attracts 30,000 people. This is in spite of media hysteria and demonisation of the protests in the run-up to it.

A European Union summit in Barcelona on 17 March 2002 sees a resurgence of demonstrators, mainly local people, numbering 300,000, despite the number of protesters, for example from Portugal, stopped at the border in a severe clampdown. The conference centre, well outside the city, is sealed off.

In June 2002, the G8 summit is held in a venue chosen for its isolation and impenetrability – in the wilderness area of Kananaskis, near Calgary, Alberta, Canada. This is as inaccessible as Doho in Qatar, chosen for the WTO conference the previous November.

In order to hold their meetings and further the agenda of globalisation, the holders of power have had to retreat further and further away from city centres into more and more inaccessible and fortified places behind higher and higher fences.

Interpreting summit demonstrations

These summit demonstrations can be usefully analysed by drawing on the works of the American anarchist, feminist and witch Starhawk and the American theologian Butigan.

Starhawk sees summit demonstrations as allowing a central drama to unfold which provides a key 'teachable' moment to emerge. As the author of numerous books on anarchism, spirituality and magic,[3] she sees the summit demonstrations, of which she has been a prominent participant, as providing a moment of learning, of breaking through apathy. While local struggles are important, she argues, their gains can be erased in a moment by the WTO, World Bank, IMF, G8 'and all their alphabet-soup brethren'. She maintains that the places where the system can be challenged as a whole are the summit meetings of the élite, where protesters can also build alliances that can strengthen their work (Starhawk, 2002a).

In Starhawk's view, the summit actions create mass moments, where the shell of apathy that normally makes people resistant to news can be cracked. The drama, excitement and urgency of such actions draws attention and wakes people up. Without a central drama going on somewhere in the world, she argues, decentralised local protests draw only the faithful, and their impact can be magnified when a large action is taking place, concentrating media and global attention.

Butigan frames anti-globalisation demonstrations in terms of modern pilgrimages, which allow the familiar to be 'defamiliarised', exposing the brutality behind the juggernaut of globalisation. He refers to the Seattle events as a 'pilgrimage of transformation' – with pilgrimage as a process by which humans mobilise themselves in loving and relentless resistance, a process of 'bearing witness' to injustices and woundedness (Butigan, 2000: 46).

Butigan puts Seattle in a line of twentieth-century modern pilgrimages, from Gandhi's 1930 march to the sea to challenge the British monopoly on salt to Martin Luther King's 1965 pilgrimage to demand voting rights for African Americans. When tens of thousands of people journeyed to Seattle to protest against the injustice of the WTO, these modern pilgrims were drawn to

> a place that momentarily intersected with history and challenged its crushing inevitability. The urgency of this journey came from a deep intuition that the great web of violence in which we are caught today is run by large economic and political forces, and that the instructions for this 'web design' were about to be codified in a very few short days. (Butigan, 2000: 46)

He argues that the concerns of these 'modern pilgrims' go beyond the political and are deeply cultural and profoundly spiritual: those travelling to Seattle also came to reclaim lost parts of themselves and to affirm the sacredness of the earth and the integrity of the earth and indigenous peoples. The events in Seattle, he argues:

> broke the spell of the inevitability and unquestioned authority of global capital, and this in turn has laid the groundwork for a process of social and cultural transformation which has the potential to make the world more just, more ecologically sensitive, and ultimately a more peaceful place. (at p. 47)

The role of the symbolic: symbolic spaces and symbolic opposition

The insights of Starhawk and Butigan are also useful for understanding the power of the symbolic in this process of defamiliarisation.

The holders of power exploit, to a large extent unconsciously, symbolic forms in order to create, reinforce and legitimate particular systems. This is primarily achieved through the control of space, and it is how these spaces are contested – both materially and symbolically – that makes the anti-capitalist movement such a powerful force.

It is important to remember that our daily experience of space is one saturated with capitalist social relations and premised on an exploitative relationship with the natural world. Many of us live in residential streets built when the railways allowed the suburbs to expand, enabling people to work further from home in urban environments designed to facilitate manufacture, business and trade. The concentration of capital in our city centres reflects a planning system that is more devoted to the speedy movement of goods and workers than to the health and survival of local communities. It is easy to forget that for tens of thousands of years of our existence as *Homo sapiens* we had the right to land, food, water, shelter, culture and community, simply by being born into that community. Bit by bit, the history of complex and State society has seen the removal of this autonomy. We now work to pay for all the basic constituents of our lives, and for those distractions (consumerism, entertainment) that rush in to fill the gaps left by capitalism's rapid erosion of vital elements to our well-being – including a relationship with nature and the environment. We find ourselves in these built-up urban spaces or deserted agricultural monocultures, alienated from each other and the natural world which has been sanitised or concreted over.

This is the visible world we inhabit, and it is the 'defamiliarisation' and breaking open of these routinised ways of life which is so significant about contemporary protest strategies. One way of looking at these processes is through the symbolic challenges that took place on May Day in London during the years 2000 to 2002.

May Days in London

The theme of May Day 2000 is 'Guerilla Gardening'. The aim is to plant seeds and plants anywhere and everywhere, but most people aim for one convergence point on the grass of Parliament Square, a patch of grass normally hemmed in by traffic and by vast buildings, and transform it into a muddy garden with plants and a pond. The police have soaked the grass beforehand to make it muddy and difficult, hampering gardening efforts. The police squeeze people into one place, tempers begin to flare and a McDonald's becomes the scene of 'hamburger liberation'.

In what was to become a famous piece of *détournement* by turf, the statue of Winston Churchill is given a punk mohican hairstyle made out of grass. A moment of inversion is created in turf. Churchill, Britain's leader through World War II, and responsible for the deaths of many thousands of German civilians in what many see as the unnecessary bombing raids on Dresden and other German cities, is transformed into a punk – the inversion of authority figure to rebel, powerful to powerless. The image lives on, used by anarchists on flyers and other literature (e.g. on the flyer for the Anarchist Book Fair in London, October 2000, with the caption 'His finest hour').

For 2001, the theme is May Day Monopoly, using the boardgame as inspiration. The idea is to converge on Oxford Street, London's famous central shopping area. Expression is curtailed when police round demonstrators into a 'Section 60', a method increasingly used to contain protests, whereby police lines surround demonstrators and detain them. Demonstrators are trapped in Oxford Circus for hours without water, food, toilets or shelter from the rain. Symbolic action is thus limited elsewhere to smaller convergences, such as Critical Mass cyclists who take over certain roads, and a group of people with a samba band.

All plans for May Day 2002 are geared to minimising the risk of a 'Section 60' by police. The meeting point for the Anarchist Travelling Circus, and other carnivalesque themes, is Mayfair, a huge area flanked by some of London's 'ritziest' streets – Park Lane, Oxford Street, Regent Street and Piccadilly. The idea is to keep moving to prevent the police trapping people. A thousand people manage to find each other and converge (though many wander about without being lucky enough to find the main congregation). The atmosphere is one of glee and mirth at setting the terms of the meander around the streets of Mayfair.

A 'gameball' theme is effected along Oxford Street; people throw inflatable balls up for anyone to catch and pass along. Traffic is held up wherever the march goes. Without the traffic and the hectic shoppers, the streets are quiet and serene. Onlookers look more bemused and curious than hostile: the raggle taggle *mêlée* of purposeful players reclaims the space on their terms – not for consumerism, traffic or capitalist bureaucratic administration, but for play, enabling the throng of people united in wanting transformation to experience being together in reclaimed space.

May Day analysed as carnival and inversion

'Carnival' as a tool of analysis is a popular form in contemporary academia, in which the work of twentieth-century Russian theorist Mikhail Bakhtin and his writings on Rabelais are mined for the last possible iota of relevance to contemporary phenomena. For Bakhtin, carnival offers the experience of utopian freedom, community and equality, with a challenge to officialdom which is a 'contained subversion of dominant forces' rather than a real threat (Edgar and Sedgewick, 2002: 15).

May Day anarchist carnivals – and, as I show below, the symbolic actions on large summit demonstrations – are 'contained' in the sense that they are temporary and exist for the duration of the demonstration. On the other hand, they are not licensed in the way that official carnivals are, and so the experience of anarchist and anti-capitalist carnival is less 'contained' and bound up with the world of officialdom. Authorities and officials do not prepare their way, although, in the case of large summit demonstrations, permission is sought to use buildings such as schools as convergence points.

A key theme in carnival is the notion of 'inversion' – the exchange of roles. In medieval times, the king played the fool for a day and the people donned the king's clothes. In the May Days, the inversion of Churchill by turf, from 'states-man' to 'punk', continues the tradition of Rabelais's carnival. For the 2002 May Day meander by the Anarchist Travelling Circus, the space of one of the new rulers of the world – the car – is inverted and reclaimed. The fancy dress and the inflatable balls connote play, inverting the roles of consumer and the stereotypes of 'powerful bureaucrat with suit'. The people are back for the day of carnival, and on their own terms, not those of capital. The May Day carnivalesque is not 'contained' and legitimised: it counters and steps outside of the conventional and licensed format of parliamentary protest (i.e. in London, the march from Park Lane to Trafalgar Square for speeches); and it goes beyond the licensed world of official carnival. It challenges more deeply the routines of power and the use of space. The disruption of the routine of modern existence is a moment in which 'the familiar is defamiliarised'.

Extending the interpretation to the large summit demonstrations

Large summit demonstrations (Starhawk's 'central dramas') contain the ele-ments discussed above and more, with so many thousands of anti-globalisation demonstrators converging from near and far (Butigan's 'modern pilgrims'). The costumes and guises speak their message with rich symbolism.

In Seattle, November 1999, people converged dressed as turtles, butterflies, vegetables and fish. This symbolism of other species was an affirmation of their existence, and expressed opposition to the decimation of the natural world by policies of trade liberalisation and globalisation. A grim skeleton with a gas mask spelt out the effect of capitalism on its subject with the painted words 'Pollution Casualty'.

Ludic parody is used to expose and ridicule the conventions of bureaucracy and repressive society: tuxedo-dressed and evening-gowned 'Billionaires for Bush' pressed wads of money into policemen's pockets, thanking them for repressing dissent in a situationist-style tactic designed to subvert and confuse power and authorities. The Revolutionary Anarchist Clowns subverted the police's expectations of them by pretending to attack each other. They also sub-verted and parodied the standardised chants of traditional Trotskyists and other Leftists, shouting 'Three word chant!' and 'Call! Response!', satirising the con-tained and predictable behaviour of orthodox demonstrations and marches (Graeber, 2002: 66–7).

In Quebec at the 'Summit of the Americas', in April 2001, demonstrators built a huge medieval catapult and lobbed soft toys from it. They also used hockey sticks to return tear gas canisters back to police lines. The use of soft toys as launcher 'ammunition', and the use of the tools of play (hockey sticks) in a defensive role, subverts and inverts the roles of play and defence. Such carniva-lesque inversions of weapons and toys are a well-established element of anti-glo-balisation protests, with the Italian Tute Bianche and the related London

Wombles characteristically using inflatable weapons and makeshift armour made from cardboard, to protect themselves from the police.

As Graeber notes:

> Where once it seemed that the only alternatives to marching along with signs were either Gandhian non-violent civil disobedience or outright insurrection, groups like the Direct Action Network, Reclaim the Street, 'Black Block' or Tute Bianche have all, in their own ways, been trying to map out a completely new territory in between. They're attempting to invent what many call a 'new language' of civil disobedience, combining elements of street theatre, festival and what can only be called non-violent warfare – non-violent in the sense adopted by, say, 'Black Block' anarchists, in that it eschews any direct physical harm to human beings. (Graeber, 2002: 66)

The last tactic referred to concerns property damage of key symbols of capitalism – banks, shop fronts, cars – carried out by the 'Black Block'. The 'Black Block' has its origins in a number of European anarchist and Western anti-nuclear movements of the 1980s, and is a tactic and concept, not a group, since anyone can participate. Paul Hawken sees the smashing of windows by the 'Black Block' in Seattle as a tactic 'intended to break the spells cast by corporate hegemony, an attempt to shatter the smooth exterior facade that covers corporate crime and violence' (Hawken, 2000: 25). Here again is the image of breaking the spell, another symbolic act to disrupt and expose routinised ways of life. This is also echoed by Brian S., a participant in the demonstrations in Genoa, in July 2001. He describes locals out on the streets afterwards exploring the burned ruins of banks and cars:

> People were picking at a melted/smashed banking machine, curious to see what one looks like from the inside . . . In a weird way, it seemed as if everyone was totally fascinated and unable to speak. No one was really condemning it or shaking their heads. It was more like bewilderment and curiosity. It's not often that one gets to see what lies behind the sleek machines and walls that run our lives. (Brian S., 2001: 20)

Graeber stresses the way in which such tactics do not cause injury to people or animals and argues that what really disturbs the powers-that-be is not the "violence" of the movement but its relative lack of it; governments simply do not know how to deal with an overtly revolutionary movement that refuses to fall into familiar patterns of armed resistance' (Graeber, 2002: 66).

The tactics of large summit demonstrations combine direct action with symbolic action. Direct action with the goal of shutting down the talks was successful only in Seattle. Since Prague (September 2000) police and military have prevented demonstrators from reaching the summit centres. However, a wide spectrum of symbolic acts serve to temporarily reclaim space for the people.

Many of the direct action methods which characterise the anti-capitalist movement have been inspired by and learnt from those in the global South, which is a theme to which I now turn.

The influence of the global South

Many people date the inception of the anti-globalisation movement to the uprising of the Zapatistas in 1994, when the North American Free Trade Agreement
(NAFTA) pushed through policies designed to open Mexico up for globalisation
and US-subsidised food imports, destroying local indigenous economies. Direct
action in the global North has drawn on techniques of resistance and nonviolent
civil disobedience invented in the global South, from tree-hugging to Gandhian-
style direct action against corporations.

The large summit demonstrations are organised by existing non-hierarchical
networks local to each summit conference. Examples are: the Genoa Social
Forum for the G8 Summit, July 2001; the INPEG[4] in Prague, September 2000;
and the Direct Action Network in Seattle, November 1999. These global networks are co-ordinated under the auspices of the People's Global Action (PGA),
formalised at the anti-WTO meeting in Geneva Switzerland in May 1998.
Groups involved include the Southern Indian KRRS (Karnataka Raiya Ryota
Sanghe) farmers, Bolivian movements against privatisation, the Canadian Postal
Workers Union, and direct action and anarchist groups in Europe.

There is a strong input into anti-globalisation, then, not only in general from
pre-existing grassroots movements of the global South, but also from agrarian,
'peasant' and indigenous peoples' movements, each with their own protest histories and repertoires.

In the North, one prominent figure concerned with the agrarian dimension in
anti-globalisation is José Bové, long-time oppositional activist, French farmer
and producer of cheese. Bové is involved with the Confédération Paysanne, a
movement of small farmers for sustainable agriculture. Bové made international
media headlines in August 1999 when he was involved in an action to disrupt the
building of a new McDonald's branch in Millau, southern France where he lives.
Although Confédération Paysanne does possess some nationalistic elements, it
is broadly libertarian and Bové cites anarchism as a key influence, alongside nonviolent action strategies as advocated by Martin Luther King, and Gandhi's
notion of powerful symbolic actions as part of mass struggle.

Another important global network, of which the Confédération Paysanne is
a part, is La Via Campesina, an international movement co-ordinating peasant
organisations and agrarian and indigenous communities in Asia, Africa,
America and Europe. Delegates from both the Confédération Paysanne and La
Via Campesina participate in large summit demonstrations such as at Seattle.

The Indian Karnataka farmers' movement, the KRRS is also involved in La Via
Campesina. It is a Gandhian movement that works to realise the 'village repub-
lic' – autonomous, self-reliant, fully participatory village communities. The
KRRS have been active since the early 1990s in opposing neoliberalism and organisations promoting it, such as the WTO. Their formulations of direct action and
civil disobedience against corporations such as Monsanto have been inspirational
in the anti-globalisation movement. The KRRS physically dismantled the seed

unit of a plant of American corporation, Cargill, in Karnataka. They also occupied a Kentucky Fried Chicken outlet.

In 1999, the Karnataka farmers organised a 'caravan' across Europe to protest against multinational and 'free trade' institutions, and to meet others involved in common struggles. The caravan consisted of twenty buses, restored and driven by European volunteers across eight countries, and supported by local host communities (including some squatting networks).

The significance of peasant, agrarian and indigenous peoples' movements to anarchism and the anti-globalisation movement

The significance of peasant and agrarian ways of life to anarchism is sometimes overlooked. Marxists look mainly to urbanised working-class or national struggles for their 'revolutionary subjects', many despising peasants as much as they do anarchists. Anarchists, on the other hand, have often seen peasant and agrarian ways of life as examples of anarchism in action. Murray Bookchin, though devoted to modernity and municipalism, nonetheless stresses the communal and self-reliant basis of peasant communities in late medieval Europe (Bookchin, 1996b: 24–5) as well as better-known examples like the seventeenth-century English Diggers movement. Bookchin (1994: 10–11) also attests to the importance of agrarian pre-capitalist structures of the Spanish countryside as both vitally nourishing and being nourished by anarchism in the decades prior to the Civil War. This was also true of nineteenth-century Russia which boasted a considerable peasant populism based around the 'mir', followed by the Makhnovist-organised agrarian communes in post-Revolutionary Ukraine until they were crushed by the Bolsheviks. Interestingly, the relative longevity of the agrarian tradition in France is sometimes cited as being one of the reasons behind the extraordinary political mobilisation of 'May 1968'. According to Bookchin (1998: 14–15) the redistribution of land after the French Revolution helped block industrial capitalist development, and maintained a decentralised, self-sufficient, agrarian-based peasant economy highly resistant to manufacturing and large-scale development. Thus even in the mid-twentieth century, France was still relatively backward in terms of the capitalist modernisation process. This has led some participants of 'May 68' to suggest that this facilitated a stronger reaction than in other countries in the world.[5]

Graeber has cited the 'extraordinary importance' of indigenous peoples' struggles in the anti-globalisation movement, and notes that: 'it almost always seems to be peasants and craftsmen – or, even more, newly proletarianised former peasants and craftsmen – who actually overthrow capitalist regimes; and not those inured to generations of wage labour' (Graeber, 2002: 73). With new communication technologies, it is possible now, he argues, for indigenous peoples' movements to be included in global revolutionary alliances, and they should play a profoundly inspirational role.

There is certainly a long history of radical peasant revolts in Europe, though many have been crushed and their gains have been limited. Graeber's point that most of us in the industrialised world have been wage labourers for so long that we barely notice it and that this has narrowed our visions of future possibilities is an important one. However, I would extend this argument by highlighting the stark contrasts between the industrialised world and small-scale agrarian, peasant and other indigenous traditional ways of life, to ask whether the kind of critiques offered by anti-capitalists and anarchists go far enough.

A critique of industrialism and modernisation

Anarchists and anti-globalisation activists are united in their opposition to neo-liberalism, and in their defence of the right of people to keep their indigenous, smaller-scale ways of life. What concerns me, however, is the problem of consistency, in that the majority of anarchists and anti-capitalists envision a more decentralised, more democratic, less environmentally destructive version of a large-scale modern industrial society. In their vision, the large-scale and urban-ised structures created for the needs of capitalism, the machines, factories and roads for the (restricted) use of motorised transport would remain, albeit in a less rampant form.

This is a view shared by the Marxist writers Hardt and Negri, whose book *Empire* (2000) attempts to analyse the contemporary world system and to under-stand the rise of the anti-globalisation movement, or what they refer to as the politics of 'the multitude'. Yet, here too, according to Los Ricos, is a clear posi-tion on ideas of progress:

> Tracing the corrupt roots of civilisation could have led to an anti-civilisation ten-dency within a Marxist doctrine. That would be heresy, though. The thought that civilisation was a wrong turn in the evolution of *Homo sapiens* is a blasphemy against everything progressive-minded people believe. Western civilisation is the logical, only possible course for human development. Never mind the rivers of blood and the spreading desertification, deforestation and homogenisation of eco-systems civilisation has brought to the world. (2001: 24)

Similar assumptions exist behind the 'participatory economic' theories (or 'parecon') of writers such as Michael Albert (2002), who envisions processes of democratisation of economics taking place within a large-scale industrial society.

This critique of modern Western civilisation and the 'progressivists' who take it as given, requires different relationships with the land by those in the global North and a more explicit critique of modern industrialisation. Such a critique intersects with the strands often referred to as 'primitivist', 'anti-civilisation' or 'anti-technological'. These positions draw on the deep past as an analytic tool.

Radical anthropologists such as Stanley Diamond (1983) and Marshall Sahlins (1972) have argued that human existence is characterised for all but the last fraction of its history by guaranteed access to all the elements of livelihood – culture, community, land, water, food and shelter. Hierarchical relations, ranging from the 'big man' to the 'king', result in differential access to the fruits of people's work. As Sahlins has showed, left to their own devices, people will produce for their own subsistence needs unless forced to produce a surplus for the powerful. The more intensely hierarchical societies are based on slavery (a constituent of early 'civilisations' such as those of Mesopotamia, Egypt, Greece and Rome, but also less bureaucratic societies such as those of 'Iron Age' Europe).

With the advent of industrial capitalism, imperialism and finally globalisation, there is a rupture, a breakout of what in non-capitalist societies is a fundamental connection between person, land and livelihood. Industrial capitalism began in England, where enclosure of land gathered pace from the eighteenth century onwards, and the number of landless labourers swelled rapidly. The pace was accelerated in the nineteenth century, when cheap food imports further threatened the stability of agriculture, and when agricultural labourers, no longer able to find work, were forced to seek employment in cities and factories. This process is the same one happening now in the global South, such as in the Chiapas in southern Mexico, where farmers are becoming wage slaves in tuna-canning factories.

'Anti-civilisation' thinking extends the anarchist critique of capitalism and the State to include a critique of large-scale systems, industrialism and modern technology. Los Ricos (2002: 25), for example, suggests that a key motivation of people in the Russian, Mexican, Chinese, Vietnamese and American revolutions was the desire to grow their own crops and control their land rather than control the industry created by the imperial powers. Such an argument therefore has consequences for thinking about revolution and how it often depends on particular notions of 'progress'.

Reclaiming a relationship to land and livelihood

The implication of the above position is that both the North and the South need to engage in a process of de-industrialisation, reclaiming land and reinstigating a direct and participatory relationship with the environment, with our livelihoods, from food to water to shelter, and smaller-scale communities with locally-based economies. A number of steps can assist this.

Permaculture

Since the human population in all but a few regions of the world is too dense to enable a return to gathering and hunting, we will require a form of horticulture and animal 'husbandry' to provide for our needs. Permaculture, a method of diverse crop-planting based on perennial plants and working in harmony with regional conditions, can enrich both monocultural agricultural land and urbanised spaces, and could play an important role both in the here and now and in a transitional period to social and economic transformation. It is a method of land use which can even enrich environments for other species, and, with its principles of multi-tiered cropping (including trees and shrubs), can facilitate the emergence of areas of wilderness, even in the most innocuous settings.

Technology

Technological 'advancement' and machinery are essential to capitalism, since competition between businesses to survive creates a dynamic of continual innovation. While some anarchists argue that technology is neutral, many now see technology as highly deterministic, as shaping and constituting a particular way of life and social environment. One of the main exponents of this position is David Watson (1999), long-time writer for the US journal *Fifth Estate*, which draws on the work of Lewis Mumford (1969) and Jacques Ellul (1965) to develop a critique of civilisation and technological society. Ellul (1965) argued that contemporary societies were technological rather than capitalist (see Millett, in chapter 4, for a full treatment of this position) and that they organised our consciousness *in terms of* the oppressive technological systems. Mumford (1969) contrasted 'democratic technics' – technology under the control of the craftsman or farmer – with 'authoritarian technics', the form of technology which predominates once the bulk of the agrarian population are forced from the land into factories in cities. Authoritarian technics allows a more complex suppression of pre-capitalist communities and their associated value systems, and the final ascendancy of the State-economic/technological complex.

Countering capitalist relations therefore means reclaiming our relationship with the land and each other; undoing the enclosures and reclaiming the commons and access to land and livelihood. Attitudes to technology must be consistent with this and must transcend commonplace arguments such as 'it is not cars that are the problem, but car culture'. The emerging strand of anti-technological anarchism suggests that it is indeed cars that are the problem; and cars are but one aspect of the complex of machines, factories, mines, quarries that constitute alienated life and the degradation of the earth.

When so much is being taken away by the intensifying globalisation process, it is easy to overlook the genuine small-scale initiatives that have occurred. However, in the wake of the attacks on America on 11 September 2001 and the subsequent 'War on Terrorism' the opportunities and possibilities for these autonomous ways of living are by no means certain.

Post-11 September 2001 and the international political scene

The repression of dissent and curtailing of civil liberties – through legislation like the US 'Patriot Act' – that escalated after 11 September 2001, had, in reality, already begun before. For example, in a report to the US Congress in May 2001, the FBI had earmarked the 'carnival against capitalism' as well as Reclaim the Streets as part of a potential terrorist threat.[6] Yet 11 September successfully distracted attention away from issues that had previously been gaining ground in the months before, such as the US refusal to sign the 1997 Kyoto Protocol (intended to reduce the effects of global warming), even in its watered-down-to-ineffectual state and its embrace of carbon trading. Where the summer of 2001 had seen a growing disquiet about climate change, with numerous demonstrations in London, the aftermath of 11 September saw most energy diverted to 'Stop the War' (against Afghanistan) movements and the 'human shield' initiative by International Solidarity Movement activists in Palestine.

The principles of anarchist philosophy, however, are more relevant than ever, as successive summits revealed governments shirking any responsibilities towards maintaining peace and towards halting environmental and climate degradation. In the World Summit on Sustainable Development in Johannesburg, South Africa, August 2002, there was a mass protest by those attending a speech by US Secretary of State, Colin Powell: his speech was met with continual jeers, and a banner proclaimed 'Betrayed by Governments'.

The US military build-up and propaganda for the wars on Afghanistan and Iraq is redolent of German Nazi military build-up. An American television advertisement proclaims the US Army to be 'the best in the world'. 'America Über Alles' is a slogan seen on the Internet in critical commentaries. The collapse of the former super-power rival, the communist bloc, and the integration of Russia and China into the global marketplace, is widely seen as leaving the United states with no constraints on its drive for economic and military domination. For one vice-admiral of the American military 'the Cold War ended on September 11, and from now on the main fight will be over globalisation . . . the task for the US is to defeat the enemies of globalisation' (*Newsnight*, 23 May 2002).

Globalisation has become a buzzword for modernisation, development and global market dominated by US and/or Western interests in the 'free trade' system of neoliberalism. Nation states increasingly show themselves to be acting in the interest of international finance and capital, even as they destroy environments and local indigenous and traditional cultures. The holders of power are increasingly exposed as having only the interests of power at heart. As Mr Social Control notes:

> In a world governed by stock prices the buck stops nowhere. It passes from Tokyo to London to New York and back to Tokyo again. Why should they care if the whole world is turned into a radiation soaked desert? If no human beings can ever see the light of day with their own eyes? What does it mean to them if every beautiful and useless creature in the world is exterminated forever? If we are reduced to drinking our own piss miles underground, dependent on them for every breath of oxygen we take? And if they are willing to save the biosphere at this late hour then why do the greenest amongst them proclaim that the rainforests should be rescued only in order that the plants be used to make herbal shampoo? If they care about

the quality of life that their underlings lead, then why are millions starving in the south to feed the debts imposed by the bank in the north? The truth is that the ecological disasters would be a stroke of luck for those that benefit from the domination of our lives. (Mr Social Control, early 1990s – no specific date)

The more radical strands of the anti-globalisation movement recognise the force of domination that is destroying people's autonomy across the globe. The alliance of primarily urban movements of the North with peasant and indigenous movements of the South is a significant innovation. The network recognises that people's land, water and food is being sold to the highest bidder. The pursuit of power and profit by the few, always the leitmotif of industrial capitalism, now runs more and more out of control.

A recognition of the need all over the world to reclaim the elements of life, there for us humans for the first 100,000 years of our existence on the planet, is a vital element in all oppositional movements. This will inevitably involve the gradual recreation of more agrarian, more local and smaller-scale ways of life. Anti-globalisation and anarchist demonstrations of current years continually re-enact this reclamation of space in urban environments: examples are the UK anti-road protest movements of the 1990s, and those opposing genetically modified crops, quarries, mines, dams and other development projects. Grassroots movements for self-determination such as the Zapatistas in Mexico continue to give inspiration to similar struggles across the world.

Conclusions

Anti-capitalist and anti-globalisation movements, with their commitment to non-hierarchical organisation, symbolic action and carnival, and their direct action, are highly visible examples of anarchism in action. It is difficult for traditional theorists of the Marxist Left fully to acknowledge the significance of anarchism as the leitmotif of anti-globalisation, the most important oppositional movements for many years. Anarchist and anti-capitalist demonstrations reclaim, albeit temporarily, space and disrupt the routine of modern capitalist living, allowing moments that expose, delegitimate and challenge those routines.

Agrarian 'peasant' movements of the global South also form a significant component of the anti-globalisation movement, which recognises the importance of helping defend traditional and indigenous ways of life from the onslaught of globalisation. These can be usefully located within the rural and peasant aspects of anarchist history.

Anti-globalisation activists need to take on board the current commonality of all humans on the planet, whereby those of us who are not part of the financial élite are reduced to the status of wage slaves. What is happening now in the Chiapas, southern Mexico, is an accelerated version of the process carried out in Europe in the last few centuries. It is important to block these 'development' schemes driven through by globalisation, but it is also vital to 'undevelop' the modernised, industrialised world and to create smaller-scale social relations and local economies. This is increasingly recognised within strands of anarchism that challenge the entire premise of industrial civilisation and modern technology, not just hierarchy, capitalism and the State.

Despite the post-11 September clampdowns and intimidation, anarchists and anti-globalisation movements have shown resilience and have continued to speak out and demonstrate. It is easy for the public to turn a blind eye to horror in the world and the threat to life from environmental degradation and global warming. Consumer and media lifestyle culture seduces them to console themselves with reading about celebrities, or purchasing new cars and mobile phones. The reality is that the worship of money, technology, consumer goods, modernisation and development is not creating happiness. The domination of nature and of humans has left a gaping void in people that no amount of spectacular glitter, speed and technology can fill.

As a contrast, here are the words of Luther Standing Bear, chief of the Native American Oglala Sioux:

> We did not think of the great open plains, the beautiful rolling hills, and winding streams with . . . tangled growth as 'wild'. Only to the white man was nature a 'wilderness', and only to him was the land 'infested' with 'wild' animals and 'savage' people. To us it was tame. Earth was bountiful and we were surrounded with the blessings of the Great Mystery. Not until the hairy man from the east came and with brutal frenzy heaped injustices upon us and the families we loved was it 'wild' to us. When the very animals of the forest began fleeing from his approach, then it was that for us the 'Wild West' began. (cited in Hoff, 1994: 297–8)

Notes

1 Contrary to many accounts, Seattle was not the first demonstration against the WTO; rather they began in Geneva, Switzerland during 18–20 May 1998.
2 *It's a Knockout* and *Dad's Army* are British television programmes from the 1970s; the former was a popular game show, the latter a comedy set during the Second World War.
3 These include *Dreaming the dark: magic, sex and politics* (Boston: Beacon, 1988) and *Truth or dare: encounters with power, authority and mystery* (San Francisco: Harper San Francisco, 1988).
4 INPEG is a Czech acronym for the alliance Initiative Against Economic Globalisation, formed in September 1999 (see Chesters and Welsh, 2002).
5 This argument was offered by S. Hayes (2000).
6 The FBI Pressroom statement to Congress can be found at www.fbi.gov/congress/congress01/freeh051001.htm.

Good news for Francisco Ferrer – how anarchist ideals in education have survived around the world[1]

Introduction

This chapter discusses the educational ideas of Francisco Ferrer, as expressed in his book *The origin and ideals of the Modern School* (1913) and compares these ideas with actual practice in anarchist schools early in the twentieth century. I suggest that a parallel movement grew up during the last century in the progressive or democratic schools which was in many ways closer in spirit to Ferrer than these early anarchist schools. This chapter reviews the fundamental principles of a free education before describing how these may be observed in practice in some of the many schools around the world that may be described variously as democratic, non-authoritarian, non-formal or free. The examples chosen come from many different cultures, and they differ widely from each other, but all are based on respect for the child as a person with the same rights as anyone else. In such schools, ignorant of Ferrer though they may be, many of his ideas have been proved by experience.

The Modern School

Education in Spain in the early 1900s had been dominated by the clergy for centuries. However, the times were changing. The foundation of Ferrer's *Escuela Moderna* in Barcelona, and the publication of his book *The origins and ideals of the Modern School* led to a movement which spread rapidly through Spain and France and even reached the United States.

'In every country,' wrote Ferrer, 'the governing classes, which formerly left education to the clergy, as these were quite willing to educate in a sense of obedience to authority, have now themselves undertaken the direction of schools' (Ferrer, 1913: 26). He described the resulting system as follows:

> One word will suffice to characterise it – violence. The school dominates the children physically, morally and intellectually, in order to control the development of their faculties in the way desired, and deprives them of contact with nature in order

to modify them as required. This is the explanation of the failure; the eagerness of the ruling class to control education and the bankruptcy of the hope of the reformers. 'Education' means in practice domination or domestication [Editors' note: probably a mistranslation of 'domesticar' which means 'to tame']. (Ferrer, 1913: 28)

Ferrer's reaction was to assert that 'the whole value of education consists in respect for the physical, intellectual and moral faculties of the child', and 'the true educator is he who does not impose his own ideas and will on the child, but appeals to its own energies' (p. 28).

Such ideas might appear in the prospectus of any modern progressive school, but some of Ferrer's views are even more advanced. On the subject of punishment, he said:

The teachers who offer their services to the Modern School, or ask our recommendation to teach in similar schools, must refrain from any moral or material punishment, under penalty of being excluded permanently. Scolding, impatience and anger ought to disappear with the ancient title of 'master'. In free schools all should be peace, gladness and fraternity. We trust that this will suffice to put an end to these practices, which are most improper in people whose sole ideal is the training of a generation fitted to establish a really fraternal, harmonious and just state of society. (p. 31)

'We are convinced', he said, 'that the education of the future will be entirely spontaneous.' This suggests support for the idea of leaving it to the children to choose when to learn, but he immediately stepped back a little from such an extreme position:

It is plain that we cannot wholly realise this, but the evolution of methods in the direction of a broader comprehension of life and the fact that all improvement involves the suppression of violence indicate that we are on solid ground when we look to science for the liberation of the child. (p. 28)

He was, of course, not the only anarchist of his time to believe that his views could be justified scientifically (see Woodcock (1975: part 1)), and he goes on to state his faith in rationality:

We shall develop living brains capable of reacting to our instruction. We shall take care that the minds of our pupils will sustain, when they leave the control of their teachers, a stern hostility to prejudice; that they will be solid minds, capable of forming their own rational convictions on every subject. (pp. 15–16)

The children's minds are to be hostile to prejudice, but their brains are to react to their teachers' instruction, and the pupils themselves are, until they leave the school, to be under the control of the teachers. Ferrer goes on to put this even more explicitly:

This does not mean that we shall leave the child at the very outset of its education, to form its own ideas. The Socratic procedure is wrong if it is taken too literally. The very constitution of the mind, at the commencement of its development, demands that at this stage the child should be receptive. The teacher must implant the germ of ideas. (p. 16)

Here is the reforming teacher's dilemma: how can you change the world for the better without preaching?

Over the last century, as I shall show, it has been demonstrated in many different contexts that preaching is unnecessary. Children have a natural curiosity and eagerness to learn and a natural concern for the well-being of the people around them. They do not need preaching; they need freedom.

Ferrer was only part of the way towards this understanding, but that was already a great deal further on than the ordinary representative of the governing classes. What Ferrer says in criticism of the educational practice of his time is still largely true today:

> Much of the knowledge actually imparted in schools is useless; and the hope of reformers has been void because the organisation of the school, instead of serving an ideal purpose, has become one of the most powerful instruments of servitude in the hands of the ruling class. The teachers are merely conscious or unconscious organs of their will, and have been trained on their principles from their tenderest years, and more drastically than anybody, they have endured the discipline of authority. Very few have escaped this despotic domination; they are generally powerless against it, because they are oppressed by the scholastic organisation to such an extent that they have nothing to do but obey. (p. 27)

Ferrer felt that the reformist teachers of his time, who were hoping to improve schools from the inside, were merely using better methods of imposing views required by the authorities, and that a more fundamental change was necessary. What we see nowadays in Britain is that the would-be reformist teachers inside the system, of whom there used to be many, are being driven out of the profession altogether.

'"The school" is the cry of every party,' wrote Ferrer (p. 27), and so it is today, but because the establishment does not understand the importance of freedom – because, indeed, they regard it with a kind of horrified dread and associate it with rioting and delinquency – they persist in imposing restrictive legislation which make rioting and delinquency more likely.

Ferrer's own school was closed by the authorities in 1906, after only five years of existence. Ferrer himself was executed in 1909 for allegedly leading a rebellion in Barcelona, and the Modern Schools all over the world died out over the next thirty years. The last Modern School in Britain, the International Modern School in Whitechapel, London, ran only from 1921 to 1928.

The New Schools movement compared with anarchist schools

The New Schools movement in Britain, which must be distinguished from the Modern Schools movement, was founded by middle-class teachers looking for an alternative to the public school system. It included Bedales (Hampshire), Abbotsholme (Derbyshire) and King Alfred's (north London) – all expensive private schools which are flourishing today. They were joined by the progressive

schools of the 1920s, of which the sole survivor is Summerhill, though
Dartington Hall School in Devon lasted until 1987. Most of the New Schools
drifted away from their original more radical ideas, in the same way as people
often do as they get older, and this drift was strengthened by the demands of
parents for more and better exam results. Only Summerhill (currently in Suffolk,
East Anglia) successfully resisted this trend.

Summerhill still exists, but the Ferrer schools have gone.

John Shotton, whose book, *No master high or low* (1993), gives a fascinating
account of what he defines as 'libertarian education and schools, 1890–1990',
makes a distinction between 'libertarian education' and 'progressivism'. He
states that there is a considerable overlap, but adds: 'This has more to do with
the rhetoric of progressivism than its practice. This is because, while claiming to
be child-centred, in reality progressivism was and is teacher-centred' (p. 9).

I would argue that many of the anarchist schools at the beginning of the twen-
tieth century were at least as teacher-centred as the progressive schools. La
Ruche, Sébastien Faure's school at Rambouillet in France, much admired by
Emma Goldman (1907: 390ff.) had the following timetable:

	Morning	*Afternoon*
Monday	Grammar	Mental arithmetic
	Dictation	Geometry
	Construing	Explanation of reading
		Music
Tuesday	Vocabulary	Shorthand
	Composition	Recitation
	Corrections	Maths
		English
Wednesday	History of civilisation	Outing
	Geography or history	
	Preparation	
	Drawing	
Thursday	Science	Esperanto
	Dictation	Metric system
	Corrections	Handwriting
		Music
Friday	Geography	Drawing
	Composition	Maths
	Corrections	Problems
		English
Saturday	Reading	Baths
	Study – overview of all the working week	Sewing
		Ironing, cleaning, etc.

Source: Faure, 1915: 41 (cited in Grunder, 1993: 87).

This hardly seems like a timetable devised by children. The photographs of the school in the same book have no feeling of cheerful informality. There is one of an actual lesson (Grunder, 1993: 96) which shows children crammed into desks, sometimes three to a double desk, all with their heads turned towards a teacher who is delivering some kind of explanation, clearly the most important person in the room. The photograph may be posed, but the situation represented is presumably what was thought to be ideal.

At the Liverpool Anarchist-Communist Sunday School (1908–16), which was organised to ' . . . break down prejudices that are set up in the weekday school . . . To teach a child to think and act for itself . . . To spread the idea of Internationalism' (cited in Shotton, 1993: 44), there were frequent lectures on political topics. Even Nellie Dick, organising her own school in the East End of London at the age of 13, said that when they started they 'sang songs and talked about anarchism' (cited in Shotton, 1993: 38). The adults who ran such schools taught anarchism in the belief, shared by many anarchists of their time, that they were not expounding a doctrine, but only exposing children to the scientific truth (see also Woodcock, 1975: part 1). Writers who discuss schools of any kind generally discuss the ideas of the adults running them rather than the experiences of the children attending them. In accounts of anarchist schools, the names of Sébastien Faure, Nellie Dick and Francisco Ferrer are inevitably seen to be more important than the names of their pupils.

The difference between the ideals of the progressives and the anarchists was more to do with politics and class than with the relative status of adults and children. They were all aiming for the same kind of relationship, but the anarchist schools were for the working class. Most of the progressive schools were obliged, because of the State's reluctance to support innovation, to depend on parents who could afford to pay fees.

Summerhill suffered the same fate, even though one of the major influences on A. S. Neill was Homer Lane's Little Commonwealth, a home for young orphans and adolescents referred either by the courts or their own parents, which was supported by the Home Office. Homer Lane believed in innate goodness and individual freedom. The Little Commonwealth was governed by a citizen's court, and the only rules were made by the citizens themselves (Bridgeland, 1971: 102ff.). The same could be said of Summerhill, but Summerhill could only survive as an independent school. Neill once said, 'My school could be run with proletariat pupils without any change of method and principle' (Neill, 1945: 96) but later he so far forgot his mentor's work that when Mary Leue, founder of the Albany Free School in New York State, asked for his advice about starting a Summerhill school with working-class children, he said he thought she would be mad to try (cited in Appleton, 2001, from a personal communication between Neill and Mary Leue in 1968).

About most other aspects of education, the progressives and the anarchists spoke with one voice. It is interesting to match quotations from Ferrer with others from progressive educators of the 1920s:

I would rather have the free spontaneity of a child who knows nothing than the verbal knowledge and intellectual deformation of one that has experienced the existing system of education. (Ferrer, 1913: 29)

I would rather see a school produce a happy street cleaner than a neurotic scholar. (A. S. Neill, cited in Lamb, 1992: 9)

Having . . . started from the principles of solidarity and equality we are not prepared to create a new inequality. Hence in the Modern School there will be no rewards and no punishments. (Ferrer, 1913: 30)

We find ourselves departing, for purely educational reasons, from the tradition that marks and competition are necessary in order to secure an adequate standard of effort and efficiency. (Curry, 1934: 59)

We can destroy whatever there is in the actual school that savours of violence, all the artificial devices by which children are estranged from nature and life, the intellectual and moral discipline which has been used to impose ready-made thoughts, all beliefs which deprave and enervate the will. (Ferrer, 1913: 29)

Therefore no corporal punishment, indeed no punishment at all; no prefects; no uniforms; no Officers' Training Corps; no segregation of the sexes; no compulsory games, compulsory religion or compulsory anything else; no more Latin, no more Greek; no competition; no jingoism. (Young, 1982: 131)

I have found no reference to Ferrer in the writings of the progressives. The quotation from Curry above comes from a book edited by Trevor Blewitt called *The modern schools handbook*, published in 1934. Unselfconsciously he used the term 'modern schools' to describe a collection of variously progressive independent establishments. The rebellion against the public school system described by Michael Young seems to have remained ignorant of the rebellion against the clerical education in Spain described by Francisco Ferrer, even though their manifestos are so similar.

A wide range of schools

This mutual unawareness has continued up to the present day, not only between progressives and anarchists but also between individual organisations. Teachers in non-authoritarian schools are usually far too busy with their pupils to spend time on theory and comparison. My own experience of free education was first teaching at Dartington Hall School and then, when it closed, at Sands School, which was founded to develop the tradition. When I retired from Sands School in 1992, I knew of only half a dozen other similar schools, mostly in the United Kingdom. Now I have had the time to get to know of something approaching a hundred, all round the world, but my hundred will not be the same as anyone else's hundred, and most of my hundred know little or nothing about each other. IDEC, the International Democratic Education Conference, has been bringing different people together every year since 1993, but it is not well known, and even those attending a conference will only have time to get to know a few of the other participants. In case the word 'democratic' shocks anarchists, I should say that the two 15-year-old students who were running the IDEC at Sands in 1997 chose the name. They did not like the name, but could not think of a better one, and it has been generally accepted because of its 'PR' value – no government or newspaper could comfortably object to the idea of democratic education, whereas 'libertarian', 'free', 'progressive' or 'anarchist' education would be under immediate attack. Most of the schools that attend the conferences have some kind of formal meeting where the students participate in decision-making, but some places have no rules, and all are committed to the idea of respect for the individual child.

To illustrate the diversity of the modern scene, here is a scattering of relevant schools and organisations: Sudbury Valley School, Massachusetts; the School of Self-Determination, Moscow; Tokyo Shure, Japan; le Centre Energie, Madagascar; Krätzä, Berlin; Tamariki, Christchurch, New Zealand; Highfield Junior School, Plymouth, England; la Fundación Educativa Pestalozzi, Quito, Ecuador; Sands School, Ashburton, England; the Democratic School of Hadera, Israel; Dr. Albizo Campos Puerto Rican High School, Chicago; the Butterflies organisation for street and working children, Delhi; Moo Baan Dek children's village, Thailand.

I have met people from all these places, and visited all but three of them. They are different from each other in their social composition and in their geographical position and in many details of organisation. The list includes three government-supported schools, two organisations for street children, five fee-paying schools and three places that depend on charitable support. There are urban and rural schools, boarding and day institutions, climates ranging from the tropical to the Muscovite and a combined age range from 2 to 20. They are all highly individual and most would probably be inclined to resist being lumped together with the others; they would emphasise their differences rather than their similarities.

However, in spite of this individualistic attitude, and in spite of the fact that they have developed in countries with cultures as different from each other as those of Japan, India and Soviet Russia, they share a central core of common values. As far as I know, none of these schools started from anarchist principles, but what they have in common with each other they also have in common with Francisco Ferrer. I match their guiding principles here with quotations from *The origin and ideals of the Modern School*:

1 Reliance on reason rather than doctrine.

'Education is not worthy of the name unless it be stripped of all dogmatism' (Ferrer, 1913: 28).

2 Self-government or shared responsibility.

'Every pupil shall go forth . . . into social life with the ability to be his own master and guide his own life in all things' (p. 30).

3   Freedom to choose.

'The education of the future will be entirely spontaneous' (p. 28).

4   Equality.

'Having admitted and practiced the co-education of boys and girls, of rich and poor – having, that is to say, started from the principle of solidarity and equality – we are not prepared to create a new inequality' (p. 30).

5   Respect for and trust in the individual child.

'The whole value of education consists in respect for the physical, intellectual, and moral faculties of the child' (p. 28).

These principles manifest themselves in different ways in different places (and are described in greater detail in *Real education: varieties of freedom*, and *Lifelines*, both by David Gribble). For example, at Sudbury Valley there are no lessons. Staff members are not supposed to propose activities, because that would influence the students; the students must decide for themselves what they want to do. On the other hand, there are numerous rules and regulations, and the Justice Committee, which deals with breaches of these, often imposes punishments, such as exclusion from a particular area, or additional work for the community.

Sands School, on the other hand, has a full timetable of (voluntary) lessons, as few rules as possible, and no system of punishment. When the school started, Andrew Edwards, one of the students, formulated this disciplinary policy in one simple sentence: 'Common sense takes the place of rules.'

At the Fundación Educativa Pestalozzi, staff members are told that teaching, explaining, guiding, motivating, persuading, anticipating and pointing out are not adequate interactions between an adult and a child. There is a prepared environment with a variety of opportunities for learning and playing within which the children are left absolutely free to choose whatever they want to do. The fact that most of the time they play is considered appropriate.

At the Puerto Rican High School, in an area of Chicago where gang warfare is rife, every student who comes to the school is expected to attend a full timetable of lessons. Outside the school there is aimlessness and danger; within the school the students welcome the security they find in a structured day. There is an easy-going and affectionate relationship between staff and students, and students show the self-respect resulting from the confident assertion of national identity and personal rights. There is a twice weekly school meeting, chaired by students, which is informal and co-operative.

Even non-authoritarian schools usually keep a record of attendance, and require all students to attend every day, unless they have some good reason for absence. Tokyo Shure, on the other hand, is a school for school-refusers, so children who are enrolled there do not have to attend. The building is simply open until 7 o'clock in the evening each weekday, and there are classes and other activities available for those who choose to come. When I visited the school there were a hundred children on the roll, but usually only fifty or so present at any given time.

The Butterflies organisation for street and working children in Delhi goes even further – it does not even have a school building. The street educators work in public places, and the children who want to learn take time off from their rag-picking, portering, shoe-cleaning or other work in order to come to them. Many of the adults around would prefer the children to continue working, and actively discourage them from taking part.

Of the organisations I have visited, only two regularly engage in formal political action – the Puerto Rican High School in Chicago and Butterflies in Delhi. The American students protest about political prisoners and police violence, demonstrate in support of funding for youth and take part in programmes to raise awareness about sexually transmitted diseases. The Delhi children march to protect their own rights and to protest against children being locked up in so-called observation homes; they organise press conferences and public meetings to air their problems; and during the war with Pakistan (the 1999 Kargil conflict) they collected money from their pitiful wages to support child victims.

Children at an ideal anarchist school should presumably be left to decide for themselves whether they should take part in political protest. At Butterflies and the Puerto Rican High School, the opportunity to do so is part of the culture.

Students from other, more sheltered environments are less active, but their experience of a community that is at least attempting to create an environment of justice usually leads them to socially responsible attitudes. They are seldom motivated by acquisitiveness, and when they leave school a disproportionate number become teachers, artists or social workers, or join the medical profession. In Britain, many take up ecological issues or become members of organisations such as Amnesty International, Greenpeace or the Campaign for Nuclear Disarmament (CND), but perhaps their comfortable schooling has not given them enough reason to rebel. In 1945, A. S. Neill wrote the following about ex-students of Summerhill: 'Politically most of them are left wing, and some have joined the Communist Party, while others, though left, cannot subscribe to the Party Line because they value their inner freedom too much' (Neill, 1945: 87).

The philosophies and practical models on which these organisations are based also vary widely. Rebeka and Mauricio Wild of the Fundación Educativa Pestalozzi were inspired by, among others, Maria Montessori and the English primary schools of the 1960s; several schools acknowledge a debt to A. S. Neill and Summerhill, and Moo Baan Dek explicitly bases its practice on a Buddhist interpretation of Neill; the Centre Energie in Madagascar and many South American street children's organisations were started by Roman Catholics, who seem to have abandoned the idea of clerical authority and taken Christianity back to such apparently un-Catholic texts as 'Love thy neighbour as thyself', and 'Go and sell that thou hast, and give the money to the poor'; David Wills ran the Barns Hostel in Scotland in the 1940s, where thirty evacuee boys, thought to be too unruly to be billeted on any ordinary family, ran their own community for a period of eight months without intervention from the staff – he was a Quaker; and Sudbury Valley acknowledges a debt to Neill, but bases its constitution on the New England town meetings.

Not theory, but practice

The projects described above originate from an enormously wide variety of starting-points, and the range becomes even larger when you include the schools that do not acknowledge any particular inspiration. Such schools emerged, not as practical examples of educational theory, but as solutions to problems, and they developed pragmatically. Many, but not all, have emerged in Third World countries were education for the poor is almost unobtainable.

Seliba Sa Boithuto, in Lesotho in southern Africa, is self-study centre. It provides learners with a quiet, comfortable place to learn, materials (books, pamphlets, computers and videos) to learn from and tutors for advice and help. It offers no courses. The tutors do not teach, but they encourage students to learn together and to learn from each other. Most of the learners are young people who cannot go to school, either because of lack of funds or because they are semi-employed, but there are also adults taking correspondence courses, secretaries who wish to obtain computer skills, and people who wish to improve their English.

Tokyo Shure was founded to help some of the large numbers of children for whom the academic pressure, the conformity and the bullying by other children and by staff in the conventional Japanese State schools was unbearable; it was not just a problem of school refusal, it was a problem of frequent child suicide. It started with a series of negatives – no uniform, no punishment, no pressure and not even any obligation to attend. It offers a curriculum which changes from month to month, according to the requests of its students. It is run, like most of the schools I have mentioned, by a school meeting where staff and students have equal status.

The Kleingruppe Lufingen, in the Swiss Canton of Zurich, was founded as part of an experiment to help the children thought to have problems too severe for even the special schools to cope with. The children were divided into groups of six, each of which had one teacher and a building of its own. Here too they started with a strong negative: the buildings were not to be associated with schools. Jürg Jegge, who ran the Kleingruppe Lufingen, treated his pupils as friends and allowed them to do whatever they liked, as long as they did not interfere with each other. One of the things they liked to do was to learn, and in between pottery and chat and theatre visits and keeping rabbits and cooking meals and restoring an old car and a hundred other things, these young people learnt self-respect, and they learnt to read and write.

The Butterflies organisation was founded to meet the needs of the street and working children in Delhi. (The distinction is that street children have no homes to go to, whereas working children live with their families.) Rita Panicker, the founder of the organisation, told me,

> Participation is a difficult thing because each one of us has been socialised in different ways. And one of the socialisations is that elders never consult. They talk at you. Therefore every day I have to ask myself, Did I consult the children? 'Did I listen to what they were saying? Or was I just hearing a little bit, and I made my own decisions?'

The inspiration does not come from any educational theorist, but from the children themselves.

The Puerto Rican High School in Chicago was founded by a group of eight students who had all been expelled from the local high school for fomenting a student strike. The strike had been in protest against the sacking of two teachers who had been teaching Puerto Rican history and culture, and speaking Spanish in the classroom. The State high schools existed to teach children to be good Americans, not to discover their own roots. The Puerto Rican High School started with volunteer teachers working in a church basement. Many of the students had family problems, drug problems, gang problems or all three. Leading figures from the district came in to talk about these issues, and to help the students to regain their self-respect. The curriculum was decided by the students. The teachers found a new role as organisers rather than authority figures.

Evolving out of diversity

The cultures from which these different schools have emerged also vary widely. The Japanese writer Yoshiaki Yamamura has commented that:

> Christian cultures, with their view of human beings as fallen creatures, who can regain an honest life only a little at a time and with divine assistance, seem to regard human nature as inherently evil. The same may be said for Freudian concepts, with their identification of sexual desire and aggressiveness in children. In contrast, the Japanese tend to think of children as inherently good. (Yamamura, 1986: 35)

At the same time, the Japanese attach enormous importance to conformity and hierarchy, whereas Westerners tend to admire the exceptional and to resent authority. In Thailand it is disrespectful to raise your head above the level of the heads of your superiors. The consequent behaviour looks servile to a Western eye, but in Thailand is merely courtesy.

In Delhi the street children are regarded as worthless urchins, but nevertheless they are shocked by the treatment of the street children in parts of South America. The School for Self-Determination in Moscow was founded in Soviet Russia, before *glasnost* and *perestroika*, whereas Dartington Hall School was an expensive independent school in a democracy. Tokyo Shure is in an office building in a huge city; Moo Baan Dek is in a loose group of specially designed buildings in a forest beside the banks of the river Kwae; Butterflies has no classrooms at all. Summerhill reached England in 1924, after three years as an international school in Germany; England in the 1920s was a very different place from England in 1987, when Sands School was founded. The Democratic School of Hadera is in Israel, where its open-heartedness stands out in what is often a brutally nationalistic community.

In spite of these wide variations in inspiration, methods and context, all these places have come to share a common set of values, and I think Ferrer would have felt at ease in any of them. Although they are not explicitly based on anarchist ideals, they present examples of such ideals in practice. The fact that similar systems have evolved from such varied beginnings, and in particular that they have evolved in situations presenting such apparently intractable problems, suggests that the common approach must have some universal validity.

A really fraternal, harmonious and just state of society

In a passage I quoted at the beginning of this chapter, Ferrer stated that: 'In free schools all should be peace, gladness and fraternity.' He went on to say that for teachers in a Modern School the 'sole ideal is the training of a generation fitted to establish a really fraternal, harmonious and just state of society'.

This, then, was Ferrer's primary aim. The primary aim in most, if not all, of the places I have described, is helping individual children to retain or to regain their natural self-respect, eagerness to learn and interest in and concern for the general welfare. In these schools, too, all should be peace, gladness and fraternity.

Should the development of the individual child come first, or the development of society? In their enthusiasm for the latter, the early anarchist educators overlooked the importance of the former.

The concept of anarchist education is self-contradictory. The word education on its own suggests control, and as soon as you attach an adjective to it – religious education, physical education – it attracts a ring of the pulpit or the parade ground. No matter how sound your principles, from an anarchist standpoint it should be wrong to require others to accept them. One of the nineteenth-century headmasters of Eton is alleged to have said, 'I will have happy, smiling faces around me if I have to flog every boy in the school to achieve it.' Although Ferrer denounced the flogging, he expected to find happy smiling faces as a consequence of instruction and example – an only slightly more rational idea. He apparently failed to understand that you can only create an atmosphere 'peace, gladness and fraternity' by such methods as are practised in the non-authoritarian organisations I have been describing.

Rules and punishments

Where Ferrer went further than many of the progressive schools was in ruling out punishments. Many supposedly non-authoritarian schools do in fact have many rules, and punish those who break them.

Sudbury Valley, about which Daniel Greenberg, one of the founders, has written a book called *Free at last* (1987), has so many rules that they need a book to contain them. I was told that it was easier for adults to step in when there was a crisis, because they could refer to rules and not have to wait for some communal decision.

Summerhill uses one of its two weekly meetings to deal with breaches of rules and to impose punishments. One explanation given is that the rules are devised by the children themselves, and the breaches of rules are dealt with by the whole community, not merely by the adults. Another is the fear that if you have no rules then the adults will simply take over. A third is that children like making rules and feel protected by them.

There is no doubt that children at schools like Summerhill and Sudbury do really feel that they are free and in charge of their own lives; they have a dignity and self-possession that is rare in any child from a conventional school. (It is also true that many of the rules at Sudbury are descriptive of administrative systems rather than restrictions on behaviour. At Summerhill, by contrast, most of the rules are about behaviour – bedtimes, going into the town, borrowing bicycles, building camps or whatever happens to be fashionable at the time.) There are, though, schools which exemplify Ferrer's principle by managing perfectly well without punishments, and even without rules, and some have made clear statements about the reasons for this.

The 1994/95 prospectus for Mirambika, the Sri Aurobindo school in Delhi, states:

> Punishment does not help the child to surmount difficulties. It builds a wall, creates divisions and an atmosphere in which it is very difficult to listen to the inner truth. Answering negative behaviour of children crudely with restriction means that at that very moment we give up our belief in basic goodness. Let us remember that sometimes the child has to experiment a little with a dark corner in himself in order to consciously choose and own light.

Lois Holzman, one of the directors of the Barbara Taylor School in New York, explains that it is wrong to punish children for their failures because, firstly, we are all responsible for each other, so the failings are the school's and not the child's; secondly, to exclude children is to deprive them of the one environment that is therapeutic for them; and thirdly, people who punish avoid having to discuss, and discussion is what leads to change.

David Horsburgh, describing Neel Bagh, the school in rural Bangalore which he ran for twelve years from 1972 until his death in 1984, wrote this: 'No punishments are given, either as a retaliation for some supposed offence, or as a deterrent to some future one; nor is there a school council to award punishments which the teacher does not like to give himself' (p. 3).

David Wills, of the Barns evacuee hostel, listed many reasons for avoiding punishment:

1. It establishes a base motive for conduct.
2. It has been tried, and has failed; or alternatively, it has been so mis-used in the past as to destroy its usefulness now.
3. It militates against the establishment of the relationship which we consider necessary between staff and children – a relationship in which the child must feel himself to be loved.
4. Many delinquent children (and adults) are seeking punishment as a means of assuaging their guilt-feelings.

But that is not all; there is still another. When the offender has 'paid for' his crime, he can 'buy' another with an easy conscience. (Wills, 1945: 22)

Wills also made the astonishing assertion that punishment shifts responsibility for behaviour onto the adult, instead of leaving it with the child (Wills, 1942: 9). On reflection I find I agree with him.

At even a Utopian school there must be occasions when a child disrupts the desired atmosphere of peace, gladness and fraternity. At the *Escuela Moderna* there was to be neither moral nor material punishment, said Ferrer, and scolding, impatience and anger were to be unknown. This left explanation and discussion as the only alternatives, and Ferrer explicitly stated this:

If any child were conspicuous for merit, application, laziness, or bad conduct, we pointed out to it the need of accord, or the unhappiness of lack of accord, with its own welfare and that of others, and the teacher might give a lecture on the subject. Nothing more was done. (1913: 30)

David Horsburgh, after describing what seems like an ideal situation, omits to say what was done when there was anti-social behaviour. The answer may be that he himself was regarded with such respect that his disapproval was enough. This may well not have been what he intended, but when I interviewed an ex-pupil, Vijayalakshmi, she told me about an occasion when she tore out the last page of her exercise book in order to get a new one:

And he asked me, 'What happened to this page?' And I said, 'I tore it.'
    And he said, 'No, never do that. Because everything has its own value.'
    That's it. He never scolded, but that was enough. (Gribble, 1998: 121)

Charismatic figures cannot shed their charisma. W. B. Curry at Dartington, Daniel Greenberg at Sudbury Valley and Jürg Jegge at the Kleingruppe Lufingen are other examples of highly articulate and powerful personalities at the head of free schools. Their personal convictions make it extremely difficult for them not to assert their views in ways which dominate the argument, and may prevent children from developing their own moral ideas. Charisma can help to make valuable ideas known in the public sphere, but it is nearly always damaging to those nearest to it. In a school, teachers and children may be prevented from exploring their own ideas, and fall back on unquestioning acceptance and a complacent intellectual idleness.

It is difficult for any adult to stand back and allow children to work things out for themselves. 'It would be so much quicker and easier,' a teacher is inclined to feel, 'if I simply told them.' With a charismatic adult it would indeed be quicker and easier, but the essential aim is neither speed nor ease, but understanding. There is a vital difference between recognising right behaviour because one understands what is right about it, and recognising right behaviour because one remembers what has been told by some dominant personality.

Freedom or neglect?

Another question that has to be answered if genuinely anarchistic education is to develop, is where the boundaries are between freedom and neglect. Are adults not to intervene when a 10-year-old has still not shown any interest in learning to read? Are playground fights to be allowed to run their course, even if there is plainly bullying involved?

Reading

Some schools insist that children will learn to read and write in their own time, without any pressure or support. Sudbury Valley and the Fundación Pestalozzi in Ecuador claim success for that view after several decades of experience. However, in A. S. Neill's time at Summerhill, children occasionally left at the age of 16 unable to read, with Neill still maintaining that they would learn to read when they needed to. Summerhill has now changed its views, as has the Democratic School of Hadera, which also started out believing that reading did not have to be taught. Tamariki School, in New Zealand, has a more explicit policy:

> In this school a very clear pattern of learning to read has emerged. About 35% of children learn to read with minimal or no instruction, usually by 7, about 50% with a fair degree of teacher support and input, usually by 9 to 9½, and the remaining 15% require intensive teacher help. Teachers should be alert from 8 years on to identify children in this last group. While no firm guidelines can be given and each child's difficulties must be carefully evaluated, remedial assistance should be given as soon as the child will permit. (Tamariki, 1989)

Most children who go to the Butterflies street educators learn to read in six months, but, although disadvantaged, they are highly motivated, and may possibly be a self-selecting group of above-average ability.

I quoted earlier the weekly timetable at La Ruche, the school so enthusiastically approved by Emma Goldman. It included one session for reading, two for dictation, one for handwriting and three for corrections. The idea of leaving it to the children to decide when they were going to learn to read and write does not seem to have arisen.

A hundred years later, experience has shown that a rigid timetable like that at La Ruche is unnecessary, but there are still differences of opinions as to the degree of adult intervention that is helpful.

Maintaining order in the community

Over what in a conventional school would be called 'disciplinary issues' there are also wide variations. At the Barbara Taylor School, the whole community is held responsible. At Summerhill, individuals are judged by the community and often punished. At Sudbury Valley and Hadera, the judgement is made by a committee consisting of several children and one adult. At Tamariki, children call together small meetings of three or four people to deal with disagreements on the spot.

Where the atmosphere is really one of peace, gladness and fraternity there are very few behaviour problems. When the only children present are the ones who have chosen to be there, a lesson is not likely to be interrupted, and if it is interrupted, the other members of the group are likely to intervene. When children can leave the room to go to the lavatory without asking for permission, a common source of stress is removed. When adults don't have to pick on children for wearing the wrong clothes or for talking in the corridors, they are able to form genuine friendships. When the premises really belong to the children, they will tolerate a greater degree of mess than is acceptable to adults, but most will share in a sense of responsibility for keeping the place at least comfortable and usable. When children are free, they pursue their own personal aims, and usually these aims require an orderly environment if they are to be fulfilled.

Order in non-authoritarian schools is generally maintained by relying on the good sense of the free child, and when that fails, the will of the community usually prevails. The way this is expressed varies from one organisation to another, but there is ample evidence for the success of this approach.

Conclusion

Over the last hundred years there has been increased recognition of the merits of freedom in schools, but it has not been under the anarchist flag. Even Bonaventure, a small school on the Ile d'Oléron off the west coast of France (sadly closed down in 2002), which happily proclaimed itself to be libertarian and was financially supported by, among others, anarchists and anarchist organisations, was cautious about using the word anarchist in describing its own practice. One of the reasons was a disapproval of the teaching of any doctrine. (Ferrer also disapproved, but he believed at the same time that the teachers should be in control and should 'implant the germ of ideas'.) Another reason is the way anarchy is misunderstood, and the harsh public attitude to the word anarchy. A third is ignorance: very few teachers in the schools I have been describing have any idea of how close their methods are to anarchism. A fourth reason is that most of the long-lived free schools (in Britain, at least) have had to be independent from State control, and have therefore had to charge fees, so inevitably creating a division based on wealth that is unacceptable to any principled anarchist.

Nevertheless, there have been examples of State support for non-authoritarian initiatives for children in Britain: the Barns Hostel (Peebles, Scotland, 1940 to1944), Countesthorpe College (Leicestershire, from 1970), the Conisburgh experiment (Derbyshire, September 1971 to September 1973), Risinghill (London, early 1960s), the White Lion Street Free School (London, 1972 to1990), Prestolee (Lancashire, 1918 to 1951), Highfield Junior School (Plymouth, transformation of the school effected by Lorna Farrington, during her headship, starting in 1991) and many others, though they have often had to try to avoid public notice in order to continue to do what they think right. The Free School movement of the 1960s also flourished briefly in Britain (see Shotton, 1993).

Outside Britain there are many schools and organisations supported by charity in the Developing World that have offered lifelines to children living in great deprivation. In Israel, surprisingly, the Institute for Democratic Education is working on the democratisation of over a hundred schools. In Guatemala, the government is taking advice from the Collegio Naleb, a school that developed its own variety of freedom after attempting to start as an exclusive school for able children. In Thailand, the government has decreed that all schools must produce plans for changing over to child-centred education – a sudden change that may well be doomed to failure because it is being attempted in a country where most teaching depends on rote learning and teachers do not understand what is being asked of them. The *Netzwerk für selbstbestimmtes Lernen* (Network for autonomous learning) in Austria has twenty-seven member schools. Scandinavia's State education is already liberal, but even so there are schools like the Forsøksgymnaset in Oslo, Norway, which was started by students who were unsatisfied with the education they were receiving. There are so many independent free schools in Denmark that they have a separate organisation of their own recognised by the State, the Dansk Friskoleforening (although how many of these are genuinely libertarian or liberating remains uncertain).

The freedom that reigns in many of these schools is in some respects wider than anything imagined by Faure or Ferrer. The absence of the red and black flag should not disguise the fact that anarchist ideals have been and are being developed and their relationship with democracy is being explored in a practical way in hundreds and perhaps thousands of schools and other organisations for children around the world. The success of these experiments must surely be a prelude to wider change.

Notes

1 I would like to thank Craig Fees at the PETT Archive for his help in chasing up references (Planned Environment Therapy Trust Archive and Study Centre, Church Lane,
   Toddington, near Cheltenham, Gloucestershire GL54 5DQ, United Kingdom. 01242
   620125. www.pettarchiv.org.uk).

I I Bronislaw Szerszynski and Emma Tomalin

Enchantment and its uses: religion and spirituality in environmental direct action

Introduction

What are the uses of enchantment? From an anarchist perspective, are forms of spiritual belief and practice always to be considered as a surrendering of personal autonomy, an enslavement to irrationality? We will suggest otherwise – that spirituality can be a source of personal empowerment. Our title contains an implicit reference to Bruno Bettelheim, who argued that fairy tales were useful for children, in that they contributed to their psychological development (Bettelheim, 1976). While we will not take a similarly psychological route in defence of eco-spirituality – with the implication that spiritual beliefs cannot be true but only useful – we make here a parallel argument: we believe that spiritual forms of belief and action empower individuals in the life of protest.

Firstly, we will introduce environmental direct action, particularly as it developed in Britain in the 1990s for specific political and cultural reasons. Secondly, we will explore the tensions between the spiritual and the secular in this movement, in the context of a critique, broadly shared within the movement, of mainstream Western religion as hierarchical and ecologically malign. Thirdly, drawing on detailed qualitative research regarding environmental direct activists in the 1990s,[1] we argue that, despite these struggles over religion, activists routinely draw on cultural resources in order to give meaning to their values, identities and actions in forms that are – sometimes implicitly, sometimes explicitly – religious in nature. We explore the uses of this 'de-regulated religion' in three different dimensions of direct action, namely beliefs, identity and action.

The environmental direct action movement

During the 1990s in the United Kingdom there emerged a new wave of direct action against activities considered to be environmentally destructive. In particular, the issue of road building attracted the attention of activists and heralded a number of lengthy battles with local authorities, the police and construction companies. Examples include the M3 extension at Twyford Down (1991–93) and the M11 extension in East London (1993). At the time, these activities received high levels of media attention and it became common for newspaper front pages to bear pictures of dreadlocked protesters being dragged from trees by security guards or police (Szerszynski, 2003). Other protests sprang up around the country in objection to perceived environmental threats, such as housing schemes or open cast mining (for a useful overview, see Seel *et al.*, 2000).

In many ways reminiscent of the anti-nuclear protests of the 1970s and 80s, the core of many of these protests was the existence of semi-permanent camps. Activists, frequently having little or no previous contact with the area, set up camp with the aim of physically stopping whatever activity they objected to, building tree houses and digging tunnels to prevent road contractors from clearing wooded areas (see Wall, 2000, for a useful analysis of different kinds of direct action). While social protest for the protection of the environment was not a new phenomenon in the United Kingdom, the scale of activity and the emergence of 'communities of direct action' added a new chapter to British environmental history. A sector of society had decided that the usual channels of political lobbying and Party politics had been ineffective in securing any substantial indication that the environment was to become a priority in national politics.

By the end of the 1990s, although never completely dying out, this type of environmental protest had become less common and media interest in it had diminished. The large-scale actions against road building, for instance, had become virtually unheard of by the time that Labour beat the Conservative Party in the 1997 general election. Prior to the Labour victory, there had been a shift in the Tory policy on road building and a number of proposed projects were halted while others were abandoned, signalling to activists that their innovative and sustained campaign had achieved some degree of success. Since then, much of the energy that was channelled into environmental direct action has been directed into campaigns against 'genetically modified' crops and for the anti-capitalist and anti-globalisation movement which has been growing since the protests against the 1999 World Trade Organisation meeting in Seattle.

Environmental direct action in the 1990s was well known for its emphasis upon non-violence to humans (although not to property). Moreover, the communities that developed were important in that, although they physically represented an impediment to road building, they were also significant in themselves. It was not the case that activists put in a good day's protesting and then returned to their ordinary lives: for many, the community was their life. However, by their very nature, direct action communities were temporary and transitory: people came and went; some stayed for one night; others were more involved in organising the protest on a day-to-day basis and lived there for the duration. Some communities were highly organised with meal times, work schedules and frequent meetings; others were less integrated, with individuals or small groups acting more or less autonomously.

This radical environmental network was maintained largely by word of mouth, freely distributed printed literature and a circuit of festivals and gatherings which individuals attended throughout the year. Beyond this active maintenance of the movement, activists were bound together by both a distrust of mainstream politics and a belief that the environment needed protecting. For activists, the Earth was of 'ultimate concern' (Tillich, 1957), the protection of the environment being the ultimate goal underpinning the movement. Whilst for some activists the 'ultimacy' of the Earth was simply a symbol of a wider political struggle against the forces of capitalism, for others this 'ultimacy' of the Earth was expressed in spiritual terms: actions were rooted, metaphorically, in 'sacred ground' (Taylor, 1997b). Through religious forms of action such as rituals and ceremonies, activists with an explicitly 'spiritual' self-understanding sought to aid the battle against environmental destruction. It is in these kind of actions that the religious dimensions of this form of protest politics are most apparent – yet, as we argue below, the 'uses' of religion and spirituality within the movement go beyond these most visible manifestations, and perform various roles in the maintenance and activity of the movement.

Religion and irreligion in direct action

It may seem counterintuitive to try to draw links between environmental direct action movement and religion. Like other anarchist-inspired social movements, direct activists are generally disaffiliated from and critical of many mainstream values and institutions, including those of religion. As such, environmental direct action might be seen as a form of *ir*religion, as a reaction against the traditional forms of authority and belief that the churches exemplify. Following Ulrich Beck's analysis of the emergence of what he calls 'reflexive modernity', one might see the rise of environmental critique as a manifestation of what he terms a second Reformation, as individuals are increasingly 'set free from the certainties and modes of living of the industrial epoch – just as they were "freed" from the arms of the Church into society in the age of the Reformation' (Beck, 1992: 14). According to this interpretation, unthinking trust of and deference towards authority is increasingly undermined by individualisation and secularisation, so that scientific claims and political decisions are not simply accepted due to their originating from experts, but are subjected to stringent social critique and contestation. According to this analysis, anarchist thought and practice in general and environmental direct action in particular might be seen as at the vanguard of a new round of secularisation, as quasi-religious deference towards expertise is replaced by more contestatory, critical and active forms of citizenship.

However, as has been argued by writers such as Norman Cohn (1970) and Murray Bookchin (1982), the history of anarchism is interwoven with that of religious movements such as millenarianism. The beliefs and practices of such movements have provided important cultural resources for challenging the accepted dualistic codings of a dominant social order – between how things are and how things could be, between private and public actions, between leaders and led (Purkis, 2000: 107–8; Szerszynski, 2002: 56). Furthermore, just as was the case with earlier forms of anti-ritualism and iconoclasm in religious history, environmental direct action has developed its own rituals, symbols and narratives. Whilst these may not be understood by the activists as 'religion', nevertheless pockets of ritualised action and mythic forms of understanding are important features of the movement (Szerszynski, 2002).

A key term used to capture this dimension of the movement's praxis is 'spirituality', a term increasingly used by individuals in Western societies to denote a belief in 'something more' than the empirical, material world while at the same time avoiding what are seen as the stultifying features of traditional 'religion' (see Taylor, 2001). Zinnbauer *et al*. (1997) conducted a survey of 346 individuals from a wide range of religious backgrounds into whether they saw themselves as 'spiritual' or 'religious'. They found that those who saw themselves as 'spiritual but not religious' 'rejected traditional organised religion in favour of an individualised spirituality that includes mysticism along with New Age beliefs and practices' (p. 561). They conclude that '*religiousness* is increasingly characterised as "narrow and institutional", and *spirituality* is increasingly characterised as "personal and subjective"' (p. 563).

This analysis is consistent with that of Woodhead and Heelas (2000), who argue that the religions and spiritualities that are faring best are those which help to resource the individual, that are concerned more with the here and now than with the afterlife, and that nurture the unique, individual, lived life rather than simply promoting life in a particular prescribed social role. Whilst support for the Christian church is in decline, there is evidence to suggest that many people are turning to a style of religion that allows them to choose the beliefs, practices and lifestyles that feel right for them. Thus, via a process of *bricolage*, individuals select, borrow and interpret diverse religious symbols and ideas for novel purposes (Beckford, 1990; Roof, 1999).[2]

Many environmental direct activists articulate their spiritual commitment to direct action in terms of a belief in the sacredness of the Earth. It is common for them to refer to the Earth as 'Mother', the 'Goddess' or simply the divine. However, in general, activists are strongly against 'religion' and prefer to call themselves 'spiritual', blaming Christianity for the environmental crisis because of its separation of man from nature. By contrast, activists see themselves as adopting styles of spirituality that stress the interconnectedness of the divine with humanity and the natural world. A female protester at the Buddha Field Festival expressed her doubts about 'religion', 'I could see the same mistakes being made again and again . . . I worship wherever I am even if it is concrete.' She saw religious traditions as having lost an idea of the sacred, and as relying on hierarchy, exclusion and dishonesty.

Just as with Zinnbauer *et al*.'s (1997) respondents, the 'personal and subjective' nature of direct activists' understandings of spirituality means that it is often used to describe their experience and way of life without any explicit reference to what may be considered as the usual indicators of religiosity, such as the divine, the supernatural or the afterlife. This is echoed by Bloch, who argues that, 'simple, daily life actions to preserve the Earth could be viewed as "spiritual" activities' (Bloch, 1998: 59). Whereas activists identified 'religion' with the discrete, established, traditional religious systems, spirituality' was frequently used by protesters to describe their entire way of life and social vision. The line between the secular and the sacred was often difficult to draw, with activists frequently choosing to use similar language and to value particular symbols whether or not they considered themselves an explicitly spiritual person (Deudney, 1995; Taylor, 1996).

In their suspicion of mainstream religion, direct activists echoed the main thrust of the academic literature on environment and religion which dates back to the 1967 article 'The historical roots of our ecological crisis' by the historian Lynn White Jr. This seminal essay traced responsibility for the environmental crisis back to the displacement of paganism by Christianity, arguing that the latter religion's emphasis on the transcendence of God over creation (and by extension of humanity over nature) desacralised nature and opened the way for human beings to transform and domesticate nature. In this literature it is commonly argued that non-Christian religious cultures – whether animistic (Native American), pantheistic (Ancient Greek) or monistic (Buddhist or Taoist) – view nature as sacred and are therefore far more cautious and respectful in their dealings with the natural world (see Gottlieb, 1996 for a selection of such readings).[3] This 'critical environmental discourse' is popular within the environmental direct action movement, which shares many characteristics with a New Age religious outlook (Heelas, 1996) as well as with the more secular 'anarchistic' tendencies of many new social movements.

However, there are many within the movement who believe that spiritual ritual and symbolism detract from serious political engagement with the issues. At one Earth First! gathering a disagreement broke out during a group meeting. About fifty people were present, sitting in a circle discussing the pros and cons of non-violent direct action. At the summation of the meeting, one participant suggested that everyone praise the 'Mother' and he began a song to the 'Earth Goddess'. This was greeted with some ridicule, and resulted in the departure of a number of participants who felt that it was all a bit 'silly' and unnecessary. This did not deter the singers who continued their worship.

Clearly, despite the widely shared critique of Western 'religion' within the movement, there are differences over the relevance of explicit 'spirituality' to political activism. Nevertheless, as we argue below, even the more apparently 'secular' wing of the direct action movement is amenable to analysis in religious terms.

For both the spiritual and the non-spiritual within the movement, a critique of Western religions of transcendence frequently accompanies a strongly felt identification with cultures considered to exemplify holistic and environmentally friendly lifestyles. Those protesters who are explicitly spiritual in their approach to protecting the Earth are attracted to the religious traditions of cultures who lived 'close to nature' such as Native America Indian traditions or other 'tribal' or 'Eastern' cultures, thus developing a form of 'Do It Yourself' religion that has become a common style of religiosity in contemporary Western society. However, even for those who are not explicitly spiritual, lifestyles, dress and professed values frequently echo an allegiance to 'tribal' or pre-industrial cultures across the globe, in an effort to turn away from capitalism and to 'regain' some of the simplicity of pre-industrial lifestyles (Szerszynski, 1997, 2003).

Religion as a cultural resource

Within this general context of creative ambivalence about religion, we perceive that religious forms of action and thought are used as a resource for sustaining the involvement of the individual and the group within the movement. Direct action pushes individuals to their physical and psychological limits. Protesters tread a precarious path between positive personal transformation and achievement and serious risk to mental and physical health, or 'burn-out'. Many employ direct action tactics such as lock-ons, walkways, tunnels and tripods, putting themselves at risk to disrupt and delay construction work (Doherty, 2000). Against the background of these disincentives to participation, the motivation to remain involved is often more than a rational, intellectual response to deteriorating environments and the social injustices thus generated; it is also often deeply emotional (Milton, 2002).

This perhaps partly explains why a strong element of spirituality emerges within the direct action movement. As Deudney suggests, 'appeals to higher self-interest or long-run self-interest may be insufficient to motivate sufficient action. The appeal of Earth religion is that it helps motivate behaviour respectful of the Earth that otherwise would be difficult to achieve' (1995: 290). We believe that religious resources such as myths, quasi-religious self-understandings and ritual action operate partly as what Michel Foucault (1988) calls 'technologies of the self'. Although much of Foucault's work analyses the production of selves by forms of expert knowledge – the way that administrative procedures and institutions such as medicine, law and the Catholic confession produce certain kinds of subjectivity in people – in his later work he also became interested in techniques whereby people work on and transform their *own* subjectivities. From such a perspective, spirituality in the direct action movement can be seen as an ensemble of technologies of the self, ones which shape protesters' subjectivities to fit them for a life of resistance and protest.[4]

In this section of the chapter we identify three dimensions to this 'use of enchantment' within the environmental direct action movement: firstly, the language which protesters use to express the core beliefs of the 'figured world' of environmental direct action; secondly, the way protesters understand their own identities; and thirdly, the way that forms of action are used to express and reinforce movement commitment and belonging.

Beliefs, myths and values

Alberto Melucci (1989, 1996) has argued that social movements act as social laboratories, enclaves of experimentation within which individuals enact different 'forms of life' that contest and alter society's dominant codes. Movements offer their own 'figured worlds', in which participants can come to experience the world in a particular but shared way (Holland, Lachicotte, Skinner and Cain, 1998). Sometimes the shared understandings of the world take explicit 'religious' form, but, even when they do not, they lend themselves to analysis in religious terms. For instance, most religious traditions have developed means for adherents to distinguish themselves from the outside world, from those who do not belong to the tradition. Similarly, direct activists frequently refer to society as 'Babylon', the name for the spiritually bereft exile of the ancient Hebrews and more recently the Rastafarian term of derision for Western society. Babylon is used not only in a substantive sense but also adjectivally: for example, 'Babylon drugs' (Western medicine) or 'Babylon press' (mainstream media). In line with previous uses of the term, this suggests that something was felt to be lacking in 'straight' society that could be found in the exiled group and, at the most basic level, this missing element could be seen as a lack of awareness of the 'ultimate' significance (or even sacredness) of the Earth. However, there also exists a very strong feeling amongst activists that 'Babylon' is oppressive and that mainstream society with its hierarchies and consumerist culture subdues and traps the individual.

Another, 'implicitly religious' theme is the tendency for activists to articulate the status of the movement in mythic form.[5] Particularly popular are myths concerning the dawning of a 'new age', often described in terms of a battle between the forces of good (the protesters) and the forces of evil (the government, capitalism, globalisation) or 'Babylon'. For example, a male activist in his mid-fifties interviewed at the Wandsworth 'Ecovillage' explained how the movement had been 'called by the Mother Earth' to fight in a cosmic battle to save the planet from the forces of greed and evil which dominate society. He saw the fight to save the planet as not just a material struggle, but as a spiritual quest, linked to fundamental issues concerning the nature of human existence. Many other activists similarly tended towards such a mystical and soteriological interpretation of their actions.

In particular, certain Native American myths which prophesy the dawning of a new age were recounted within the movement. One popular myth prophesies that a time will come when children of the white people will come and seek the wisdom of the 'Elders', wearing long hair and beads. This will signal a time of purification. Another Native American myth, retold on a number of occasions, involves a prophecy surrounding the birth of a female white buffalo that will signal the proximity of world peace and the dawning of a new era – a sign of rejuvenation. Many protesters tended to talk about the emergence of the movement in such prophetic terms, as if it were inevitable. For such individuals the environmental direct action movement was part of a millenarian rejuvenation. Indeed, some activists believed that the white buffalo had been born (on 20 August 1994 in Janesville, Wisconsin, on Heider Farm) and that the world was therefore on the cusp of change.

Some writers have expressed concern over the adoption and adaptation of myths from other cultures.[6] Such concerns aside, such myths clearly play an important role in the understanding of movement members of themselves as agents of ecological defence. Such meta-narratives of ecological decline and renewal help to connect the times of protesters' own concrete actions with the more abstract time of 'world-historical transformation' (Jasper, 1997: 22; Szerszynski, 2002). The identification of activists with oppressed groups such as Native Americans also serves to ground their identity as a revolutionary and emancipatory force in a much wider 'imagined community' (Anderson, 1983), seeing themselves as part of a wider resurgence of oppressed groups reasserting their values and way of life in the face of the homogenising forces of global capitalism.

Identity, conversion and personal transformation

In order for movement membership to play a significant role in participants' lives, it has to become a meaningful and significant part of whom they take themselves to be – their *identity*. Identity is shaped by the experience of practice (see the next subsection), by an oppositional stance to the wider world, and can be grounded in mythic meta-narratives (see the last subsection – 'Activism and non-violence'). However, identity is also understood in terms of personal narrative, and in the context of social movements, the biographical narrative is generally a discontinuist one, where the narration of their passage from pre-movement life to movement involvement is an important way in which individuals situate their present selves (on conversion in religious movements, see Lofland, 1966). As James Jasper argues, once individuals are part of a social movement, they tend to rewrite their personal biography, using the narrative of their own conversion not just as a straightforward description of past events, but as a symbolic resource to affirm their alignment with movement values (Jasper, 1997: 82). Whether overtly spiritual or not, activists frequently talk about their entry into the movement in terms of a conversion experience. Many activists experience their conversion to a new set of values and responsibilities as a revelation, of something to which they were previously blind. This life-changing moment or phase is arguably a factor central to the ability of activists to hold values which often put them at odds with mainstream society and to engage in activities which may endanger their safety or place them in breach of the law.

Protesters' belief in the possibility of persuading others to change is partly grounded in the examples of personal transformation experienced within the movement. As one female protester at the Big Green Gathering admitted: 'If I really thought that people still wouldn't care even if they knew the facts then I would drop out of society and become more Buddhist or meditative. The social protest movement really believes people will change. People who are involved are transformed.' Protesters revelled in stories about 'locals' who remained involved and interested in direct action even when the protest in their locality was over. A female activist who had been involved in the M11 anti-road protest in East London excitedly explained that there had been some 'suburban housewives' in Wanstead who were affected by the proposed road plans and joined the protesters in objection: 'they are still wandering around dressed like hippies a year after everyone has gone and they are still political, like fighting the CJA.[7] People wake up, the most unlikely people, suburban housewives!'

Personal accounts of transformation and conversion are invariably spoken of in highly emotional terms. Many activists attested to the fact that taking part in direct action had changed their lives. At the Earth First! Gathering, Joe explained that it was through the protests against the (then proposed) Criminal Justice Act in 1994 that he had first become involved in direct action and had lived at many protest sites including Newbury and Wandsworth. However, he said that now he cannot imagine living any other way; direct action had become a way of life, his way of life. Similarly Green Dave stressed that 'I've never been happier or healthier' since adopting this lifestyle. Protesters attest not only to a sense of satisfaction from feeling that they are contributing to positive social change but also claim that they benefit from the personal challenge. There is an atmosphere of immediacy amongst protesters, a sense that their political stance, both in terms of lifestyle and forms of action, is necessary in order to save the planet from environmental destruction.

Action, healing and ceremony

Religion is not just about the cognition and articulation of certain beliefs and values; it is also about action. Similarly, activities within the environmental direct action movement of the 1990s also served to confirm and validate key movement meanings. Here we explore three different kinds of action in this way: healing, worship and celebration, and direct action protest itself.

Healing

Gatherings attended by activists tended to include a 'healing area' where a wide range of therapies including homeopathy, *reiki*, acupuncture and crystal healing, as well as spiritual disciplines from Paganism, to Buddhism and the Hare Krishna were on offer. As the programme for the 1996 Big Green Gathering explains:

> In this 1996 Big Green Gathering we in the healing area will be coming together to celebrate and enhance the joy of life, but also to recognise ourselves as witness to

the deterioration of our environment which threatens the quality and even the very fabric of life itself. As consciousness and self-awareness increases we will be able to learn and grow together in an atmosphere of loving support.

One Earth First! Gathering offered a number of workshops on health issues, including 'Camp Living and its Attendant Diseases' (which involved the sharing of experiences on how to live in a camp and stay healthy, first-aid, self-defence sessions, discussions on how to avoid 'burn-out' and information on diet and the effects of toxic pollutants). Additionally, the gathering had a formal healing area, a space at the centre of the field within which a large bender had been erected where individuals ran sessions on Earth healing and meditation as well as offering massage and other therapies.

Many activists had made protest sites their homes, often for months on end, living with the constant anxiety that at any moment their tree houses, benders or whole communities could be demolished. Coupled with the personal invest-ment in the cause itself, the stress of this lifestyle brought immense pressure to bear upon individuals. It was not uncommon for people to become depressed and dependent, with alcoholism and drug abuse emerging as serious problems within the movement. Activists highlighted the importance of attending gather-ings and festivals as an opportunity to 'chill out' away from the pressures of the eco-battlefield and this is also a reason given for the existence of healing areas or 'sacred' spaces at such events as well as within protest communities. The protest movement cannot survive if individuals are unbalanced or out of touch with themselves and lose sight of their goals.

The 'return' to traditional or holistic healing arts can be seen as a broader reaction within this alternative community against contemporary Western med-icine, which is considered to concentrate on the physical at the expense of the other aspects of human nature. 'Alternative' traditional methods stress that healing cannot be successful unless it considers the whole person. Healing, in this broad sense, is considered by many to be fundamental to the underlying ethos and ultimate success of the movement. For example, at the Earth First! Gathering, Ash, a woman in her twenties expressed concern about the health of members of the direct action movement and felt that it was an area needing attention. One of her primary interests was making people more aware of camp illnesses, including visitors to protest sites, and in encouraging people to take better care of themselves. She also drew attention to the stresses of a life of protest and the fact that people often drink too much in order to block out the pain of evictions. She was training in *reiki*, learning about different herbal rem-edies ('as most people are shy of Babylon drugs') and attempting to introduce health as a serious issue into the camps where she stayed.

Some rituals were considered to have a direct power to heal the Earth. 'Eco-magic' or Earth healing aims to access the divine powers inherent in nature and the individual, and to direct them towards healing the Earth. A session at an Earth First! Gathering, called 'Healing Ourselves Healing the Planet' was organ-ised by three local female healers. They built an altar at the centre of a bender with flowers and candles arranged upon it and invited us all (there were about twenty people present) to sit in a circle and begin meditating. The guided healing ritual required us to visualise a bright light, allowing it to enter at the top of the head and to bathe the whole body. The light was then allowed to pass out of the head and progressively fill the room, the world, the planet, the cosmos. Finally, this energy was visualised as spreading from the centre of the Earth to its surface and filling the rocks, the plants, the animals and people. This ritual reflects the belief that humanity not only has the capacity to destroy nature but also directly to heal nature. For the healers this was seen as a necessary and important element in saving the environment, reflecting the interconnectedness of creation not only in terms of a physical link but also through an energy pervading everything.

Worship and celebration

Many of the rituals at gatherings and protest sites served not so much to heal as to reaffirm common values. At the 1996 Big Green Gathering, a group called 'Tree Spirit' organised a tree planting ceremony where thirteen trees associated with the eight seasonal festivals were blessed in preparation for planting as a sacred grove. Celebration of the eight seasonal festivals and the thirteen annual full moons are popular amongst activists, and individuals may travel to sacred sites or conduct their own rituals at protest camps. However, there was no set formula: celebration during these periods involved anything from a big party to carefully planned rituals and prayers. The ceremony included praise to the Goddess and to the spirits of each tree as an expression the re-sacralisation of nature. According to Glennie Kindred, a founder member of Tree Spirit,

> throughout the world, trees have been revered as divine sources of wisdom and worshipped as deities. The ancient people believed that trees were sacred and contained a spirit who could be talked to. There are many documentations of ceremonies for felling trees, warning the tree spirit, or asking for its forgiveness. Trees were honoured and thanked for their gifts and treated with respect and awe. (Kindred, 1995: 3)

Shortly after the tree planting ritual there was a Druidic ritual at a nearby set of standing stones, erected during the previous gathering, and in a far corner of the healing area followers of the International Society for Krishna Consciousness (ISKCON) were chanting. Many individuals attended all the above rituals as general expressions of Earth spirituality, as re-affirming the sacredness of the Earth.

Activism and nonviolence

Activism itself was also considered by some individuals as a ritual expressing love and respect for the Earth. As such, environmental protest activity is largely nonviolent. In general, protesters would not deliberately use physically violent strategies in the course of their actions. This is one of the features of environmental protest that for many observers locates it clearly in the Western anarchist tradition, which distinguishes itself from other forms of revolutionary politics by its conviction that means should always be consistent with goals, and that action should be 'prefigurative'. As one activist, Josh, argued, 'social transformation requires personal transformation. We need to become the type of person we would like to live in our communities.' Activists also often justify nonviolence in contrast to Babylon, which, as mentioned previously, is considered to use aggressive means to control nature and humanity. If physical violence is used then the protesters would be playing by Babylon's rules; if Babylon is to be fundamentally challenged, then alternative, nonviolent strategies must be employed.

However, activists also refer to the example of Mahatma Gandhi and the Indian idea of *ahimsa* (nonviolence or non-harm). Gandhi extended this traditional Indian teaching to the domain of political protest where he emphasised that fighting the aggressors, the British, with their own tactics, violence, was not as effective as approaching them nonviolently. It could be argued that Gandhi resorted to this traditional idea as a strategic measure because his followers did not have the resources to wage a violent battle against the colonial army and indeed this is suggested by some activists as a good reason to adopt a nonviolent approach. However, Gandhi's freedom movement drew great support and was eventually successful in bringing about an independent India. Despite the suggestion of this as a tactical move, it is generally believed that the movement was at least partially successful because of its adherence to the spiritual teaching of *ahimsa* (Chapple, 1995; Gupta, 1995).

Conclusion

Environmental direct action shares with organised religion the characteristic of reflecting what Paul Tillich (1957) called the 'ultimate concern' of the individual. Whilst for some activists their ultimate concern is articulated in a secular way, for many others it is expressed in the language of spirituality, in terms of belief in the sacredness of the Earth or of love for the Mother Earth goddess. We have argued that this internal diversity within the direct action movement is an intensified form of broader 'spiritual' critiques of organised religion in many sectors of wider society, in which 'religion' is seen as connoting the formulaic and the oppressive, and 'spirituality' is used to refer to beliefs and practices seen as expressing and nurturing the individual, lived life. Virtually all activists share this critique of 'religion', but only some see explicit 'spirituality' as a desired alternative.

However, we went on to suggest that, across this spectrum within the direct action movement, there is a widespread use of religious forms of belief and action to 'resource' groups and individuals in their commitment to the protest cause, to shape their subjectivities for the life of protest. Firstly, we looked at the way that certain forms of belief about the movement and wider society serve to express and sustain their sense of calling to a higher cause. Secondly, we explored the importance of conversion and a sense of personal transformation for the maintenance of commitment amongst movement members. Thirdly, we discussed how the performance of practices such as healing, ceremony and direct action are fundamental to maintaining the strength of the movement.

We opened with one reference to the term 'enchantment', that of Bruno Bettelheim. However, it was Max Weber, who first gave us the term 'the dis-enchantment of the world', *die Entzauberung der Welt*. He used the phrase to describe the way that, in modern societies, people withdraw from public life into the private sphere in accordance with their substantive 'core' values, leaving public life to be organised around notions of instrumental rationality and bureaucratic efficiency (Weber, 1989: 14, 30). Although Weber lamented some of the side-effects of this dis-enchantment, he was enough of an Enlightenment thinker to nevertheless see it as a necessary part of human progress and emancipation. Anarchist writers – Murray Bookchin (1982) included – have largely aligned themselves with this tradition of thought, one that sees progressive forces in society as always on the side of the secular against the religious or spiritual. Using the example of environmental direct action, we have argued that the story is more complex, that forms of enchantment can have their uses, in constituting subjects suitable for civil disobedience in defence of the Earth.

Notes

1 The ethnographic material in this chapter is based on fieldwork undertaken by Emma Tomalin from May to October 1996 at a protest sites and related gatherings and festivals: the Wandsworth 'Eco-village' (South London, May–October 1996); the 'Big Green Gathering' (24–28 July 1996, Longbridge Deverill, Wiltshire); the 'Buddha Field Festival' (17–20 July 1996, near Shepton Mallet, Somerset); and an Earth First! Gathering (12–15 June 1996, North Wales) (see Tomalin (2000)). Activists' names have been changed.

2 The term '*bricolage*' in anthropology was originated by Levi-Strauss (1962). For a useful discussion of the general phenomenon of *bricolage* in social movements, see Hetherington (1998: 28; 2000: 98–9).

3 The accuracy of this view is doubtful. Whilst many cultures have religious practices or teachings associated with the natural world, such traditions of *nature religion* ought to be distinguished from *religious environmentalism*. Religious environmentalism is limited because it is a product of Western ideas about nature, in particular a 'romantic' vision of nature as a realm of purity and aesthetic value. Although in India, for example, people worship certain trees, this is not evidence of an inherent environmental awareness if only because such practices are very ancient and predate concerns about a global environmental crisis (Tomalin, 2002; Milton, 1996; Pederson, 1995).

4 Cruikshank (1999) considers various forms of participatory democracy in order to argue that, while they ostensibly seem to empower the powerless, they in fact serve as technologies of the self which at once create and regulate governable citizens. By contrast, the spiritual technologies of the self explored here, we argue, are less amenable to such a critical reading.

5 Such mythmaking is of course a perennial feature of political communities (see Anderson (1983); Hobsbawm and Ranger (1983)).

6 These myths do have their origins in Native American culture, but the form in which activists know them originates in the 'Rainbow Family', an alternative social movement originating in the United States in the early 1970s, originally influenced by Native American traditions which were later overlaid by elements of European Paganism as the movement spread to Europe (Niman, 1997). Niman is concerned at the way that the Rainbows 'have written themselves into Hopi prophecies' (p. 134), considering this process as tantamount to 'ethnocide' (p. 146). By contrast, Taylor argues that this process is unexceptional in religious life: 'some cross-cultural borrowing, reciprocal influencing and blending is an inevitable aspect of religious life – thus at least some of the hand-wringing over appropriation and syncretic processes is misplaced and over broad' (1997: 206).

7 In the United Kingdom, the Criminal Justice and Public Order Act (1995) criminalised most forms of direct action.

Jonathan Purkis and James Bowen

Conclusion: how anarchism still matters

Introduction

As possibly the most idealistic, complicated and contradictory political philosophy to have emerged from the Enlightenment, anarchism occupies a unique and under-acknowledged place in the history of ideas. The chapters in this volume have engaged with and critiqued much of what is taken by mainstream academics and commentators to *be anarchism*. In the era that we have called that of 'global anarchism', the classical anarchist canon has come under attack from a variety of perspectives which have posited different interpretations of history and the use of power based on narratives of gender, ethnicity, sexuality, environment, technology, social psychology and anthropocentrism. The consolidation of these critiques – all of which have long histories – has reinvigorated anarchism and allowed a constructive dialogue with the classical-era theories of Bakunin, Proudhon, Godwin and Kropotkin *et al*. At the beginning of the twenty-first century, anarchism is extremely theoretically diverse, with considerable fragmentation based on different philosophical premises, each attempting to formulate strategy utilising enduring anarchist principles such as the need for consistency of means and ends and opposition to hierarchy. It is these parallel versions of anarchism that have led to calls for the term *anarchisms* to be employed instead, or indeed to re-embrace the word anarchy as an idea which many groups work towards but which holds no central organising premise. There is considerable evidence to suggest that, although this may defy consensus, as a description of the practical manifestations of libertarian and antiauthoritarian projects it is hard to fault.

Anarchism has been arguably most recently visible at the many economic and political summits hosted by the rulers of the richest countries and corporate bodies, from Seattle, November 1999, onwards. However, the evidence from this book suggests that we cannot limit our concerns to this particular strand of global anarchism and all of its cross-cultural and cross-continental networks. The variety of anarchist projects on education, media, community activism, ecology, art and literature or sexual liberation is extensive, and these are far from limited to isolated pockets of the West, although there is considerable work still

to be done, for instance, in putting African anarchism 'on the map'. Yet in order
to maximise the influence of anarchism so as to impact more meaningfully on
the destructive economic and political agendas of the powerful, some reflection
as to the constituency of anarchist process and its relationship with the non-
anarchist world is needed.

The following discussion considers how we might begin to theorise this relationship, the opportunities for influence and the difficult question about consistency of means and ends of actions. We suggest that the possibilities for
resistance to power and the construction of what Dennis Hardy (1979) has called
'practical utopias' are actually increasing in the wake of the post-11 September
2001 clampdowns and repression, despite anecdotal evidence to the contrary.
This is particularly the case with contemporary debates about the future of
'democracy', given the emergence of new political forces in the developing world,
declining electoral participation in the West and the increasing intervention that
unaccountable corporate bodies such as the World Trade Organisation are
having on everyday life. The spaces that open up as a result of the contradictions
and complexities of social life are also important in realising the potential that
can be actualised through considering popular culture as an area where anarchism matters. To fully appreciate these possibilities, along with many other
areas of likely intervention and influence, we suggest that the kind of anarchism
(or even anarchisms) that is required for the future should be a non-dogmatic,
flexible, inclusive one. This must be based upon an adaptability at seeing anarchist theory and practice as something that engages with as many areas of
society and culture as is practically possible, rather than existing only as a marginalised and somewhat élitist political force.

In order to arrive at this conclusion, we review the different ways that anarchism can be seen in terms of its often under-acknowledged role in political
change. In particular, we suggest that anarchism can serve as a 'conscience' to
many non-anarchist or marginally anarchist milieus in terms of the influence of
its central ideas. Moreover, the idea that contemporary anarchism is extremely
flexible in its impact and manifestations can also be supported by the anti-dualistic philosophical positions adopted by each of the contributors. Such a situation allows much more theoretical, and therefore practical, leeway.

Anarchism as the 'conscience of politics'

One of the key themes that run through anarchist literature is the existence of
an alternative account of historical change, based on everyday acts of co-operation, voluntarism and spontaneity. The so-called naturalness of these actions has
underpinned many anarchist arguments over the best part of two centuries from
Kropotkin to Bookchin, just as Bakunin argued for the 'naturalness' of rebellion
in his book *God and the state* (1985). There is, according to all of the writers in
Changing anarchism, a sense that the potential for anarchist action lies barely

beneath the surface of everyday life, if indeed it is not overtly taking place in many contexts on a daily basis. This is an important methodological point that allows us to move away from traditional histories of anarchism that concentrate on key events such as the Paris Commune of 1871, the Haymarket martyrs of 1886, the Russian and Spanish Revolutions through to 'May 68' in France and beyond. It also needs to be acknowledged that the *idea of anarchism* has an appeal that extends far beyond the radical political milieus of this world, many of which are outlined in this collection. We would suggest that especially, but not exclusively, in the last four decades, anarchism has enjoyed a close relationship with a number of political movements that are not openly anarchist, yet maintain many characteristics associated with anarchism. This is particularly the case with the new social movements discussed in the chapters by Morland and Purkis (chapters 1 and 2), the structures and critiques of which have been linked to anarchism (Cahill, 1992; Welsh, 1997, 2000). These processes have intensified with the huge networks known as the 'alternative globalisation movement' (Chesters, 2003). It is in these contexts that anarchism acts as a cultural resource and as a form of 'political conscience', irrespective of whether or not the organisations in question formally acknowledge this.

The invisible hand of anarchism

Firstly, it is worth extending the aforementioned point about the wider influence of anarchist ideas, to note how easily such aspects of 'social movement culture' can be overlooked in popular and academic accounts. The full ramifications of this cannot be discussed here, but the crucial point to note is that it is the less visible dimension of political movements, rather than their explicit protest intentions which are frequently the location for the transmission and diffusion of ideas. We have seen how in chapters by Heckert, Goaman, and Szerszynski and Tomalin (chapters 5, 9 and 11), protest camps and actions frequently constitute transformatory experiences leading to the creation of new forms of political identity. Moreover, these cultural practices are occurring not in isolated movements but as part of a wider set of networks and social relations. The Dutch sociologist Bert Klandermans (1993) calls this 'the multi-organisational field', a space where political cultures interact, exchange members, form alliances and share resources. Our argument is that this is actually the norm rather than the exception within much of politics, and that within these fields anarchism has a greater influence than is often acknowledged, whether the networks concerned are officially anarchist or just implicitly so. Yet, from both a theoretical and practical point of view, these incidents of cultural cross-fertilisation are particularly difficult to research, a situation which is often made more difficult by the fact that the ideological outlook of individuals comprising supposedly clearly differentiated groups is actually closer than is often imagined. One now well-established case in point is the impact that the radical environmental Earth First! network has had on their more established environmental counterparts.

As Derek Wall documents (2000), the reaction to the emergence of the UK Earth First! network in the early 1990s from groups such as Friends of the Earth and Greenpeace was one of initial distrust if not hostility, partly on account of the drift towards 'respectability' and increasing bureaucratisation of these once-pioneering organisations. Such attitudes were to a certain extent reproduced on a micro-sociological level, yet in some political cultures, such as those of large northern English cities, issues of tactics, joint participation in actions and the sharing of resources were much more complex (Purkis, 2001). This relationship of dialogue between different movement cultures – one anarchist, the other not – eventually resulted in the decentralist direct action politics of Earth First! and other radical environmental networks actually beginning to influence the direction of their more moderate counterparts. By the late 1990s, both Greenpeace and Friends of the Earth had begun to examine their own structures and strategies. The former's high-profile campaign of direct action against genetically modified crops in the United Kingdom during this time appeared to signal a keenness to encourage wider participation in such actions from its members (many of whom had tended to be little more than fundraisers in the past). Whilst one would be hard-pressed to elicit a response from a major non-governmental organisation that mentioned anarchist praxis in a favourable light, the repositioning of moderate organisations in reaction to their more marginal radical counterparts is certainly not a new phenomenon (see Scarce, 1990).

In terms of its impact on a wider political consciousness, it is important to note that the anarchist politics of the early twenty-first century implicit in the chapters in this book is frequently alliance-based, involving networks of co-operatives, umbrella or popular front campaigns on specific issues, sometimes across countries and continents. Whether organising around education, sexuality, environmental destruction, development issues, narcotics, conflict resolution or bearing witness, the question of influence and diffusion becomes highly pertinent in terms of what *form of anarchism* is being advocated. We regard it as significant that each of the contributions here addresses the deconstruction of particular conceptual dualisms, which can assist in the development of a much more theoretically and practically flexible notion of anarchism. With this in mind, it is vital that this project acknowledge the gradual dissolution of one of the most insidious dualisms to have dogged radical politics, that of 'reform' versus 'revolution'.

Reform or revolution?

In the nineteenth-century political world, the forces of oppression were much more visible and more obviously manifested than in the era of global anarchism. Society was more polarised, opposition was more clear-cut, and the political choice or 'reform or revolution' seemed a realistic and pertinent one. However, with twenty-first century eyes, the dualism is both deterministic and mechanistic regarding what political change actually *is* and *who* carries it out. The subtleties of political influence and the fact that anarchism is a process not an event is noted in the chapters by Heckert and Bowen (chapters 5 and 6) and the theoretical possibilities offered by poststructuralism and complexity are discussed by Morland and Purkis respectively (chapters 1 and 2). Gribble's documentation (chapter 10) of libertarian education further invalidates this dualism, given the incredibly precarious institutional 'grey areas' within which the projects described are frequently located, as does Craig's depiction (chapter 7) of the complex decisions involved in making an anarchist position on narcotics. As Todd May has argued:

> The distinction between reform and revolution should not be the tired one of 'mere reform' vs. 'real revolution.' It should instead be an issue of how much and how deep of a change is going on. In fact, I think the term is often used as a banner, a mark of one's radicalism, and an unconsidered way of marking out one's distinction from liberalism. As such, it hides the question, which we should be asking; what needs to be changed and how does it need to be changed? (2000: 3)

In a sense, the fluidity and flexibility of political movements and their strategies have always been more complex than many with vested interests on the anarchist or Marxist Left have been willing to admit. Social-psychological approaches to political movements have sometimes emphasised the highly contingent nature of individual political participation (see Klandermans, 1997), and this can also be applied to movement tactics. A useful illustration of this is Szerszynski's concept of 'dual-legitimacy' (2002), whereby a movement pursues more than one strategy at the same time: one course of action may be aiming to influence the general public, whilst another is couched in terms appropriate to fellow activists or even the media. So, on the one hand it might *appear* to be the case, if, for instance, a campaign emerges in opposition to a particular piece of legislation, that this is a 'reformist movement'. However, the consequences of such a mobilisation are, as we have indicated, multi-faceted, providing new skills, solidarity and what French sociologist Alain Touraine calls 'positive assertions of freedom' (2000: 297). That the actions might inadvertently lead to reform is merely one particular outcome of many possible ones.

So far we have suggested that anarchism frequently *has* an influence that is sometimes under-acknowledged. This builds on David Graeber's (2002) point that anarchism is the heart beating at the centre of the alternative globalisation networks, a notion that has been picked up by several of our contributors. However, whilst it is possible to argue that anarchism does act as the conscience of *some* political formations, with relevant 'monitoring' of 'hierarchical drift', the complexities of these contemporary alliances do also pose a number of problems for anarchists.

This position tends to assume a form of ideological unity which, in such a diverse milieu, is unlikely. Whilst there are always anarchist enclaves within these wider networks who adhere to 'pure' anarchist principles, alliance politics are a much messier affair. The experienced activist knows that one has to accept limited rather than absolute victories, to campaign on issues which one knows in the short term may be unsuccessful yet, in time, will be of lasting importance. Thus self-identified anarchists may find themselves in protest situations whereby they might not be acting completely in ways consistent with the principles of classical anarchism. For example, the aforementioned 'dual (or multi)-legitimacy' strategies of network cultures might sometimes necessitate an occasional dipping of the ideological standards in exchange for meaningful alliances. This is a trade-off that many of the contributors to this book appear to be sympathetic to and has no doubt been reproduced on many occasions throughout 'revolutionary' history. Heckert's argument (chapter 5), that it is better to take affirmative action in support of 'positive' projects than needlessly opposing authority without an outcome gain, is a case in point. Perhaps more important is the need to acknowledge the influence of anarchism in unexpected areas of society and why developing alternative forms of socialisation such as those described by Gore and Gribble (chapters 8 and 10) is a crucial, if slightly unglamorous, process. Yet, in terms of the ethical agonies about taking action in more 'mainstream' political contexts, one should not ignore the fact that the kinds of models of power that have begun to replace the ones from the era of classical anarchism do not necessarily invalidate action of this kind.

Anarchism as communication

The preceding argument can be seen less as an abandonment of anarchist praxis and more as an attempt to avoid reproducing the mechanistic and potentially exclusionary strategies of the era of mass anarchist movements. Instead there is a real need to theorise in a manner appropriate to the era of globalisation and complex configurations of power, yet also where intervention and influence are possible and beneficial. To accomplish this, it is useful to revisit the notion of contemporary anarchist subjectivity, outlined in highly different ways by Moore, Morland, Heckert, Szerszynski and Tomalin, Millett and Gore. The reason for this is twofold: firstly, there needs to be a re-evaluation and deconstruction of the classic dualism of individual and collective; and secondly, that the impact which power has on the individual may influence subsequent strategy. We suggest that an understanding of these aspects of anarchist identity becomes a prerequisite for communication and building what we have called 'discursive bridges' between anarchist and non-anarchist spheres of action.

New interpretations on old dualisms

The individual and collective dualism is central to all political theory, but is more starkly realised in anarchist thought because of its antiauthoritarian sensibilities. It is also a problem which many theorists have tried to find ways 'around' or reinvent for the purposes of a more constructive anarchist praxis. One such author is L. Susan Brown. In *The politics of individualism* (1993) she posits something of a conceptual bridge by differentiating between 'instrumental individualism' (whereby individual liberty can be 'achieved' even if it entails using people for gain) and 'existential individualism' (whereby individual freedom must not be achieved at other people's expense). Thus 'existential individualism' – similar to Paul Lichterman's concept of 'personalism' which opposes materialism as a way of self-actualising (1996: 6) – utilises the anarchist ethic of equating the means of an action with its ends. Whilst there are problems with Brown's endorsement of existentialism (see Morland, 1997), her framing of the means and ends of actions in this way is useful. It is also commensurate with poststructuralist theories of identity, which reject the liberal construction of the autonomous free rational agent as 'natural' and look to the social construction of the subject by society. This critique is also central to Moore's article on Max Stirner, which also offers a 'way out' of this particular dualism.

As indicated in our introduction, Stirner's controversial place in intellectual history has recently been revised, as poststructuralist theorists have seized on his rejection of universal truth and 'fixed ideas', and associated his ideas with contemporary notions of contingency, plurality and dynamism (Koch, 1997: 105). As Moore's chapter (chapter 2) demonstrates, it is this constant uncertainty and absolute rejection of any imposition on Stirner's notion of the self ('ownness') which has led to his arguments being wrongly perceived as completely rejecting any form of collectivism. By implication, this reading of Stirner suggests that a 'union of egos' *can* provide a meaningful (rather than impossible) dialogue between the individual and collective. Thus, even in the most collaborative of circumstances, the unique signature of the individual – ownness – is not lost. This is the true intersection of the egoist and the union of egos: the individual needs the support of the 'affinity of egos', yet the collective cannot exist without acknowledging the unique creativeness of the individual ownnesses that drive it. Such ordinary processes are part of the hard work that is required in all areas of human interaction and which is in need of further theorisation.

Power, subjectivity, principles

The logic of both Brown's and Stirner's arguments is that extreme individualism is not incompatible with either collective action or advocating a consistency of means and ends of actions. This is an important point for the kind of alliance politics and networks comprising contemporary anarchism. When there is the need for cross-cultural co-operation, the different emphases and assumptions placed on individuality and collectivism may well require maximum flexibility. In such circumstances, an awareness of the different forms of power that have shaped individual expectations is also a crucial ingredient for meaningful change on a collective level.

The chapters in this book offer a wide range of observations and analyses of the impact of power on the individual, some of which evoke deeper processes than the often-observable injustices of political economy. Here it is important to note the development of the psychological dimension to anarchism through analyses of the history of civilisation and human relationships with technology and the environment. The critiques underpinning the chapters by Goaman, Millett and Moore are challenging in terms of the alienation that they bestow on the contemporary psyche. Not unexpectedly then, strategies for 're-enchanting' the world (as Szerszynski and Tomalin put it) or 'becoming' rather than 'being' (Moore) are to be encouraged. However, there is the need to acknowledge the difficulties which the re-instatement of concepts such as 'totality' or 'complexity' into an anarchist critique pose for the organisation of strategic thinking and communicating between the different anarchist 'subjectivities'. This is most clearly evident in terms of the need to re-assess founding anarchist principles in the light of such diversity.

Earlier we made the point that sometimes a temporary 'dipping' of anarchist standards might be acceptable for the sake of particular network politics. However, we would suggest that on an individual level, a sureness of anarchist principles is necessary, both for the purposes of 'ontological security' and to inform and monitor any collective actions that drift too far away from anarchism. In this respect it is useful to note the criteria suggested by Benjamin Franks (2003) that set anarchism apart from socialist and Marxist politics (a distinction that, given the frequent presence of such groups in alliance politics, is no bad thing). He argues that anarchist actions should always be 'pre-figurative' with the means being equivalent to the ends; they should never attempt to represent other groups (even oppressed ones) in a paternalistic manner; all forms of power are to be opposed but none prioritised; and actions should be carried out non-hierarchically.

Discursive bridges I – cultural resources

Franks's criteria, whilst obvious to many, are worth reiterating simply because our concerns in this section are to explore the different strategies that might be involved in influencing 'non-anarchist' areas of society. Whilst we accept the value of tactical positioning on the margins (as well as anarchism's own influence there!), anarchism's direct impact on global issues remains marginal, and as a result other courses of action are worth pursuing. The aforementioned awkwardness about consistency of principles within alliance politics is equally of relevance when dealing with the suggestion of anarchist strategies and analyses in 'everyday life'.

Initially, we would suggest that there are a number of cultural resources upon which anarchists can draw in terms of engaging with 'non-anarchist' spheres. Firstly, there are the arguments for the 'natural' co-operative (yet also antiauthoritarian) dimension to human nature, which classical anarchist theorists emphasised and which continue to be important. Clearly, these are essentialist and inflexible concepts, as poststructural anarchists like Koch (1997) have rightly pointed out, but as a resource, debates about which societies have tended towards co-operative rather than egoistic (in the despotic rather than Stirnerian sense) organisation are useful.

Secondly, it is important to emphasise the question of prefiguration in terms of the things that are *already in place* or are currently being developed in communities around the world as part of a resistance to the economic, climatic and epidemiological contradictions of the current global order. This has been particularly true of agriculture and food production and how local circumstances quickly generate all kinds of associated political movements. New forms of food production, distribution and activism reveal the reaction of the 'global local'. In the UK, small-scale 'farmers' markets' have politicised networks isolated by agribusiness, which, as Goaman notes (chapter 9), is also a facet of the politics of Indian farming communities. Where national economies have collapsed, such as in Argentina in 2001, extensive networks of local assemblies as well as distribution networks have erupted, proving that even in a highly divided society many things are possible (Klein, 2003). One of the significant points about these incidents is that they tap into many people's existing disenchantment with the global economic and political order and show how ordinary people change the world.

A third area that can act as a resource is the area of popular culture, which might seem strange given the many criticisms from anarchists in recent years about the so-called 'turn to culture'. Yet, as Jude Davies has argued (1997), ignoring such a huge part of everyday life is to overlook the possibilities of anarchist intervention and mobilisation; indeed, considerable opportunities exist alongside, and inform rather than replace, critiques of political economy and other forms of power. Engaging with, rather than rejecting, aspects of popular culture can provide space for those who have been both extremely compromised by, or alienated from, it. Another reason for doing so, is that the appeal of anarchism in the contemporary alternative globalisation movement and related milieus has sometimes come *from* popular culture. In the United Kingdom, for instance, a familiarity with hi-profile radical folk/punk bands such as Chumbawamba, The Levellers and Rage Against the Machine has been evident, all of whom have campaigned against legislation such as the Criminal Justice and Public Order Act of 1994 and the Terrorism Act of 2000. As Allan Antliff has recently noted (2003), anarchist street art, video work and comics such as *World War 3* have, in various North American settings, managed to blur some of the existing boundaries between 'culture' as passive and culture as politically proactive. Such forms can, if allowed to flourish, revisit the kind of radicalism of 'community arts' that Gore discusses in her contribution to the book (chapter 7) and connects to points made about revolutionary form made here (and elsewhere) by Moore (1998).

Equally crucial in terms of the idea of 'discursive bridges' and culture is the matter of communication between different generations, and here it is important to pick up issues raised by Bowen, Gore and Gribble (chapters 6, 8 and 10) concerning the centrality that education has in determining anarchist praxis. It is interesting to note how a number of the contributors to the volume *Anarchism today* (Apter and Joll, 1971) argue that the apparent lack of theoretical sophistication of the late 1960s counter culture was on the grounds that it was too preoccupied with youth concerns and hedonism. In this respect, the arguments made by Gore about the importance of the revolutionary imagination and overcoming particularly stultified views of reality, including the importance of play, speak volumes about the relevance of this area for future work.

Discursive bridges II – communication

Anarchists may be able to draw upon a range of cultural resources to facilitate better communication, but *how* that communication takes places is of primary importance. Moreover, communication strategies need to be considered both in terms of the political language used and the way in which particular protest actions communicate to non-participants. As Heckert comments in his chapter (chapter 5), the issue of means and ends becomes pertinent here. He notes how the rhetorical strategies adopted by some campaigners can be extremely violent, raising an uncomfortable issue about alienation; those who are trying to do the persuading are equally 'damaged' by the system. This calls for sensitive strategies, and here we would suggest that the building of discursive bridges between different social spheres and political realities ought to begin with couching notions of resistance in terms of 'common sense'.

Here we deliberately utilise the term as developed by Antonio Gramsci (1971) to mean the consensual worldview secured by the dominant classes as represented in language and culture. However, this is only a starting-point, since the models of power offered by Gramsci are largely inappropriate for the contexts within which the contributors to this book are working. This is particularly the case with respect to the relationship between language and ideology. From a poststructuralist perspective, language is extremely differentiated, context dependent and, importantly, not so determined by monolithic power interests. The flexibility of language, we would suggest, provides opportunities for establishing 'bridge points' within particular discourses between anarchist communicators and listeners. 'Bridge points' might be a facet of debate that is controversial in nature, but not a direct threat to the act of communication or the interaction itself. Once established, it becomes feasible to introduce newer ideas. In a sense this is an interpersonal version of the model of political 'dual legitimacy' outlined above, and, as with political tactics, requires appropriate and non-alienating forms of behaviour (not least, good listening skills).

To take an example: as both Millett and Goaman have documented (chapter 4 and 9), one of the most controversial and complex issues within contemporary anarchist thought is the oppressive nature of technology, and the extent to which it is 'neutral' or inextricably connected to relations of power. Trying to construct a 'bridge point' on this issue is difficult, and a more useful conversational strategy than the matter of the 'neutrality of technology' might be *psychological dependency* on technology. This is partly because the existing research on the addictive properties of entertainment and communications technologies, combined with established positions on the impact of workplace and transport technologies on health, are so readily available within the public domain that as a 'resource' they offer considerable potential. Thus an identification with concepts such as unsustainability or obsolescence would comprise a useful starting-point, not least because, as argued by German sociologist Klaus Eder (1996), environmental politics have become a significant framework within which much political debate now takes places. Basing a discursive bridge upon the newly developed frameworks of ecological policy (whatever the actual limitations) is consistent with 'common sense'. From this point on, the potentially oppressive impact of technological systems, gene, seed and DNA patenting, control of seed and so forth, could be introduced into dialogue. Dealing with such issues as *technique*, the biological versus technology dualisms raised in the discussions by Craig (narcotics), Heckert (sexuality) and the contradictions of using mobile phone and internet technologies to plan the actions discussed by Goaman, would come, along with all of the other questions one might raise, later.

Many of the matters raised above can be seen to apply to the communication that takes place during public protest. As noted by Heckert and Goaman, the opportunities which the symbolic and practical occupation of public spaces provide are considerable, yet there is always the danger of creating hierarchies between protesters and 'ordinary people' through non-inclusive forms of action. Here it is interesting to note the rediscovery by some alternative globalisation protestors of Jacques Camatte's essay 'On organisation' (1995), which argues against the dominance of political 'gangs' who monopolise political protest culture and create more barriers between themselves (as experts) and the general public. In this respect, the communicative and liberatory possibilities offered by art and aesthetics raised by Goaman and Gore on protest tactics and socialisation respectively are all the more important, as is the legacy of the Situationist International.

The fluidity of communication, the indeterminacy of influence in such circumstances, these and other factors further support the above refutation of the 'reform and revolution' dualism. As with consensus decision-making, the ideal praxis of direct action, anarchist and alternative globalisation cultures, these processes take time, patience and understanding. How one extrapolates this into global terms is something that also requires consideration.

Towards a global anarchist *realpolitik*

In a famous television debate in 1980, Noam Chomsky and Michel Foucault argued about the extent to which international laws on human rights or the United Nations were forms of moral and political advancement. Whilst the respective opinions are interesting – Chomsky thought this was a form of progress, Foucault did not – the reasons for positioning oneself, as an anarchist, on matters of international governance and legislation, would appear to be a strange and largely irrelevant one. However, just as we have suggested that the 'reform versus revolution' debate is unhelpful, we would extend this to requiring that there is a need for a globally relevant anarchist *realpolitik* that amounts to more than the theory and practice of 'we told you so'. This is a controversial but necessary step in terms of arguing the usefulness of anarchism on stages that its European founders could not possibly have envisaged.

Through African eyes

In the time since the aforementioned Chomsky versus Foucault debate, 'democracy' as the political cornerstone of the West has began to lose its legitimacy, and why this has happened needs to be understood. The reason for exploring this political avenue is because the debates around its usefulness provide a significant political opportunity, as well as a warning to those who would adopt isolationist forms of anarchism. The challenges have come from a number of quarters. Firstly, the corporate onslaught on local government decision-making and the public sector, especially in Europe (see Monbiot, 2000), has weakened the processes of accountability of decision-making as well as letting corporations have free rein over the planning of urban life and communities. These processes are also occurring at an international economic policy level, as the World Trade Organisation passes legislation that can challenge social and environmental policies of a nation state, on the grounds that they interfere with free trade. In poorer parts of the world, such as sub-Saharan Africa, politics has increasingly played second fiddle to the neoliberal economic agenda, with the International Monetary Fund insisting that health and public service cuts are necessary to encourage economic growth and loan repayments.

In this respect, a secondary attack on democracy, by Western social movements with much more participatory agenda, requires consideration from the point of view of those countries that have had to endure post-colonial dictatorships or structural adjustment policies as their 'public spheres'. Such a quick dismissal of the viability of a political system that has, in the West to a very limited degree, provided some protection from the ravages of capitalism needs contextualising. So, when we talk about the crises of representative democracy (Mulgan, 1994), we need to remember this point, as well as the fact that, as Bowen notes in his chapter (chapter 6), one simply cannot 'graft' on to certain political cultures a set of ideas that are assumed to be universally relevant. There is a danger, as the neoliberal hegemony unravels, that the proposed solutions to its contradictions will simply adopt Western political models. To follow this might well be to reprise the mistakes that radical feminist groups in the 1970s and 1980s did, in terms of trying to universalise the experience of women without always being as culturally sensitive as they might have been. Anarchism, like democracy, under such circumstances, may simply be another form of imperialism.

With this in mind, the North–South alliances discussed in Goaman's chapter (chapter 9) become crucial to try and facilitate an understanding of differing political perspectives. To some extent these things are occurring through the alternative globalisation movement, as well as other fora that attempt to facilitate relationships outside of the 'scramble for Africa' actions of development and aid charities who sometimes actually hinder conditions. The absence of a Zapatista-type of struggle around which Western anarchists can mobilise and express solidarity might be a contributing factor to the lack of visibility of 'African anarchism'.

If useful relationships with African networks need to be made, why is it that anarchists have often (both politically and personally) supported the boycotts of 'problem countries' such as South Africa in the 1980s, Nigeria from the mid-1990s and currently Zimbabwe? Here the observation made by Craig (chapter 7) in relation to narcotics and the tactical support by Left-wing people for State-approved actions, is a useful reference-point. Surely, from an anarchist point of view, forging individual and informal networked relations is more meaningful and a lot more direct in impact than blindly following a State, political party or union-derived decree. A classical anarchist position has been to organise regardless of what institutional forces are doing; perhaps this is an opportunity to develop a consistent yet unpopular anarchist *realpolitik*.

For social ecology

The preceding remarks about non-Western perspectives are a crucial part of a future anarchist praxis, yet this should not obviate considering the possibilities for a *realpolitik* that engages with the possibilities of transforming existing democratic structures within Europe, North America, the Antipodes and parts of the Pacific Rim. Although anarchists might not want to formally campaign for devolution of political power, proportional representation, regional assemblies and other current alternatives to centralised party politics, they should have something to say about these things. Given the increasing calls for these institutions, we feel that it is time to reclaim aspects of Murray Bookchin's work that are tangible to these debates. Locked into sectarian exchanges about mysticism, primitivism, postmodernism, technology or individualism, Bookchin and his detractors have, to the point of tedium, often overlooked the communicative possibilities that the philosophy of social ecology offers for anarchism.

Bookchin has for decades been an advocate of town meetings, municipalism, urban communities and the practicalities of encouraging libertarian dialogue within some of the existing structures (Bookchin, 1992). Contemporary debates within the field of social ecology include explorations of the different decision-making 'powers' that autonomous communities might have, the different types of delegation that may be required to effectively co-ordinate the relative interests of say a collectivised workplace and wider community participation. These kinds of decisions are pivotal to any anarchist community and in this respect, whilst clearly problematic in completely idealistic terms, they provide an engagement with political questions that can be 'discursively bridged' without too much difficulty. As Gribble notes in his chapter (chapter 10), 'democratic' has been an ugly word for anarchists, but if, in the context of libertarian education, it has to be used as part of a survival strategy, so be it. Given some of the academic material beginning to emerge on notions of 'discursive' and 'deliberative' democracy' (Dryzek, 2002), the potential for intervention in these debates is significant.

In a similar vein, within the debates about alternative or ecological economics, whether the LETS (local exchange and trading) systems that are in operation in many Western countries, the advocacy of the 'participatory economics' (Albert, 2002) or through the existing co-operative movement, there are the opportunities for the discursive bridges outlined above. Equally, there are less progressive events that force us to take a stance and to try and forge alliances, bridges and to take the victories that we can.

Bearing witness again: from 9/11 to 15/2

Many words have already been written on these events by anarchists (see, for example, Gemie *et al.*, 2002) and it is not our intention to revisit debates about terrorism, conspiracy or why the United States has made enemies. Our interest primarily is in the implications of these events for political mobilisation and the need to 'bear witness' to the crimes that are committed 'in our name'.

If anything has really come out of the events in America, Afghanistan and beyond during the autumn of 2001, it is that the mechanisms of power have suddenly become much more visible. This is whether we are speaking of Western foreign policy and all of its unholy alliances or the new domestic clampdowns on civil liberties and increased levels of surveillance that the populations of the developed and developing worlds have been subjected to. As both Goaman and Craig have pointed out (chapters 7 and 9), the consequences of these developments do not make for an optimistic vision of change. The asymmetrical wars of metaphor that have replaced Cold War logic have successfully targeted all kinds of opposition to the neoliberal economic hegemony, not just those elements which might choose to employ 'terrorist actions'. There are, however, a number of hopeful possibilities. Firstly, as the Western media attempted to forge some kind of consensus on the imminent American and British invasion of Iraq in February 2003, millions of school children walked out of lessons to occupy city centres in countless cities and towns across the globe. What was surprising to their parents' generation was the energy and inventiveness with which these actions were carried out. Secondly, the political literacy of this generation suggests that the hasty attempts by Western governments to concoct paranoid and repressive pieces of legislation, will, like on so many occasions in the recent past, fail to deter people from resisting.[1] As noted in different ways by both Gribble and Gore (chapters 10 and 8 respectively), the politicisation of young people has proved to be particularly powerful on many occasions. In the post '9/11' climate of fear and repression, the mobilisations on the 15 February 2003 might be considered to be a massive call for more accountable political systems and an end to the new era of oil-company-sponsored problem-solving through force.

There are always possibilities for change, cracks in the system, news stories that suddenly spur a previously cynical person on a personal quest to challenge a pharmaceutical company, or to be a witness in the Occupied Territories with the International Solidarity Movement or to give up their car.

During the writing of this book, one of our contributors noted how their 80-year-old ultra-conservative father had begun to ask the kinds of questions that the contributor had long believed impossible, about vested interests and the impact of the war in Afghanistan on the environment and Western consciousness. Mainstream television reports of the protests on '15/2' seemed to relish the fact that they were interviewing people who 'had never been on a protest in their life'.

In Britain during the last decade, the Blair Government has successfully transformed the language of communitarianism into something consistent with its endorsement of the free market, utilising phrases such as 'citizenship', 'responsibility' and 'participation'. Whilst this has all the hallmarks of the 'political contract' between State and subjects, as theorised by Enlightenment liberals, a more useful formulation for anarchist *realpolitik* is to begin with the 'duty' of *individuals* to act in their own long-term best interests. This includes everything from unmasking the powerful, challenging attempts to dismantle the limited avenues for expression and participation that exist, to taking control of their own localities with a keen eye on the predatory global forces. If 'bearing witness' is something that has tended to be applied to being present to observe *excessive* uses of power (usually force), we would suggest that an anarchist appropriation of the idea is one that monitors *any use of power whatsoever*.

The view from the sports hall

On many Friday evenings over the last decade, the editors of this book have played five-a-side football at a local village sports hall. The team is made up of an assortment of builders, plumbers, social workers, lecturers, teachers, council workers, computer programmers and even poets, all over 30 years old, some nearer 50. Based on nothing more than a 'block booking' made sometime in the late 1980s and word of mouth, this venture has led to many friendships and provided the space for modestly talented people to stay a lot fitter than they otherwise might have done. There is no referee and the rules have adapted with the wishes of those playing rather than what is seen on Match of the Day. It is fast and furious, but if somebody oversteps the mark and plays dangerously they are told so, just as anyone who feels entitled to a 'free kick' for a foul is allowed one. Prior to this year, any injuries incurred were mostly accidental and when particular grievances were felt (such as who should represent the 'team' in occasional tournaments) meetings were actually convened to discuss them (once with an outside facilitator!). Such an environment might seem a strange forum for the implementation of libertarian practices, but as an example of how difficult 'doing anarchism' can be, it provides some useful closing thoughts.

In early 2003, a player was deliberately punched and was hospitalised with a broken nose. The perpetrator and his closest associate (who appeared to claim that the victim had deserved the action) were banned. Everyone was shocked by the events, but also thrown into huge dilemmas as to future courses of action, particularly since no one had ever been banned before. There was the additional problem that the two players in question had been at the heart of every difficult incident over the previous year or so. For many people it was felt that in the long run it was for the good of everyone that they did not play.

Meetings and phone calls ensued, letters were sent to the banned players and the possible cancellation of the 'block booking' loomed large owing to the connections one of the banned players had with the relevant committee. A range of philosophical issues reared their heads. What was the best course of action for the majority? Would it be better to stay principled and lose the block booking rather than reinstate the players if the committee (who would be over-stretching their powers) decided to expel us if we didn't? Did the fact that the perpetrator's associate was well known for alienating other local football teams prejudice the outcome? Was it simply a question of 'cultures clashing' and that attitudes to playing football competitively were so different that it was a waste of everybody's time trying to resolve the situation at all?

Whilst the number of possible solutions to this problem was limited, the implications of any of the courses of action were more extensive, particularly in terms of the exercising of power. Who actually had the right to make the decision to ban the players and for an indefinite period of time? To what extent should the decision be arrived at 'democratically' and did the fact that some players absolved themselves of responsibility for taking part in any decision mean that attempts at a consensus were impossible? Should a meeting be held to air all grievances and under what circumstances could it take place? Did the fact that no one really advocated a meeting mean that the intensive discussions and collective letter writing was just a smoke screen for the fact that, in some people's eyes, the end (keeping the football going) justified the means (expelling the two players indefinitely)?

Although in material terms there were clearly winners and losers in this example, from the point of view of libertarian practice, it felt as though everybody had lost, since the implications of the actions weighed heavy on people's consciences. Acting in fair, principled, anarchist ways *is* difficult, and whilst compromise and consensus can be sought on every occasion, the end results are seldom ideal. There are presumably thousands of small town ventures and community groups who have similar stories to tell. The point is that the effort *is* made at precisely this interpersonal level and better practice consequently evolves from it.

What we have tried to do in this book is to provide a flavour of many of the existing projects that are changing anarchism in different ways, whether adding to the complexities of existing critiques or providing an inspirational moment around which people can mobilise. We have noted the need for flexibility and non-sectarian positions, which do their level-best to build bridges in everyday as well as extraordinary settings. We have suggested that anarchism has an influence in many areas of everyday life that is often largely unrecognised and that it is important not to take dogmatic stances about the 'right' sort of anarchism and to reinvent nineteenth-century dualistic thinking about revolution versus reform. The complexity of global society requires resistance in ways appropriate to dealing with the specific problems in question and we must be careful about exporting our concepts if they do not fit. Nevertheless, evidence from our contributors suggests that there are many 'practical utopias' in existence across the world and the distances between them are becoming smaller all the time.

The view from the sports hall is not entirely beautiful, but to date the anarchist football continues and the editors try not to kick each other too much.

Notes

1 The reaction in Britain to the extremely draconian 1994 Criminal Justice and Public Order Bill is a case in point (McKay 1998).

Glossary

Alternative Globalisation Movement (AGM)   A general term, used in prefer-
ence to 'anti-globalisation', for the diverse network of largely autonomous
groups who have contested the *neoliberal* economic and political agendas of the
world's leading industrial powers and corporations since the early 1990s. Often
believed to have emerged at the World Trade Organisation summit in Seattle,
United States, November 1999, the movement's roots lie in the reaction to the
impact of the North American Free Trade Agreement, particularly on the
Zapatistas in the Chiapas area of Mexico, in 1994. The AGM includes farming
groups, campaigners against debt, squatters, indigenous peoples organisations
as well as high-profile Western groups such as Reclaim the Streets, Tute Bianche,
Globalise Resistance and Black Block.

Anarcho-communism   Arguably the most enduring strand of anarchism,
closely associated with the struggles of European and Russian movements in the
nineteenth and early twentieth century in particular, as well as writers such as
Kropotkin, Proudhon, Bakunin. Particularly strong in Britain in the post-World
War II era. Some debate exists as to the extent of its close relationship with
anarcho-collectivism.

Anarcho-individualism   A philosophy based on the premise that the individual
should attempt to minimise the way that authority impacts on them personally in
pursuit of freedom. Culturally strong in the United States at the turn of the twentieth century, it sometimes draws right- as well as left-wing anarchists to it. Most
famously advocated by the writings of *Max Stirner*, it is often seen to be a somewhat self-indulgent form of anarchism, but continues to have many followers.

Anarcho-primitivism (see *Perlman, Zerzan*)   A critique of civilisation, initially
based on the work of *Perlman*, which synthesises an advanced analysis of the
existing forms of power within society with a re-evaluation of the concept of the
'primitive'. Increasingly highly regarded among some anarchists and publications (*Green Anarchist* in Britain, *Fifth Estate* in the United States), it has also

been criticised for fetishising a primitive 'golden age' and failing to address economic factors.

Anarcho-syndicalism Political philosophy which rejects the State as a tool of capitalist oppression, and which advocates *direct action* and political and social organisation based on the workplace under the direct democratic control of the workers. Developed by such thinkers as Georges Sorel, it was a particularly important movement in southern Europe and the Americas before World War I, and it was an important revolutionary tool in Spain in the 1930s.

Anti-roads movement UK-based 1990s network of groups opposed to extensive plan of road building initiated by Conservative administrations. Effectively formed at Twyford Down in 1992, the movement, which included *Earth First!*, opposed dozens of high-profile road (and airport) schemes reaching a peak in 1996. The anti-roads movement was successful at generating a significant ecological counter culture around the protest camps and associated lifestyles.

Bakunin, Mikhail (1814–76) Russian anarchist, most famous for his rejection of the *Marxist* model of 'Dictatorship of the Proletariat' and his criticisms of *Marx* and the First International, as a result of which he has come to symbolise anti-authoritarianism among some anarchists. A complex and often contradictory theoretician, he is, however, rightly regarded as one of the founders of modern anarchism, particularly due to his development of a 'collectivist' model of social organisation.

Bey, Hakim Idiosyncratic and prolific contemporary American writer, best known for his concept of the Temporary Autonomous Zone, deconstruction of existing anarchist frameworks and an evocative prose style.

Bookchin, Murray (b. 1921) American eco-anarchist whose impact on anarchist thought since the 1970s has been unparalleled but who has accordingly drawn criticism from many quarters (principally *anarcho-primitivists*). He has written widely on themes including liberatory uses of technology, green movements, freedom and citizenship. Perhaps best known for development of the philosophy of *Social ecology* and the creation of the Institute for Social Ecology in Vermont, United States.

Camatte, Jacques French radical communist writing mostly in the 1960s and 1970s whose rethinking of certain aspects of *Marx*'s work succeeded in formulating new ways of understanding the power of capitalism to enslave all aspects of human life. Influential on the *Fifth Estate* collective and early *anarcho-primitivism*, his writings on political organisation have also had a more recent impact on radical environmentalist and *alternative globalisation* groups.

Chomsky, Noam (b. 1928)   Prolific and influential American academic, political commentator and anarchist, initially famous for his linguistic theories, but who has tirelessly worked to expose the brutality and hypocrisy behind Western (principally US) foreign policies. He has undertaken thorough critical analyses of the role of the modern media and their creation of the illusion of democratic debate.

Complexity   Scientific theory emerging in the 1970s that proposes the differentiated, fluid and highly unpredictable organisation of matter and energy. Seized on by social scientists as well as managerial theorists to explain non-hierarchical structures and networks within everyday life (and business!) during the late 1980s. Eco-anarchists have looked to complexity to legitimate many of their theories, especially in conjunction with the much earlier work of *Kropotki*n.

Conrad, Joseph (1857–1924)   Polish-born English writer, best known among anarchists for the lasting damage which his stovepipe-hatted and black-caped terrorist character Karl Yundt (in *The secret agent*, 1907) has done to damage the image of anarchism.

Dada   More explicitly political than subsequent *avant-garde* movements, this was a nihilistic artistic movement of the early twentieth century which flourished in many major cities in Europe and the United States. Its visual and literary forms found inspiration in the bizarre, the irrational, the iconoclastic and the fantastic, and its protagonists developed it as an expression of disgust at bourgeois values and in vehement opposition to World War I.

Deep ecology   Wide-ranging and sometimes controversial ecological philosophy, prominent from the 1980s, particularly in North America and associated with the *Earth First!* network. Sometimes tending towards the spiritual, its non-anthropocentric critique of the relationship between people and the planet (particularly the impact of industrial society) has sometimes been interpreted as an excuse for misanthropy.

Deleuze, Gilles and *Felix Guattari*   Highly influential poststructuralist French thinkers, writing in the 1970s and 1980s, whose ideas about the constitution of power in contemporary societies have began to appeal to anarchists on account of their move away from deterministic forms of analysis.

Détournement   An action or event in which (symbolic) meaning is inverted, often in a humourous or ridiculous way so as to make a political point.

Direct action   This is where activists take control of their political milieu by acting only for themselves, rejecting representation or other indirect forms. It can range from the smallest of everyday actions to major social and political events, but at all times, protagonists act only for themselves and their shared aims.

Dualism A philosophical term originating from Rene Descartes' juxtaposition of the mind and the body, which has been incorporated into the analysis of ideology in the humanities and social sciences. Essentially applicable to any sufficiently polarised concepts (nature/culture; Self/Other) it has been particularly used by feminists and poststructuralists to illustrate the highly context-dependent nature of power.

Earth First! Direct action-oriented grass-roots environmental movement whose decentralist and non-hierarchical structures are strongly influnced by anarchism. Initially arising in North America in the 1980s, but spread to Europe in the 1990s, and has been involved in the defence of wilderness areas, opposition to road building programmes, and questioning the sustainability of modern consumer capitalist societies.

Ellul, Jacques French American social theorist whose book *The technological society* has become one of the single most influential ideas on *anarcho-primitivism*. Essentially it reinterprets the materialist analysis of history to argue that it is technology, not capital or classes, which organises the lives and consciousness of human populations.

Enlightenment, The Rationalist European intellectual movement of the seventeenth and eighteenth centuries which held that the goals of rational human beings were knowledge, freedom and happiness, and that these could be achieved by a synthesis of reason, religion, nature and humanity. Rationalist thought developed critiques of the arbitrary, authoritarian nature of the State, and it was out of this movement that much modern, democratic, liberal, socialist and anarchist political philosophy emerged. Much *Enlightenment* philosophy is now taken for granted as common sense, as well as being criticised by *postmodernists* and *anarcho-primitivists*.

Existentialism Philosophical movement concerned with the relationship of human beings to their world in terms of individual self-development. It contests that humans are capable of becoming (or choosing not to become) whatever they like, essentially being unfettered by anything other than their own creativity and desires.

Ferrer Guardia, Francisco (1859–1909) Pioneering Spanish educationalist of the late nineteenth and early twentieth century, whose ideas and work have influenced generations of libertarians and progressives. Best known for his book *The origins and ideals of the modern school*, and setting up his own school, he was framed and executed by the Spanish Government in 1909.

Foucault, Michel (1926–84)   Historian of ideas, principally concerned with exploring concepts of truth, power and self. His innovative tracing of the genealogy of certain discourses – including madness, crime and punishment, knowledge, sexuality and medicine – has had a profound impact on the social sciences and political and cultural theory.

Frankfurt School of Critical Theory   Developed principally in the post-World War II period by Theodore Adorno, Herbert Marcuse and others, this theoretical school rejected past philosophy for its search for some ultimate human identity or primacy, arguing that to do so would be to 'reify' the human subject and render it subject to exploitation. The task of Critical Theory is to challenge all conceptual distinctions so that they cannot deform the true nature of reality. It is often seen as having turned Western Marxism away from direct engagement in politics towards academic and cultural issues. Often used as a reference point in debates about the effects of the mass production of culture on audiences.

Gandhi, Mahatma (1869–1948)   Indian political leader, famous for his organised campaigns of civil disobedience and direct action against both the injustices of his own government and against British rule in India. Also an opponent of the caste system and materialism, his philosophies on peace and nonviolent protest have inspired countless anarchists.

Godwin, William (1756–1836)   Writer and radical usually acknowledged as the founder of British anarchism with his *Enquiry concerning political justice* (1793), an extremely sober but radical book of its time. Married to proto-feminist Mary Wollstonecraft and father of Mary Shelley.

Goldman, Emma (1869–1940)   Jewish-American anarchist famous for her tireless propaganda work for the anarchist cause on both sides of the Atlantic. Her goals of freedom, equality and pleasure have inspired generations of anarchists, feminists and other radicals.

Inclusive democracy   Contemporary political theory that prioritises the need to critique capitalism as fundamental to the success of any ecological future. Associated with the journal *Democracy and Nature* and the writings of Takis Fotopoulos, it bears some relationship to *Social ecology* in terms of its suggestion for local participatory decision-making, although its critique is less rooted in ecological theory.

Kropotkin, Peter (1842–1921)   Russian prince, geographer and anarchist, renowned for his writings on mutual aid in evolution, Russian literature, history and geology. His theories on decentralised communities resonate strongly through *anarcho-communist* and *Social ecology* movements.

Liberalism   Political philosophy which believes in the maximisation of individual liberty and that the primary function of the State is to protect the rights of citizens. Liberalism is an ambiguous term, however, since at one extreme it can be interpreted as advocating totally unregulated *laissez-faire* capitalism (see *neo-liberalism*), where the market is unfettered by the State; at the other extreme, it provides a basis for Socialism where the State is regarded as the promoter and defender of citizens' rights and as the provider and distributor of welfare.

Malatesta, Errico (1853–1932)   Italian anarchist working in the anarcho-communist tradition, initially in the First International with *Bakunin* and subsequently in many uprisings around the world. Primarily an activist, he wrote very little, but his pamphlet *Anarchy* has been translated into many languages and is regarded as a very clearly argued political tract.

Marx, Karl (1818–83)   Jewish-German political philosopher whose writings (along with Friedrich Engels) provided a comprehensive socio-economic analysis of the phases of capitalism as well as the basis for much socialist and communist thought over the last century and a half. Criticised by many for being too historically deterministic, Marx has also long been criticised by anarchists, from *Bakunin* to the present, for the authoritarian tendencies inherent in *Marxist* revolutionary political structures.

Marxism   Political philosophy developed by *Marx*, Engels and others which interprets history in terms of the tensions between the socio-economic classes. Capitalism is regarded as an inevitable phase in human history in which the majority (the proletariat) work to produce surplus value which is appropriated by the minority (the bourgeoisie). The proletariat, driven to rebel against this injustice by their extreme alienation, are historically destined to unite behind a common goal of healing the divisions of humanity and creating a classless society.

'May 68'   A significant event in anarchist history, owing to the variety of spontaneous and leaderless occupations and experiments with new forms of political organisation that took place. A huge general strike in France involving most social classes – initially sparked by student radicals – came close to toppling the régime of Charles de Gaulle. Other radical activities ensued in the United States, Germany and Britain, and although in the short term few real political advances were achieved, the events of 1968 are regarded by anarchists as symbolically important regarding the rise of the New Left, in providing a basis for political criticism and change in modern Western democracies, and in moving political focus away from the relations of production towards a sense of the importance of consumption. Also seen as influential in the formation of modern environmental movements.

May, Todd   Contemporary American writer who has done much to rejuvenate anarchist theory by looking at the potential which *poststructuralist* perspectives have for anarchist critiques of power.

Millenarianism   Doctrine arising out of Christian theology which has often been popular at times of rapid social change and which believes that good or catastrophic (or both) events are imminent, particularly with approach of numerically relevant historical dates. Owing to its inherently fatalistic nature, millenarians are often involved in marginal and unconventional social movements, including anarchism.

Modernism   A defining philosophical sensibility of the late nineteenth and early twentieth century, arguably either rooted in *Enlightenment* principles or a reaction to them, it is associated with the emergence of the Social Sciences, the political theories of Socialism and anarchism and various artistic movements. Essentially a philosophical assault on orthodox 'realist' methods of cultural representation, it embraced the political and industrial turbulences of its time with a self-conscious style, but remained committed to the search for absolute truths.

Montessori, Maria (1870–1952)   Radical Italian educationist whose practices seek to develop individual, spontaneous, exploratory and self-motivated learning in young children through offering a stimulating environment and no coercion. Particularly of interest to libertarians as a successsful innovator in non-directive educational practice.

Mumford, Lewis   Wide-ranging social theorist, writing principally in the 1950s, whose views on technology and the emergence of civilisation have been extremely influential on ecological anarchists and *anarcho-primitivists*. Best known for his theory of the 'megamachine' and his notion of the differentiation between authoritarian and democratic technics.

Neill, A. S. (1883–1973)   Scottish educationist and writer who, influenced by the work of Sigmund Freud among others, founded Summerhill free school in the 1920s with an evolving radical educational philosophy which sought to liberate children and education based on 'freedom not licence', respect, love and direct democracy. Summerhill still exists, and Neill's influence continues to resonate in radical education projects across the globe.

Neoliberalism   Economic philosophy which emerged after the Oil Crisis of 1973 emphasising the usefulness of classical *laissez-faire* theory for preventing the stagnation of State-managed economic policies. Influential in many Western countries throughout the 1980s and 1990s, it has helped to legitimate continuing globalisation, with attendant costs on populations and eco-systems world wide. Has become one of the focuses for the emerging *Alternative globalisation movement*.

Paddick, Brian   Controversial openly gay British police chief well known for his public endorsement of liberal drug policies and for suggesting that anarchism has a particular philosophical appeal!

Perlman, Fredy (1934–84)   Key founder of *anarcho-primitivist* theory, best known for his *Against his-story, against Leviathan!* (1983), but also prominent in production of *Fifth Estate* and influential on debates about the emergence of civilisation, technology and the nature of power.

Postmodernism   This challenges many philosophical premises of the *Enlightenment*. Extremely controversial, it emerged from an architectural milieu in the 1980s, celebrating eclecticism, pastiche, popular culture and philosophical iconoclasm, often from a perspective of absolute relativism. Despite being disregarded by many on the Left for its rejection of political and moral absolutes, it has also been welcomed by many (including some anarchists) for its theoretical openness, its opposition to determinism and dogmatism, and its sense of humour.

Poststructuralism   This rejects explanations (such as those found in *Marx*) that the human condition can be explained solely with reference to underlying structures, such as economics, that are subject to objective analysis outside the discourse that constructs these structures. The emphasis placed by poststructuralist writers on the fluid, non-deterministic and micro-sociological manifestation of powers of power have provided some interplay between anarchists and theorists such as *Michel Foucault, Deleuze* and *Guattar*i and *Todd May.*

Proudhon, Pierre-Joseph (1809–65)   French anarchist, printer and scholar who originated the phrase 'property is theft'. Active during the revolutionary 1840s, he proposed a transformation of society, believing that, as humans become morally more mature, restrictions of government and law become redundant and can be dispensed with.

Situationism   Political philosophy dating from the 1950s and 1960s which rejects much of modern technological and consumer society for its reduction of individuals into commodities, and which emphasises alienation experienced through consumption as much as production. Essentially a synthesis of Marxist and anarchist thought and developed principally by Guy Debord and Raoul Vaneigem, situationism succeeded in updating revolutionary political ideas for the post-World War II world with attacks on faceless bureaucracy, commodification and the depersonalisation and pacification of people in 'the Spectacle'.

Social ecology   An ecological philosophy, pioneered by *Murray Bookchin*, which gained critical attention in the late 1980s. It maintains that the domination of nature is rooted in humanity's domination of itself through hierarchical relationships and advocates an eco-centric organisation of society based upon an integrated balance of human and natural ecosystems.

Stirner, Max (Johann Kaspar Schmidt) (1806–56)   German *individualist* philosopher, poet and school teacher, advocated a society of 'egoists' whereby all aspire to equality through total assertion of the self as ungovernable, individual and independent. Criticised by many anarchists for advocating élitism and anti-social values, but recently rehabilitated into the anarchist 'canon'.

Ward, Colin (b. 1924)   High-profile English anarchist thinker, writing in the tradition of *Kropotkin*, who has succeeded in achieving a certain respectability for anarchism through his extremely readable and practical books and his media contributions. Best known for *Anarchy in action* (1988).

Weber, Max (1864–1920)   Pioneering German sociologist best known for his work on the class structures of industrial societies, theories of rationality and bureaucracy and his controversial claims that it was the protestant ethic that facilitated the growth of Western capitalism.

Zapatistas   Indigenous movement for autonomy in the Chiapas province of Mexico, whose 'uprising' in 1994 captured the attention of the world's radical media and has become a founding moment for the struggle against *neoliberalism*.

Zerzan, John   One of the leading contemporary *anarcho-primitivist* thinkers, long-associated with the magazine *Fifth Estate*, whose eclectic and readable accounts of the impact of technology and civilisation on the human condition, have begun to enjoy wider influence owing to his association with radical environmental networks and the *Alternative Globalisation Movement*.

Bibliography

Abelove, H., Barale, M. A. and Halperin, D. M. (eds.) (1993) *The lesbian and gay studies reader*, New York: Routledge

Adorno, T. and Horkheimer, M. (1979) *The dialectic of enlightenment*, London: Verso

Albert, M. (2002) *Parecon: life after capitalism*, London: Verso

Amster, R. (1998) 'Anarchism as moral theory: praxis, property and the postmodern', *Anarchist Studies* 6 (2), 97–112

Amnesty International (1996) 'China – no one is safe' at www.amnesty.org/ailib/intcam/china/china96/report/cc5.htm

Anderson, B. (1983) *Imagined communities: reflections on the origin and spread of nationalism*, London: Verso

Anonymous (2001) 'being busy' in *On fire* (2001)

Anthias, F. (1998) 'Rethinking social divisions: some notes toward a theoretical framework', *Sociological Review* 46 (3), 505–35

Antliff, A. (1997) '1918: Russian artists of the anarchist revolution' in *Fifth Estate* 32 (1), 10–13

Antliff, A. (2001) *Anarchist modernism: art, politics, and the first American avant-garde*, Chicago: University of Chicago Press

Antliff, A. (2003) 'Anarchy in art: strategies of dissidence', *Anarchist Studies* 11 (1), 66–83

Appleton, M. (2001) 'Myths of education', *The Journal for Living*, October, also at www.jflmag.com

Appleton, M. *The journal for living* (October 2001), quoted in a personal email from Mary Leue

Apter, D. (1971) 'The old anarchism and the new: some comments' in Apter and Joll (1971)

Apter, D. and Joll, J. (eds.) (1971) *Anarchism today*, London: Macmillan

Armitage, J. (1999) 'From modernism to hypermodernism and beyond: an interview with Paul Virilio', *Theory, Culture & Society* 16 (5–6), 25–55

Armstrong, G. (1993) 'Like that Desmond Morris?' in Hobbs and May (1993)

Arts Council of Great Britain (1974) *Community arts: the report of the community arts working party June 1974*, London: The Arts Council of Great Britain

Atkinson, P. (1990) *The ethnographic imagination*, London: Routledge

Atton. C. (1999) '*Green Anarchist*: a case study of collective action in the radical media', *Anarchist Studies* 7 (1), 25–50

Bakunin, M. (1973) 'God and the State' in Lehning (1973)

Bagguley, P. (1992) 'Social change, the middle class and the emergence of 'New Social Movements': a critical analysis', *The Sociological Review* 40 (1), 26–48

Bagguley, P. and Hearn, J. (eds.) (1999) *Transforming politics: power and resistance* London: Macmillan

Bakunin, M. (1985) *God and the State*, (reprint) London: Bash'em Books

Bakunin, M. (1990) *Statism and anarchy*, Cambridge: Cambridge University Press

Ball, T. and Dagger, R. (1991) *Political ideologies and the democratic ideal*, New York: HarperCollins

Baudrillard, J. (1972) *For a critique of the political economy of the sign*, New York: Telos Press

Baudrillard, J. (1983) *Simulations*, New York: Semiotext

Bauman, Z. (1987) *Legislators and interpreters*, Cambridge: Polity Press

Bauman, Z. (1988) 'Is there a post-modern sociology?', *Theory, Culture and Society 5*, 217–35

Beck, U. (1992) *Risk society: towards a new modernity* (translated by Mark Ritter), London: Sage

Beck, U., Lash, S. and Giddens, A. (1994) *Reflexive modernization*, Cambridge: Polity Press

Beckford, J. A. (1989) *Religion and advanced industrial societies*, London: Unwin Hyman

Beckford, J. A. (1990) 'The sociology of religion and social problems', *Sociological Analysis* 51 (1), 1–14

Beevor, A. (2001) *The Spanish civil war*, London: Cassell Military

Berg, C., Durieux, F. and Lernout, G. (eds.) (1995) *The turn of the century: modernism and modernity in literature and the arts*, Berlin/New York: Walter de Gruyter

Berman, M. (1992) 'Why modernism still matters', in Lash and Friedman (1992)

Bettelheim, B. (1976) *The uses of enchantment: the meaning and importance of fairy tales*, London: Thames and Hudson

Bey, H. (1991) *TAZ: the temporary autonomous zone, ontological anarchy, poetic terrorism*, Brooklyn: Autonomedia

Bey, H. (1994) 'Ontological anarchy in a nutshell' in *Immediatism*, Edinburgh: AK Press

Bijker, W., Hughes, T. P. and Pinch, T. (eds.) (1987) *The social construction of technological systems*, Cambridge, Mass.: MIT Press

Black, B. (1997) *Anarchy after Leftism*, Colombia, Mo.: CAL Press

Blewitt, T. (ed.) (1934) *The modern schools handbook*, London: Gollancz

Bloch, J. P. (1998) 'Alternative spirituality and environmentalism', *Review of Religious Research* 40 (1), 55–73

Bluechler, S. M. (1993) 'Beyond resource mobilization: emerging trends in social movement theory', *The Sociological Quarterly* 34 (2), 217–35

Bookchin, M. (1974) *Post-scarcity anarchism*, London: Wildwood House

Bookchin, M. (1980) *Towards an ecological society*, Montréal: Black Rose Books

Bookchin, M. (1982) *The ecology of freedom: the emergence and dissolution of hierarchy*, Palo Alto: Cheshire Books

Bookchin, M. (1989) 'New social movements: the anarchic dimension', in Goodway (1989)

Bookchin, M. (1992) *Urbanization without cities: the rise and decline of citizenship*, Montréal: Black Rose Books

Bookchin, M. (1994) *To remember Spain: the anarchist and syndicalist revolution of 1936 essays*, Edinburgh: AK Press

Bookchin, M. (1995) *Social anarchism or lifestyle anarchism: an unbridgeable chasm,* Edinburgh and San Francisco: AK Press

Bookchin, M. (1996a) *The philosophy of social ecology,* Montréal: Black Rose Books

Bookchin, M. (1996b) *The Third revolution: popular movements in the revolutionary era: vol. 1,* London: Cassell

Bookchin, M. (1998) *The Third revolution: popular movements in the revolutionary era, vol. 2,* London: Continuum

Bookchin, M. and Foreman, D. (1991) *Defending the earth,* Boston: South End Press

Booth Davis, J. (1993) *The myth of addiction,* New York: Harwood Academic Publishers

Bornstein, K. (1996) *Gender outlaw: on men, women and the rest of us,* New York: Routledge

Bottomore, T. B. (ed.) (1991) *A Dictionary of Marxist thought,* Oxford: Basil Blackwell

Bottomore, T. B. and Rubel, M. (eds.) (1963) *Karl Marx: selected writings in sociology and social philosophy,* Harmondsworth: Penguin (texts translated by T. B. Bottomore)

Bové, J. (2001) 'A farmer's international', *New Left Review* 12, Nov.–Dec., 89–101

Bové, J. and Dufour, F. (2001) *The world is not for sale: farmers against junk food,* London: Verso

Bowen, J. (1997) 'The curse of the drinking classes' in Purkis and Bowen (1997)

Boyd, W. (ed.) (1944) *Evacuation in Scotland: a record of events and experiments,* Bickley, Kent: the Scottish Council for Research in Education XXII and University of London Press

Bradford, G. (1981) 'Marxism, anarchism and the roots of the new totalitarianism', *Fifth Estate* 306, July, 9–10

Bradford, G. (1983) 'Choose your poison', *Fifth Estate* 312, Spring, 6

Bradford, G. (1984a) 'A system of domination – technology', *Fifth Estate* 315, Winter, 11

Bradford, G. (1984b) '1984: Worse than expected?', *Fifth Estate* 316, Spring, 1–8

Bradford, G. (1988) 'We all live in Bhopal' in Zerzan and Carnes (1988) (originally in *Fifth Estate,* Winter, 1985)

Bradford, G. (1990) 'Revolution against the megamachine', *Fifth Estate* 333, Winter, 5–11, 32

Bradford, G. (1992) 'The triumph of Capital', *Fifth Estate* 339, Spring, 7–20

Brady, J. (2002) 'The public sphere in the era of anti-capitalism' in Schalit (2002)

Brewer, J. (2001) Evidence to the Home Affairs Select Committee (Questions 563–579), 27 November: www.parliament.the-stationery-office.co.uk/pa/cm200102/cmselect/cmhaff/318/1112708.htm

Brian S. (2001) 'reporting from the front line' in *On fire* (2001: 17–22)

Brickell, C. (2000) 'Heroes and invaders: gay and lesbian pride parades and the public/private distinction in New Zealand media accounts', *Gender, Place and Culture* 7 (2), 163–78

Bridgeland, M. (1971) *Pioneer work with maladjusted children,* London: Staples Press

Bristow, J. and Wilson, A. R. (eds.) (1993) *Activating theory: lesbian, gay and bisexual politics,* London: Lawrence and Wishart

Brown, L. S. (1993) *The politics of individualism: liberalism, liberal feminism and anarchism,* Montréal: Black Rose Books

Brubaker, B. (1981) 'Community, primitive society and the state', *Fifth Estate* 306, July, 18–19

Brubaker, B. (1983) 'Reply to letter headed "Do odious tasks"', *Fifth Estate* 314, Fall, 2

Bruun, O. and Kalland, A. (eds.) (1995) *Asian perceptions of nature: a critical approach,* Richmond, Surrey: Curzon Press

Buick, A. (1987) 'Bordigism' in Rubel and Crump (1987)

Bulmer, M. (1984) *The Chicago school of sociology*, Chicago: University of Chicago Press

Burawoy, M. (ed.) (1991) *Ethnography unbound*, Berkeley: University of California

Butigan, K. (2000) 'We traveled to Seattle: a pilgrimage of transformation' in Danaher and Burbach (2000)

Cahill, T. (1992) 'New social movements and anarchism: a green perspective', paper to the *Northern Anarchist Research Group*, Bradford 1 in 12 Club, 19 September 1992

Califia, P. (2000) *Public sex: the culture of radical sex*, San Francisco: Cleis Press

Camatte, J. (1975) *The wandering of humanity*, Detroit: Black & Red

Camatte, J. (1995) 'On organisation' in *This world we must leave & other essays*, New York: Autonomedia

Campbell, D. (2001) 'Anarchy in the USA', *The Guardian*, (2) 18 April, 1–4

Campion, D. (1988) 'A reply to the syndicalists: anarchy and the sacred', *Fifth Estate* 328, Spring, 16–18

Capra, F. (1982) *The turning point*, London: Wildwood House

Carroll, J. (1974) *Break out from the crystal palace: the anarcho-psychological critique: Stirner, Nietzsche, Dostoevsky*, London: Routledge and Kegan Paul

Carter, A. (1989) 'An anarchist theory of history' in Goodway (1989)

Carter, A. (1993) 'Some notes on "anarchism"', *Anarchist Studies* 1 (2), 141–5

CDF: Community Development Foundation (1992) *Arts and communities: the report of the national inquiry into arts and the community*, London: Community Development Foundation

Chan, A. (1995) 'Anarchists, violence and social change', *Anarchist Studies* 3 (1), 45–68

Chapple, C. K. (1995) *Nonviolence to animals, earth, and self in Asian traditions*, New Delhi: Sri Satguru Publications

Chaplin, E. (1994) *Sociology and visual representation*, London: Routledge

Chesters, G. (2003) 'Shape shifting: civil society, complexity and social movements', *Anarchist Studies* 11 (1), 42–65

Chesters, G. and Welsh, I. (2002) 'Reflexive framing and ecology of action: engaging with the movement for humanity against neoliberalism', Research Committee 24: Globalisation and the Environment, XV World Congress of Sociology, 6–13 July 2002, Brisbane, Australia

Chomsky, N. (1969) *American power and the New Mandarins*, Harmondsworth: Penguin

Chomsky, N. (1970) 'Introduction' in Guérin (1970)

Chomsky, N. (1991) interview in *Anarchy: a journal of desire armed*, Summer 1991

Chomsky, N. (1997) *Media control: the spectacular achievements of propaganda*, New York: Seven Stories Press

Churchill, W. (1999) *Pacifism as pathology: reflections on the role of armed struggle in North America*, npp. Canada: Arbeiter Ring Publishing

Clark, J. (1984) *The Anarchist moment*, Montréal: Black Rose Books

Cleaver, H. (1994) 'Kropotkin, self-valorization, and the crisis of Marxism', *Anarchist Studies* 2 (2), 119–35

Clifford, J. and Marcus, G. (eds.) (1986) *Writing culture: the poetics and politics of ethnography*, Berkeley: University of California Press

Cohn, N. (1970) *The Pursuit of the millennium: revolutionary millenarians and mystical anarchists of the middle ages*, London: Pimlico

Connell, R. (1995) *Gender and power*, Cambridge: Polity Press

Connell, R. (1997) 'Sexual revolution' in Segal (1997)

Conrad, J. (1978) *The secret agent* (first published, 1907), Harmondsworth: Penguin

Cooper, D. (1967) *Psychiatry and anti-psychiatry*, London: Tavistock

Coppock, V. and Hopton, J. (2000) *Critical perspectives on mental health*, London: Routledge

Corner, J. and Pels, D. (eds.) (2003) *Media and political style: essays on representation and civic culture*, London: Sage

Cruikshank, B. (1999) *The will to empower: democratic citizens and other subjects*, Ithaca: Cornell University Press

Currie, E. (1993) *Reckoning*, New York: Hill and Wang

Curry, W. B. (1934) 'Dartington Hall School' in Blewitt (1934)

D'Anieri, P., Ernst, C. and Kier, E. (1990) 'New social movements in historical perspective', *Comparative Politics*, July, 445–58

Danaher, K and Burbach, R. (eds.) (2000) *Globalise this! The battle against the World Trade Organisation and corporate rule*, Monroe, Maine: Common Courage Press

Davies, J. (1997) 'Anarchy in the UK: anarchism and popular culture in 1990s Britain', in Purkis and Bowen (1997)

Day, D. (1998) 'Sad termination of a life-saving project', *The Times*, Trenton New Jersey, 25 December, 13

Debord, G. (1987 [1957]) *The society of the spectacle*, London: Rebel Press

Deleuze, G. and Guattari, F. (1984) *Anti-Oedipus: capitalism and schizophrenia*, London: Athlone Press

Deleuze, G. and Guattari, F. (1988) *A thousand plateaux: capitalism and schizophrenia*, London: Athlone Press

Deleuze, G. and Guattari, F. (1994) *What is philosophy?*, London: Verso

Dellar, R., Leslie, E., Watson, B. and Curtis, T. (eds.) (2000) *Mad pride: a celebration of mad culture*, London: Spare Change Books

Derrida, J. (1976) *Of grammatology*, Baltimore: Johns Hopkins University Press

Deudney, D. (1995) 'In search of Gaian politics: Earth religion's challenge to modern Western civilisation', in Taylor (1995)

Devall, B. and Sessions, G. (1985) *Deep ecology: living as it nature mattered*, Salt Lake City: Peregrine Smith

Diamond, S. (1983) *In search of the primitive: a critique of civilisation*, New Brunswick: Transaction Books

Dickson, M. (ed.) (1995) *Art with people*, London: AN Publications

Do or Die (2000) issue 9, December, c/o Prior House, 6 Tilbury Place, Brighton.

Dobson, A. (1990) *Green political thought*, London: HarperCollins

Doherty, B. (2000) 'Manufactured vulnerability: protest camp tactics' in Seel, Paterson and Doherty (2000)

Dolgoff, S. (ed.) (1973) *Bakunin on anarchy*, London: George Allen & Unwin

Dreyfus, H. L. and Rabinow, P. (1982) *Michel Foucault: beyond structuralism and hermeneutics*, Brighton: Harvester Press

Drugscope (2002) 'Results from the British Crime Survey 2000' at www.drugscope. org.uk/news_item.asp?intID=473

Drugscope (2002a) 'Afghan opium production 1400% higher than before war' at www.drugscope.org.uk/news_item.asp?a=3&intID=840

Drugscope (2002b) 'Is drug use mainly in deprived, inner city areas?' at www.drugscope. org.uk/druginfo/drugsearch/faq_template. asp?file=%5Cwip%5C11%5C1%5C2%5Cdeprived.html

Drug War Facts at www.drugwarfacts.org/racepris.htm

Dryzek, J. (2002) *Deliberative democracy and beyond: liberals, critics, contestations*, Oxford: Oxford University Press

Durkheim, E. (1970 [1897]) *Suicide: a study in sociology*, London: Routledge and Kegan Paul

Duyvendak, J. W. (1995) *The power of politics: new social movements in France*, Oxford: Westview Press

Dyncorp-sucks.com (2002) www.dyncorp-sucks.com/cia_cocaine.htm

Eagleton, T. (1996) *Literary theory: an introduction*, Oxford: Blackwell

Eder, K. (1996) 'The Institutionalisation of environmentalism: ecological discourse and the second transformation of the public sphere' in Lash, Szerszynski and Wynne (1996)

Edgar, A. and Sedgewick, P. (2002) *Cultural theory: the key thinkers*, London: Routledge

Edwards, D. (1998) *The Compassionate revolution: radical politics and Buddhism*, Totnes: Green Books

Ehrlich, H., Ehrlich, C., De Leon, D. and Morris, G. (eds.) (1979) *Re-inventing anarchy*, London: Routledge and Kegan Paul

Eisinger, P. (1973) 'The conditions of protest behavior in American cities', *American Political Science Review* 67, 11–28

Ellul, J. (1965) *The technological society*, London: Jonathan Cape

Ellul, J. (1969) *Violence*, London: Seabury Press

Ellul, J. (1970) 'From Jacques Ellul . . .', in Holloway (1970)

European Monitoring Centre into lifetime prevalence of drug use across European schools (2001) Annual Report at www.annualreport.emcdda.org/pdfs_data_library/school_lifetime_prev.pdf

Evans, M. (1994) *A change of mind: sociological insights into mental disorders*, Pennsylvania: Dorrance Publishing Company

Faure, Sébastien (1915) 'Propos d'Educateur' in Grunder (1993)

Federal Bureau of Investigation (2001) *Congressional Statement on 'Threat of terrorism to the United States'*, May 10 at www.fbi.gov/congress/congress01/freeh051001.htm

Ferguson, A. (1991) 'Managing without managers: crisis and resolution in a collective bakery' in Burawoy (1991)

Ferkiss, V. (1993) *Nature, technology, and society: cultural roots of the current environmental crisis*, London: Adamantine Press

Ferrer Guardia, F. (1913) *The origin and ideals of the Modern School*, London: Knickerbocker Press

Feyerabend, P. (1979) *Science in a free society*, London: Routledge

Feyerabend, P. (1988 [1975]) *Against method: outline of an anarchistic theory of knowledge* (revised edition), London: Verso

Feyerabend, P. (1995) *Killing time* (autobiography) London: University of Chicago Press

Fifth Estate (1978) 'Technology and the state: an introduction', *Fifth Estate* 290, March, 2–7

Fifth Estate (1979a) 'Fifth Estate slips quietly into 14th year', *Fifth Estate* 296, 29 January, 5, 15

Fifth Estate (1979b) 'Searching for the culprit', *Fifth Estate* 298, 19 June, 6

Fifth Estate (1983) 'Notes on "Soft Tech"', *Fifth Estate* 312, Spring, 4

Fifth Estate (1986) 'Renew the earthly paradise', *Fifth Estate* 322, 20/3, Winter/Spring, 10–11

Fillingham, L. (1993) *Foucault: for beginners*, London: Writers and Readers Publishing Incorporated

Fischer, M. (1982) 'Tensions from technology in Marx's communist society', *Journal of Value Inquiry* 16, 117–29

Fotopoulos, T. (1997) *Towards an inclusive democracy*, London: Cassell

Fotopoulos, T. (2000) 'Systems theory and complexity', *Democracy and Nature* 6 (3), 421–46

Foucault, M. (1972) *The archaeology of knowledge* (translated by A. M. Sheridan Smith) London: Tavistock

Foucault, M. (1980) *Michel Foucault: power/knowledge* (ed. C. Gordon), Hemel Hempstead: Harvester Wheatsheaf

Foucault, M. (1982) 'Afterword on "The Subject and Power"' in Dreyfus and Rabinow (1982)

Foucault, M. (1988) 'Technologies of the self' in Martin, Gutman and Hutton (1988)

Foucault, M. (1990) *The history of sexuality, vol. 1*, New York: Vintage

Fountain, J. (1993) 'Dealing with data' in Hobbs and May (1993)

Franks, B. (2003) 'The direct action ethic', *Anarchist Studies* 11 (1), 13–41

Freire, P. (1972) *Pedagogy of the oppressed*, Harmondsworth: Penguin

Fulano, T. (1981a) 'Against the megamachine', *Fifth Estate* 306, July, 4–8

Fulano, T. (1981b) 'Uncovering a corpse: a reply to the defenders of technology', *Fifth Estate* 307, Nov., 5–8, 21

Fuss, D. (1989) *Essentially speaking: feminism, nature and difference,* London: Routledge

Gare, A. (2000) 'Systems, theory and complexity', *Democracy and Nature* 6 (3), 327–41

Gemie, S. Creagh, R. Chomsky, N. CNT of Fraga, von Hosel, J. Istanbul Anarchist Platform, Goaman, K. (2002) 'Neither soldiers nor terrorists: anarchism after 11 September', *Anarchist Studies* 10 (1), 1–23

Giddens, A. (1991) *Modernity and self-identity*, Cambridge: Polity Press

Giedion, S. (1969) *Mechanization takes command*, New York: W. W. Norton

Goaman, K. (1999) 'Endless deferral . . . simulation, surveillance, social postmodernism, postsocialism . . .', *Anarchist Studies* 7 (1), 69–74

Goaman, K. and Dodson, M. (1997) 'A subversive current? contemporary anarchism considered', in Purkis and Bowen (1997)

Goaman, K. and Dodson M. (2000) 'Habermas, the postmodern turn and their (ir?)relevance to anarchism', *Anarchist Studies* 8 (1), 75–80

Goff, S. (1999) 'Inside US counterinsurgency: a soldier speaks' at www.consortium-news.com/1999/122299a.html

Goff, S. (2001) 'Is Colombia the next Vietnam?' at www.anncol.com/July/3007_IS_COLOMBIA_ THE_NEXT_VIETNAM.htm

Goff, S. (2002) 'The infinite war and its roots' at www.fromthewilderness.com/free/ww3/082702_infinite_war.html

Goffman, E. (1961) *Asylums: essays on the social situation of mental patients and other inmates*, London: Penguin

Goldman, E. (1907) 'La Ruche', *Mother Earth*, in Grunder (1993)

Goldman, E. (1977) *Living my life*, New York: Meridian

Goldner, L. (1999) 'Communism is the material human community: Amadeo Bordiga Today', www.geocities.com/CapitolHill/Lobby/2379/gold62.html, March

Goode, D. (1991) 'Kids, culture and innocents' in Waksler (1991)

Goodman, P. (n.d., originally 1966) 'The psychology of being powerless', New York: A. J. Muste Memorial Institute Essay Series No. 10

Goodman, P. (1971) *Compulsory miseducation*, Harmondsworth: Penguin

Goodway, D. (ed.) (1989) *For anarchism: history, theory and practice*, London: Routledge

Gottlieb, R. S. (1996) *This sacred earth: religion, nature, environment*, London: Routledge

Graeber, D. (2002) 'The new anarchists', *New Left Review* 13, Jan.-Feb. 2002, 61–73

Graham, R. (1989) 'review Michael Taylor's *The Possibility of Co-operation*' (1987), *Bulletin of Anarchist Research* 18, 17–20

Gramsci, A. (1971) *Selections from the prison notebooks*, London: Lawrence and Wishart

Green, M. (ed.) (1989) *Black letters unleashed: 300 years of enthused writing in German*, London: Atlas Press

Greenberg D. (1987) *Free at last*, Framingham: Sudbury Valley School Press

Green Party (2002) 'Results from the British Crime Survey 2001' at www.greenparty.org.uk/drugs/news/survey2002.htm

Gribble, D. (1998) *Real education: varieties of freedom*, Bristol: Libertarian Education

Gribble, D. (2003) *Lifelines*, Bristol: Libertarian Education

Grunder, H.-U. (1993) *Theorie und Praxis anarchistischer Erziehung*, Grosshöchstetten and Bern: Sonnmatt Verlag

Guérin, D. (1970) *Anarchism: from theory to practice*, New York: Monthly Review Press

Gupta, R. K. (1995) *Social action and non-violence*, New Delhi: Indian Council of Philosophical Research

Habermas, J. (1981) 'New social movements', *Telos* 49, 33–37

Haggerty, K. D. and Ericson, R. V. (2000) 'The surveillant assemblage', *British Journal of Sociology* 51 (4), 605–22

Hall, P. (1988) *Cities of tomorrow*, Oxford: Basil Blackwell

Hamilton, C. V. (1995) 'Anarchy as modernist aesthetic' in Berg, Durieux and Lernout (1995)

Hardt, M. and Negri, A. (2000) *Empire*, Harvard: Harvard University Press

Hardy, D. (1979) *Alternative communities in nineteenth century England*, London: Longman

Harper, C. (1987) *Anarchy: a graphic guide*, London: Camden Press

Harrison, P. M. and Beck, A. J. (2002) 'Prisoners in 2001', *US Department of Justice Bureau of Justice Statistics*, Washington DC: US Department of Justice, July

Hart, L. (1997) 'In defence of radical direct action' in Purkis and Bowen (1997)

Hawken, P. (2000) 'Skeleton woman visits Seattle' in Danaher and Burbach (2000)

Hayes, S. (2000) unpublished discussion paper on 'May 68', *Talk May Day Conference*, 30 April, London

Heckert, J. (2000) 'Beyond identity? questioning the politics of pride', Department of Sociology, Edinburgh: University of Edinburgh, also at www.moebius.psy.ed.ac.uk/~heckert/MSc.html

Heelas, P. (1996) *The New Age movement: the celebration of the self and the sacralization of modernity*, Oxford: Blackwell

Herdt, G. (1982) *Rituals of manhood: male initiation in Papua New Guinea*, Berkeley: University of California Press

Herdt, G. (1987) *Guardians of the flutes: idioms of masculinity*, New York: Columbia University

Herman, E. S. and Chomsky, N. (1988) *Manufacturing consent*, New York: Random House

Hetherington, K. (1998) *Expressions of identity: space, performance and the politics of identity*, London: Sage

Hetherington, K. (2000) *New Age travellers: vanloads of uproarious humanity*, London: Cassell

Hill, D. (2003) 'UN: Population Division says Eastern Europe's population to fall by half in some areas', Centre for Defence Information www.cdi.org/russia/246-18.cfm

Hippler, B. (1993) 'Fast times in Motor City – the first ten years of the *Fifth Estate*: 1965–1975' in Wachsberger (1993)

Hobbs, D. and May, T. (eds.) (1993) *Interpreting the field: accounts of ethnography*, Oxford: Clarendon Press

Hobbes, T. (1968) *Leviathan*, Harmondsworth: Penguin

Hobsbawm, E. and Ranger, T. (1983) *The invention of tradition*, Cambridge: Cambridge University Press

Hoff, B. (1994) *The Tao of Pooh and The Te of Piglet*, London: Methuen

Hoggart, R. (1957) *The uses of literacy*, Harmondsworth: Penguin

Holland, D., Lachicotte, W. Jr., Skinner, D. and Cain, C. (1998) *Identity and agency in cultural worlds*, Cambridge, Mass.: Harvard University Press

Holland, J., Ramazanoglu, C., Sharpe, S. and Thomson, R. (1998) *The male in the head: young people, heterosexuality and power*, London: Tufnell Press

Holloway, J. Y. (1970) 'West of Eden' in Holloway (1970)

Holloway, J. Y. (ed.) (1970) *Introducing Jacques Ellul*, Grand Rapids: William B. Eerdmans

Holmwood, J. (1999) 'Radical sociology: what's left?' in Bagguley and Hearn (1999)

hooks, b. (1984) *Feminist theory: from margin to center*, Boston: South End Press

Hopton, T. (2000) 'Tolstoy, god and anarchism', *Anarchist Studies* 8 (1), 27–52

Horsburgh, D. (n.d.) *Neel Bagh* (privately printed description, no publication details)

Huston, S. (1997) 'Kropotkin and spatial social theory', *Anarchist Studies* 5 (2), 109–130

Hutchinson, J. and Smith, A. D. (eds.) (1994) *Nationalism*, Oxford: Oxford University Press

Illich, I. (1971) *Deschooling society*, London: Calder and Boyars

Illich, I. (1990) *Tools for conviviality*, London, New York: Marion Boyers

Intercourse: talking sex (2002) 'Give yourself a hand: an introductory guide to masturbation' at www.intercourse.org.uk/masturbation.html

International Communist Current (1992) *The Italian Communist Left 1926–45*, London: ICC

Jasper, J. M. (1997) *The art of moral protest: culture, biography, and creativity in social movements*, Chicago: University of Chicago Press

Jazz (2001) 'the tracks of our tears' in *On Fire* (2001)

Jenkins, R. (1996) *Social identity*, London: Routledge

Johnston, L. (1997) 'Queen(s') street or Ponsonby poofters? Embodied HERO parade sites', *New Zealand Geographer* 53 (2), 29–33

Joll, J. (1979) *The anarchists*, London: Methuen

Jones, A. (1987) 'The violence of materialism in advanced industrial society: an ecological approach', *Sociological Review* 35 (1), 17–47

Joppke, C. (1993) *Mobilizing against nuclear energy: a comparison of Germany and the United States*, Berkeley: University of California Press

K (2001) 'being black block' in *On fire* (2001)

Kamura, V. (2001) 'love changes everything' in *On fire* (2001)

Kellner, D. (1989) *Jean Baudrillard: from Marxism to postmodernism*, Stanford, Ca.: Stanford University Press

Kelly, O. (1984) *Community, art and the state*, London: Comedia Publishing Group

Kesey, K. (2003) *One flew over the cuckoo's nest*, Harmondsworth: Penguin

Kindred, G. (1995) *The earth's cycle of celebration*, Brassington, Derbyshire: Glennie Kindred

Klandermans, B. (1993) 'The social construction of protest and multi-organizational fields' in Morris and Mueller (1993)

Klandermans, B. (1997) *The social psychology of protest*, Oxford: Blackwell.

Klein, N. (2000) *No logo*, London: Flamingo

Klein, N. (2003) 'Argentina: a new kind of revolution', *Guardian* (Weekend) 25 January, 14–23

Koch, A. (1993) 'Poststructuralism and the epistemological basis for anarchism', *Philosophy of the Social Sciences* 23 (3), 327–51

Koch, A. (1997) 'Max Stirner: the last Hegelian or the first post-structuralist?', *Anarchist Studies* 5 (2), 95–108

Kohn, A. (1992) *No contest: the case against competition*, Boston: Houghton Mifflin Company

Koopmans, R. (1995) *Democracy from below: new social movements and the political system in West Germany*, Oxford: Westview Press

Kriesi, H., Koopmans, R., Duvendak, J. and Giugni, M. (1995) *The politics of new social movements in Western Europe*, Minneapolis: University of Minnesota Press

Kristeva, J. (1984) *Revolution in poetic language*, New York: Columbia University Press

Kropotkin, P. (1988) *Act for yourselves: articles from 'Freedom' 1886–1907*, London: Freedom Press

Kropotkin, P. (1993) *Mutual aid: a factor in evolution*, London: Freedom Press

Kurzman, C. (1991) 'Convincing sociologists: values and interests in the sociology of knowledge' in Burawoy (1991)

Laclau, E. (1988) 'Politics and the limits of modernity' in Ross (1988)

Laing, R. D. (1978) *The politics of experience*, Harmondsworth: Penguin

Lamb, A. (ed.) (1992) *The new Summerhill*, Harmondsworth: Penguin

Lash, S. and Friedman, J. (eds.) (1992) *Modernity and identity*, London: Sage

Lash, S., Szerszynski, B. and Wynne, B. (eds.) (1996) *Risk, environment and modernity*, London: Sage

Lassman, P. and Velody, I. (eds.) (1989) *Max Weber's 'Science as a Vocation'*, London: Unwin Hyman

Lehning, A. (ed.) (1973) *Michael Bakunin: selected writings*, London: Jonathan Cape

Le Guin, U. (1974) *The dispossessed*, London: Victor Gollancz

Levi-Strauss, C. (1962) *The savage mind*, London: Weidenfeld

Lichterman, P. (1996) *The search for political community*, Cambridge: Cambridge University Press

Light, A. (ed.) (1998) *Social ecology after Bookchin*, New York: Guildford Press

Lofland, J. (1966) *Doomsday cult: a study of conversion, proselytization, and maintenance of faith*, Englewood Cliffs: Prentice-Hall

Lorber, J. (1991) 'Dismantling Noah's Ark' in Lorber and Farrell (1991)

Lorber, J. and Farrell, S. (eds.) (1991) *The social construction of gender*, London: Sage

Los Ricos, R. (2002) review of M. Hardt and A. Negri's *Empire* in *Anarchy: a journal of desire armed*, Spring–Summer, 23–5

Lovekin, D. (1977) 'Jacques Ellul and the logic of technology', *Man World* 10, 251–72

Lyman, S. (ed.) (1995) *Social movements: critiques, concepts, case-studies*, Basingstoke: Macmillan

McAdam, D., McCarthy, J. and Zald, M. (eds.) (1999) *Comparative perspectives on social movements*, Cambridge: Cambridge University Press

McCarthy, J. D. and Zald, M. N. (1977) 'Resource mobilisation and social movements: a partial theory', *American Journal of Sociology* 82 (6), 1212–41

McKay, G. (ed.) (1998) *DIY culture: party and protest in nineties Britain*, London: Verso

McKechnie, R. and Welsh, I. (1994) 'Between the devil and the deep green sea' in Weeks (1994)

Macauley, D. (1998) 'Evolution and revolution: the ecological anarchism of Kropotkin and Bookchin' in Light (1998)

MacCoun, R. J. and Reuter, P. (2001) *Drug war heresies: learning from other vices, times, and places*, Cambridge, Cambridge University Press

Maffesoli, M. (1996) *The time of the tribes*, London: Sage

Malatesta, E. (1974) *Anarchy*, London: Freedom Press

Maple, E. B. (1982) 'For a non-administered world', *Fifth Estate* 309, June 19, 2–7

Maple, E. B. (1983) Response to 'FE Sidesteps' and 'Do Odious Tasks', *Fifth Estate* 314, Fall, 2

Maple, E. B. (1993) 'The Fifth Estate enters the 20th century. We get a computer and hate it!', *Fifth Estate* 342, Summer, 6–7

Maple, E. B. and Clark, E. (1976) 'On Organization: two reviews of the Camatte/Collu pamphlet', *Fifth Estate* 279, December, 6–10

Marcuse, H. (1968) *One dimensional man*, London: Sphere Books

Marsh, M. S. (1981) *Anarchist women 1870–1920*, Philadelphia: Temple University Press

Marshall, G. (2001) 'High consumption lifestyles and their contribution to climate change', *Rising Tide Gathering* (Workshop Notes, October) at www.risingtide.org.uk/pages/lifestyl.html

Marshall, P. (1992) *Demanding the impossible: a history of anarchism*, London: HarperCollins

Martin, L. H., Gutman, H. and Hutton P. H. (eds.) (1988) *Technologies of the self: a seminar with Michel Foucault*, Amherst, Mass.: University of Massachusetts Press

Marx, K. (1976) *Capital, vol. I* (translated by Ben Fowkes), Harmondsworth: Penguin

May, T. (1994) *The political philosophy of poststructuralist anarchism*, Pennsylvania: Pennsylvania State University Press

May, T. (2000) 'Interview with the author', *Perspectives on Anarchist Theory*, 4, Fall, 2–5

Melucci, A. (1989) *Nomads of the present: social movements and individual needs in contemporary society*, London: Hutchinson Radius

Melucci, A. (1996) *Challenging codes: collective action in the information age*, Cambridge: Cambridge University Press

Menninger, D. (1981) 'Politics or technique? a defence of Jacques Ellul', *Polity* 14, 110–27

Merleau-Ponty, M. (1962) *The phenomenology of perception*, London: Routledge and Kegan Paul

Meyer, D. S., Whittier, N. and Robnett, B. (eds.) (2002) *Social movements: identity, culture and the State*, Oxford: Oxford University Press

Meyer, M. (1995) 'Social movement research in the United States: a European perspective' in Lyman (1995)

Miller, D. (1984) *Anarchism*, London: Dent

Miller, D. L. (1995) *The Lewis Mumford reader*, Athens: University of Georgia Press

Millett, S. (2003) 'Divergence and disagreement in contemporary anarchist communism: social ecology and anarchist primitivism', unpublished PhD dissertation, University of Central Lancashire

Milstein, C. (2000) 'Reclaim the cities: from protest to popular power' in *Perspectives on Anarchist Theory* 4 (2) at www.flag.blackened.net/ias/8Milstein.htm

Milton, K. (1996) *Environmentalism and cultural theory: the role of anthropology in environmental discourse*, London: Routledge

Milton, K. (2002) *Loving nature: towards an ecology of emotion*, London: Routledge

Mitcham, C. and MacKey, R. (1971) 'Jacques Ellul and the technological society', *Philosophy Today*, 15/2, 102–21

Monbiot, G. (2000) *Captive state: the corporate take-over of Britain*, London: Macmillan

Moore, J. (1988) *Anarchy and ecstasy: visions of halcyon days*, London: Aporia

Moore, J. (1997a) 'Anarchism and poststructuralism', *Anarchist Studies* 5 (2), 157–61

Moore, J. (1997b) 'Armed dialogue: language, poetry and rebellion', *Green Anarchist* 47, Summer, 1997, 21–3

Moore, J. (1998) 'Composition and decomposition: contemporary anarchist aesthetics', *Anarchist Studies* 6 (2), 113–22

Moore, J. (1998a) 'Maximalist anarchism/anarchist maximalism', *Social Anarchism* 25, 37–40

Moore, J. (2002) 'The Insubordination of words: poetry, insurgency and the situationists', *Anarchist Studies* 10 (2), 145–64

Moore, M. (2002) *Stupid white men . . . and other sorry excuses for the state of the nation*, London: Penguin

Morland, D. (1997) 'Anarchism, human nature and history: lessons for the future' in Purkis and Bowen (1997)

Morland, D. (1997) *Demanding the impossible? Human nature and politics in nineteenth-century social anarchism*, London: Cassell

Morin, J. (1998) *Anal pleasure and health*, San Francisco: Down There Press

Morris A. and Mueller C. (eds.) (1993) *Frontiers in social movement theory*, New Haven: Yale University Press

Mouffe, C. (1988) 'Radical democracy: modern or postmodern?' in Ross (1988)

Mr Social Control (early 1990s – no specific date) *Away with all cars*, London: BM Jed

Mulgan, G. (1994) *Politics in an anti-political age*, Cambridge: Polity Press

Mumford, L. (1969) *The myth of the machine: vol. 1, technics and human development*, London: Secker and Warburg

Mumford, L. (1971) *The myth of the machine: vol. 2, the pentagon of power*, London: Secker and Warburg

Mumford, L. (1988) 'Authoritarian and democratic technics' in Zerzan and Carnes (1988)

Naess, A. (1973) 'The shallow and the deep, long-range ecology movement', *Inquiry* 16, 95–100

Naess, A. (1989) *Ecology, community and lifestyle*, Cambridge: Cambridge University Press

National Coalition of Anti-Violence Programs (1997) *Anti-lesbian, gay, bisexual and transgendered violence in 1997*, San Francisco: NCAVP

Neill, A. S. (1945) *Hearts not heads in the school*, London: Herbert Jenkin

Neill, A. S. (1962) *Summerhill*, Harmondsworth: Penguin

New, C. (2001) 'Oppressed and oppressors? The systematic mistreatment of men', *Sociology* 35 (3), 729–48

Newman, S. (2001) 'War on the State: Stirner's and Deleuze's Anarchism', *Anarchist Studies* 9 (2), 147–63

Niman, M. I. (1997) *People of the rainbow: a nomadic utopia*, Knoxville: The University of Tennessee Press

Offe, C. (1985) 'New social movements: challenging the boundaries of institutional politics', *Social Research* 52 (4), 817–68

On fire: The battle of Genoa and the anti-capitalist movement (2001) npp: One-Off Press

Onion, The (2001) 'Gay-Pride parade sets mainstream acquaintance of gays back 50 years', www.theonion.com/onion3715/gay_pride_parade.html (accessed July 2002)

Orwell, G. (1949) *The road to Wigan Pier*, London: Secker and Warburg

Orwell, G. (1984) *Down and out in Paris and London*, Harmondsworth: Penguin

Palast, G. (2003) *The best democracy money can buy*, London: Robinson

Payne, M. (1993) *Reading theory: an Introduction to Lacan, Derrida and Kristeva*, Oxford: Blackwell

Pederson, P. (1995) 'Nature, religion and cultural identity: the religious environmentalist paradigm', in Bruun and Kalland (1995)

Perlman, F. (1983) *Against His-story, against Leviathan!*, Detroit: Black & Red

Perlman, L. (1989) *Having little, being much: a chronicle of Fredy Perlman's fifty years*, Detroit: Black & Red

Perlman, T. (1992) *Anything can happen*, London. Phoenix Press

Piven, F. Fox and Cloward, R. A. (1977) *Poor people's movements: why they succeed, how they fail*, New York: Pantheon

Plant, S. (1992) *The most radical gesture: the Situationist International in a postmodern age*, London: Routledge

Plows, A. and Wall, D. (2001) *'Let our resistance be as transnational as capital!': charting the influence of generational diffusion, grassroots action and cross-movement alliances on UK activists' anti-globalisation strategies and discourses*, paper presented at the 5th Conference of the European Sociological Association, Helsinki, Finland

Plummer, K. (1997) *Telling sexual stories: power, change and social worlds*, London: Routledge

Porter, A. (2001) 'it was like this before' in *On fire* (2001)

Proudhon, P. J. (1923) *The general idea of revolution in the nineteenth century*, London: Freedom Press

Purchase, G. (1994) 'Chaos and anarchism', *Anarchist Studies* 2 (2), 162–8

Purkis, J. (2000) 'Modern millenarians? Anticonsumerism, anarchism and the new urban environmentalism' in Seel, Paterson and Doherty (2000)

Purkis, J. (2001) 'A sociology of environmental protest: Earth First! and the theory and practice of anarchism', PhD thesis, Department of Sociology, Manchester Metropolitan University (electronic copies available from the author: jonathan purkis@yahoo.co.uk)

Purkis, J. and Bowen, J. (eds.) (1997) *Twenty-first century anarchism: unorthodox ideas for a new millennium*, London: Cassell

Rahman, M. (2000) *Sexuality and democracy: identities and strategies in lesbian and gay politics*, Edinburgh: Edinburgh University Press

Randle, M. (1994) *Civil resistance*, London: Fontana Press

Rapp, J.A. (1998) 'Daoism and anarchism reconsidered', *Anarchist Studies* 6 (2), 123–151

Read, H. (1970) *Education through art*, London: Faber and Faber

Redding, A. (1988) *Raids on human consciousness: writing, anarchism and violence*, Columbia, S.C.: University of South Carolina Press

Ribbens, J. (1993) 'Fact or fictions? Aspects of the use of autobiographical writing in undergraduate sociology', *Sociology* 27 (1), 81–92

RIP WTO (2000) (activist video), Eugene, Oregon: Pickaxe Productions

Roberts, M. (2000) 'The last 69 to Chingford' in Dellar, Leslie, Watson and Curtis (2000)

Roof, W. C. (1999) *Spiritual marketplace: babyboomers and the remaking of American religion*, Princeton: Princeton University Press

Rooum, D. (1990) 'Myself and the working class', in *The Raven*, 3 (3), July–September, 235–8

Roseneil, S. (1995) *Disarming patriarchy: feminism and political action at Greenham*, Buckingham: Open University Press

Roseneil, S. (2000) *Common women, uncommon practices: the queer feminisms of Greenham*, London: Cassell

Ross, A. (ed.) (1988) *Universal abandon? The politics of postmodernism*, Minneapolis: University of Minnesota Press

Roudiez, L.S. (1984) 'Introduction' in Kristeva (1984)

Rubel, M. and Crump, J. (eds.) (1987) *Non-market socialism in the nineteenth and twentieth centuries*, Basingstoke: Macmillan Press

Rubin, G. (1993) 'Thinking sex: notes for a radical theory of the politics of sexuality' in Abelove, Barale and Halperin (1993)

Ruggiero, V. (2000) 'New social movements and the "centri sociali" in Milan', *The Sociological Review* 48 (2), 167–85

Sader, E. (2002) 'Beyond civil society: the Left after Porto Alegre', *New Left Review* 17, 87–99

Sahlins, M. (1972) *Stone age economics,* Chicago: Chicago University Press

St Jacques, C. (1981) 'Technological invasion', *Fifth Estate* 306, 17 July, 22–23

St Jacques, C., Kaplan, D. and Solis, P. (1980) 'Fifth Estate & readers debate technology', *Fifth Estate* 304, 31 December, 3–14

Scarce, R. (1990) *Eco-Warriors: understanding the radical environmental movement*, Chicago: Noble Press

Scarce, R. (1994) '(No) trial (but) tribulations: when courts and ethnography conflict', *Journal of Contemporary Ethnography* 23 (2), 123–49

Schalit, J. (ed.) (2002) *The anti-capitalism reader: imaging a geography of opposition*, New York: Akashic Books

Schumacher, F. S. (1976) *Small is beautiful*, London: Sphere

Scott, J. C. (1985) *Weapons of the weak: everyday forms of peasant resistance*, Newhaven, Cn: Yale University Press

Seel, B., Paterson, M. and Doherty, B. (eds.) (2000) *Direct action in British environmentalism*, London: Routledge

Segal, L. (ed.) (1997) *New sexual agendas*, London: MacMillan

Seidman, S. (ed.) (1996) *Queer theory/sociology*, Oxford: Blackwell

Seidman, S. (1997) *Difference troubles: querying social theory and sexual politics.* Cambridge: Cambridge University Press

Seidman, S. (1998) *Contested knowledge: social theory in the postmodern era*, Oxford: Blackwell

Shiva, V. (1991) *The violence of the green revolution: Third World agriculture, ecology and politics*, London and New Jersey: Zed Books

Shotton, J. (1993) *No master high or low*, Bristol: Libertarian Education

Slyk, J. (2000) 'Smashing Seattle: how anarchists stole the show at the WTO', *Anarchy: a journal of desire armed*, Spring–Summer 2000

Singer, P. (1997) *How are we to live? Ethics in an age of self-interest*, Oxford: Oxford Books

Smith, R. D. (1998) 'Social structures and chaos theory', *Sociological Research Online* 3, (1), at www.soccresonline.org.uk/socresonline/3/1/11.html

Solis, P. (1985) 'Bhopal and the prospects for anarchy', *Fifth Estate* 320, Spring, 24–26

Stafford, D. (1971) 'Anarchists in Britain today' in Apter and Joll (1971)

Stanley, L. and Wise, S. (1993) *Breaking out again: feminist ontology and epistemology*, London: Routledge and Kegan Paul

Starhawk (2002a) 'The G8 June meeting in Kananaskis: a strategic moment', 26 May, cited at www.ainfos

Starhawk (2002b) *Webs of power: notes from the global uprising*, Gabriola Island, B.C. Canada: New Society Publishers

Stevenson, H. (ed.) (1986) *Child development and education in Japan*, New York: Freeman

Stirner, M. (1967) *The false principle of our education*, London: Ralph Myles

Stirner, M. (1993) *The ego and its own* (translated by Steven T. Byington), London: Rebel Press

Szasz, T. (1974) *The myth of mental illness: foundations of a theory of personal conduct*, New York: Harper and Row

Szasz, T. (1996) *Our right to drugs: the case for a free market*, New York: Syracuse University Press

Szerszynski, B. (1997) 'The varieties of ecological piety', *Worldviews: Environment, Culture, Religion* 1 (1), 37–55

Szerszynski, B. (2002) 'Ecological rites: ritual action in environmental protest events', *Theory, Culture and Society* 19 (3), 305–23

Szerszynski, B. (2003) 'Marked bodies: environmental activism and political semiotics,' in Corner and Pels (2003)

Taghi Farver, M. and Milton, J. P. (1972) *The careless technology: ecology and international development*, New York: Natural History Press/Garden City

Tamariki (1989) official policy document (typescript)

Tarrow, S. (1994) *Power in movement*, Cambridge: Cambridge University Press

Taylor, B. (1996) 'Earth First! From primal spirituality to ecological resistance', in Gottlieb (1996)

Taylor, B. (1997a) 'Earthen spirituality or cultural genocide? Radical environmentalism's appropriation of Native American spirituality', *Religion* 27, 183–215

Taylor, B. (1997b) 'On sacred or secular ground? Callicott and environmental ethics', *Worldviews: Environment, Culture, Religion* 1 (2), 99–111

Taylor, B. (2001) 'Earth and nature-based spirituality (part I): from deep ecology to radical environmentalism', *Religion* 31 (2), 175–93

Taylor, B. (ed.) (1995) *Ecological resistance movements*, Albany, NY: State University of New York Press

Taylor, M. (1982) *Community, anarchy and liberty*, Cambridge: Cambridge University Press

The Onion (2001) 'Gay-Pride parade sets mainstream acceptance of gays back 50 years' at www.theonion.com/onion3715/gay_pride_parade.html

Tillich, P. (1957) *Dynamics of faith*, London: Harper and Row

Tomalin, E. (2000) 'Transformation and tradition: a comparative study of religious environmentalism in Britain and India', PhD, Department of Religious Studies, Lancaster University

Tomalin, E. (2002) 'The limitations of religious environmentalism for India', *Worldviews: Environment, Culture, Religion* 16, 12–30

Tomlinson, A. and Fleming, S. (eds.) (1995) *Ethics, sport and leisure: crises and critiques*, CSRC: Brighton: University of Brighton

Touraine, A. (1981) *The voice and the eye*, Cambridge: Cambridge University Press.

Touraine, A. (2000) *Can we live together? Equality and difference*, Cambridge: Polity Press

Trotter, A. (1995) 'Introduction' to Camatte (1995)

UK Parliament (2002) 'The Government's drugs policy: is it working? Options for change', www.publications.parliament.uk/pa/cm200102/cmselect/cmhaff/318/31806.htm#a18

Unabomber Manifesto (2001) 'Industrial society and its future' at www.panix.com/%7Eclays/Una/

Urry, J. (2003) *Global complexity*, Cambridge: Polity Press

Van Steenbergen, B. (1990) 'Potential influences of the holistic paradigm on the social sciences', *Futures*, December, 1071–83

Vanderburg, W. H. (ed.) (1997) *Perspectives on our age: Jacques Ellul speaks on his life and work*, Concord, Ontario: House of Anansi Press

Vaneigem, R. (1967) *The revolution of everyday life*, London: Left Bank/Rebel Press

Vaneigem, R. (1994) *The movement of the free spirit*, New York: Zone books

Vidal, G. (2002) *Perpetual war for perpetual peace*, Glasgow: Clairview Books

Wachsberger, K. (ed.) (1993) *Voices from the Underground: – vol. 1, insider histories of the Vietnam era underground press*, Tempe, Ariz.: Mica's Press

Waksler, F. C. (ed.) (1991) *Studying the social worlds of children*, London: Falmer Press

Walford, G. (1990) 'Class politics: and exhausted myth', *The Raven* 3 (3), July–September, 225–30

Wall, D. (2000) 'Snowballs, elves and skimmingtons? Genealogies of environmental direct action' in Seel, Paterson and Doherty (2000)

Wall, D. (2000) *Earth First! and the anti-roads movement*, London: Routledge.

Walter, N. (1979) 'About anarchism' in Ehrlich, Ehrlich, De Leon, and Morris (1979)

Ward, C. (1982) 'Play as an anarchist parable' in Ward (1988) [*Ed. Note:* Author's references are to an earlier edition of Ward (1988)]

Ward, C. (ed.) (1988) *Anarchy in action*, London: Freedom Press

Ward, C. (1992) 'Anarchist sociology of federalism', *Freedom*, June–July (also at www.nothingness.org)

Warner, M. (2000), *The Trouble with normal: sex, politics and the ethics of queer life*, Cambridge Mass.: Harvard University Press

Watson, D. (1992) '1492–1992: The Fall of the 500 year Reich', *Fifth Estate* 340, Autumn, 1, 14–15

Watson, D. (1995) 'Catching fish in chaotic waters', *Fifth Estate* 345, Winter, 8–12

Watson, D. (1996) *Beyond Bookchin: preface for a future social ecology*, New York: Autonomedia

Watson, D. (1999) *Against the megamachine: essays on empire and its enemies*, New York: Autonomedia

Webb, G. and Waters, M. (1999) *Dark alliance: the CIA, the Contras, and the crack cocaine explosion*, New York: Seven Stories Press

Weber, M. (1930) *The Protestant ethic and the spirit of capitalism*, London: George Allen and Unwin

Weber, M. (1989) 'Science as a vocation,' in Lassman and Velody (1989)

Weeks, J. (ed.) (1994) *The lesser evil and the greater good*, London: Rivers Oram

Weeks, J. (1995a) *Invented moralities: sexual values in an age of uncertainty*, Cambridge: Polity Press

Weeks, J. (1995b) *Sexuality*, London: Routledge

Weir, D. (1997) *Anarchy and culture: the aesthetic politics of modernism*, Amherst: University of Massachusetts Press

Weizenbaum, J. (1984) *Computer power and human reason*, Harmondsworth: Penguin

Welsh, I. (1997) 'Anarchism, social movements and sociology', *Anarchist Studies* 5 (2), 157–61

Welsh, I. (1999) 'New social movements yesterday, today and tomorrow', *Anarchist Studies* 7 (1), 75–81

Welsh, I. (2000) *Mobilising modernity: the nuclear moment*, London: Routledge.

Welsh, I. and McLeish, P. (1996) 'The European road to nowhere: anarchism and direct action against the UK roads programme', *Anarchist Studies* 4 (1), 27–44

Werbe, P. (1996) 'The history of the *Fifth Estate* part 1: The early years', *Fifth Estate* 347, Spring, 1– 9

Weston, K. (1998) *Long slow burn: sexuality and social science*, London: Routledge

White, L. Jr. (1967) 'The historical roots of our ecological crisis', *Science* 155, 1203–7

Whittier, N. (2002) 'Meaning and structure in social movements', in Meyer, Whittier and Robnett (2002)

Wilchins, R. (1997) *Read my lips: sexual subversion and the end of gender*, New York: Firebrand Books

Willis, P. (1990) *Moving culture: an enquiry into the cultural activities of young people*, London: Calouste

Wills, W. D. (1942) 'Barns house: a hostel for difficult boys evacuated from Edinburgh', in Boyd (1944)

Wills, D. (1945) *The Barns experiment*, London: Allen and Unwin

Wilson, E. (1993). 'Is transgression transgressive?' in Bristow and Wilson (1993)

Winick, C. (1962) 'Maturing out of narcotic addiction', *Bulletin on Narcotics* 14 (1), 1–7

Winner, L. (1977) *Autonomous technology: technics-out-of-control as a theme in political thought*, Cambridge, Mass.: MIT Press

Wolff, R. P. (1998) *In defence of anarchy*, London: University of California Press

Woodcock, G. (1975) *Anarchism: a history of libertarian movements and ideas*, Harmondsworth: Penguin

Woodhead, L. and Heelas, P. (eds.) (2000) *Religion in modern times: an interpretive anthology*, Oxford: Blackwell

Woolgar, S. (ed.) (1988) *Knowledge and reflexivity*, London: Sage

Yamamura, Y. (1986) 'The child in Japanese society' in Stevenson (1986)

Yorganci, I. (1995) 'Researching sport and sexual harassment: the ethics of covert participant observation and open methods' in Tomlinson and Fleming (1995)

Young, M. (1982) *The Elmhirsts of Dartington*, London: Routledge and Kegan Paul

Zerzan, J. (1982) Reply to letter under heading 'Does *Fifth Estate* view mean "War Or Big Brother"?', *Fifth Estate* 309, June (19), 2

Zerzan, J. (1988) *Elements of refusal*, Seattle: Left Bank Books

Zerzan, J. (1991) 'The catastrophe of postmodernism', *Anarchy*, Fall

Zerzan, J. (1994) *Future primitive*, New York: Autonomedia

Zerzan, J. (1995) 'Youth and regression in an infantile society', *Alternative Press Review*, Summer

Zerzan, J. (1995) *Future primitive*, reprint by Dead Trees Earth First!, Prior House, 6 Tilbury Place, Brighton, E. Sussex, England

Zerzan, J. (1999) *Elements of refusal*, Columbia: C.A.L. Press
Zerzan, J. and Carnes, A. (eds.) (1988) *Questioning technology*, London: Freedom Press
Zinnbauer, B. J., Pargament, K. I., Cowell, B. J., Rye, M. and Scott, A. B. (1997) 'Religion and spirituality: unfuzzying the fuzzy', *Journal for the Scientific Study of Religion* 36 (4), 549–64

Index